# CLASS THEORY AND HISTORY

# CLASS THEORY AND HISTORY

## Capitalism and Communism in the USSR

*Stephen A. Resnick & Richard D. Wolff*

Routledge
New York and London

Published in 2002 by
Routledge
29 West 35th Street
New York, NY 10001

Published in Great Britain by
Routledge
11 New Fetter Lane
London EC4P 4EE

Routledge is an imprint of the Taylor & Francis Group.

Copyright © 2002 by Routledge

Printed in the United States of America on acid-free paper.

10 9 8 7 6 5 4 3 2 1

All rights reserved. No part of this book may be reprinted, reproduced, or utilized in any form or by any electronic, mechanical, or other means, now known or hereafter invented, including photocopying and recording, or in any information storage retrieval system, without permission in writing from the publishers.

Library of Congress Cataloging-in-Publication Data

Resnick, Stephen A.
    Class theory and history : capitalism and communism in the USSR / Stephen A. Resnick and Richard D. Wolff.
    p. cm.
    Includes bibliographical references and index.
    ISBN 0-415-93317-X (hard) — ISBN 0-415-93318-8 (pbk.)
    1. Social classes—Soviet Union. 2. Communism—Soviet Union. 3. Soviet Union—Social conditions. 4. Soviet Union—Social policy. 5. Communism. 6. Capitalism. I. Wolff, Richard D. II. Title.

HN530.Z9 S6394 2002
305.5'0947—dc21

2001058940

# Contents

Introduction ............................................................................................ ix

## Part 1: Communism

**Chapter 1: A General Class Theory** .......................................... 3

    The Classical Tradition  5
    Our Basic Terms  8
    Utopia and Communism: A Brief Digression  10
    A Concrete Communism  13
    Communist Class Structures: Centralization versus Decentralization  16
    Culture, Politics, and Economics of Communism  20
    Appendix: How Societies Differ—A Methodological Problem  42
    Notes  44

**Chapter 2: The Many Forms of Communism** .......................... 51

    Class and Property  52
    Class and Markets  59
    Class and Power  65
    Classless Communism and Proletarian Dictatorship  71
    Socialism and Communism  74
    Notes  79

## Part 2: State Capitalism

**Chapter 3: A Class Theory of State Capitalism** ........................ 85

    Capitalisms and Exploitation  85
    Justifying the Label "Capitalist"  88
    Value Analysis for State Capitalism: A Technical Digression  92
    Capitalisms, Communisms, and Socialisms  95
    Notes  101

## Chapter 4: Debates over State Capitalism — 104
Conflicting Concepts   104
Power as the Theoretical Key   111
Weaknesses of Power Theories   119
Notes   126

# Part 3: The Rise and Fall of the USSR

## Chapter 5: Class Structures and Tensions before 1917 — 133
The Fundamentals: Feudal, Ancient, Capitalist, and Communist   133
The Complexities   143
The Contradictions and the Revolution   146
Notes   153

## Chapter 6: Revolution, War Communism, and the Aftermath — 156
Changing the State and Class Structures   158
Organizing the New Class Structures   164
A Class and Value Analysis of War Communism   169
Class Contradictions after War Communism   175
Notes   179

## Chapter 7: Revolution, Class, and the Soviet Household — 183
Bolshevik Class Blindness   185
New Economic Policy/Old Household Policy   192
Notes   202

## Chapter 8: The New Economic Policies of the 1920s — 206
Relations between Agriculture and Industry: An Overview   209
The NEP in Class and Value Terms   213
A History of NEP Contradictions   222
Adjusting State Industrial Capitalism   227
Revolution and NEP as a Transition to State Capitalism   229
Notes   231

## Chapter 9: The Transformations of the 1930s — 237
New Complexities and Contradictions   238
Communism in Agriculture   243
State Capitalism and Industry   257
The Industrial Workers   262

Stalinism and Class   268
Appendix A: The Value Equation for Collective Farms   273
Appendix B: The Value Crisis of Collective Farms   274
Notes   275

## Chapter 10: Class Contradictions and the Collapse        281

Class Structures after World War Two   282
Postwar Culture   286
Postwar Politics   298
Postwar Economy   310
State, Enterprise, and Household Transitions   316
The Collapse   321
Appendix A: The Value Equation for Military Expenditures   325
Appendix B: The Value Equation for International Terms of Trade   326
Notes   326

## References        335

## Index        347

# Introduction

This book offers a new interpretation of the USSR's birth, evolution, and death. We rely on the available literature in important ways. However, the "surplus" theory of class we find in Marx and use to analyze Soviet history differs sharply from the theories used by both its defenders and its critics. Thus, our focus on the multiple class structures that interacted across Soviet history enables us to extract and construct an argument not found in the available literature. That argument develops two especially controversial points: (1) that a particular kind of capitalist class structure comprised the actual class content of Soviet "socialism," and (2) that communism occurred only in very limited, subordinated realms of the Soviet economy and took the form of a communist kind of class structure. Our stress on class builds on earlier work (Resnick and Wolff 1986, 1987). Therefore, below, we only summarize the distinctive "surplus" concept of class that we deploy throughout. Applying our class analysis to communism, to a state form of capitalism, and to Soviet history continues the effort to insert class—in its particular "surplus" definition—into both popular and scholarly discourses on how societies work and especially on how they ought to be changed. Confrontations between capitalism and socialism/communism, globally as well as in the USSR, were a central part of twentieth-century history. In highlighting certain class dimensions of the lessons and legacies of those confrontations, we hope thereby to give this century's confrontations a more developed class consciousness.

Unlike other studies, this book begins (part 1) with a systematic, new kind of class analysis of what a communist economic system is and how it works. We elaborate a concept of communism, based on Marx, that defines it as a distinct, non-exploitative class structure. Whatever other kinds of communism Marx and others may have gestured toward (e.g., "classless" or "need-based"), the kind developed on the basis of Marx's class analysis is itself a distinct *communist class structure*.[1] Our goal in developing the concept of a communist class structure and exploring some of its variant forms is to pose and answer this question: Did the USSR ever establish any forms of a communist class structure, and if so, where, when, and what happened to them?

Part 2 offers a quite parallel analysis of a capitalist class structure and its variant forms. Among the latter, we single out the private and state forms. We explore the possibilities and implications of social arrangements where state officials, rather than private individuals, appropriate the surpluses generated by laborers in productive enterprises. In distinguishing private from state capitalisms (in terms of how they organized surplus production and distribution), we construct a specification of state capitalism very different from most of those produced and applied to the USSR before. We devote chapter 4 to clarifying that difference. Our goal in developing a new concept of state capitalism is to pose and answer the question: Did the USSR establish a state capitalism, and if so, where, when, and with what consequences for the evolution of Soviet socialism?

The two opening sections of the book enable the much larger part 3 to argue that the USSR never attempted, let alone achieved, communism (not as a class structure and still less as classlessness) on a society-wide basis. Instead, the USSR represented, across its entire history, chiefly a state form of capitalism. The Bolshevik revolutionary state replaced the private form of capitalism that had prevailed in industry to 1917 with a state capitalism. As we shall show, Lenin said as much and also stated his hope to go further toward a nonexploitative class structure variously designated as socialism or communism. Stalin and subsequent leaderships abandoned that hope and rather redefined Soviet state capitalism as "socialism." In their conception, socialism was a largely classless society led by a workers' vanguard party that controlled the state.[2] That plus the state's ownership and operation of industry made this society the opposite (and the transcendence) of capitalism. Their socialism was an early step on the road to the more fully developed future they called "communism," where work would be based on ability and product distribution on need. Our goal instead is to show that Soviet socialism was not a step to communism but rather a state capitalist class structure.

From 1917 through the 1960s, Soviet state capitalism overcame several serious economic crises with remarkable successes. It mobilized its own resources as the world's first claimed and sustained, albeit surrounded, socialism. It built a global support network based on opponents of capitalism everywhere. And its definition of its own state capitalism as socialism—and thus the negation of capitalism—became the standard conception for the twentieth century's confrontation between the "two great systems" for most people on both sides. However, Soviet state capitalism eventually encountered a set of problems that proved insurmountable. As the economic downturn of the 1970s matured into a general social crisis in the 1980s, it spelled collapse. As we shall argue, the USSR had come full circle. Where the 1917 revolution had replaced private with state capitalism, the collapse of the 1980s served to accomplish the reverse shift. In such an oscillation, Russian capitalism displayed swings between private and state forms of capitalism that have likewise characterized capitalism in other countries (including the state capitalisms of the USSR's allies).

The class analysis used in crafting this book's arguments derives from the Marxian tradition, but not in the usual way, nor with the usual results. Marxism is now the richest, most developed repository of class-based critiques of capitalism. It became that over the last hundred years, as it spread from Europe to become a globally dispersed accumulation of many theoretical and practical efforts aimed at anticapitalist class transformations. The Marxian tradition's deepening diversity has made it an indispensable analytic resource. From among its contesting theories, we deploy one—the kind of class analysis we have found most persuasive—to criticize the other theories used by the defenders and critics of the USSR over at least the last seventy years.

The key distinction between our kind of class analysis and theirs lies in the different concepts/definitions of class itself. Official Soviet—and most other—conceptions of class define it chiefly in terms of property and/or power. In the property definition, populations are divided into classes according to how much and what kind of property they do or do not own: the rich versus the poor and so on. In the power definition, populations divide into those who give versus those who take orders: the rulers versus the ruled. In short, these class analyses focus on the social distributions of property and/or power. In the classic economic formulation: capitalism represents *private* property and *private* market transactions, while socialism and communism represent *state* property and *state-planned* distributions. Here, socialism arrives once the state, *as the representative of the whole population,* has (1) taken property from its private owners and socialized it, and (2) abolished private market transactions (and hence the power of private transactors) and substituted state planning (state power) as the mechanism for distributing all resources and products.

In contrast, we define class differently. For us, class refers to how society organizes the production, appropriation, and distribution of surplus. Stated simply, this definition of class presumes that in all societies, one part of the population interacts with nature to produce a quantity of output. The total quantity of output always exceeds the portion that is returned to this part of the population (the workers) for its consumption and reproduction. This excess is the "surplus." A second part of the population immediately receives this surplus from the producers. Finally, a third part of the population obtains distributions of portions of the surplus from the second part. Any society's class structure refers to how it organizes its population in relation to the surplus as (1) surplus producers, (2) surplus appropriators (and hence distributors), and/or (3) recipients of distributed shares of the surplus.[3]

As part 1 shows in considerable detail, a communist class structure is then one in which the producers and appropriators are the same people, whereas the class difference of capitalism is precisely that the appropriators are different people from the producers. The appropriators of the surplus *exploit* its producers—appropriate the latters' surplus product—insofar as and precisely because they are not also producers themselves. Part 2 then shows how a capitalist class structure can take either of two forms. In private capitalism, one or more persons with no official position in the state apparatus function as surplus appropriator/exploiter, whereas in state capitalism, the surplus appropriator/exploiter consists of one or more state officials.

The overwhelming preponderance of other analysts of socialism and communism, both advocates and opponents, have defined class in terms of who owns what property and who wields what power. The USSR was thus socialist or communist in economic terms *because* it abolished private property and the market (private power), replacing them with collective property and state planning. Critics of the USSR have questioned its socialist or communist credentials chiefly on the same two grounds: it had not genuinely or sufficiently abolished private property and markets and/or it had not genuinely or sufficiently empowered the workers to control the state and production. Most analysts on all sides have ignored the social organization of the surplus. A small minority have paid it scant attention as something secondary to and derivative from the key issue of how property and power were distributed.

Our analysis, by contrast, foregrounds the social organization of surplus. We therefore investigate how the 1917 revolution changed the production, appropriation, and distribution of the surplus. After determining how property and power distributions were changed, for us the key question remains: How did those changes affect the social organization of surplus? The USSR's actual property and power changes do not render that question irrelevant, nor do they answer it. Changes in the social distribution of property and power, important in themselves, do not determine how the social organization of surplus has changed.

As this book shows, the Soviet revolution's alterations of property and power distributions did not abolish the basic organization of surplus—the way Soviet people were divided into producers and appropriators of surplus and recipients of shares of that surplus distributed to them by the appropriators. The USSR's organization of its industrial surplus—the priority focus of Soviet economic policy throughout its history—remained capitalist. The USSR did change the form of the capitalist class organization from a private to a state capitalism. For example, in place of private boards of directors appropriating the surplus produced by industrial workers, the USSR substituted state officials as the appropriators. The mass of industrial workers, as before 1917, produced a surplus appropriated by others and distributed by the latter to still others.

The insights yielded by a definition of class in surplus rather than in property and power terms are what this book seeks to demonstrate. We believe that this definition of class, a central contribution of Marx's work, was largely lost to the Marxian tradition after him. Reviving, developing, and applying it systematically generates the new interpretations of communism's distinctive class structure, of capitalism's oscillations between private and state forms, and of the USSR's rise and fall that this book presents.

The histories of Marxism and that of the USSR are deeply intertwined. This is hardly surprising given the Bolsheviks' Marxism and the subsequent leaderships' commitments to particular Marxian theories of history, economy, and their own policies. Those Marxian theories defined class in property and power terms. Soviet leaders powerfully and effectively urged just those definitions and theories on others. Remarkably, the critics of Soviet socialism—Marxian and non-Marxian—almost always shared the same definitions and theories, no matter how much the conclusions they reached clashed with those of Soviet supporters. Since we reject their shared property and power definitions of class and deploy instead a surplus definition, our assessment of the capitalism/socialism confrontation and its embodiment in the history of the USSR is different from all of theirs. Thus, this book is unavoidably a critical engagement within Marxism as well as with the received histories of the USSR.

Given such objectives, this introduction should clarify what are *not* included among our goals. We are not historians and this is not, in the main, a work of empirical history. We appreciate and acknowledge the wealth of empirical history available to us from diverse perspectives.[4] If our reconceptualization stimulates others to undertake close empirical research of Soviet and other histories, we will be gratified, but that research is not the task here.

Our purview is further limited by our focus on the USSR's class structures: their interactions with and influences upon the larger Soviet society. Hence we concentrate on internal aspects of Soviet history rather than the external forces that helped to shape it. No denigration of the latter's importance is intended. Similarly, we are only tangentially concerned with the qualities and quantities of outputs produced across Soviet history (matters of great importance to other theorists). Our focus is rather on the class dimensions, that is, on the relations among the Soviet people as they produced, appropriated, and participated in the distribution of surpluses. Of course, we are interested in property and power (alongside culture, religion, and many more aspects of Soviet society), but primarily in terms of their relationship to class in its surplus sense. Because class in that sense is missing from other accounts, we foreground it here. The point is to integrate the social organization of surplus into the analytic frameworks used henceforth to grasp the ongoing conflict between capitalism and socialism.[5] We approach the particular history of the USSR as an important chapter in that conflict.

Nor are we primarily moralists (as were and are so many on all sides who have analyzed the USSR). Little attention is paid to the moralities entailed, for example, in Czarist policies before 1917 or in the practices of "Nepmen" and kulak farmers in the 1920s or in the policies of the USSR's Cold War enemies. Likewise, we try to keep the approach analytical rather than moral when considering abandonment in the 1920s of early Bolshevik commitments to socialized housework or the collectivization of agriculture in the 1930s or the privileging of the bureaucracies of state and party. Yet a moral concern does animate the book. The realization that a capitalist class structure survived and thrived in the modern society ostensibly most committed to its abolition touched our sensibilities and fueled our analysis. Provoked by the USSR's failure to overcome capitalism—and aided by important steps a few other Marxists took to begin to explain this failure—we believed that a basic and radical reconceptualization was needed.[6] For present and future social movements aimed at advancing human society beyond capitalism, this book presents some basic lessons, both theoretical and practical, drawn from the Soviet experience.

## Notes

1. We have shown elsewhere how Marx's work enables the specification of a distinctly communist class structure (Resnick and Wolff 1988). We believe that such a communist class structure is not only implied by Marx's economics, but is also the appropriate model for what any possible communism in the USSR could have exemplified. It is clear to us that the kind of communism prefigured in the notions of classlessness (ability-based work systems and need-based distribution systems) were never germane descriptions of what actually happened in the USSR. Indeed, its leaders typically recognized this by referring to the Soviet actuality as socialism and its ultimate, future goal as communism. In contrast, communism conceived as a class structure in which the same people who produce the surplus are also its collective appropriators, differentiates it usefully from all exploitative class structures to which it is an alternative. Thus, for example, in capitalist, feudal, and slave class structures, the persons producing the surplus are not the same as those who appropriate and distribute it. Part 1 of this book elaborates and systematizes the definition of such a communist class structure.
2. Stalin's and his successors' use of "classless" underscores the difference between their concept of class (which they derive from Marx) and the class concept informing this book. In their definition, class is a matter of property ownership, specifically property in means of production. A class system is one in which some people own more than others. Thus the USSR's leaderships eventually decided that since they had socialized property—i.e., made it all (or nearly all) into collective property—they had thereby abolished classes. This view contrasts starkly with our approach in which any redistribution of property still leaves open the issue of whether and how the production, appropriation, and distribution of surplus have changed. For example, if the property collectivization leaves some groups in the society as producers and others as appropriators, our class analysis rejects any notion—such as that prevalent in the USSR—that classes were abolished.
3. Marx describes these three parts for capitalism as follows: "[W]e regard the capitalist: 1. as the person who immediately appropriates the whole surplus-value created; 2. as the distributor of that surplus-value created between himself, the moneyed capitalist, and the proprietor of the soil" (1969, 108).
4. This book makes special use of historians of the USSR whose interests and theoretical sensitivities provided us with material closely related to our class analytical interests. Many of these were Marxian, such as Dobb, Carr, and Baykov; some were not, such as Nove. While new data and literature have since became available—some of which we cite—the alternative theoretical frameworks applied to Soviet history have not changed much for quite some time. Thus our selection among secondary sources was governed more by historians' substantive approaches than by their dates of publication.
5. We seek to persuade both those who ignore all concepts of class and those who use other class concepts yet ignore or marginalize the surplus notion of class.
6. Throughout the text, we cite many Marxists (as also many non-Marxists) whose work has been useful in various ways to construct our argument. However, we acknowledge a special debt to one writer, Charles Bettelheim (1976b, 1978). His different kind of class analysis (defining class in power rather than surplus terms) informed a remarkable understanding of the USSR and what he saw as its failures to build a communist economy and society. What we learned from him clarified why and how we had to proceed differently.

# PART 1

# Communism

CHAPTER 1

# A General Class Theory

This chapter presents what neither Marx nor Engels ever provided: a systematic, nondeterministic class analysis of communist societies. To be clear, Marx, Engels, and others within and without the Marxian tradition did produce diverse conceptualizations of communism, and they still do.[1] Indeed, the idea of communism as the "good life" existed for centuries prior to the works of Marx and Engels. Consider, for example, the believers for whom true Christianity arrived only when individuals renounced their worldly property and affirmed the distribution of material wealth to others on the basis of their needs.[2] Closer but still before Marx and Engels, the "utopian socialists" argued for establishing communal societies ruled by reason and good will in contrast to the anarchy and greed they saw in the ruthless capitalism of their day.[3]

We hold that all theorizations of communism so far have lacked two key qualities. First, no systematically nondeterminist (i.e., antiessentialist) perspective has been applied to define and elaborate a concept of communism. Secondly, no class perspective has been applied where class refers to the social organization of surplus: how it is produced, appropriated, and distributed in a distinctively communist way. Such a nondeterminist, class conceptualization of communism was missing not only from theorizations but also from the socialist and communist movements associated with them.

In part 1 of this book, in order to focus on developing the basic class analysis, we treat socialism and communism as roughly synonymous. However, toward the end of chapter 2 we will show how that class analysis enables and implies a new understanding of the profound differences between socialism and communism and the consequences of those differences. Parts 2 and 3 develop still further the differences between communism and socialism.

Among non-Marxist accounts of communism, the absence of class analysis—in its surplus labor definition—is not surprising. However, it is initially puzzling within Marxian conceptualizations since they usually do refer to class. But closer inspection shows that Marxism includes multiple, different notions of class and hence of class analysis. For us, one of the most significant contributions of Marx was conceptualizing class as the production, appropriation, and distribution of surplus within society (Resnick and Wolff 1987, ch. 3). Yet this conceptualization has never yet been used to theorize that particular society—communism—that Marxists themselves have preferred. The existing Marxian treatments of communism, as we show below, used exclusively other, different concepts of class, those defined in terms of property and power rather than surplus. Thus they reached conclusions about communism, socialism, and the history of the USSR radically different from the conclusions of this book.

We believe that the absences of the surplus labor notion of class and of nondeterminist reasoning within most Marxian conceptualizations of socialism and communism have imposed profound costs on the diverse movements favoring them over the last century. Those absences helped to thwart the revolutionary potential of the regimes these movements sometimes created: a possible transition from a capitalist to a communist class structure. Those absences contributed, as we show in part 3 below, to the widespread belief that the Bolshevik revolution had established either communism or at least a socialist transition to communism. We do not share that belief, since we do not agree with the conceptualizations of class upon which it depends. We reject both the criticisms that find Soviet socialism and communism to have "failed" and the defenses that affirm that socialism or communism "succeeded" in the USSR. For us, the communist or socialist alternative to capitalism never prevailed there.

In this and the following chapters, we offer a definition and theorization of communism and socialism that differs radically from those prevailing among both their proponents and detractors. This different theory yields a correspondingly different way to interpret events occurring within regimes claiming to have produced socialism or communism. We shall illustrate this difference by focusing on what most have considered to be the preeminent socialist/communist revolution in the twentieth century—that which occurred within the USSR.

The first section of this chapter presents the basic terms of our theory of communism with some attention to how it differs from other major theories, especially the traditional or classical Marxian view. Despite our rejection of the latter's typically deterministic rendition of capitalism (in which inner economic laws of motion inevitably entail the revolutionary action of the proletariat), we nonetheless respond to that discourse in a specific way. Our analytical focus on class, conceived as the appropriation and distribution of surplus labor, and our commitment to overdetermination (rather than a determinist approach), comprise our responses to the different analytical approaches that have prevailed within the complex, contested history of Marxism (Resnick and Wolff 1987, ch. 1 and 2).

## The Classical Tradition

Before we use our concepts of class and overdetermination to construct a new Marxian view of communism, it will be useful to summarize traditional notions of socialism and communism, especially on the Left. Common to most are two characteristics: collectivity and classlessness (Bernstein 1961; Bettelheim 1976b, 1978; Bottomore 1990; Bukharin and Preobrazhensky 1969; Dobb 1966; Engels 1969a; Kautsky 1971; Lenin 1969; Marx and Engels 1978; Muqiao 1981; Preobrazhensky 1966; Sweezy and Bettelheim 1971, 1985a, 1985b; Tugan-Baranowsky 1966). *Collectivity* characterizes a society devoted to fostering its social nature more than its private. For example, socialist/communist societies collectively establish and secure communal rather than private rights of ownership to property, above all to the means of production. They promote conditions of collective intervention in the economy. Collective planning replaces individuals' private-market decisions in regard to the distribution of resources—means of production and labor power—and of produced wealth. Culturally, there is the hegemony of a collective over a private, individualistic consciousness in regard to notions of equity, fairness, and the "good life" for all citizens. Politically, true democracy arrives, meaning that power rests securely in the collective hands of the people.

*Classlessness,* in the traditional view, characterizes a society that has eliminated its class divisions *understood in terms of inequalities in the distribution of property and/or of political power*. Placing (1) collective rights of ownership in the hands of those whose work yields the wealth of society and (2) effective power in the democratic collectivity of citizens removes the ultimate causes—unequal property and power distributions—of class divisions.

In the language of classical Marxism, posed most clearly in Engels's *Socialism: Scientific and Utopian* and Kautsky's *Class Struggle*, the essence of a socialist society becomes its achievement of a fully collectivist power both over the means of production (including labor power) and the distribution of wealth.[4] The classical authors tended either to equate socialism and communism or to see the former as a way station to the latter. In this century socialism and communism became concepts and labels distinguishing often warring factions among the critics of capitalism—although the basic foci on collectivity and classlessness remained common to all. By contrast, our class analysis changes and therefore differentiates the two terms in a new way.

In the traditional view, the socialist/communist revolution, by transforming private to fully social (collective) ownership, eliminates capitalism. Capitalism's privateness, in this view, had become a fetter on human history. While it had developed great new production techniques (socializing masses of people in great factory and office conglomerations), it could not realize their potential to generate wealth. The reason was private ownership and its attendant markets, profit motives, and so forth. To secure their private profits and unequal distributions of wealth, income, and political power, the capitalists systematically blocked the full utilization of the very means/forces of production they had developed.

For these classical writers, the socialist/communist revolution thus restores a social harmony (correspondence) between the forces of production (technology) and the relations of production (property distribution). That restoration, a new socialist/communist economy, then determines its superstructure of communist politics and culture. The new economy, having socialized productive property, permits the forces of production to renew their march forward, thereby ushering in an age of plenty. The classical theorists conclude, in direct contrast to Adam Smith's alternative utopian vision, that it is socialism/communism, and not capitalism, that finally will liberate human society from poverty and its social consequences.

For Lenin (1969), this revolution enables as well the withering away, but not yet the complete disappearance, of the state. For although its singular cause—class division—has been eliminated (because the private ownership of the means of production was abolished), "bourgeois rights" still remain. Lenin meant that in the first stage of postcapitalist society, the distribution of wealth would depend on the labor performed by each worker. Only later could the basis of distribution become individual needs—the definition of a specifically communist society. In the initial postcapitalist "first phase of communist society," a fundamental inequality remains in society: despite radically different individual needs, rewards nonetheless depend on individual labor performed. Since this distribution is not based on needs, it breeds tension and conflict in all societies where it occurs. Managing these creates the need for a transitional state.

True communism or the "higher phase of communist society" awaits, for Lenin, the unfolding of socialism, defined as the lower phase. Socialism's historic role is to enable the pouring forth of vast wealth from the no-longer-constrained socialized forces of production and to create a new human being finally liberated from the alienation bred by capitalism. Only when the higher phase has been achieved, when the constraints of capitalist poverty and capitalist human nature are finally broken, will there be the elimination of the underlying need (cause) of a state. Only then can Marx's famous aphorism apply and be extended from the economic to include also the political and cultural aspects of social life: "from each according to ability, to each according to need."

The classical tradition's view of communism has received its challenges over the years. Perhaps the most important, from a leading Marxist theorist at the beginning of this century, was Eduard Bernstein's *Evolutionary Socialism* (1961). His emphasis shifted from property distribution (the relation of haves to have-nots) to power distribution (the relation of rulers to ruled). The central issue became democracy.[5] Whether or not aware of Bernstein's arguments, many subsequent writers conceived communism to be a society that embodied full equalization of power, i.e., "true" economic, political, and cultural democracy for its citizens. Power largely displaced property in definitions of class and hence of the difference between capitalism and communism.

Although most writers affirmed that collectivity and classlessness defined a communist society, their different interpretations of Marx, Engels, Kautsky, Bernstein, Lenin, and others produced different conceptions of communism/socialism. Some emphasized property distributions while others stressed matters of politics and democracy. These differences often coexisted within the same groups, parties, and individuals, stimulating debates in the growing left movements. Sometimes they erupted into fierce oppositions and played central roles in splits within the movements.

For example, most leftists defined communism in terms of more or less collectivized ownership of the rights to the means of production *and* more or less democracy. To these notions of collectivity, others (e.g., Engels 1969a; Kautsky 1971) added the collectively planned (rather than market) distribution of resources and products. For them, removing private ownership of the means of production removed the need for as well as the desirability of private markets as means of distribution.

Replacing markets by collective distributions managed by state agencies became a definitive signature of socialism/communism over capitalism. Yet other formulations (e.g., Lenin 1969; Sweezy and Bettelheim 1971) moved this discussion in somewhat different directions. For them the key issue was whether effective state power really (and not just formally) lay in the collective hands of workers. Defined as true democracy, that became *the* criterion of genuine socialism as a transition to communism. In their view, much more important than collective ownership of the means of production and collective mechanisms of distributing output, the essential issue concerned who within the collective possessed effective power (over wealth, the state bureaucracy, workers, cultural life, and so on).

Increasingly, across the twentieth century, the terms of debate over socialism and communism shifted. While there was a continuing focus on property and production, the emphasis increasingly settled on power and democracy. These became the more fundamental, focal criteria of whether or not a society was socialist/communist.

Interestingly, the shift to concern with how power is distributed in society was echoed in non-Marxian accounts of socialism and communism. For example, Nove (1983) proposes a "feasible socialism" that prioritizes the distribution of power in society and its consequences.[6] His socialism combines workers' collectivized rights to the means of production with a competitive market economy. The bad sides of markets (business cycles and unequal income distributions) would be offset by state planning and collectivized property ownership. These two kinds of collective interventions represent what is good about socialism. Socialism's bad sides (power concentrated in an omniscient state's planning board) would be swept away by decentralizing power into the individual hands of market-related buyers and sellers. Nove's notion of socialism—the "good life"—offers Engels's collectivized property ownership, but now tempered by Bernstein's full economic democracy and Smith's competitive markets.

## Our Basic Terms

We differ with all these writers from whom we have learned much. Because we understand Marx's social theory—and especially his class analytics—differently, we produce a different notion of socialism and communism. The notion of class we glean from Marx is neither defined as nor derived from unequal distributions of property or power. Such factors, although interactive with any society's class structure, are nonetheless fundamentally different from it.

By class we mean, in the first place, a process in society where individuals perform labor above and beyond ("surplus" to) that which society deems necessary for their reproduction as laborers (Resnick and Wolff 1987, ch. 3). In simplest terms, one part of the population does such necessary and surplus labor and receives back the fruits of the necessary labor for their own reproduction. These laborers deliver the fruits of their surplus labor—the "surplus"—to another part of the population that then distributes it to still another part. A class analysis in this sense *classifies* individuals in a society in terms of their relationship to this surplus. It asks who performs the necessary plus surplus labor, how is this socially organized, and how does the organization of the surplus impact the larger society? Secondly, a class analysis asks who first receives the surplus from the laborers, to whom do these receivers then distribute it, for what purposes, and how do these distributions affect the larger society? The analysis is particularly concerned with whether it is the same or different groups of people who respectively perform, appropriate, and/or receive distributions of the surplus. It is likewise interested in exploring the interdependence among these groups and how multiple, different organizations of the surplus may coexist within a society. Finally, after specifying a society's arrangements for producing, appropriating, and distributing surplus—i.e., its class structures—this kind of analysis explores how nonclass processes of society (political, cultural, and so on) interact with the class processes in a mutually constitutive way.

This concept of class defined in surplus labor terms is very different from the other concepts that have prevailed in discussions of socialism and communism to date. As we noted, in such discussions class has typically meant a grouping of individuals within a community according to the property they own or the power they wield.[7] Our writings have emphasized the theoretical and political consequences that flow from these alternative definitions of class (Resnick and Wolff 1986, 1987). In our judgment, many class analyses have missed completely the unique surplus labor notion of class offered by Marx and thus could not appreciate how alternative systems of surplus labor shape society differently. Too many agendas for social change have excluded the transformation of how surplus labor is produced, appropriated, and distributed. The history of the USSR exemplifies the disastrous consequences of such exclusions for the project of moving beyond capitalism.

The second key difference between our approach and those prevailing in the debates over capitalism, socialism, and communism concerns the issue of determinism. As argued elsewhere, we have found persuasive a consistent, if minority, perspective within Marxism (associated especially with Lukacs, Gramsci, and Althusser) that rejects determinism (Resnick and Wolff 1987, ch. 2). Thus, one aspect of society is not the ultimate determinant of the others. A superstructure of politics and culture is not reducible to being the effect of an economic base.

The goal of social analysis is not to find the key, determinant cause or causes that "explain" social structures or historical change. By contrast, in our view, most discussions of communism and the USSR have been determinist.

We affirm instead the Marxian notion of "overdetermination": the proposition that all aspects of society condition and shape one another. Hence it is not possible to reduce society or history to the determinant effect of some one or a subset of its constituent aspects. What theory or explanation does—all it can do or has ever done—is to select and draw attention to some aspects and some relationships of whatever object it scrutinizes. That object's overdetermined complexity and ceaseless change place a comprehensive grasp beyond any theory's reach. All theories and explanations remain partial, open to ceaseless addition, contestation, and change. This is because, to be intelligible, they can focus on only a few aspects. They necessarily leave out most of the other aspects.

Thus, our analysis, which is focused on class in terms of surplus labor, is distinguished by *not* asserting that class is what determined the rise and fall of the USSR. Ours is not a determinist class analysis intended to confront alternative analyses arguing that what determined Soviet history was politics, bureaucracy, technical productivity, or any other essentialized cause. Instead, we produce a class analysis of communism and the USSR to draw attention to aspects that other analyses overlooked and to relationships that they missed.

Even those who did use a concept of class in their studies of communism and its relation to the USSR rarely if ever used class defined in surplus terms used here (Dobb 1966; Preobrazhensky 1966; Sweezy and Bettelheim 1971; Bettelheim 1976b, 1978; Muqiao 1981; Mandel 1985). For them, class refers to groups of people who wield unequally and unfairly distributed power and/or property. For the property theorists of class, capitalism disappears and classlessness arrives once productive property is fully socialized. For the power theorists, the same result depends instead on the achievement of a fully egalitarian, democratic distribution of power. Communism and socialism are, then, societies that have abolished or are abolishing power and/or property elites.

This chapter offers a surplus labor–based definition of socialism and communism. A communist class structure exists if and when the people who collectively produce a surplus are likewise and identically the people who collectively receive and distribute it. As we shall argue, this is the relevant concept of communism for assessing efforts over the last century to establish communist societies. This concept of communism likewise serves well to demarcate it from the other major social organizations of surplus (capitalist, feudal, slave, and individual self-employment).

Finally, this concept of communism is especially well suited to craft a systematic differentiation of socialism from communism and to organize the economic history of the USSR as the interaction of different, coexisting class structures presented in part 3 below.

Our theorization of specifically communist class structures (in terms of surplus labor) will show that they can coexist with a vast range of different political, cultural, and economic arrangements—a vast range of nonclass processes. That is, communist class structures interact with the other nonclass aspects of the societies in which they exist. They cannot and do not alone determine them. Hence societies with communist class structures may exhibit varying political forms ranging from those that are fully democratic in nature to those that are clearly despotic. They may display property ownerships that range from the fully collective to the very private. They also may exhibit radically different ways of distributing resources and wealth, from full scale central planning to private markets, including markets in labor power and means of production. Chapter 2 explores these forms in some detail.

We refer to property, markets, planning, power, politics, and culture in general as processes that together comprise a communist society's nonclass structure. The term *communism* thus refers to a communist class structure interacting with the nonclass structure that comprises its social context. The interaction between the class and nonclass structures changes both in a continual process of development. It thus follows that there are countless forms of communism corresponding to all the possible ways in which nonclass structures can affect a communist class structure with which they interact. Indeed, it is also possible that the interaction will go further and produce a transition from a communist to a different class structure. The important methodological issues raised by the problem of conceiving of social structures and changes in this way are treated in the appendix to this chapter. We will use this approach to specify what communist and noncommunist class structures existed in the USSR and how they interacted and evolved across its history. That will provide the basis for our conclusions, explaining why communism never came to Soviet industry, why its place in Soviet agriculture was so limited, and why Soviet socialism was actually a state form of capitalism.

## Utopia and Communism: A Brief Digression

Debates about communism have always proceeded in the shadow of a certain utopian sense of the word. Utopia here refers generally to images of societies that are striving to produce or have arrived at a certain fullness and perfection of community. Utopia can be simply "the desire for a better way of being" (Levitas 1990, 8) or "the assumption that there is nothing in man, nature or society that cannot be so ordered as to bring about a more or less permanent state of material plenty, social harmony and individual fulfillment" (Kumar 1991, 29).

Before and after the Soviet revolution, communism meant for many a society in which inequality and injustice generally were eradicated (with "socialism" perhaps a society in transition thereto). Communism often embodied utopian longings for societies that did more than just equally distribute wealth and power. Inequalities of gender, race, and ethnicity would likewise be gone. Even the more elusive cultural forms of inequality and injustice would be eradicated by a communism that made tolerance, nurturance, honesty, artistry, openness, and love the dominant features of interpersonal relations.

Many Bolsheviks inside the USSR, as well as sympathizers outside, understood Soviet policies and actions at least partially in utopian terms. Their goal of communism meant quite literally a completely just, democratic, and personally free social order in which every individual achieved full self-realization in the context of a loving community. The formulation that sometimes captured these longings was the equation of communism to "classlessness" (Resnick and Wolff 1988). While for some, utopian formulations served merely as lofty rationales for narrowly self-interested policies, for others honest utopian longings were central to their commitments to Soviet policies. Of course, Bolsheviks and other radical activists were hardly unique in mixing utopian longings into their practically oriented discussions and projects. Liberals, conservatives, and reactionaries likewise have always had their utopian images of just societies. They too justified their policies, more or less honestly, in terms of moving society closer to their utopian images.[8]

We respect the utopian longings within social analyses and programs. Indeed, we share many of those on the Left. However, we also differ from them in two ways. First, we wish to *add* a notion of class conceived as the social process of producing and distributing surplus labor. That notion has largely been missing in the utopian as well as the more practically oriented understandings of communism.[9] Theorizations of utopia rarely include direct, explicit attention to reorganizing the production and distribution of surplus labor in communist rather than other kinds of social arrangements. Instead, they focus on and essentialize one or another nonclass process as defining utopia and therefore serving as the goal for utopians. For many, Sir Thomas More's *Utopia* provides the canonical definition. His utopia would banish inequalities by abolishing private property (1964, 53). It would reorganize labor time to produce abundant wealth (chiefly by making a larger proportion of the population do labor): "if you consider how large a part of the population in other countries exists without working" (71). Finally, when wealth is abundant and "everything belongs to everybody" (146), wealth can be distributed according to "what he and his require and, without money or any kind of compensation, carries off what he seeks" (77).

Taken together, the reorganization of property ownership, labor time, and wealth distribution define the utopian economic structure for More. Missing is any notion of how utopia would reorganize the production, appropriation, and distribution of the surplus (not surprising in a book published 350 years before Marx).[10] What remains puzzling, however, is why after Marx's contribution so many utopian theorizations—and particularly those interested in connecting notions of utopia to communism—continue to ignore the social organization of the surplus.[11] Beyond our desire to add class to utopian thought, we differ from most utopian discourses in a second way derived from our commitment to overdetermination. Thus we do not fasten on any one aspect of a communist society (utopian or otherwise) in the belief that achieving it will necessarily or automatically achieve all the other aspects. Thus, achieving a collective ownership of wealth does not guarantee achieving, for example, either a democratic political system or a communist class structure. Likewise, achieving the latter does not guarantee or entail the former.

From the standpoint of overdetermination, utopians cannot rely on some socially determinant essence: change it and all the rest of the utopian and/or communist vision will necessarily fall into place. Utopians have to struggle for all the dimensions of the society they desire; achieving any subset does not guarantee achieving the rest.

On the one hand, our understanding broadens the utopian communist vision by adding a class-as-surplus-labor perspective ignored or missed heretofore. Yet it also detracts, because it recognizes communist forms that could include features far removed from utopian longings. If economic, political, and cultural inequalities and injustices could characterize variant forms of communism, why should left theoreticians and activists struggle for a communist future? Might theoretical and political energies be better spent on reforming rather than overthrowing capitalism? How should we choose between a more equal, more democratic capitalism and a less equal, less democratic communism?

We offer no facile answers to these real concerns. For us, communist instead of exploitative class structures comprise a worthy goal in themselves. This is a moral, ethical, and even aesthetic judgment. The same holds for the other, nonclass elements of our utopian vision. Both the class and nonclass elements of a communist utopia have to be won and sustained since neither guarantees the other; at the same time, their coexistence is much more desirable than either without the other.

Our theoretical commitment to overdetermination has still further implications for how we think about the relation of communism and utopia. If each part of society is overdetermined by all the other parts that push and pull it in all manner of directions, that influence it this way and that, that partly combine to sustain it and partly to disintegrate it, then each part embodies all these diverse, contesting, sustaining-yet-also-undermining determinations. In short, the class and nonclass parts of any society and the relation between them are *contradictory* (Resnick and Wolff 1987, 5–7). The Marxian theory we deploy thus finds contradictions in all societies, not only in capitalism. Communism in all its forms will, we presume, likewise display its distinctive contradictions. We cannot imagine a communism, however utopian, without its contradictions.[12] Even a utopian communism would contain contradictions within and between its class and nonclass dimensions. It would change as these contradictions have their effects including all sorts of struggles over change.

The quest for utopian community that has haunted and enticed human societies for millennia has not always been the same quest. Utopias, as mental constructs of living persons, are likewise overdetermined, hence contradictory, and hence always changing. Utopian visions help to change societies just as social changes helped to change utopian visions. Their dialectical interplay has always changed them both. Our argument here, then, reacts to recent social changes by yet again altering the meanings and social impacts of communism and utopia.

The history of the USSR, like the histories of many other movements with strong utopian components, represents bold experiments to alter fundamentally the way property is owned and controlled, goods are produced and distributed, cultural life is experienced, and power is wielded. We have little quarrel and much agreement with most of the utopian aims. While the USSR in particular did take certain initial steps after 1917 in the direction of some utopian aspects of communism—radically diminishing inequalities of wealth, power, and cultural freedom—it did not, with rare exception, take steps in creating communist class structures. We shall argue that the failure to create communist class structures and the resultant lapse into state capitalist structures instead contributed to the reversal of even those steps toward utopia that were taken initially. The absence of communist class structures helped to undermine, in the Soviet case, the utopian dimensions of the Bolshevik movement and revolution and many of the utopian impulses beneath them. The costs of conceptual blindness toward the organization of surplus labor proved extremely heavy.

## A Concrete Communism

Marx's analysis of capitalism in *Capital* concentrated on the particular kind of capitalism dominant in his day and in the minds of his readers. While acknowledging that other kinds and forms of capitalism could and did exist, he devoted secondary attention to them. We propose likewise to begin our analysis of communism in this chapter by concentrating on the particular kind that strikes us as closest to most reader's notions about the term. However, we will be more interested in the variant forms of communism—tangentially in this chapter and then more systematically in chapter 2.

The communism we begin with thus exhibits two familiar qualities widely associated with communism: (a) state-managed distribution of resources and products, as the antithesis of market-allocated resources and wealth, and (b) collectivized as opposed to private ownership of means of production. In other words, such a communism has organized property ownership and the distribution of resources and products in these particular ways. The question for us, then, is to ask how it has organized the production, appropriation, and distribution of its surplus.

To answer this question, we turn first to the already developed literature on the basic alternative ways to organize the surplus (Resnick and Wolff 1987, ch. 3). These are the capitalist, feudal, slave, ancient, and communist class structures: the five major kinds of class structure recognized and analyzed in the Marxian tradition. Each class structure is a distinctive combination of a unique fundamental class process (producing and appropriating surplus labor) and its subsumed class process (distributing the appropriated surplus). Of particular importance to Marx and to us, the feudal, slave, and capitalist class structures exhibit exploitation. This is defined as a fundamental class process (by definition entailed by certain class structures) in which the performers of surplus labor are not also the appropriators and distributors of the surplus. Serfs, slaves, and proletarians produce surpluses appropriated and distributed not by themselves but rather by feudal lords, slave masters, and capitalists. By contrast, the ancient class structure—in which an individual produces, appropriates, and distributes his/her own surplus individually—while not exploitative by definition is also not collective, communal, or communitarian in the way central to Marx's communist project. In each class structure, the appropriator generally distributes the surplus so as to reproduce that class structure.

A communist *fundamental* class process, as we noted earlier, is defined as one in which the same individuals who perform the surplus labor collectively also receive it collectively. As Marx wrote: "they [the workers] *themselves* appropriate this surplus either of the product or of the labor" (Marx 1971, 255, Marx's emphasis). A communist *subsumed* class process is one in which these collective receivers of surplus labor also collectively distribute it. They do so to pay for the performance of nonclass processes (political, cultural, and so on) deemed necessary for the existence of the communist fundamental class process.[13] These might include surplus distributions to lawyers, teachers, entertainers, security personnel, and others to provide the specific services that comprise the conditions of a communist class structure.

Communist appropriation differs in general from noncommunist appropriations in that (1) the producers are also the appropriators of their surplus, and (2) the appropriation is done collectively, not individually. Thus, in a capitalist class structure, for example, different individuals typically occupy the two fundamental class positions: one group performs the surplus labor while a different group appropriates the surplus.[14] In the class structure of individual self-employment, while the same person is both the producer and receiver of surplus, the appropriation is individual, not collective. It is thereby differentiated from communism which alone has both collective appropriation and an identity between the collectivities of producers and appropriators.

Corporate kinds of capitalism actually entail a kind of collective rather than individual appropriation (notwithstanding the individualism celebrated by most capitalist societies). A collectivity of individuals, namely the corporation's board of directors, appropriates surplus labor. However, this capitalist collectivity is *not* identical to the collectivity that would appropriate in a communist class structure; it is not the *same* collectivity as that which produces the surplus labor. That is why, unlike a communist class structure, corporate capitalism represents a form of exploitation.

Specifying communist fundamental and subsumed class processes in this way defines a communism without exploitation but with classes and hence with class conflicts. People in such a communism struggle over the size of the communist surplus and over its distribution. Some people secure their livelihoods by being collective producers and appropriators of the surplus, while others live by receiving distributions of it. These two groups of people occupy different communist class positions. In our view, Marx provided the analytical basis for as well as gestured toward this class notion of communism. The specification of such a communist class structure enables the rethinking of Soviet history presented in part 3. Finally, we develop and explore this notion of communist class structure because it has rarely received the attention in Marxist literature that it deserves.[15] Many of the complexities and diversities of communism have therefore been missed.

One group of individuals in a communist class structure labor collectively for a certain number of hours per day producing the basic goods and services that Marx called use-values. One portion (x) of these hours—the "necessary" labor—yields a bundle of use-values that is returned to these laborers for their consumption, for the reproduction of their capacity to work. It is necessary in the sense that it comprises the quantity of output laborers require to work. What is "necessary" depends on the unique history of each time and place.

However, the laborers work for additional hours (y) above and beyond the necessary hours (x). Following Marx, these additional hours worked (y) comprise their surplus labor. In a communist class structure, the product of this surplus labor—the surplus—is received collectively by these same laborers. It is not received as profits by another group of people as would be the case in a capitalist class structure. The label *communist* applies to this class structure because it specifies how the surplus labor and its fruits are appropriated: collectively by those who have produced it.

Once received by the workers who have produced it, the surplus is distributed to secure whatever nonclass processes are deemed necessary to ensure that this collective organization of the surplus, the communist fundamental class process, continues to exist. In other words, this distribution aims to secure those nonclass processes of social life (political, cultural, and economic) that induce, inspire, or compel communist laborers to work those extra hours (y) beyond what is necessary (x) to their reproduction as laborers.[16] This distribution of the received surplus labor warrants the label *communist subsumed class process* because the workers who produced the surplus labor not only received it collectively—the communist fundamental class process—but also distribute it collectively to secure the conditions of existence of this communist class structure. Those who received such distributions were thereby paid and equipped to perform various nonclass processes (teaching, policing, politically mobilizing, etc.) designed to secure the specifically communist organization of surplus production and appropriation. Such recipients are thus communist subsumed classes.

This initial discussion has thus added a conception of the social organization of the surplus to the conventional notion of communism with which we began. That notion understood communism as collectivized (rather than private) property in the means of production and planning (rather than markets) to distribute resources and products. Our addition produces a particular kind of communism characterized by a communist class structure as well as collectivized property and planning. The next step in our argument is to explore the combinations of political, economic, and cultural conditions (nonclass processes) that would be needed to generate and sustain such a communism and especially its communist class structure. However, before undertaking that task as the final discussion of this chapter, we offer a digression on the relationship between a communist class structure and two rather opposite criticisms that have long plagued discussions of communism: (1) that only small producing units could ever be organized communistically, and (2) that communism necessarily entails a highly centralized economy.

## Communist Class Structures: Centralization versus Decentralization

Can we conceive the existence of these communist (fundamental and subsumed) class processes in relatively large-sized, technologically advanced, and secular societies, like the United States, or are they viable only in small, technologically simple, kinship-dominated and/or religiously motivated societies?[17] Or, on the other hand, must communist class structures entail highly centralized economies? On a general level, we reject the premises of both of these critical questions. This follows from the notion of overdetermination central to our work. That notion refuses to essentialize any one or a subset of nonclass processes that must be present to enable a communist class structure to exist. Hence a communist class structure does not depend essentially on this or that particular condition: a limited number of participants, their religious fervor, specific spatial conditions, degrees of centralization, and so forth.[18] What matters is only whether and how the totality of nonclass processes combine to overdetermine a particular class structure. Not the presence or absence of this or that *essential* cause, but rather how the presence or absence of any one social condition interacts with all the others in the society: that interaction overdetermines what kind(s) of class process will exist and survive there. Communism is, then, a feasible alternative for those class structures currently prevalent in United States society. It is not limited to small units nor does it necessarily entail centralization. To demonstrate these points, we shall consider how different social conditions can yield different kinds of communist class structures.

Although communism is defined by an identity between the collectivities of surplus labor producers and appropriators, their geographic locations may differ, depending on the specific social and natural conditions in the society. This means that communist production of surplus can occur in one space while its appropriation happens elsewhere. Part of the complex variation taken on by communist class structures can be attributed to this kind of difference in spatial locations occupied by communist surplus labor producers and appropriators.[19]

Such variations reflect a continuum of possibilities. In a decentralized arrangement, surplus production and appropriation occur at the same local production site. In a partially centralized arrangement, surplus labor appropriation is aggregated across particular subsets of producing units (regions, industries, and so forth). In a completely centralized arrangement, appropriation is aggregated across all producing units, irrespective of their location in society. To explore this continuum, we first consider cases in which collective appropriation and production occur within the same producing unit. Then, we consider examples in which appropriation and distribution are aggregated across many units. As we shall see, each of these variations is feasible under differing technological conditions, size of populations, and so forth.

Suppose our producing unit refers to a single communist industrial or farming enterprise, an individual household, or a band of hunters. Whichever it is, the fruit of the communist surplus labor performed in that space is also appropriated there by that unit's surplus labor performers who literally come together as a collective to receive it. In some historical cases, this decentralized appropriation entails members of the producing unit meeting at particular intervals to receive as a group the surplus portion of the use-values produced by that unit. This surplus is physically gathered so that they may then collectively distribute it to local or distant recipients.

In different historical circumstances, it may not be practical or desirable to assemble the collective appropriators and the physical surplus in one place at one time. Because receipt of the surplus is always a social and not merely a physical designation, specific procedures and understandings would then have to be developed, including dissemination of all relevant information, to ensure the social positioning of the producers of the surplus as likewise its collective receivers and subsequent distributors. In such cases, communist workers' appropriating and distributing positions would be like those held by members of boards of directors in modern industrial corporations. Even if these workers never physically received the surplus, they might nonetheless function and be understood to function as the first receivers and distributors of that surplus.

The cultural, political (legal), and economic processes would have to be in place to ensure that the workers occupied those communist class positions. In this regard it is worth recalling that capitalist corporate boards of directors can and do delegate functions to subordinates while the board alone functions as the appropriator and distributor of surplus labor ("profits"). The communist collective of workers can alone retain their class position as appropriator even while delegating some functions to subordinates (to avoid, say, assembling physical surpluses, etc.). The tensions that might arise between appropriators and subordinates in the two different class structures would reflect their differences.

One kind of decentralized communist class structure can be found in a growing—if still relatively small—number of family households in the United States (Fraad, Resnick, and Wolff 1994, ch. 1). In them, certain household members collectively perform household labor and appropriate its surplus portion. They assemble collectively to distribute the surplus. For example, suppose a family household composed of several members. Collectively, they perform x hours of labor producing a bundle of use-values (prepared meals, cleaned rooms and clothes, repaired appliances, doctored family members, and so forth) that are considered necessary for their consumption—i.e., their reproduction as communist household laborers.

Collectively they also perform y hours above and beyond that. The communist class nature of this household depends on the proceeds of this surplus labor being received collectively by the same household members who produced it.[20]

These family appropriators then collectively distribute the proceeds received (a communist subsumed class process) to secure the communist class structure within their household. For example, portions are distributed to individuals (within or outside the household) to perform nonclass processes needed to sustain household communism: maintaining household accounts, establishing and enforcing the rules of collective behavior there, producing and inculcating doctrines that legitimate or sanctify the collective surplus labor production and appropriation by all family members, paying taxes, etc.

This example of decentralized communist appropriation in a family household could occur under varying social conditions. For example, it might coexist with a household technology that is relatively simple in nature, a Christian theology affirming that true Christianity is communal, and a relatively large family membership. These are at least three of the specific conditions described in accounts of eighteenth- and nineteenth-century American communist households within the Shaker, Amana, Harmony, and other like societies (Nordhoff 1970). They may be contrasted with the advanced household technology, feminist theories, and much smaller family units characterizing communist households operating in the United States today (Fraad, Resnick, and Wolff 1994). Another example of decentralized communism can be provided by certain independent industrial or farm enterprises. There, collectives of workers would appropriate and distribute their surpluses in enterprises displaying the entire range of possible technologies and sizes. Although communist appropriation and production of the surplus occur in the same producing unit, some enterprises may not assemble all communist appropriators and the physical surplus at one location and time. Hence we may expect subordinate managers to appear within these enterprises as agents under the direction and control of the communist appropriators. They would receive a distributed share of the surplus for performing this management which has become a condition of existence for this communist class structure.

Despite wielding a degree of power over production and also over the surplus within such a decentralized communist class structure, these managers are not surplus appropriators. Power is one thing; appropriation is another. Hence, although communist producers-appropriators rely upon managers (perhaps enabling the latter to exercise some power over the produced surplus products), other social processes—laws, courts, schools, cultural traditions, and so forth—operate within society to secure the communist producers-appropriators as the only collective appropriators in society.

Of course, some social circumstances might arise enabling managers to become the actual appropriators and thereby displace the communist producers-appropriators. If this occurred, the identity between producers and appropriators of the surplus would have been broken. In the formal terms of Marxian class analysis, a communist subsumed class of managers would have transformed a communist into a noncommunist class structure with themselves in the new noncommunist class position of appropriator of surplus labor rendered by others. Instead of receiving a distributed share of the communist surplus from others, such former managers would then appropriate surplus and make distributions from it themselves.

Such a transition to a noncommunist class structure is found in the history of the collective farms established in the USSR under Stalin. As detailed below in part 3, their producing members were initially the collective receivers of the surplus they produced there. However, the surplus was not physically delivered to them. Instead, managers were assigned specific tasks in relation to the surpluses, but they were subordinate to the communist collective farmers who appropriated and distributed the surpluses. Portions of the communist surplus were distributed to the managers themselves as their income and as means for the discharge of their duties; portions also were distributed to Soviet state officials who secured other conditions of existence for the communist collective farms, and so on. For some time, managers, party, and state officials wielded considerable power over surpluses, but the communist collective retained the functions of appropriation and distribution: a communist class structure. While the collective farmers remained the sole appropriators and distributors of the surplus, they shared power in determining its overall size and the sizes and destinations of its distribution with the managers, party, and state officials. Eventually heavy state intervention displaced collective farm members as appropriators of the collective farm surpluses. Communist class structures gave way to state capitalist class structures as state officials replaced producers as the appropriators of surpluses. The name "collective farm" was all that remained of the initial communist class structures.

We may conclude this discussion of decentralized modes of communist surplus appropriation with an example drawn from the anthropological literature on "primitive communism." Consider a band of hunters appropriating and distributing the fruit of their surplus labor at the same location in which it is produced. Unlike most of the previous examples, the technology used is likely to be relatively simple. On the other hand, distributions of the surplus may be every bit as complex as in the other institutional forms. Similar to them, portions may be received by individuals located elsewhere in society, as when shares of the surplus are distributed to a headman located in the village, to village elders, or to still others there—i.e., warriors, priests, healers, traders, and so forth—to sustain activities believed necessary to the success of the hunt.

We turn now to a more centralized form of communism where production of surplus labor is local but its appropriation occurs on a more aggregated basis. To illustrate this form of communist appropriation, consider surpluses produced, respectively, in an industrial and a farming enterprise. We may assume that in both enterprises highly skilled workers operate advanced technological processes. The surpluses collectively produced in each enterprise are appropriated by a collective comprising both sets of workers. That collective might appropriate (literally gather) the surplus in a central location different from both the industrial and farming enterprises. This example could be extended to increasingly aggregated communist appropriators across many communist enterprises and beyond them to communist households as well. Once again, subordinate managers might well be needed to organize the class structure so that its communist form prevails: that the producers continue collectively to appropriate and distribute surpluses.

It is, of course, quite possible that a society could contain more than one kind of communist fundamental class process. For example, it might display both centralized appropriation across its enterprises, while decentralized appropriation occurs within its households. Similarly, some so-called tribal societies may be characterized by the norm of centralized communal appropriation in most activities save perhaps the particular ones of hunting and household production of manufactures. In the latter, local producers practice local collective appropriation. Nor is there any reason to doubt that cultural and political processes may generate all manner of tensions, conflicts, and changes as members of a communist society determine whether, where, and when centralized versus decentralized appropriation is preferred.

This initial, brief discussion of decentralized and centralized kinds of communist class structures already suggests two noteworthy qualities of communism. First, it can display an immense range of variation in and coexistence among its forms: centralized and decentralized, high-technology and low-technology, large and small producing units, and so forth. Second, communism displays its own particular tensions, contradictions, and changes: for examples, in the mix of decentralized and centralized appropriation, in the delegation of subordinate management tasks, and in the ways noncommunist class structures can arise and displace communist class structures. To the variations and internal contradictions mentioned so far, many more will be added as our discussion proceeds. However, the primary focus and space limitations of this book preclude our exploring another whole level of variations and contradictions: those arising when communist class structures coexist socially with noncommunist class structures. A comprehensive study of communist class structures would have to include such situations. In addition, any concrete examination of an actual society would have to identify and explore interactions and contradictions among its multiple class structures—as we undertake in part 3.

## Culture, Politics, and Economics of Communism

Now that we have outlined some basic class analytics of communist class structures and initially explored a small portion of their range of possible variations, we turn to the cultural, political, and economic contexts needed for such structures to exist. We will assume a modern industrial society with numerous industrial enterprises and households. Centralized communist surplus labor appropriation occurs across its enterprises, while decentralized communist surplus labor appropriation occurs within each of its households. In the enterprise economy, the collectivity of individuals who participate in the communist fundamental class process located within any given industrial enterprise appropriates surplus labor aggregated across all such enterprises. In the household economy, each household's members produce surplus labor collectively, but they also only appropriate their own household's surplus.

Given this particular combination of communist class structures, we propose to consider some specific nonclass processes that would support such a communism. We presume that particular combinations of culture, politics, and economics must be present to overdetermine the existence of this assumed society's particular communist class structure. In other words, we seek to explore what nonclass dimensions of such a society would motivate individuals within its enterprises and households to collectively produce surplus labor and to collectively appropriate it. In short, what are the specific nonclass conditions of this communist society?

Asking what motivates individuals to participate in a communist fundamental class process might seem to invite an obvious answer: they "naturally" desire to appropriate all that they have produced. Yet, if this were indeed natural, then the existence of noncommunist fundamental forms of surplus labor appropriation—capitalism, feudalism, and slavery—would be problematic. For in these forms of appropriation, individuals produce surplus labor for the collective or individual appropriation of others. Giving the fruits of surplus labor to another—with nothing in return—is the precise meaning that Marx attached to those kinds of fundamental class processes that he grouped under the concept of exploitation (1990, ch. 9). Why might individuals prefer a situation in which they produce surplus labor for others rather than for themselves?

One possible answer is that individuals may believe communism to be an evil, perhaps a social arrangement hostile to religiously sanctioned, long-standing traditions. Or they might understand it to be inconsistent with or a danger to their freedom. In such circumstances, there might be little desire to participate in communism. People might well prefer capitalism, feudalism, or slavery even if they admitted that they would be exploited there.

A preference for capitalism might depend significantly on belief in a theory of capitalism that denies that it entails exploitation. Conceptualizing capitalism in terms of an inherent harmony among its parts, each contributing to production and drawing its rewards (incomes) in proportion to that contribution, legitimates capitalism as ultimately fair, equitable, and just. In such a conception, workers in capitalism are not exploited; they give no more than they get; profits are not a surplus they produce, but rather a reward to the resources and efforts provided to production by capitalists; and so forth. Communism is contrastingly depicted as inherently opposed to human nature: it refuses to recognize individuals' differing capacities and qualities and to provide for correspondingly different rewards. Hence it is unfair, oppressive, and economically inefficient. With communism depicted in this way, a preference for capitalism hardly surprises.

A good example of this kind of theorization is found in the United States over recent decades. Even when exploitation, however theorized, is admitted to have existed there, it is relegated to a distant feudal, slave, or even "robber baron" capitalist past. Even when criticisms are directed against capitalism today, class exploitation is rarely if ever included. Thus communism does not now represent an alternative, nonexploitative social organization offered as part of a solution to U.S. social problems. Exploitation is conceptually invisible even to most of capitalism's current critics. Thus it vanishes as a "problem" of the United States needing a solution. Absent the issue of exploitation, the concept of communism has all the more easily been dismissed as not only no solution, but as an unrealizable utopian fantasy that, if actually attempted, yields an altogether inferior economic, political, and cultural arrangement exemplified by the USSR.

In this context, we can understand what an advocacy of communism in households and enterprises evokes in the United States. It is virtually equivalent to arguing for the introduction of a social cancer that would destroy the fabric of American life. Communist households would erode and then destroy those personal relationships between men and women within patriarchal families that form the bedrock of American society. Communist enterprises pose a parallel danger. By implanting a foreign agent in the economic body, communism would frustrate and then destroy individuals' different abilities to produce and reap wealth. Communism stifles humans' ability to act rationally; it spells economic ruin and irrationality. Advocating its establishment in society is the same as arguing for the underdevelopment of that society, an act that is mad or devious.

Even if other societies were understood as exploitative, whereas communism were understood to exclude exploitation, individuals might still prefer one or more of them to communism. They might see the latter and its "communal appropriation" as impracticable albeit perhaps charming utopian dreams. The best social arrangement "realistically possible" might be a relatively humane and democratic capitalism against less desirable forms of capitalism and against feudal and slave social formations.

A culture can also develop that affirms both that capitalism is undesirable and that communism is unrealizable. This would provide important conditions of existence for a class structure different from both. Individual self-employment—what Marx called the "ancient" mode of production (Gabriel 1990)—might then become the desirable alternative to capitalism and communism. Unlike capitalism, here the producer and appropriator of surplus labor is the same person; unlike communism, neither production nor appropriation is collective, it is individual. Self-employment can emerge—as it has throughout the history of the United States, for example—as the real or fantasized alternative, typically manifested in workers' desire to leave capitalist employment, open a small business, and thereby work for themselves rather than for others.

For communism to exist and survive, all such systems of meaning—such cultures—would have to be displaced in favor of others.[21] Just as capitalism typically requires a culture rendering it as fair and just (and contrasting alternative class structures as evil, inefficient, and/or unrealizably utopian), so too communism would likely require a different culture interpreting it as the "good society" and attacking alternatives to it for their injustice and lack of freedom. A communist culture would entail nonclass processes of producing and disseminating meanings that help to support communist fundamental class processes. Some of these processes would presumably seek to convince individuals laboring in enterprises and households that surplus labor appropriation is as real a part of human existence as are the other social processes that they recognize and take seriously. Fundamental class processes would then become as relevant to them and their lives as are processes of speaking, eating, laboring, loving, thinking, child-rearing, voting, and so forth. In other words, individuals would become conscious not only of nonclass but also of class processes—in surplus labor terms—in their daily lives. In a word, they would develop a particular class consciousness.

In addition, communist cultural processes would likely affirm values that portray the replacement of capitalist, feudal, and slave appropriation by communal appropriation as the elimination of a kind of social theft in society, exploitation, that breeds misery and despair. The goal would be to have such theft viewed generally as a kind of evil—much as slavery is now so recognized—that distorts and constrains human development in concrete ways. A parallel set of arguments would likely be directed against individual self-employment as, for example, destructive of the collectivity and community solidarity needed to achieve economic efficiency and a democratic politics.

Such arguments would also celebrate communal appropriations by those who produce the surpluses as providing a way, a possibility, for a new and more desirable era of human behavior to develop. They would connect economic freedom from exploitation—be it capitalist, feudal, or slave—to the liberation of society from many of the recurrent social miseries that have haunted it. To survive, communist class processes would require that individuals be persuaded that freedom from exploitation is consistent with and a condition for a new system of political and cultural freedoms that permit all individuals to struggle effectively and participate fully in social life.[22]

For communist class structures to exist and survive, then, a communist culture would have to emerge hegemonic in place of cultures that had supported noncommunist class structures. To take the United States as an example again, individuals would have to be persuaded that relationships between men and women in its traditional households display a form of class exploitation (Fraad, Resnick, and Wolff 1994, ch. 1). Such a class-conscious culture would stress how women's provision of surplus labor to husbands constitutes an injustice that damages women and men inside households and in their relationships outside as well. Household exploitation would come to be understood, like physical or psychological abuse, as intolerably distorting the interactions among men, women, and children within their diverse relationships.

Likewise, a communist class consciousness would likely require different understandings of enterprises from those now dominant in the United States. Capitalism would be understood as a system whose enterprises annually yield a small group of capitalists trillions of dollars of surplus value—fruits of their workers' surplus labor.

The injustice per se of this class structure would be stressed, as would its deleterious social consequences, from extreme inequalities of wealth and income to ostensibly democratic political processes systematically corrupted by those using them to sustain capitalism. Additionally, such a communist culture would likely criticize the enterprises of the self-employed (ancient) class structure as yielding less success and freedom than physical exhaustion and loneliness.

Cultural processes that produce such consciousness about class would incline individuals toward the communal appropriation of surplus labor. Communist class structures would then be viewed as indispensable to genuine community and democracy in their broadest terms. They would likewise be associated with systematic improvements in the quality of individuals' lives inside and outside their households. Such a communist culture would also likely motivate those individuals to struggle against the continued existence or reemergence of noncommunist class processes.[23]

Individuals who would produce and disseminate these meanings in schools, films, books, songs, and so on, would thereby sustain such a culture. In return, they might receive a distributed share of communist surplus labor as payment for their effort and for the supplies they need to be effective. They would thereby occupy communist subsumed class positions in this society. Without the subsumed class labor of these individuals, performing these nonclass cultural processes, the communist surplus labor in households and in enterprises might not be forthcoming and thus the survival of communist class structures might thereby be jeopardized.

Culture is always complex, diverse, and overdetermined by many aspects of a society other than the latter's class structure. Our argument is not that a communist class structure could or would alone determine a culture that was functional to its survival (any more than any other class structure could do that). Cultures always contain incompatible, contradictory meanings and impulses; they interact with multiple, often contesting class structures within a society. We seek only to establish the point that for communist (or indeed any other) class structures to exist and survive, their cultural contexts must provide some of the requisite conditions, however complicated by cultural crosscurrents. Yet even this point needs to be qualified, for beside the cultural, there are also the political and economic conditions of the existence of class structures. Where cultural conditions are minimal or absent, sometimes political and economic conditions can suffice to sustain a class structure, and vice versa. It is never this or that particular condition that is the essential condition, the essential determinant of a class structure. It is rather the particular ensemble of cultural, economic, and political conditions that together determine—or rather, overdetermine—what class structure will exist. Thus, our initial sketch of some likely cultural conditions of existence of communist class structures, now appropriately qualified, leads next to a parallel consideration of some political and economic conditions.

Political processes include the creation, application, and adjudication of disputes over rules, laws, and procedures that order individuals' behavior within society. Whereas exploitative class structures partly rest on laws, rules, and procedures that empower collectivities or single individuals with the right to receive the surplus proceeds produced by others, a communist class structure would require a radically different set of rules, laws, and procedures. These would empower the collectivity of individuals who produced the surplus with the sole right to receive it. But legally establishing and enforcing this exclusive right of appropriation is only one of the many sorts of political processes that might secure the existence of a communist class structure. Such laws may range from restricting the ownership of all means of production to the collectivities of communist producers/appropriators of surplus labor to rotational rules circulating individuals between communist fundamental and subsumed class positions. Rules and procedures might range from valuing to distributing the wealth produced by communist class structures in enterprises and/or households.

As communist class structures depend on cultural processes to exist and survive, they also depend on such laws, rules, and procedures—on such political processes. However, the dependence of class structures on political processes raises a special problem. The reason for this problem, as we noted earlier, is that many Marxian and non-Marxian social theories essentialize political processes. Particular political processes do not merely take their place along with other social processes in securing the conditions of existence of a particular society. Instead they take on the privileged causal role of being the essential conditions whose presence must be secured for that society to exist. Thus, we need to stress here that while communist class structures may well be supported by laws mandating collective rather than private property and state planning rather than markets, such laws are not ultimate or necessary conditions of existence for communist class structures. In chapter 2 we shall consider how private property and markets could, under some conditions, support a communist class structure.

Given the prevalence of approaches that essentialize property ownership rules and rules governing markets and planning, we need here to stress that no particular property or power distribution is the absolutely essential precondition for a communist class structure to be in place. Rather, we shall emphasize how particular political processes—especially those essentialized in most other formulations—need not be present to sustain a communist class structure (so long as other conditions are present to do that). We shall also emphasize how political processes that function to support a particular class structure can simultaneously work to undermine it.

We begin with collective rather than private ownership of the means of production. Suppose that political processes—in particular, laws written and enforced—effectively give all individuals in a society collective power over property in all or most of the means of production, whether used within its enterprises or households. Hence such collectivized productive assets could not be privately rented, sold, or passed on to heirs. These political processes of property ownership would, especially if combined with communist cultural processes, likely undermine exploitative class structures and provide support instead to communist class structures.

For example, once productive workers within capitalist enterprises become collective co-owners of the productive assets used in their enterprise, their willingness to continue to provide surplus labor to the enterprise's board of directors might wane or disappear. If the workers now view themselves as owners and the board as their agents, they could well decide to reduce the surplus labor they perform or replace the board with themselves or perhaps both. Such possibilities and tendencies are ways in which collectivization of ownership in means of production can (although not necessarily) contribute to undermining capitalist class structures and provide conditions of existence for communist.[24] Such collective property laws could also undermine forms of feudalism insofar as serfs no longer separated from ownership might well refuse to perform surplus labor for lords. Within traditional households for example, women positioned in class terms as serfs may be less apt to deliver feudal surplus labor to their husbands as lords when women become, along with their husbands, collective owners of the means of production used therein.[25] Collective ownership can undermine slavery as a class structure even more directly. Finally, enforcing such ownership laws would also problematize ancient (self-employment) class structures to the extent that individuals may be precluded from individually obtaining access to the collectively owned means of production. The cult of individuality at the core of the ancients' very existence would be challenged, if not undermined. Besides laws enforcing collective ownership of the means of production, we may suppose another set of laws in our concrete example of that form of communism that approximates the historical stereotype. This set directly prohibits private market transactions such as the sale and purchase of commodities including labor power. The presence of political processes establishing and enforcing both sets of laws could undermine the possibility of particular (but not all) kinds of capitalisms. Market mechanisms to enable acquisition of inputs and sales of outputs would have been destroyed; market-mediated values, prices, surplus values, and profits would have vanished.

Such laws constrain the freedom of individuals. In parallel fashion, feudal serfs and slaves lacked the freedom to sell what they did not own—their own labor power and often other productive property as well. Because particular nonfreedoms characterize our example of a communist society as well, it may lose its appeal as an alternative to those who live under capitalism. Certainly, few would wish to recreate in a communist society some of the more onerous conditions of either a feudal or a slave society. After all, transitions from the latter types of societies to capitalism have long been celebrated for ridding human existence of those very unfree conditions.

However, capitalist societies have their particular freedoms and unfreedoms too. These opposites are always intertwined, albeit in different ways and combinations in different societies. The communist nonfreedoms listed above—the inability to privately own the means of production or to buy and sell commodities including labor power—are political conditions of existence for its communist class processes. Similarly, capitalist nonfreedoms, such as the inability of laborers to appropriate the fruits of their own surplus labor or to collectivize productive property without compensation, help to secure the freedom of capitalists to appropriate others' surplus labor. These are some political conditions of the exploitation of some individuals by other individuals. In contrast to this, the inability to alienate property and labor power (via market exchange) in communism helps to undermine the freedom to exploit. The other side of this unfreedom is the freedom from exploitation. Where communism denies the freedom to exploit, capitalism, feudalism, and slavery secure it.

By contrast, non-Marxian approaches conceptualize freedom in class-blind ways; that is, they typically theorize freedom without reference to class. For example, they often conceptualize a set of freedoms as essential conditions for the achievement of maximum feasible wealth and happiness of a society's citizens. They determine that only a capitalist society can foster the institutions—specifically private market exchange and private property—capable of producing and maintaining these freedoms and this potential wealth and happiness. Freedom is thus an absolute and functions as an absolute standard of social organization.

In contrast, Marx and Engels (1978) argued that the particular freedoms of capitalism (private enterprise, markets, and so on) helped to secure its unfreedoms (exploitation, subjection to business cycles, and so on), and that these unfreedoms had deeply negative effects on the social wealth and happiness of capitalist societies. We might extend those initial insights as follows: each kind of society generates contesting standards, measurements, and comparisons of the wealth, productivity, freedom, and happiness in itself and in such alternative kinds of societies as it can recognize or imagine. For a capitalist class structure to survive, these standards, measurements, and comparisons will usually need to conclude that capitalism is preferable to any feasible alternatives. For a communist class structure to survive, a correspondingly different set of standards, measurements, and comparisons would likely have to be hegemonic. In short, there will have to be particular interactions among political processes establishing freedoms and unfreedoms and cultural processes ascribing particular meanings to them to secure any class structure. It is not this or that political or cultural process that is ever, by itself, a condition of existence of a particular class structure. It is always a matter of how particular combinations of political and cultural (and also, as we shall see below, economic) processes interact to overdetermine a particular class structure.

Besides the laws and rules concerned with the collective ownership and nonmarket distribution of resources and products, political processes favoring the existence of communist class structure must establish and enforce other decision-making procedures. These would determine which individuals shall occupy this particular communism's various class and nonclass positions, what shall be the relative magnitudes of necessary and surplus labor, where and when that surplus will be appropriated and distributed, to whom for what purposes, how all such determinations might be altered, and so forth.

Let us pursue our example of a concrete communism by examining first the law that might detail communist class behavior within enterprises. It might, for example, direct that only producers of the surplus shall participate in its collective appropriation and distribution that shall occur four times a year at schools or community centers located near producers' households. There and then, surplus producers will gather to discuss, debate, and vote in particular ways on how the surplus they have received is to be divided and distributed, to whom in society, and for what purposes.

Such political processes, to be effective as intended, require more than the establishment and enforcement of laws. An entire conglomeration of cultural, economic, and other political processes must be in place for such a communist class structure to function in this way. Part of that culture, for example, helps to induce a class consciousness in the society that makes all individuals participate in this kind of appropriating and distributing behavior as a normal, desirable, highly valued aspect of life. In this concrete communism, the culture and politics would overdetermine surplus labor producers to understand themselves and act as citizens endowed with two kinds of "inalienable rights"—to borrow and extend a political idiom from the United States. In addition to their right (and civic obligation) to decide who shall govern them in political office, the producers have the right (and civic obligation) collectively to receive and distribute the surplus they produce.

As part of this political-cultural apparatus, we also shall assume that information is regularly produced and disseminated to workers regarding the estimated size of the surplus produced and received by them over the previous three-month interval as well as a history of previous appropriations and distributions, their results, and so forth. Such information might include forecasts of expected surpluses and expected consequences forthcoming from differing possible surplus distributions.

This kind of surplus-labor decision making, undertaken by workers in communism, is different from but no more or less problematic or contradictory than that of decision-making groups in societies with noncommunist class structures: for example, capitalist corporate boards of directors. Against losses in production from long, difficult meetings, communist class-structured enterprises would see gains in effort and motivation from workers' participation in such hitherto unthinkable ways. Communist enterprises' changes in technology, product mix, work rules, and so on would have a vast array of effects on economic performance as they ramified across the society and over time. It is, of course, impossible ever to garner complete information about *all* the infinite causes or consequences of any event in society. No net result, weighing all the ramifications of a change from capitalist to communist class structures, is thus calculable. No unambiguous, absolute measure of efficiency exists. All efficiency measurements reflect and depend upon the measurer's mechanisms of selecting which of the infinite causes and consequences of any event to measure.[26]

An overdetermined world is one of ceaseless change for each and all of its processes, a change without a telos or endpoint (defined as equilibrium or otherwise) that governs or determines its development. If, then, the process of surplus labor and all other interconnected processes *exist in change*, there is no way to capture at any moment the nature, let alone all the social effects, of that which is always becoming different from what it was. Measurements of an economic event always confront a radical uncertainty as to what happened, is happening, and will happen as a result of the event.[27] Hence the required surplus labor information produced and then provided to the communist producers/appropriators in our concrete communism must be, like all information in all societies, inevitably partial and fleeting, inevitably selective in ways reflecting the particular economic, political, and cultural conditions at that moment. The production and dissemination of information, embodying their own overdetermination, will then add their influence to all the other processes overdetermining the decisions of workers, creating thereby a specific surplus labor distribution.

We may consider next a law covering power distributions in households with communist class structures: only producers of the surplus within each household shall participate in the collective appropriation and distribution of that household's surplus. For this law to have the effect of sustaining a communist class structure, other social processes must also be in place. These would have to counter the patriarchal processes of power and the cultural processes of gendering that help to sustain women's laboring for the benefit of men within the exploitative class structures of many traditional households. They would also have to create a new political and cultural environment for men and women in which each becomes willing to labor collectively, inside the household, as part of intimate life, for the collective benefit of both.

Our discussion of cultural and political conditions conducive to the existence of communist class structures needs now to focus on the individuals charged with providing those conditions. In class analytic terms, such individuals perform nonclass processes that provide those conditions. Their personal incomes and the costs of their activities are defrayed by distributed portions of communist surplus labor. They are communist subsumed classes, obtaining portions of the surplus from the producers/appropriators who seek thereby to secure the conditions of existence of their communist class structures. Such individuals occupying communist subsumed class positions include persons who formulate and disseminate meanings in society (e.g., teachers, artists, clerics, and publicists), persons who write, enforce, and adjudicate laws and rules of behavior (e.g., state office holders, political party personnel, and social workers), and so on.

The individuals occupying these subsumed class positions—performing nonclass processes—may be assumed to spend their full working time doing so. If so, they may constitute a bureaucracy. Given the importance ascribed by others to this phenomenon in relation to communism, its location within our approach requires attention. As specified above, a political/cultural bureaucracy occupies a subsumed class position within a communist class-structured society. If social conditions warrant, the bureaucracy's subsumed class activities will operate smoothly: securing specified conditions of existence and receiving in return a distributed share of communist surplus labor. Under different conditions, this situation can and will change in many possible ways. For example, conflicts and struggles *within* the subsumed bureaucracy may undermine its ability to continue to provide conditions of existence to communist class structures, even as such a bureaucracy demands and perhaps obtains ever larger distributed portions of communist surplus. Eventually, this situation explodes, possibly communist class structures break down, and a transition to noncommunist class structures may unfold. To take another example, if communist producers/appropriators allocate distributions to the bureaucracy that it finds to be inadequate for discharging its political and cultural tasks, it might respond by directly challenging those distributions. The resulting struggles might resolve themselves in new, mutually agreed-upon relations between the fundamental and subsumed classes such that the communist class structure would thereby be maintained. Alternatively, a difficult or even violent conflict might develop from which the bureaucracy might not only emerge victorious but able and interested to achieve a transition from the communist into one or another noncommunist class structures, perhaps with top bureaucrats themselves in new, exploitative, surplus-appropriating class positions.

Neither the presence, strength, or relative social position of a bureaucracy is uniquely determined by a communist class structure. No equation of communism and bureaucracy is necessary or warranted since bureaucratic power is hardly unique to communism (as attested by, for example, the histories of absolute feudalism in Europe and monopolistic capitalism in recent decades). Any class structures may (but need not necessarily) come to depend upon individuals occupying subsumed class positions in a bureaucracy—whether the bureaucracy is located within the state or elsewhere (for example, in a church apparatus). All class structures face the possibility that bureaucrats may one day achieve power sufficient to determine the sizes and distributions of surpluses appropriated by others or perhaps even to displace those others and become surplus appropriators themselves.

In capitalism, for example, the state bureaucracy's relationship to appropriating capitalists has been ambiguous and contradictory. At times it has exhibited a somewhat subservient role securing private capitalists' diverse conditions of existence in return for modest taxes on the appropriated surplus. When either the business cycle or war seemed to threaten the viability of such private forms of capitalism, the state has taken on a more powerful role by raising taxes on capitalist surpluses and intervening directly in markets. National emergencies have even elevated state power to determining both the sizes of capitalists' surpluses (via wage and profit limitations) and how much of capitalists' appropriated surpluses should be destined to capital accumulation or managers' salaries. In particularly revolutionary conjunctures (as we shall show in the following chapters), state officials have gone so far as to displace private capitalists and occupy the *capitalist* appropriating position themselves. Then a state capitalism has replaced a private capitalism.

These possibilities underscore the illogic of presuming the state to occupy a necessarily weak or passive position in capitalism and a necessarily powerful or even dictatorial position in socialist or communist societies. Still further from our perspective would be any theory that literally defines communism in terms of bureaucratic dictatorship by collapsing the communist class structure and a powerful bureaucracy into a necessary and universal identity.

Struggles over power occur not only between bureaucracies and whatever fundamental classes they coexist with (capitalists and proletarians, communist producers/appropriators, and so on). They can also occur within bureaucracies, between fundamental classes, and within a fundamental class. Different class structures provide *different* contexts for all such struggles over political power and its distributions. The outcomes of all such struggles, for example, the power of any bureaucracy, depend on all of the dimensions—both the class and nonclass processes—of each struggle's social context.

Yet another political process that can provide a condition of existence for a communist class structure concerns decisions about how individuals are to occupy its different class positions. For example, one rule might be for individuals to prepare themselves, perhaps via public education, to occupy one class position in a lifetime: fundamental class producer/appropriator *or* subsumed class receiver of a distributed share of communist surplus (in a political bureaucracy *or* cultural apparatus).

There is a considerable tradition in Marxism that expresses suspicion that such fixity of class positions is *not* conducive to the maintenance of a communist class structure. The notion here is that such an arrangement risks hardening the inevitable tensions and conflicts among communist fundamental and subsumed classes into explosive oppositions rather than resolving them to the advantage of communism. The proposed solutions have been various forms of rotation of personnel. The idea is that individuals should occupy different fundamental and subsumed class positions during a lifetime and/or multiple class positions simultaneously in particular patterns of rotation.[28] Enabling all citizens to see the problems of communism by rotating through such multiple class positions is thought to be an important condition of existence of a communist class structure. Processes creating, organizing, and enforcing rotational patterns—as well as a culture celebrating their importance—would, from this perspective, be added to the other political and cultural conditions deemed necessary for the existence of communist class structures.

The final set of nonclass social processes we consider in our example of a concrete communism are economic processes other than the class processes in which surplus is produced and appropriated (fundamental) and then distributed (subsumed). Such nonclass economic processes can include the mechanisms of producing and distributing communism's goods and services, distributing its productive resources, credit and monetary relations, and so on. For the communist fundamental and subsumed class processes to exist, there must be in place transformations of inputs into outputs (production sites) that, in turn, require that means of production be distributed to these sites and products from them to final users of such products. Such final users include those who reproduce labor power and resources so that they can function as inputs for the next round of production. All of these nonclass economic processes can be performed in ways that help to sustain the communist class structure.

A communist fundamental class process is also partly an effect of the division of labor in society. Let us assume, in the concrete communism specified so far, that some of its laborers produce only food in rural farm enterprises while others specialize in the production of cloth in urban industrial enterprises. Consequently, rural communist producers/appropriators spend their $x + y$ hours laboring to produce only food whereas their town cousins spend their $x + y$ hours producing only cloth. Assuming that both food and cloth comprise the means of subsistence required to reproduce such laborers (and thus their participation in the communist class processes), food must be distributed to the specialized cloth producers and cloth to the specialized food producers. In other words, use-values must flow between town and country—a nonclass economic process—in particular ways to support the communist class structure built on this division of labor.

We shall assume that these flows do not happen by mechanisms of market exchange. Assuming their absence (and, as we shall see in a moment, the presence of administered distributions) does not mean that communist class structures necessarily or universally imply the absence of market exchange. In fact, we shall demonstrate in chapter 2 how a communist class structure could interact with a market exchange economy that secured its conditions of existence. We assume away markets in beginning our discussion here only because the traditional literature has so rigidly dissociated communism from market mechanisms for distributing resources and products. Once we have theorized the familiar dissociation, we will be in position to show its contingency and how the presence of markets need not imply nor cause the demise of a communist class structure.

Although farm and industrial enterprises produce, respectively, food and cloth for partial distribution to one another, the precise quantities of and values assigned to those distributions are shaped in part by an officially administered rather than a market determined process. By "administered" we mean that this communist society establishes some kind of state agency whose function is to administer—that is, to plan, organize, supervise, and execute—the required distributions of labor, means of production, and produced goods and services. Individuals within this agency who perform the processes needed to effect these distributions (designing, executing, monitoring, and adjusting them) thereby secure conditions of existence of the communist fundamental class process within enterprises. Their labor involves participating in cultural and political processes as well as economic processes. For example, the production and allocation of goods and services among enterprises require plans and documents announcing, clarifying, interpreting, and justifying how communism is served by the particular ways in which this production and allocation are achieved. Similarly, agency personnel may establish accounting rules for computing and assigning values and/or prices to resources and products, instructions to be given, orders to be carried out, and so forth. Like any complex activity, "administration" (or "planning") as a general concept or activity, irrespective of where in society it takes place, cannot be reduced merely to its economic components (Ruccio 1986a). Individuals who perform these functions take their place along with the other subsumed classes we already have considered. Like them, they too receive a distributed share of the communist surplus, in this case for securing the administration of resources and outputs in ways conducive to communist class structures.

We shall assume that these planners and managers use Marxian value categories (and the literature that elaborates them) to define values of food and cloth.[29] They do this by attaching to outputs specific quanta of the "socially necessary abstract labor times" required to produce each output unit. They also develop accounting rules for calculating and assigning values in this way (e.g., output value equals the average sum of living labor expended plus labor embodied in materials and tools used up in production of this output). Under such circumstances, food and cloth stand in an administered value relationship to one another: exchanges and allocations in an administered market would be accounted for at those values.

As we understand Marx's value theory, values are signs, socially contrived designations of the worth of produced wealth. Values are overdetermined rather than being essentially reducible to a single determinant.[30] They reflect technical and natural conditions of production, economic conditions of distribution, political conditions, and cultural conditions. These last—the system of meanings produced and circulated in any society—include the conceptions and calculations that comprise the "values" assigned to objects. In private capitalisms with markets, for example, culture operates in overdetermining values (or prices in the preferred code of most private capitalisms) through shaping the desires, manipulations, and negotiations of private buyers and sellers. In the communism depicted here culture operates through the planning agency's deployment of Marxian value categories and the derived accounting rules.

In private capitalisms with free markets, the values/prices that get assigned to outputs reflect the social conditions of private buyers and sellers including the appropriating capitalists' technical conditions of production, their expectations, economic strategies, political considerations, business interpretations, racial and gender objectives and constraints, ideological biases, and so forth. In our concrete communism with only administered markets, values reflect the Marxian theories and calculations of the state planning agency, their interpretation of political trends and information on buyers' and sellers' shifting desires, communist appropriators' technical conditions of production, their development strategies, regional, ethnic, and gender goals and constraints, adjustments to the vagaries of weather, and so forth.

In both capitalism and communism, values are overdetermined by their social contexts. Those contexts are different in private capitalism as compared with the concrete communism we have constructed here. In this communism, the collective of workers who produce the surplus replace capitalists as appropriators of that surplus; the collectivity of citizens displaces private individuals as owners of the means of production; planners displace private buyers and sellers as distributors of the wealth produced in society. Thus, the sets of values assigned to resources and products in each society are differently constituted and play different social roles.

The administered values may rise if communist appropriators undertake a development strategy requiring that more machines and tractors be used, respectively, in cloth and food production (a rise of the indirect labor requirements). If this same strategy enhances the productivity of workers in all enterprises (a fall in the direct labor required per unit of output), the administered values might decline. Concrete political and cultural factors also affect values. Responding to perceived threats to communism, communist appropriators may prolong the length of their own work week to increase their output and surplus for military purposes. Similarly, they may work longer hours to expand the surplus to meet rising subsumed class demands for, inter alia, accumulative, educational, or supervisory purposes. Values will change if ethnic and regional differences persuade enterprises to employ more rather than less direct labor to produce outputs at particular production sites. If education or factory supervision increases communist workers' own productivity, values per unit of output may fall generally (less direct labor is required).

In private capitalism, the impacts of comparable economic, political, and cultural changes upon values will be different because of the different social context. In private capitalisms with markets, the phenomena of market competition will help to shape values, whereas the absence of that kind of competition and the presence of other kinds of competition will help to shape communist values differently. The point is to recognize the different determinants constituting the different kinds of values in the two different kinds of societies.

There are differences between capitalist-market and communist-administered values for produced inputs and outputs. There are thus parallel differences between capitalist-market and communist-administered surplus values calculated by means of those values; and the same applies to profit rates.[31] Categories such as values, surplus values, and profit rates require distinguishing adjectives—communist-administered or capitalist-market—to signal their different conjunctural contexts and hence different social definitions and roles. *Communist-administered* values, surplus values, and profit rates are being identified with the communist regime assumed here in which free, private markets and private property are absent. *Capitalist-market* values, surplus values, and profit rates would be correlated with a private capitalist regime such as the United States in which those two institutions are present.[32]

Besides determining the values attached to produced goods, individuals occupying the subsumed class state agency positions will perform other nonclass tasks. Perhaps in conjunction with other subsumed classes, likely in consultation with communist workers, they will decide how much surplus labor workers will perform, the technical conditions of their labor, and how much social product will be returned to the workers for their consumption. The latter (along with the administered value assigned to that product) determines the value of their wages, if indeed wages are the form in which laborers receive their incomes. These decisions add their contribution to creating and reproducing the communist fundamental class process. The collectivity of workers requires them if it is to be in a position to appropriate the very surplus it has produced. That is why it distributes portions of its appropriated surplus to sustain these along with still other diverse activities.[33]

The difference between the administered values of the total output and the values of used-up materials and workers' wages yields the *administered* surplus value that is received by the collectivity of workers positioned to perform that surplus appropriating function. The ratio of this surplus value to the values of wages and used-up materials yields administered rates of profit for each communist enterprise (and, of course, an economy-wide average rate of profit, too).

Communist subsumed classes can allocate inputs and outputs according to such profit rates: for example, favoring the higher than average profit enterprises at the expense of the lower than average. Alternatively, such profit rate calculations might be demoted to the status of merely one among other—perhaps *many* other—variables taken into account in determining resource allocations (e.g., military survival of communism, minimizing ethnic and national conflicts within communism, attaining specific cultural goals of communism, etc.). If those charged with the task of allocation view profit calculations per se in deeply negative terms, they might not respect profit very much in reaching their decisions.[34]

If we presume that administered profit rates are at least one among the criteria of those enterprises' performances, there might well be competition for profitability among them: communist enterprise competition.[35] This competition, while different, is somewhat analogous to that among private capitalist enterprises. As is well recognized, competitive strategies among private capitalist enterprises can focus on price and advertising as well as rapid accumulation of means of production and labor power, reducing supervisory costs, vertical and horizontal integration, expanding research and development, reducing local taxes, bribes to state officials, and so forth (Chandler 1962). Competitive strategies among communist enterprises can share some of these foci while including others such as overachieving state-administered quotas, excluding price and advertising competition, and avoiding unemployment. Competition exists in both social arrangements, but communist forms of competition will differ from capitalist forms. The differences will reflect the ways in which these different class structures participate in overdetermining the specifics of competition in each concrete situation.

Parallel to what occurs in private capitalism, the complex, multiple, and contradictory effects of communist enterprises' competitive strategies will ramify throughout the communist economy. Consequently, competitive acts within a communist class structure will provoke all manner of associated shifts in administered values and profits (costs and benefits, gains and losses). As in a private capitalist economy with markets, it is never possible to isolate and count all the resulting benefits and costs over all the impacted domains and over all the relevant time periods so as to reach an unambiguous final judgment on the net results of any particular competitive strategy or act. It is an illusion to think that either a market or a planned economy can transform this impossibility into a possibility. Capitalists and communists always face incomplete information in regard to costs and benefits.[36]

Inside communist households, we might presume that flows of resources and produced use values do not occur together with an exchange process. Instead, household members organize, monitor, and adjust such flows in terms of physical quanta alone. The communist household surplus appropriators may distribute a share of the surplus to some members for their managing the conditions of existence for household communism. If those household members double as producers/appropriators as well as managers, then they occupy both communist fundamental and communist subsumed household class positions.

Of course, these household managers could decide to attach values to household output. Quite parallel to the case of administered values of enterprise outputs, they would then attach specific quanta of socially necessary abstract labor times to household products. A special state agency might provide households with the applicable information, rules, and methods parallel to those developed for assigning administered values in enterprises. Thus, for example, the value of, say, cooked meals might be defined as the average sum of living labor expended plus labor embodied in the raw materials and household equipment used up in producing such meals. The unlikelihood of such household valuations does not invalidate their possibility and their logical parallel to the attachment of administered values to enterprise products.

Communist fundamental class processes also are overdetermined by labor productivity: the ratio of labor time inputs to physical units of output. For example, a rise in such productivity, whether in enterprises or households, will increase the quantity of goods and services to be distributed and may thereby facilitate the reproduction of communism in each site. However, like changes in other economic processes (flows of use-values, division of labor, etc.), changes in the productivity of labor are distinct from changes in class processes. A growth in productivity need not alter the relation of necessary to surplus labor time. Indeed, the contradictory quality of relations among social processes, presumed by the overdeterminist theoretical framework of this book, alerts us to yet another possibility. The increase in productivity, and the enhanced wealth it brings to the communist society, may, in some circumstances, become a danger to the continued existence of the communist class process there. Communist enterprises whose workers experience rising productivity, for example, might therefore demand higher wages than other workers obtain at enterprises without rising productivity. One can imagine social circumstances where such agitation might eventuate in demands for a transition from communist to noncommunist class structures.

The nonclass economic processes described above can become objects of struggles—these would thus be nonclass struggles—in a society with a communist class structure. The logic here parallels that of our previous discussions of cultural and political conditions of existence. Thus, for example, tensions may evolve into acute struggles over (1) the terms of flows between rural and urban production units, (2) the use of market versus administered valuation mechanisms, (3) the distribution of gains from rising productivity, and so on. We are concerned to keep distinct such nonclass struggles from class struggles in communist societies. The latter are struggles over the quantitative and qualitative dimensions of surplus labor's production, appropriation, and distribution. Nonclass struggles over economic, political, and cultural conditions of existence have no necessary relation to a society's class structure or its class struggles. Struggles over such nonclass processes as, for example, educational curricula (culture), voting procedures for state office (politics), and credit allocations between enterprises and households (economics), will surely affect the communist class structures in such a society. However, there is no basis for presuming what that effect will be. Contradictions, tensions, or struggles within any nonclass process may strengthen or weaken the communist class structure. They may provoke or resolve class struggles—that is, struggles over the communist class processes. The contradictions within and among nonclass and class processes, the class and/or nonclass struggles they may provoke, and the outcomes of these struggles all develop in ways depending on the entire social context. In each historical moment it is that social totality that uniquely overdetermines those contradictions and their evolution.

We have so far assumed, for the particular form of communism that this first chapter analyzes, that enterprises and households are the only places in society where the communist fundamental and subsumed class processes occur. However, we can now extend our analysis to encompass a communist subsumed class located elsewhere. Keeping in mind the traditional literature on communism, our example of such a communist subsumed class is the state in a society with predominantly communist class structures.[37] We shall assume that state officials perform various cultural, political, and/or economic nonclass processes that provide conditions of existence of communist class structures inside enterprises and households. To defray the costs of this state apparatus, communist appropriators distribute portions of their surpluses to the state. The state officials receiving these distributions thereby comprise a communist subsumed class.

The state becomes simply another site in this society interacting with communist enterprises and households. On the one hand, the state is one determinant (provider of conditions of existence) of this society's communist class structures. On the other hand, the state likewise depends partly upon distributed shares of the communist surpluses. This state is thus no more or less important than the communist class structures to the survival of the particular form of communism under discussion.

Affirming this mutual dependence of communism's class structure and its state diverges from the traditional Marxian view (Marx 1986; Lenin 1969). It interpreted the state's existence as proof that communism had not (yet) been achieved. In Lenin's work (1969), for example, the existence of a state necessarily reflects (is an effect of) the existence of exploitative class divisions in society. Where such capitalist, feudal, or slave class divisions have been abolished, a continued state presence reflects merely a temporary or transitional need that is literally withering away. The final disappearance of exploitation—the arrival of what Lenin called the second or "higher" phase of communism—is the death knell of the state.

In our contrasting view, the existence of a state in many forms of communism is perfectly consistent not only with the absence of exploitation, but also with securing that very absence. In such cases, a withering away of the state could jeopardize communist class structures and possibly enable the return of the exploitation that Lenin and other Marxists abhor. We believe that this rather stark difference in theorizing the state and its relation to class is significant.

We have argued elsewhere (Resnick and Wolff 1987, ch. 5) that Lenin's and many other Marxists' theories of the state are essentialist. They reduce its causes to one essential economic determinant (exploitation) and reduce its activities to pursuing one essential economic goal (preservation of the exploitative class structure). This is an application of the classical Marxian metaphor that the economic base of society determines in the last instance the functions and survival of the social superstructure. Because causation runs only in one direction—class causes state—communism conceived as the *absence* of class is therefore the *absence* of any need for a state or only a temporary, "transitional state" (Lenin 1969, 74).[38]

In this last view, the state's death is prolonged because inequities still persist in the transition from the "lower" to the "higher" phase of communism. Lenin refers explicitly to the fact that produced wealth will still be distributed on the basis of labor performed—an inherited "bourgeois right" that continues "to rule"—rather than the ultimate communist basis of "need" (Lenin 1969, 77). The tensions among workers resulting from need-blind distribution require the intervention of a state to maintain social peace while helping to move the society toward full communism when need-based distribution withers the state out of existence. In terms of these roles and functions, such a state was termed "a dictatorship of the proletariat." This classical Marxian theory of the state was often taken another step by adding the idea that so long as capitalists and others committed to exploitative class structures remained active anywhere on the earth, a dictatorship of the proletariat was also needed to prevent them from reestablishing exploitation wherever the proletariat had removed it.

Unlike this essentialist view, we do not understand the existence and duration of the state to be a mere epiphenomenon of society's class structure. Instead, we treat the communist state, as we do any other institution in a communist society, as an overdetermined social construct, depending on and helping to cause other similarly overdetermined sites. We reject essentialist views of the state and its relationship to class in favor of a notion of the mutually overdetermining interaction between any communism's institutions and its class structures.

From our perspective, changing a process—no matter whether it be a class or nonclass process—in any one of these sites changes the character of all the others.

So, for example, replacing private exploitation in enterprises and households with communist class structures there would change the entire society. Our previous discussion covered many of the possible changes. However, such changes by no means necessitate or guarantee the absence of a state. Rejecting essentialism and affirming overdetermination means that we conceive a state's absence or presence as the effect of an infinite set of causes (class and nonclass processes). The state is not reducible to being the effect of one essential cause.[39] Communisms can exist with and without state apparatuses of all sorts; the relation between state and class in communism (as also in all other class structured societies) is overdetermined by the historically specific contexts of that relation.

While rejecting Lenin's economic determinism, we agree with his general view that the main issue is not whether state ministries, police, parliaments, bureaucracy, and so forth exist under communism, but rather the completely new ways in which they would exist and operate. We made a similar point when discussing the existence and meaning of value categories. States, like values, require a modifying adjective to reflect their conjunctural context and hence their particular meanings and social functions. The latter vary under different conditions such as different class structures. Communist values, we noted, differ from capitalist values—whether these are market or administered values. Likewise, a communist state differs from a capitalist state.

This contextual point is so important to Lenin that he describes in some detail a number of new characteristics that must belong to a communist (as opposed to a capitalist) state's subsumed class positions: "(1) not only electiveness, but also instant recall; (2) payment no higher than that of ordinary workers; (3) immediate transition to a state of things when *all* fulfill the function of control and superintendence, so that *all* become 'bureaucrats' for a time, and *no one*, therefore, can become a bureaucrat" (Lenin 1969, 92). Items (1) and (3) aim to prevent the development of a permanent subsumed class within the state. Item (3) suggests the importance to Lenin of rotating not only the communist fundamental but also the state subsumed class positions among all members of society. We would extend Lenin's notion to establish the rotation of all members of society among *all* the communist subsumed class positions (not just the state subsumed class positions).

Item (2) is Lenin's attempt to address the problem of the distribution of income between communist enterprise workers who produce the surplus and communist state workers who are paid incomes in large part distributed directly or indirectly out of that surplus. If their incomes are unequal or have a differing relationship to their labor times or change at different rates or in different directions, tensions and conflicts might arise between them. In a cultural and political environment that stresses equality and collectivity, such imbalances might even disrupt and undermine a communist class structure. Consequently, in Lenin's mind, a communist state would have to legislate and enforce various limits on the inequality of wages across all workers irrespective of their location in communist society. Such laws, along with the election procedures and rotational rules that a communist state would likely organize, would become part of the political infrastructure overdetermining the existence of the communist class process.

These laws and procedures, and the associated culture that creates and disseminates their meaning, attempt to mitigate some of the power and income differences that can arise within communism. They seek to limit tensions and conflicts within the society and especially to preclude the emergence of an entirely new kind of class society. For example, in the absence of such laws and culture, concentrated power wielded by a few well-placed and -paid state officials could become one of the conditions that helps to transform them from communist subsumed class officials into noncommunist collective appropriators of the surplus produced by others. Once that transformation occurs, communism no longer exists in the society, and the state no longer deserves the adjective communist. Those favoring communism's survival could attempt to preclude such conditions by not permitting the same individual to occupy multiple subsumed class positions within the state, by enforcing a rotation of these subsumed class positions among all members of society, by including all kinds of sophisticated voting procedures, by establishing equal rewards for all workers, and so on. Nonetheless, despite all of these and other like-minded attempts, differences among individuals are ceaselessly overdetermined and hence changing. Those changes in turn influence changes in the class and nonclass structures of a communist (or any other kind of) society. The potential for transitions from communist to noncommunist societies is always there—as is the potential for the reverse movement. The contradictions overdetermined within and among social processes may congeal into either transition. It all depends on the particularities of such processes' historical evolution. That means it depends, in part, on what is argued in books such as this and how the arguments are understood, developed, challenged, and applied.

In the particular, concrete communism that this chapter posits, the state is subsumed to the communist class structures. It provides conditions of existence of those structures and receives distributed shares of communist surpluses. It cannot wither away without jeopardizing the communist class structure unless other social processes provide the supports previously provided by the state. At the same time, the contradictions overdetermined within the state and in its relationship to communist class structures can generate tensions, conflicts, and sometimes basic changes not only in the state but also throughout the nonclass and class processes of the society. One possible change might be the withering away of the state apparatus while other conditions of existence of communism ensured its continuation without a state. But such a withering is contingent and in no way inherent in a communist society.

The state is a site of many processes. Individuals and groups place all sorts of demands on state agencies, policies, and financial resources. These demands can and will conflict. One possible trajectory of such a network of contradictions can conclude this chapter's illustrative construct of a concrete communism.

Suppose our concrete communism organizes its state such that one group of officials, a distinct subagency, is a communist party.[40] It organizes political meetings, for example, to discuss and implement the rotation of all persons through all the various communist fundamental and subsumed class positions. It likewise disseminates its interpretations of social events. These activities aim to secure the conditions of existence of communist class structures. Party members' wages and operating budgets depend in part on subsumed class distributions to the party from the communist surpluses appropriated in enterprises and households.[41]

We shall suppose another subagency: a communist state economic ministry that plans and supervises communist enterprises. It administers the values of their outputs and inputs, allocates resources to them, and so forth. Top officials within this ministry also receive a distributed share of enterprises' surplus to sustain their activities. Still other such subagencies might include a police and military infrastructure, an educational establishment, a mass media organization, and so forth. Together, all these subagencies would comprise a communist state subsumed to the communist class structures in enterprises and households.

Suppose now that the state's economic ministry seeks to increase the portion of communist surplus going to accumulation—adding to enterprises' stocks of tools and equipment. Suppose that simultaneously the army and the state educational authorities also demand larger distributions of the surplus. All three state agencies justify their increased demands on the communist surplus on the same grounds: the increases are urgently required for these agencies to secure enterprises' communist class structures in the current social circumstances.

Of the many possible reactions (each provoking still others), we consider this one first. Suppose that the economic, military, and educational state agencies struggle for increased surplus distributions by appealing to communist ideology, alarms about foreign encroachment, manipulation of administered values and budgets, and even force. The issue becomes a subsumed class struggle in the sense that different subsumed classes contest for shares of a given surplus available for distribution.

A different reaction might involve pressuring communist producers/appropriators in enterprises to generate enough additional surplus to meet all the increased economic, military, and educational demands on the state. State officials might act alone or enlist the military, educational, and party officials to also exert such pressure. Communist laborers might respond by producing and appropriating an expanded surplus and distributing it to satisfy the increased demands. The rate of communist surplus appropriation (surplus relative to necessary labor time) would then have risen. Alternatively, the communist workers might resist, alone or with allies from others in the society. From a struggle over the size of the communist surplus, the conflict might, depending on circumstance, change and become a struggle over the nature of the class structure. Then the existence of the communist class structure itself becomes the issue.

In the concrete communism we have sketched, the possible paths of historical development are literally infinite. They flow from the endless variations in the particular nonclass processes (cultural, political, and economic) that provide the conditions of existence of the communist class processes. They flow as well from the contradictions within and between the communist fundamental and subsumed class processes. And they also flow from the contradictions between the communist class structure and the myriad nonclass processes and noncommunist class processes that comprise its social context. The overdetermination of any one social process by *all* the others renders each process contradictory because it embodies the different and conflicting pushes and pulls emanating from all those other processes. From the contradictions spring not only the change and movement of every social process—history—but also the tensions, conflicts, and struggles that motivate and erupt to punctuate that history. Our construction of a concrete communism illustrates the range of possibilities as well as the theory aimed at making them visible.

### Appendix: How Societies Differ—A Methodological Problem

Such questions directed to the history of the USSR are part of a much larger theoretical issue, namely: How does one distinguish one societal form from another? In other words, on what basis can we distinguish one form of communism from another or communist from noncommunist forms? For instance, what differentiates a communism from a capitalism when both display generalized commodity production and individual rights to property ownership? On what grounds can we reject the notion that the USSR was a form of socialism or communism when its state planning and collective rights of ownership of the means of production strike others on the Left and Right as key indexes of what they claim is precisely its socialist or communist nature?

These kinds of questions and the societal identification problem they involve are hardly unique to our argument. They exist for all social theories and not just for Marxism. Because all societies comprise infinite processes, identifications of their nature will vary according to which subsets of their processes are considered. Theories differ in terms of which subset of processes they consider definitive of a society's identity. It is not surprising, then, to find analysts debating over which subset of these processes are the ones that constitute the "right" way to identify a society or a change in a society's identity.

Consider, for example, the two opposing positions that emerged in the well known debates on the European transition from feudalism to capitalism between the twelfth and sixteenth centuries (Hilton 1976). Sweezy identified the development of commodity production, money rents, and merchant capital as marking the end of feudal Europe and the transition to capitalism. Opposing him, Dobb and Hilton concluded that these developments marked the emergence of but a new kind of feudal society (a transition from one form of feudalism to another). More was at stake than understanding when capitalism emerged from European feudalism. At issue explicitly was how to go about identifying the boundaries of feudalism and capitalism as social systems. A parallel issue, lying urgently just below the surface of debate, was how to distinguish forms of capitalism from socialism and communism and to devise political strategies accordingly.

It is clear from such debates and from our questions about the class nature of the Soviet Union that much rests on theoretical differences in distinguishing social systems. These differences matter to the central arguments of this book. We therefore need to clarify here how we will use class in surplus labor terms as our standard to theorize the nature and hence boundaries of any society.

To borrow the Hegelian idiom, this idea of class (or class structure) represents an initial thesis. As such, it is stripped of all determinations; it exists prior to the specification of all its relationships to other aspects of the society in which it is posited. It has yet no content beyond the important fact of its being posited as the opening of a discourse aimed at producing a meaning.[42] To build from an initial positing of class or class structure to an elaborated meaning of class entails showing how the initial class concepts are linked to, bounded by, their "others," namely, the nonclass aspects or structure of social life. We do this as follows: class exists as the effect of all the nonclass aspects of society. They interact to produce class, to overdetermine class. In other words, the nonclass aspects of social life form the conditions of the existence of class. To develop a Marxian understanding of class—to do a class analysis—requires linking class to all the nonclass aspects of society.

Marxian analysis, understood in this way, is necessarily never finished or complete. This is because the meaning of class and class analysis depends on the accumulating linkages drawn between class and the infinity of nonclass aspects of social life. Whenever a new linkage is drawn between class and some previously untheorized nonclass aspect of a society, new light is shed on our understanding of class; it is further concretized. However, as a result, old formulations are changed, old conclusions questioned, and new questions posed. In response, new linkages will likely be explored between class and nonclass aspects of social life. Then again the meanings of class and class analysis, as well as the analytical constructs built with them, will change. Thus, Marxian definitions of and boundaries between social systems, as constructed meanings, must be recognized as always changing.

In this context, what can identification or labeling of a society possibly mean? The consequence of deploying overdetermination as a method is to be continually presented with a different society at any moment in time. How then are we to continue to label a society as communist, if at every moment that we theorize it, it changes?

Any concrete labeling—whether of a particular process or of a cluster of processes comprising a society—necessarily compromises this ceaseless changing (Marx's dialectic). To identify an entity is to intervene in its movement and to create a momentary closure, an illusion of fixity. That is what identification or labeling means. It disrupts the process of change, for at such a moment we can say definitely what a thing "is" rather than recognizing that it exists only in a state of change, always becoming something different or other than what it is. Labeling introduces a notion of fixity that is logically inconsistent with an overdeterminist methodology. That is why identifying the boundaries of any society manifests a more general problem within nondeterminist Marxian theory.[43]

For example, in our discussion below of possible variant forms of communism we claim that the introduction of particular nonclass processes (specifying how resources and/or produced wealth are owned and distributed) yields different communist forms. We do likewise for nonclass processes of power. In theorizing this way, new forms of communism are defined, new boundaries between communism and other social systems are specified. Of course, these definitions and boundaries are relative to the particular nonclass processes we have theorized; they are different from the definitions and boundaries yielded by theorizing different nonclass processes and their relation to communism. In effect, any and all definitions and boundaries utilized in social analysis depend on what subsets of social processes are selected—privileged—by the theorist for attention. On this basis the theorist makes claims about social structures and social changes, about the presences and absences, the rises and falls of feudalisms, capitalisms, communisms, and so forth.

Privileging particular processes in this way is what makes societal distinctions possible, but does that not violate the very premise of overdetermination (DeMartino 1992, 296-305)? It would if we asserted that the definitions and boundaries resulting from the social processes we privilege in our theorizing were fixed or absolute in any way. But we do not imagine that our theorizing (or anyone else's) is anything more than a momentary intervention fixing in one particular way what is ceaselessly open and in flux. Our theory with its particular privileging and fixing is itself both an overdetermined effect of the social totality and a cause of yet further changes in it. Indeed, every theory is a transient fixing of the unfixable precisely aimed at pushing its ceaseless changes more in some directions than in others. Our theorization of communism here is, then, a momentary, illusory fixing of the social changes swirling around us undertaken with the hope of thereby inflecting them in particular directions. These directions differ from those sought by other theorists who likewise privilege and fix, but do so with other concepts.[44]

## Notes

1. Marx's writings on communism are sparse. The most developed, found in the *Grundrisse* (1973, 471-514), comprise the section known as the *Formen* or "Pre-Capitalist Economic Formations." See also his *Critique of the Gotha Programme* (1986); *Capital*, vol. 1 (1990, 477-479); *The Economic and Philosophic Manuscripts of 1844* (1968, 132-146); and *The Communist Manifesto* (1978, 469-500.) For Engels a good source is *The Origin of the Family, Private Property, and the State* (1969b). In recent years, Ollman (1979, 48-98), Avineri (1969, 220-239), Amariglio (1984), Hindess and Hirst (1975, ch. 1), Jensen (1982), Saitta and Keene (1985), and Anderson (1974, 107-111; 1975, 462-549) have produced conceptualizations useful for our approach. This was

especially true for Amariglio's original theorization of forms of communism and Ollman's critical examination of Marx's scattered writings on communism. We also benefited from modern writings on utopia and utopian thought such as Levitas (1990, 40–45), Lukes (1984, 153–167), Geoghegan (1987, 22–34), and Manuel and Manuel (1979, 697–716). Recent anthropological literature on communist or so-called primitive societies likewise proved useful, especially Godelier (1972, 1977), Terray (1972), Meillassoux (1972), Rey (1975), Sahlins (1972) and still others, together with Amariglio's analyses of them (1984, 279–329).

2. Their belief rested in part on New Testament passages: "Now all who believed were together and had all things in common, And sold their possessions and goods, and divided them among all, as anyone had need" (Acts 2: 44–45). "Now the multitude of those who believed were of one heart and one soul; neither did anyone say that any of the things he possessed was his own, but they had all things in common.... Nor was there anyone among them who lacked; for all who were possessors of lands or houses sold them, and brought the proceeds of the things that were sold, And laid them at the apostles' feet; and they distributed to each as anyone had need" (Acts 4: 32, 34–35). For the close relationship between Christianity and communism in early American communist societies such as the Shakers and the Amana Society see Nordhoff (1970), Holloway, (1966, passim), Pitzer (1984, 119–135), and several essays, especially the survey by McCrank, in Pitzer (1997).

3. Engels (1969a) criticized such utopian socialists for lacking a class perspective (conceived in surplus value terms): "One thing is common to all three [Fourier, Saint-Simon, and Owen]. Not one of them appears as a representative of the interests of that proletariat, which historical development had in the meantime produced. Like the French philosophers, they do not claim to emancipate a particular class to begin with, but all humanity at once" (1969a, 33). On early socialist and utopian socialist thought, see also Lichtheim (1969), Tugan-Baranowsky (1966), and Manuel and Manuel (1979, part 6, 581–693).

4. Diskin (1990) presents a detailed criticism of the rationalism and economic determinism informing the visions of both Engels and Kautsky.

5. Diskin (1990, 137–138) concludes: "Finally, socialism, for Bernstein, has ceased to refer to a change in class relationships, or to the process of the historical and necessary unfolding of the contradictions within capitalism. It has come to mean the process of increasingly socialized production under conditions of democracy."

6. Nove actually continues an older radical tradition in economics—arguments for "market socialism"—associated with Lange and Taylor (1964) in the 1930s and Lerner (1959) in the 1940s. Harrington's (1990) recent book represents still another part of this same tradition. Lange took generally Marxist positions, Lerner and Nove took quite opposed positions, and Harrington located himself in between.

7. Property and power definitions of class, while overwhelmingly predominant in discussions of communism and socialism, have not been the only definitions. Some Marxists make the existence of class depend on individuals' consciousnesses (Thompson 1963, 9).

8. To some extent, Right and Left utopias are reverse images of one another. The Right gives priority to the private over the collective. Its utopian images decentralize social power completely into individual hands. Free, private individuals deploy their property in their individual interest without state or other external interference. In the utopian imagery of the neoclassical economic theory dominant in the world today, the result of free individuals disposing of their property self-interestedly is maximum happiness, maximum output, social stability: the "optimum" of which they speak. The Left sees this as a dystopia, equating it with maximum exploitation, inequality, waste, and vast personal and social suffering. It counterposes socialism or communism as the overcoming of this dystopia, the utopian image of a social order that takes all its affairs—economic, political, and cultural—under fully participatory, democratic, and collective control.

9. Cullenberg (1992) argues similarly for a "thin definition of socialism": collective surplus labor appropriation plus democratic decision making over that surplus. He views that as a feasible socialism and hence preferable to some utopian communism impossible to achieve. As the text below will argue, we prefer a "thinnest" notion of communism (which defines a specifically communist class structure in exclusively surplus terms) which can then coexist with democratic or undemocratic decision-making systems.
10. More's only explicit reference to "surplus" arises in describing what farmers do in the island of Utopia: "they produce far more grain and cattle than they require for their own consumption: they distribute the surplus among their neighbors" (1964, 63). He never developed this remark into any theory of the surplus.
11. A good example is the otherwise excellent book on utopia by Levitas (1990). In discussing the relationship of Marx to utopia, she chooses four key aspects of Marx's conception of communism: "the abolition of the division of labor, the development of individual potential, the transformation of work, and the increase in material prosperity (made possible by the social ownership of the means of production)" (1990, 42). She does not recognize the production, appropriation, and distribution of the surplus, nor how their theorization is different from the few other aspects of Marx's work that she does discuss.
12. Jensen (1982) shows how class and nonclass contradictions within a concrete communism—the Wolof society of West Africa—led to basic social changes there.
13. Marx (1986) criticized the Gotha Program of the German Socialist Party because it neglected the nonclass processes. He viewed such processes as necessary to sustain a communist class structure. Moreover, they could be secured only by distributing portions of the communist workers' surpluses to those individuals charged with performing these nonclass processes. Marx listed, as examples of such nonclass processes, "replacement of the means of production used up" during that production period, "expansion of production," "reserve or insurance fund," "costs of administration," "communal satisfaction of needs," and "funds for those unable to work, etc."
14. The same individual can occupy both the positions of capitalist receiver of surplus value and of coworker alongside the other productive laborers he/she employs. However, even though the same person here produces and appropriates his/her own surplus labor, the appropriation is individual. It is not a communist class structure because the collective of workers is not identical to the collective of appropriators.
15. Some important exceptions to this neglect—and hence resources for our work—are Amariglio (1984), Hindess and Hirst (1975, ch. 1), Jensen (1982), and Saitta and Keene (1985).
16. Our term for necessary labor, the x hours worked to produce means of consumption for workers, is what Marx calls in his *Critique of the Gotha Programme* the "'diminished' proceeds" of labor that result after subtracting from labor's total product (created by $x + y$ hours of labor) the deductions (the y surplus labor hours) required to cover the nonclass processes listed in note 13. The workers' consumption is what remains "after deducting his labor for the common fund." Marx's reasoning here implies the production and existence of a surplus in communism—here designated as the portion of output allocated to the "common fund"; see Hindess and Hirst (1975, 26-27) for a similar argument. While Marx does not use the adjective *communist* to describe this surplus, this adjective would follow logically from his own analysis and his lifelong effort to persuade readers of the existence of surplus in all societies: "Surplus labor in some form must always remain, as labor beyond the extent of given needs" (1991, 958). Hence in communism too the question for Marx is not whether the production, appropriation, and distribution of a surplus exist, but rather how communism organizes those processes differently from other class systems.
17. Nordhoff (1970) discusses some small and religious American communist societies (some technologically advanced for their time). Holloway (1966) surveys American utopian experiments from

the seventeenth through the nineteenth centuries. Pitzer (1997) provides an even more extensive survey (and bibliography) of American communal experiments including the Shakers, Mormons, and New Harmony. These works' common lack of a class perspective is illustrated in Holloway's description of the moment when one society adopted communism: "The members agreed to place all their possessions in a common fund, to adopt a uniform and simple style of dress and of house, and to labour for the good of the whole body" (1966, 90). Approaches to historical communist societies sharing the approach of this book exist in the discussion of the Iroquois in Amariglio, Resnick, and Wolff (1988). See also Amariglio's (1984, ch. 3) critical review of "primitive communism" and Jensen's (1982) historical analysis of the West African Wolof.

18. See Amariglio's (1984) forceful critique of an essentialist conceptualization of communism implicit in the traditional coupling of the adjective "primitive" with the noun "communism."
19. The notion of a locational difference between the production and appropriation of surplus labor was first developed in our research work with David Ruccio.
20. As we show in part 3 below, the prevalent class structure inside Soviet households was *not* communist. Rather, the father occupied the class position of feudal lord and his wife that of serf. In any case, since no class analysis (in the surplus labor sense) was applied to households, the issue of their class structure never arose in the USSR, nor did any examination of the social consequences of Soviet households' class structures (on Soviet politics, culture, and economic development).
21. Space limits prevent us from developing here the contradictions between the cultural conditions of existence of class structures and those class structures. For example, the individualism that supports a capitalist class structure in some ways may undermine it in others, perhaps by drawing workers into self-employment. If capitalist enterprises outcompete such self-employed workers, they might then turn against capitalism. For another example, if a culture excoriates state interference in the private capitalist economy, this may undermine capitalism when a cyclical downturn requires state intervention. Those who support capitalism—its "organic intellectuals" in Gramsci's nuanced formulation—try to manage its contradictions in ways that will support capitalism. And if and when they fail—if and when cultural conditions of existence of capitalism are not secured—either economic or political supports will have to be strengthened (e.g., military compulsions introduced) to provide the supports formerly provided by culture, or else capitalism's existence may be in jeopardy.
22. Communist class structures could survive for a time without such a culture, but only if political and economic processes were in place that could then suffice to sustain communism.
23. In a society where communist class structures predominated, but with the coexistence of noncommunist class structures, a supportive culture would have to accommodate this coexistence and its contradictions. We do not here explore the rich range of possibilities this complexity introduces.
24. Workers' collective ownership of means of production introduces problems for capitalism but by no means makes it impossible. In some cases, collective ownership by workers can provoke capitalist growth and expansion. For example, in the United States today, certain groups of unionized workers accept longer hours and lower wages from boards of directors in corporations whose stocks their union pension plans own in significant quantities. In this case, collective workers' ownership is positively correlated to the rate of exploitation. Even where collective ownership is virtually complete and the elimination of a market in labor power total, workers may well continue to produce surplus for capitalists. Chapter 3 illustrates exactly this possibility. In sum, collective ownership does not, by itself, prevent or preclude capitalism.
25. On the other hand, we described elsewhere (Fraad, Resnick, and Wolff 1994, ch. 1) the prosperity of feudalism operating with collective rather than private ownership of the means of production. Property laws passed in many states endowed wives and husbands with joint ownership of the means of household production, including the house itself. This kind of collective ownership

changed but did not destroy feudalism as a mode of exploitation inside traditional U.S. households. Wives still performed surplus labor delivered to their husbands. Notwithstanding property owned collectively by husband and wife, other kinds of nonclass processes—including marriage, love, gendering, economic discrimination, and so forth—sustained feudal household class structures. Such class structures can coexist with a range of different kinds of property ownership.

26. Claire Sproul (1994) extended the overdeterminist critique of "efficiency" noted in our text to the neoclassical economic concept of "externalities." One implication of her work is that the decision making of communist workers in regard to surplus labor, while different from that of capitalists, cannot be determined to be more or less efficient in any absolute sense. Thus, each system develops its particular, relative "standard of efficiency" (mechanisms of selecting which costs and benefits to measure and how to measure them). Each then makes decisions more or less aimed at "maximizing" their respective standards. Different societies will likely generate different concepts of efficiency.

27. Douglas Vickers (1994) depicts the remarkable ways in which conventional economic theories encounter uncertainty only to flee back into certainty via probability mathematics. "For the assignment to future possible outcomes of a designated probability distribution is itself an assumption of knowledge.... In a stroke ignorance is abolished" (1994, 9).

28. In most societies, individuals occupy multiple class positions across their lifetimes; hence some pattern of rotation exists. Our point here is that in a communist class structure, such rotation might well be extended and made an explicit object of law and culture in the sense of its being a condition of communism's continuation.

29. In chapter 3 below we return to such "administered" values, prices, surpluses, and profits. However, there the class context is not communism but rather a state form of capitalism. If and when a state capitalism uses administered values and allocations instead of markets, the resulting values will not only differ from what market valuations would have been; they will also differ from the administered values emerging from a communist rather than a state capitalist class structure.

30. We think Marx coined the phrase "socially necessary abstract labor time" to signal this antiessentialist perspective. What is "socially necessary" at any moment reflects the ever changing and mutually interacting natural and social processes comprising any society. Values can then never be reduced merely to one subset of processes as in neoclassical economic theory (preferences, etc.) or orthodox Marxian theory (physical labor inputs). For sustained developments of this perspective, see Garnett (1994), who builds on the earlier works of Roberts (1981, 1987) and Wolff, Roberts, and Callari (1982, 1984).

31. Communist-administered surplus value would be calculated as follows: subtract the sum of administered values of raw materials and tools used up in production (comparable to the "c" in Marx's value equation) and the values paid to productive workers as wages (Marx's "v") from the total value of output (Marx's "w"). The result would be communist-administered surplus value (Marx's "s"). The ratio of this s to this (c + v) would yield a communist-administered equivalent of Marx's rate of profit, as explained in the text below. If the particular administration of communism introduced the use of money as a universal equivalent and if it allowed for prices of output to diverge from values, there could be communist-administered profit rates calculated on the basis of such prices.

32. Sometimes, as in wartime emergencies, private capitalism may coexist with administered prices; likewise, communist class structures can coexist with markets as argued below. Administered "prices" could be calculated and differentiated from administered "values" in ways parallel to Marx's differentiation of market values and prices in *Capital*, vol. 3.

33. If appropriating workers thought that making the decisions governing the hours, conditions, and wages of their work were as important to them as owning the means of production, they could

occupy these subsumed class planning positions where such decisions are made. Then they would distribute a portion of their appropriated surplus to themselves for making such decisions. In addition to the fundamental and two subsumed class (distributing surplus and owning means of production) positions they already occupy, their new planning position would comprise yet another subsumed class position.

34. We cannot here fully engage the apologetical and dogmatic claims that purely market-based (i.e., private capitalist) allocations of inputs and outputs necessarily yield the greatest efficiency, growth, etc. Such claims ignore the problem of "externalities" (costs and benefits not reflected in market valuations—see note 26 for further discussion) and the unresolved debates over the different meanings and measures of "profit."

35. Communist enterprises may be allowed greater or lesser autonomy from central planning and control authorities, greater or lesser freedom to compete with one another. That will depend on shifting historical circumstances. We do *not* make the degrees of such autonomy or competitiveness or the extent of markets the indices of capitalism versus socialism and communism as do others: see Sweezy as against Bettelheim (Sweezy and Bettelheim 1971, 34ff.) and Hilferding (1950).

36. Once again (see note 26), neither planning nor markets can or do count all costs and benefits. This is a logical or philosophic issue in epistemology that any economics concerned about its own foundations would have to face. Absent any possibility of total cost-benefit accounting, neither market nor state planning systems can claim any absolute efficiency vis-à-vis the other. Efficiencies are relative to the theoretical presumptions and selective counting systems of those who make the measurements. Champions of both systems continue to make absolute efficiency claims, usually while deriding epistemology as irrelevant to economics.

37. Societies typically display multiple class structures coexisting in various ways. By labeling a society communist, we mean that the prevailing class structures are communist; other coexisting class structures are not. We ignore that complexity here only to facilitate exposition of the theory of communist class structures. Part 3 below takes systematic account of multiple, coexisting class structures.

38. As noted above, the traditional Marxian class analyses proceed with a definition of class in terms of power distributions, in particular those distributions of the power to exclude others (property rights) from objects usually called "means of production." Thus, the classical Marxian theory of the state in capitalism reduces its existence to the absence of collective property and its functions to the preservation of that absence.

39. It follows that state apparatuses coexisting with communist class structures could vary in countless ways. For example, communisms might develop that favor highly decentralized over centralized state forms. State functions might then devolve upon individual households and enterprises. A class analysis of such a communism would require examining all the unique interactions, contradictions, and changes that its distinct historical evolution would display.

40. Of course, an alternative arrangement (and hence an alternative form of communism) might locate the communist party outside the state and separately subsumed to communist class structures in enterprises and/or households.

41. In this and the following examples, there is a difference between two groups of state officials that is important from a class-analytical perspective. Those state officials who receive the communist subsumed class payments into their hands are therefore occupants of communist subsumed class positions. Those whom they hire—the likely majority of employees in both party and other state agencies—do not occupy subsumed class positions because they are not the first receivers of surplus distributions. Their remuneration occurs at one remove from the processes of producing, appropriating, and distributing the communist surplus labor. To signal that position *outside* the set of class processes (outside the production, appropriation, and distribution of the surplus), we designate them nonclass workers; they occupy nonclass positions. These definitions and their

justifications and implications are developed in Resnick and Wolff (1987, ch. 3 and 5). The designation of state employees as nonclass neither demotes or denies their activities' importance for securing communist class structures; the contrary is the case. The point of the nonclass designation is locational, to show their particular relation to the nexus of surplus labor production, appropriation, and distribution.

42. The "no content" refers to the explicit linkages *yet to be drawn* between the posited entry-point concept and all other concepts that will be connected to construct its meaning. Of course, every concept used in a discourse, including an initial organizing one, comes already laden with conscious and unconscious associations that will no doubt help to shape the construction of meaning.

43. Our argument here is indebted to DeMartino's original and important analysis (1992) of identification and explanation within an overdeterminist context. While we disagree with his critique of our overdeterminist explanations, our engagement with it helped shape the formulations here.

44. Stuart Hall (1985, 93) describes as "articulation" what closely parallels our "entry-point": "If Derrida (1977) is correct in arguing that there is always a perpetual slippage of the signifier, a continuous 'difference,' it is also correct to argue that without some arbitrary 'fixing' or what I am calling 'articulation,' there would be no signification or meaning at all. What is ideology but, precisely, this work of fixing meaning through establishing, by selection and combination, a chain of equivalences?"

# CHAPTER 2

# The Many Forms of Communism

The previous chapter summarized one basic form of communism: a combination of communist class structures interacting with several particular nonclass processes. We started with that form because its nonclass processes are the familiar property distribution (collectivized means of production) and allocation mechanism (state-planned distribution of productive resources and outputs). Next we discuss some of the many other, less familiar forms of communism that are possible. We will show forms of communisms in which communist class structures coexist with (1) private ownership of the means of production, (2) undemocratic distributions of power, and/or (3) competitive markets.

As forms of communism can vary, so too can forms of capitalism. To underscore this point, chapter 3 will examine forms of capitalism in which capitalist class structures coexist and interact with collectivized property, state planning, and democratic political institutions. Thus, chapters 1 and 2 demonstrate how each possible nonclass structure can coexist with either communist or capitalist class structures yielding various forms of communism and capitalism. Were we to consider other nonclass processes (for example, religious, educational, or family structures), still more variant forms would come into view. We limit ourselves to the forms associated with property, distribution, and democracy because they establish the general point and because they figure prominently in the class history of the USSR presented in part 3 below.

The aspect common to all forms of communism is the class structure: a collective of surplus producers that also appropriates and distributes that surplus collectively. Their common class structure demarcates all forms of communism from any form of capitalism. Put simply, the forms of capitalism all display a different class structure: those who appropriate and distribute the surplus are different people from the collective of surplus producers.

This surplus-based demarcation of communism from capitalism differs from other theories' demarcations. For them, property distribution (private or collective), resource and product distribution (via markets or state planning), and/or power distribution (democratic or not) differentiate capitalism from communism. Thus, for example, when private gave way to collective property and markets to planning in any society, many defined such changes as socialist or communist. Others disagreed: only a transition from undemocratic to fully democratic societies counted as socialist/communist for them. Debates among proponents of these nonsurplus definitions of socialism and communism deeply influenced twentieth-century history, and especially that of the USSR. What they ignored—the surplus-based definition and demarcation—was equally influential by its absence.

When, for example, socialist or communist regimes of collective property and planning left workers dissatisfied and alienated and eventually provoked their opposition, what happened? In frustration, anger, and despair, many socialists acquiesced in a return to private property and markets as the only and perhaps desirable option.[1] Likewise, many enemies of socialism and communism exulted in their "failure" and the "return to capitalism" that private property and markets represented to them.

For us, one ironic lesson of Soviet history is how dependent it was on the absence of the surplus-labor approach inaugurated by Marx and developed herein. The problems associated with collective property and planning would have provoked a different response had the conceptualization of communism in class-qua-surplus terms been available and applied. Instead of returning to private property and markets, an alternative solution might have been long-overdue policy debates over—and the eradication of—exploitative class structures inside the USSR and elsewhere. That alternative pertains equally to anticapitalist regimes and movements across the world today.

## Class and Property

We begin by examining the following change that might occur in the form of communism discussed in chapter 1: collective gives way to private ownership of the means of production. For many conventional Marxian as well as non-Marxian theorists, this change alone would end communism, since they presume communism and private property to be mutually exclusive. The Marxists among them believe that changed property relations (the economic "base" of society) transform everything else in the society (its political and cultural "superstructure"). Those who lost their shares in the formerly collectivized property would necessarily become dependent on selling their only remaining asset, their labor power. Those who privatized the formerly collective property could and would therewith buy the labor power of those forced to sell it. Analyses proceeding in this way conclude that capitalism has necessarily emerged. The change from collective to private property becomes synonymous with the transition from communism to capitalism.

We disagree. As we will show, a change in property ownership need not have any one particular effect on class structures or, indeed, on any other aspects of the society in which the property ownership changes. The larger context will overdetermine how a property change will influence all the different aspects of a society in each historical case. In asking how a communism that experienced such a property change might be altered, we focus on how that change might affect the communist class structure. We argue that private property can be consistent with and supportive of a communist class structure. Notwithstanding private property in means of production, a society's rules and laws, customs and culture, wealth production and distribution could together propel individuals collectively to produce, appropriate, and distribute their own surpluses. Then private property and communist class structures could socially coexist. We can call that a private property form of communism to distinguish it from a collective property form such as that presumed in chapter 1.

Suppose individuals who privately own productive property make it available to (invest in) enterprises with communist class structures. In return, the communist appropriators distribute to such private owners portions of the communist surpluses as dividends (much like dividends paid out of capitalist enterprises' surpluses to their private share-owners). Laws and customs could make such investment in communist class-structured enterprises every bit as "normal" as investment in capitalist enterprises is now. The change from collective to private property in means of production need neither coincide with nor produce a labor power market. Individual workers might be guaranteed paid employment and allocated by state officials to communist enterprises whether or not those enterprises' means of production were collectively or privately owned. Workers deprived of their share in collectively owned means of production do not, therefore, necessarily become sellers of labor power in the classically capitalist fashion. That is a possible outcome of changes in property ownership, but it is hardly necessary, as this example shows.

Besides the dividends paid to private owners out of communist surpluses, other portions would be distributed to still other communist subsumed classes. For example, taxes to the state could pay for public education teaching the wisdom, morality, and efficiency of this form of communism: communist class structures coupled with private property in means of production. Tax flows would enable the state to make and enforce laws mandating the coexistence of communist class structures and private property. Another portion of communist enterprises' surpluses might flow as rents to landlords for making available their privately owned space. Still another portion might comprise more or less voluntary contributions to a communist party that developed and disseminated the ideological justifications for this form of communism, and so on.

No doubt the contradictions unique to a communist class structure interacting with private property would generate particular kinds of strains and tensions. We might expect problems—jealousies, resentments, movements for and against forced equality of distribution—arising out of changing distributions of private property among citizens. One response—aimed to limit or contain such tensions—might be laws requiring that all citizens, regardless of what they own, must occupy, in rotation, all communist fundamental and subsumed class positions.[2] Other laws might limit the inequality of private property distribution by progressive personal income and inheritance taxes. Yet another response might be alterations in how the culture conceives private property. With or without state or party encouragements, private property might come to be understood—via ideological training, public education, literature, theater, film—as a kind of social trust rather than an individual owner's freely disposable resource. Indeed, the same culture that celebrates while constraining private property might also depict any class structure other than the communist as unacceptably undemocratic. The slogan might be: Only and all those who produce the surplus must participate in appropriating and distributing it.

Of course, no guarantee exists that such a coexistence and mutual support of a communist class structure and private property will endure. Political and cultural processes such as those illustrated above may not suffice to contain the contradictions and tensions of this form of communism. Suppose, for example, that private owners demanded and were able to obtain ever larger distributed shares of (dividends from) communist enterprises' surpluses. Eventually insufficient surplus might remain for distributions to secure those enterprises' other conditions of existence (taxes to the state, contributions to the party, new technologies, outlays for cultural programs, and so on). Struggles might then ensue over the communist dividends paid to private property owners. The outcome would depend, of course, on the entire social context.

No presumption exists that communist class structures would necessarily survive. Perhaps the richest property owners would succeed in obtaining the right to hire relatively propertyless individuals in new, capitalistically class structured enterprises. Alternatively, the struggles might eventuate in the end of private property in favor of collective property. Then again, perhaps various compromises might be reached allowing another combination of communist class structures and private property to prosper, albeit under new social arrangements reflecting the consciousness, goals, and relative powers of the parties to such struggles.

We can illustrate how such struggles yield variations within a society that combines a particular class structure with a particular regime of property ownership by recalling capitalism's parallel history. In early European capitalism, the private capitalists who appropriated their workers' surplus also owned the means of production used in their enterprises. Later, this distribution of property changed. Joint stock corporations often replaced individuals as the capitalist appropriators of surplus, and the means of production were owned not by the appropriators but rather by an investing "public" quite removed from capitalist production.[3] This change in the social distribution of productive property affected capitalist enterprises as well as much else in the societies where it occured. However, it did not make capitalist class structures within enterprises disappear. Capitalism changed its form; it did not vanish.

Other recent property changes have likewise produced new forms of capitalism. Workers, individually or collectively (especially via their pension funds' holdings), have bought shares of the firms in which they work. Sometimes workers' holdings suffice to gain positions for them on boards of directors and/or in management. Such enterprises change, but no transition to communist class structures has occurred. The workers there still do not collectively appropriate and distribute the surpluses they produce. The cultural and political context secured a capitalist class structure while property ownership changed; workers did not even try to use their property to alter the class structure of production.

As with communism's variant forms, the tensions, strains, and struggles unique to social combinations of capitalist class structures and different property distributions might jeopardize the survival of those class structures. Workers in capitalist class structures—whether they own large blocks of shares or not—might struggle to replace them with communist class structures. A class transition structure can emerge from the struggles in any society. It depends on the overdetermining social context and how its contradictions shape the consciousness, goals, and strengths of the contending parties.

For all possible social combinations of class structures and property arrangements, we presume that contradictions exist between them. Each particular class structure both supports and undermines the property system with which it coexists, and vice versa. This contradictory relation, interacting with its larger social context, creates the social dynamic that yields the variant forms of any type of society (capitalism, communism, and so on) and the occasional transition from one type to another (capitalism to or from communism).

Here we propose to illustrate our argument by examining a hypothetical form of communism in which a centralized communist class structure interacts with the private ownership of its means of production in the form of shares. We will suppose, for simplicity, that the enterprise distributes such shares only to its productive employees. A state agency monitors these distributions and sets an initial share value. Productive workers have the right to sell such shares at whatever price they can get on a stock market, but only to other productive workers (in the same or other enterprises). Other citizens are thus excluded from productive property ownership (although not from personal or household property). This is a variant form of communism that differs from the more conventionally recognizable form in which all productive property is owned collectively by all citizens.

Now suppose a law mandating that all adults rotate through communist fundamental and subsumed class positions. Thus, while each citizen functions within a collective of workers that produces and appropriates the surplus in an enterprise (the communist class structure), that individual will obtain shares and be able to buy or sell such shares. When workers exit communist fundamental class positions, they must sell whatever shares they then own to the state agency at a value it could set in a host of different ways. Exiting workers would enjoy capital gains or suffer capital losses on their holdings, thereby possibly producing wealth inequalities alongside communist class structures. Of course, state tax policies could constrain such a development.

Income inequality might also deepen. For example, consider an individual occupying, in rotation, a communist fundamental class position in an enterprise and, therefore, receiving some of its shares. Such an individual could then receive three kinds of income. First, their individual necessary labor will be compensated—the "wage" paid to all communist productive laborers. Secondly, they will receive dividend payments if and when the communist collective allocates a portion of the enterprise's surplus to share owners (a communist subsumed class payment). Workers who had sold such shares would not receive dividends, while those who bought them would: unequal incomes emerge here. Thirdly, still further inequalities of income can arise as communist productive workers realize capital gains or losses when selling shares. The first two kinds of income derive from productive laborers' participations in communist fundamental and subsumed class incomes. We call the third kind a nonclass income because it occurs separate from (at one remove from) the production, appropriation, and distribution of surplus.

This particular private property arrangement could well support and strengthen the society's communist class structures. Since workers' incomes depend in part on the surplus portion they distribute back as dividends to themselves, they have an incentive to maximize their surplus. That incentive is strengthened to the extent that efficient surplus production enhances the value of the enterprise's shares and hence capital gains. The opportunity to amass considerable personal wealth in these ways may also make workers, especially the wealthier among them, quite enthusiastic about this form of communism.

However, all sorts of difficulties also could arise. For example, whatever portion of communist surpluses flows into dividends reduces what is left to secure other conditions of the existence of the communist enterprises. Portions of their surpluses pay the taxes that the state uses to fund the agencies, public education, police, military security, and other institutions that the enterprises need. Other portions fund technical innovation and the communist party activities aimed at securing social acceptance of a communist class structure. Still other portions pay interest on the credit that the communist enterprise periodically requires, and so on. Inescapable conflict emerges among proponents of different combinations of such surplus allocations as they differently evaluate and balance the competing demands of communist enterprise surpluses: enhancing personal incomes versus securing communist class structures and balancing among the competing ways to secure them. The everpresent threat is that failure to fund the needed nonclass processes (state and party action, credit extension, technical progress, etc.) may undermine communism itself.

Responding to conflicts over surplus distributions, workers might increase the quantity of surplus they produce by laboring more hours. Their goal might be to enable more dividend payments without reducing the other surplus allocations. Yet such a response risks worker exhaustion, alienation, and disaffection from communist class structures. It may also yield growing inequality of private wealth, if shareholding in such enterprises is restricted, and hence dividend receipts flow, to a minority of workers. Growing inequality may provoke animosities directed against that inequality and/or against private wealth per se (in favor of a return to collective wealth) and/or against communist class structures (in favor of other class structures).

Access to a stock market might also produce such difficulties. Stock market fluctuations and differing individual share-trading abilities might deepen income and wealth inequality. This could undermine the culture of equality often celebrated in communist society as crucial to its existence and survival. Diverging consumption standards, status, amd inheritances; new definitions of social power and success in society; and even new individual strategies to achieve such power and success might interact to generate a culture and a politics increasingly ambivalent about the communist class structures of enterprises.

Ambivalence may become hostility toward the communist fundamental class process. Those who became wealthy on the basis of this form of communism might confront rising hostility and opposition from those who did not. They might then decide to preserve their wealth by ending communism rather than shifting to another form of communism. Freedom, democracy, and economic efficiency, they might then insist, require that individuals with the means to do so be free to establish private enterprises in which they would appropriate the surplus labor produced by others without such means. Such voices might rediscover and proclaim Adam Smith's "invisible hand" theory (or its modern reformulation as "Pareto optimization"): that the pursuit of individual self-interest is the surest route to optimizing the welfare of the whole society. Such a theory might legitimate a transition from communist to capitalist class structures on the grounds of their greater efficiency. Freedom to start capitalist enterprises could be defended morally as a matter of rewarding the successful and as a civic virtue itself.

Our hypothetical example shows how communist class structures could enable, enhance, and strengthen private property arrangements. It likewise demonstrates how private property might induce workers to support and work hard within communist class structures. Yet the example also reveals how communist class structures in enterprises might undermine private property were increasing inequalities of wealth to clash with the collective values and turn people against private property. Similarly, the institution of private property could undermine communist class structures if it were to (1) divert too large a portion of communist surpluses to personal accumulations and/or (2) undermine workers' physical health by promoting overwork.

The logic of overdetermination in our argument implies not only that contradictions characterize the relationship between class and property. The illustrative contradictions cited above—as well as many others that constitute the class-property relation—all operate simultaneously. The *net* result of the web of contradictions—those that sustain versus those that undermine—is contingent. It depends on the total social context of cultural, political, and economic processes. They overdetermine whether and how the contradictions sustain or undermine any particular coexistence of class and property structures.

A different example can enrich the argument. Suppose a society characterized by a decentralized communist class structure. Productive workers appropriate and distribute *only* the surplus produced in their own enterprise. Ownership of each enterprise's productive property is vested exclusively in its workers. This form of communism avoids some of our first example's contradictions, but it encounters others. The communist class structure in each enterprise will yield different quantities of surplus (for reasons of weather, planning errors, technical problems, local politics, etc.). Thus, some communist workers will be able to distribute more surplus to themselves as private owners. Communist workers in other enterprises will have to settle for smaller distributions to themselves as owners. Still other communist enterprises may generate no surpluses and perhaps exhaust their workers' personal property to maintain their enterprises. If growing inequality of enterprises' performances and of wealth among communist workers results, the kinds of conflicts seen above may develop and perhaps evolve toward a change in the form of communism or even a transition out of communism.

Such transitions may never become possibilities in citizens' minds, or they might be thwarted if begun. If interacting property and communist class structures generated unequal distributions of wealth, new laws might redistribute the wealth through inheritance or other taxes and subsidies. Cultural affirmations of communism and demonizations of exploitation may succeed in making a transition away from communist class structures literally unthinkable, precluding popular support for any program to abolish communist class structures. The coexistence of communist class structures and private property might come to be viewed overwhelmingly as "the ideal balance" between collective well-being ("community" values) and personal well-being ("individual" values). The ways that communist class structures and private property undermine each other may be more than offset by the ways in which they reinforce each other.

A final example completes our discussion. First, we suppose a decentralized surplus labor appropriation and the enterprise's workers as sole owners, collectively, of its property, as in our previous example. However, we now add the legal possibility that the workers as private owners could agree to dismantle and sell the assets of their enterprises to anyone willing to buy. This might be touted as an ideally decentralized mechanism to close enterprises whose products were unwanted or whose technology was outmoded. Such asset sales would mean that communist workers had abolished their own communist class positions. The thus unemployed workers might then enter capitalist or other class structures, if no positions were available in communist enterprises. In this case, private property would have helped to undermine communist class structures. Alternatively, if the law allowed only communist class structured enterprises, no supersession of communist class structures would ensue. Perhaps new communist class structured enterprises would be required to give priority to such unemployed workers. Such a form of communism might combine efficiency and equity in a model way.

These examples support several general propositions about the coexistence of communist class structures and property structures. Property regimes ranging from the collective to the private can coexist with communist class structures. The equality of persons within the collectives of producers/appropriators within communist class structures may sustain unequal and even increasingly unequal private property distributions. At the same time, such communist class structures in enterprises can range from the decentralized to the centralized. The possible combinations of property and communist class structures yield many variant forms of communism. The interactions between coexisting class structures and property structures are contradictory. The larger social context overdetermines whether, how, and for how long each particular coexistence survives and, if it does not, to which other class and/or property structures a transition will occur.

Having shown that communist class structures can coexist with private as well as collective property, we turn next to a parallel demonstration. Communist class structures can coexist with or without markets, including a market in which labor power is exchanged for a wage payment. Productive resources and products need to be distributed among producers and consumers in all economies with developed divisions of labor. The mechanism of distribution can be administered allocations (by state, religious, communal, or other authorities) or market exchanges (with the usually associated prices, wages, and money). However, the distribution of resources and products is different from production and hence different from the class structure of production.

How resources are assembled for production and how the resulting products get distributed socially are different matters from how surplus is produced, appropriated, and distributed. Mechanisms of distribution and class structures of production interact, but that is no argument for making them identical or fixing them in only one possible relationship. The next section shows how both markets and other distribution systems—for resources including labor power and for products—can coexist with communist class structures.

## Class and Markets

To make this argument, we begin by considering two enterprises, one producing cloth, the other food. Both have communist class structures. They operate within a society whose system of distribution entails market exchanges between buyers and sellers. Workers in these communist enterprises collectively produce and sell their outputs. One portion of their sales revenues comprises the values yielded by their "necessary" labor; the collective appropriates this portion and uses it to pay wages to its individual members. The remaining portion of sales revenues, yielded by the workers' surplus labor, is collectively appropriated and distributed. In this way, communist labor has been embodied in communist commodities and communist surplus labor in those commodities' surplus values.

These commodities deserve a modifying adjective—*communist*—to indicate which class process was involved in their production. The same adjective belongs with related nouns such as *value, surplus value, price,* and *profit* when they too pertain to communist class structures and their commodity products. As Marx (1990, 953) noted, "The *commodity* that emerges from capitalist production is different from the commodity we began with as the element, the precondition of capitalist production." Here as elsewhere, he underscores the difference between precapitalist and capitalist commodities. The commodities differed because they emerged from capitalist versus noncapitalist class structures.[4] Our argument here aims to show how communist class structures can coexist with markets to yield yet more variant forms of communism.

We begin by focusing on a market in labor power, since it is so often viewed, wrongly in our opinion, as a sign of capitalism. A market in labor power means that laborers sell their labor power to buyers by mutual agreement or contract. Laborers use the revenues from the labor power commodity they sell—their wages—to purchase means of subsistence. We make the usual assumption that these means of subsistence are also commodities as, indeed, are all the products of industry. In short, our focus on the labor market presumes a generalized context of markets as the means to distribute resources and products.

In such a generalized market system, we ask the following two questions that are basic to our class analytical approach: (1) Inside the producing enterprises, who produces, appropriates, and distributes the surplus? and (2) To whom are shares of the surplus distributed and for what purposes? If we answer that a communist class structure exists inside all enterprises, that means that the collective of communist workers is both the purchaser of labor power as a commodity and the seller of its products as commodities. The collective buys each individual unit of labor power from its own members (much as it also buys tools, equipment, and raw materials for production).[5] The collective alone thus acquires the use-value of each unit of labor power sold by setting in motion the labor of these workers with other purchased means of production. In this way, the collective carries out production and then sells its output in market exchanges. It uses one portion of the revenues to pay the wages it owes its individual members. It collectively appropriates and distributes the remainder. The coexistence of such communist class structures inside enterprises with commodity—including labor power—markets defines a form of communism that we might call market communism.

As with private property, so with generalized markets: communist class structures that coexist and interact with them will display particular qualities and contradictions. For example, market communism would likely require new laws and a new consciousness among its participants. Such laws might require that laborers who sell their labor power to communist enterprises *must* thereby also become part of the collectivity of workers that appropriates and distributes their surplus labor. The new consciousness might entail workers thinking it normal and unremarkable that they are simultaneously individual sellers and collective buyers of their own labor power. This would parallel the sort of normality now conventionally assigned to market exchange transactions as the appropriate mechanism to distribute goods and services outside the family and household—alongside the abnormality associated with using a market mechanism to distribute goods and services inside the household.

A state that coexisted with generalized markets and communist class structures within enterprises would likely be pressed to help secure such laws and social consciousness. Instead of operating agencies to plan economic activity, such a state would design, enforce, and adjudicate laws that combine markets and communist enterprises in mutually supportive ways. It would likewise operate schools and other institutions, organize cultural campaigns, and so on to inculcate the norms needed for such a social combination to become routine and naturalized in the popular consciousness. We would expect that communist enterprises would make subsumed class payments to the state out of their appropriated surpluses. These might take the form of taxes on communist enterprises' realized surpluses to help pay for such state activities—rather like capitalist enterprises pay taxes for state activities aimed at securing their class structure's conditions of existence.

This argument encounters questions. Does the coexistence of generalized commodity production and communist class processes in enterprises preclude the survival of those communist class processes? What happens to the viability of communist class structures when the fluctuations endemic to markets yield high unemployment? How can the notion of collectivity among workers survive the competitive, individualist, and alienating environment of markets and exchange? Are markets not necessarily, in the last instance, linked to capitalism?

We responded to similar questions above concerning the coexistence of private property and the communist fundamental class process. There we argued that a contradictory relationship existed between them. Private property both sustained and undermined communist class structures; which effect would prevail was always contingent, dependent on the larger social context. A contradictory relationship also exists, we believe, between markets and communist class structures. It encompasses both instability and stability, concentration and competition, alienation and solidarity.

Consider first the classic notion of worker alienation as it has widely been discussed in relation to capitalist class structures. Workers who competitively sell their labor power to capitalists are thereby alienated not only from their surplus labor, but also from controlling the process of their labor as well as its fruits, from one another, and ultimately from parts of themselves. Whether or not they are conscious of their situation, it is argued, their alienation generates endless problems of low motivation and low productivity that threaten the survival of capitalist enterprises. No doubt, similar problems would also appear if workers sold their labor power to communist enterprises. Such problems could, under certain social circumstances, even contribute to undermining communist class structures altogether.

However, the problems of alienation associated with wage labor are only part of the complex, contradictory relationship between wage labor and class. Wage labor markets do not always and necessarily exert only undermining effects, regardless of the broader social contexts. Capitalist economies have found their ways to limit, mute, offset, or control the effects of wage-earner alienation. Comparable ways to manage alienation would likely emerge in societies where communist class structures prevail within enterprises. Moreover, individuals' motivations and productivities, their senses of themselves and their social relationships, are not determined solely by (reducible to) market processes. We reject such determinist/reductionist logics in favor of overdetermination.[6] We presume multiple and contradictory causes of workers' alienation. Market processes interact with all the other social processes to overdetermine how individuals feel and construe their experiences in the labor market, in production, and elsewhere. Just as the presence of a particular class structure cannot be reduced to the presence or absence of a wage labor market as its essential determinant, neither can the existence of worker alienation.

Communist class structures would, where they exist, also participate with all other social processes in overdetermining the consciousness that workers bring to their market experiences. For example, communist enterprises might well support state, party, and other activities that inculcate particular norms and values in workers. These might radically demote workers' individual market activities relative to the importance assigned to their collective production activities (producing, appropriating, and distributing the surpluses they themselves create). The latter would then function as the prioritized elements of their self-definition and sense of individual worth. What might come to matter most would be workers' proficiencies within the collective activities of enterprises rather than the wages they received. Societies with markets and capitalist class-structured enterprises often display a reverse pattern of self-definition and self-worth. In the United States, for example, education and advertising persuade many workers to define themselves minimally in terms of their labor and maximally in terms of the standards of (conspicuous) consumption that their wages and salaries make socially visible.

Of course, the contradictions within the relationship between markets and communist class structures can evolve in ways that jeopardize those class structures. Depending on the overdetermining social circumstances, markets, communist enterprises, and workers' experiences may deepen alienation, weaken collective solidarity, and thereby undermine the survival of communist class structures. Under other conditions, the interaction strengthens both markets and communist class structures. The latters' supporters will presumably intervene whenever, wherever, and however possible to maximize the likelihood of that outcome. Their efforts may succeed or fail depending on time, place, and context: no historical inevitability attaches to the contradictory relationship between markets and communist enterprises.

The same logic applies when a society in which markets and communist enterprises coexist encounters the instabilities associated with markets. Marx's analysis of market capitalism underscores how markets can fail—commodity supplies and demands unbalanced—and how their failures can lead to generalized economic crises. Markets in communism can also fail and threaten dire consequences. For example, suppose that some communist enterprises face insufficient demand for their commodity outputs to be sold at the prices needed to recoup their costs of production and realize their surplus value. Let us suppose further that they react by reducing output and employment.

Communist workers might react to high unemployment, unsalable products, and thus falling surpluses by deciding to reduce their surplus distributions, their subsumed class payments. They might, for example, cut outlays for day-care centers for workers' children or contributions to the communist party to enable their reduced surplus to maintain outlays on sales staffs seeking buyers. For some communist enterprises, this strategy may succeed in overcoming market instabilities and restoring adequate surplus realization. In other communist enterprises, the strategy may well fail. Reduced child-care boosts worker absenteeism and lowers productivity while underfunded party activities further depress worker morale and productivity. Communist enterprises experiencing these problems may be unable to continue to operate. In this form of communism, market interactions with communist class structures would have led some communist enterprises' collectives of workers/appropriators to fire some or all of their individual members.

If the unemployed were willing to take jobs producing surplus without becoming a part of the enterprise collectivity that appropriates that surplus—and if such noncommunist enterprises existed in the society—capitalist enterprises might grow. The interaction of markets and communist enterprises might in this way undermine some (or, in extreme circumstances, perhaps all) communist enterprises and provoke transitions to differently class-structured enterprises. Such a class change would then react back upon markets to alter them, and so on.

Generalized communist commodity production that produces unemployment may thereby threaten the survival of that form of communism or indeed any form of communism. However, no necessity for communism's passing follows. In societies where chiefly capitalist enterprises interact with markets, likewise no *necessity* exists for market instabilities to undermine the existing class structures. Capitalisms have long learned to survive and even prosper despite recurring periods of unemployed labor and capital. Various state policies and private sector adjustments have usually succeeded in preventing unemployment from undermining capitalist class structures. Cultural processes have aided this process. For example, economists have stressed the "positive" aspects of market downturns: they weed out the "less efficient" enterprises. In contrast, the negative aspects of lost jobs, traumatized families, wasted production facilities, and other such market inefficiencies tend to be minimized, ignored, or attributed to causes other than market instabilities.[7]

The culture of a society with communist enterprises and markets would, of course, differ from the culture of a society with capitalist enterprises and markets. Both cultures would face troublesome market fluctuations, but they would respond in different ways designed to maintain their different class structures. Thus, state officials in communist societies might well justify interventions in markets by references to a commitment "to guarantee the good life for communist workers."[8] Their interventions would include the outlawing of exploitation—much as other societies outlaw slavery, serfdom, or legal discriminations of various sorts—as well as laws fixing minimum wages, annual incomes, and so on.

Anticipating possible unemployment, such a state might require each communist enterprise to distribute some of its surplus to a central fund to sustain the unemployed. To overcome market difficulties the communist state could increase support to communist enterprises (buying communist commodity outputs, finding new export markets, and so on). The state might establish new state enterprises (of course, with communist class structures) to absorb unemployment, at least temporarily, generated in existing communist enterprises. The state might also reduce its tax demands on communist enterprises' surpluses when market difficulties reduce their realized surplus. These are but a few of the possible state policies to prevent or offset market difficulties in societies where markets coexist and interact with communist class structures. Many such policies are analogous to ones that exist in capitalist societies.

Such state interventions create new kinds of contradictions within market communism. For example, establishing state enterprises fosters new forms of competition for nonstate enterprises. Locating them within the state also provides new opportunities both for communist state officials and for workers in those enterprises possibly to achieve more favorable (powerful) positions in society for themselves vis-à-vis the private communist enterprises. To expand state service supporting private communist enterprises while reducing its taxes on their surpluses—a strong program against unemployment—would throw the state budget into imbalance. If such a deficit were to be offset by raising taxes instead on workers' incomes, this might well provoke other problems.

Market interventions that secure enterprises' communist class structures while preventing falling incomes and rising unemployment may also introduce problems often associated with "actually existing socialisms." If the state does not let communist enterprises dissolve when market conditions render them no longer viable, it may thereby block the shift of workers and productive resources to the production of other goods and services that may be more important to social progress (in terms of standards of living but also in terms of citizens' attitudes toward and support for economic change). The analogies with similarly motivated state interventions in capitalist societies are striking. The state must, in both cases, weigh the costs and benefits of its support against those of "letting the market decide." But each state weighs different costs and benefits. Thus, the communist state gives great weight to how its policies produce benefits for as against imposing costs on long-term survival and growth of communist class structures; the capitalist state clearly does not.

A communist state may intervene, rather than let the market mechanisms proceed, if, for example, it shares a broad cultural consensus that workers should control markets rather than adjust to them. If such adjustment is seen as quintessentially capitalist and hence the opposite of socialism and communism, workers may expect and state officials oblige with market-controlling state interventions. As a result, the economic development of a communist society will be different from what it would have been had markets been left alone. Moreover, it is quite possible that at another time, with a different cultural concensus, the state might not intervene when market instabilities threaten some communist enterprises. We might well expect periodic oscillations in state policy toward markets in communist societies.

Capitalist societies too have oscillated between phases of relatively active state intervention to regulate or control markets and phases where state interventions were minimized. We presume that similar oscillations in the extent of communist state interventions will likely emerge. Policy makers reach different conclusions in weighing the costs and benefits of state intervention because their ever-changing social context alters what they count as costs and benefits and how they measure them. But there is no reason to presume nor any evidence that such oscillations necessarily undermine the class structures that state policy aims to secure. Not only can communist class structures inside private enterprises coexist with markets, they can likewise coexist with more or less state intervention when those markets experience instabilities. These are thus still more forms of communism: those with markets and maximum state intervention as well as those with markets and minimum intervention.

The complex coexistence of communist class structures, markets, and a state is, as we have shown, fraught with contradictions, tensions, and instabilities. The communist enterprises and the state will seek to cope with them in ways that reproduce communist class structures. It is possible that the interactions among markets, communist class structures, and state interventions will yield difficulties that exceed their coping mechanisms and undermine the survival of the communist class structures. This could help to inaugurate a class transition. The latter remains as much a possibility for communist societies with markets and a state as it has always been a possibility in societies where capitalist class structures interact with markets and a state.

## Class and Power

Communist class structures may coexist with alternative structures of power and thereby display still more variant forms of communism. The argument here parallels our previous discussions of the coexistence of communist class structures with alternative distributions of property (private and collective) and alternative mechanisms of resource and product distribution (markets and planning). Given the politically charged associations linking communism to particular social distributions of power, we will focus on them quite closely. However, we seek only to suggest an approach; we cannot here do justice to all its implications for the relationship between class and power (a vast topic of a vast literature).

Consider a society composed of M adult individuals. Of these, a subset, N, participate as producers, appropriators, and distributors of surplus labor in the communist enterprises prevailing in this society. Thus, M-N individuals do not participate as such communist workers. We propose to examine three different possible distributions of power among the adult individuals in this society: power in the sense of effective authority to order/govern individuals' activities and relationships in this society (including their relationships to the communist class structure). The first distribution gives every one of the M adult individuals equal power. The second gives *only* the N communist workers such equal power. Finally, the third distribution that we consider allocates such power only to all or some of the individuals (M-N) who are *not* communist workers in this society.

We may call the first distribution a complete social democracy; everybody shares equally in the power to order individuals' social activities and relationships. We term the second distribution a complete class democracy (power vested in the M communist workers). The third distribution of power describes a kind of oligarchy (power in the hands of only nonworkers) that might even take the extreme form of being concentrated in one person, a despot.

The goal here is to keep separate the class processes of producing, appropriating, and distributing surplus labor from the political processes of distributing and exerting power or control over individuals' behaviors. Power—even when it is exerted on the class processes—remains separate and distinct from them. For example, consider a class democratic communism where N producers collectively produce, appropriate, and distribute the surplus *and also have* the legal power alone to decide (1) the size of that surplus and (2) what portions of the surplus will be distributed to which recipients. For a contrasting example, consider a complete social democracy: power there is distributed equally to all M citizens. They would thus decide both the size of the surplus and how it is to be distributed. Note that here, the N communist workers remain the sole appropriators and distributors of the surplus, but they would have to share, equally with all other adult citizens, the power to decide on the magnitudes and allocations of the surplus. Yet another relationship between class and power would emerge if social power were concentrated solely in the hands of the M-N subset of the population, what we termed an oligarchy. Then the individuals engaged in the communist class structures of enterprises would be excluded from power over the size and distibribution of the surplus. That is, they would continue to produce, appropriate, and distribute the surplus collectively, but the power to determine the size and particulars of the distribution would lie in others' hands. No invariant or uniquely necessary link connects communist enterprises to one or another social distribution of power.

While we focused above on alternative distributions of power over the sizes and distributions of communist surpluses, the same logic applies to power over other aspects of individuals' behaviors. Alternative social distributions of power over, for example, child rearing or voting for political leaders or designing educational curricula can likewise coexist with communist class structures inside enterprises. Power relationships and class relationships within any society are neither identical with, nor uniquely connected to, nor deducible from one another.

Each distinct coexistence of communist enterprises and a particular social distribution of power displays its unique contradictions. In complete social democracy, for example, every individual is endowed with equal rights to help shape the rules of social interactions among individuals (including their relations to communist surplus labor production, appropriation, and distribution). If such rights took the concrete forms of voting and majority rule, then that majority would decide, among other things, (1) the number and identities of the individuals comprising N, (2) the division between necessary and surplus labor, (3) what portions of the surplus to distribute to different occupants of subsumed class positions, (4) whether or not to rotate individuals through different class positions, and (5) how to organize any rotation.

Such a social democratic form of communism might become popular because every individual participates in exercising this power—making these decisions—over the class (and also the nonclass) processes comprising the society. Contradictions, however, also exist in the interaction of power and class structures. Added to the tensions and conflicts that can arise in any situation where majority votes decide, there are particular problems that may arise between the N communist surplus labor producers and appropriators and the rest of adult society (M-N). In a social democracy, the N producers of surplus must share control over the surplus with the other M-N individuals who do not perform communist surplus labor. Suppose a democratic decision mandated increased surplus labor by the N performers. They might, under certain circumstances, question or challenge the nonperformers' power over surplus labor. Complete social democracy might come to appear to the N communist producers to be grossly unfair. Its abolition might become the goal of workers' movements. Countermovements might then define their goals in terms of abolishing communist class structures as inimical to the social democracy they champion. They might, for example, endorse some version of "Jeffersonian democracy," understood as a social democracy coexisting with an ancient class structure (generalized individual self-employment). Whatever the good intentions that might lie behind establishing the egalitarianism of complete social democracy, such egalitarianism also establishes the basis for tensions and possible conflicts that could, under some circumstances, undermine either that distribution of power or the communist class structure or both.

Under other social circumstances—specifically under other culturally hegemonic values—such tensions might not arise or become socially explosive. If the requirement that communist workers share power with nonworkers—including power over how individuals relate to the communist class structure—were celebrated as the long-sought, utopian core of communism, that might minimize contradictions becoming openly antagonistic. Proponents might succeed in gaining wide acceptance of this definition of communism: a society in which enterprises have communist class structures, where all individuals rotated through all class positions, and where every citizen had equal control over deciding the rules of social behavior (including relations of individuals to the communist enterprises). Such acceptance might mute the contradictions between communist class structures and social democracy for indefinite periods.

Within socialist and communist movements, many have focused on democracy as the essential difference between capitalism and the socialist/communist alternative. They have equated capitalism with merely formal democracy and socialism/

communism with substantive, "real" democracy.[9] The prevalence of such thinking might help to secure the coexistence of communist class enterprises and social democracy by undermining other discourses that "see" democracy violated if communist producers must share power equally with nonproducers. Once again, neither discourse necessarily prevails over the other.

In the distribution of power that we labeled complete class democracy, the N producers/appropriators of surplus also have exclusive power over its sizes, dispositions, and so on. This form of communism would eliminate some of the tensions discussed above. As usual, eliminating one set of contradictions provokes another set. Concentrating power in the hands of communist workers may enable them to take actions unacceptable to others. The workers may use their power to raise their necessary labor (devoting more of their labor time to producing their own wage incomes). If we assume a constant length of the working day, this action would reduce the surplus they produce and hence the surplus available to be distributed by them to others. They may reduce distributed shares of the surplus to disfavored subsumed class recipients. In these and other ways, a class democracy could make life increasingly difficult for some or all who do not perform communist surplus labor.

On the other hand, a set of cultural and political processes may be present that constrains such actions, despite the power over the surplus allocated exclusively to the communist producers of it. A system of regular rotation of all individuals in and out of communist class positions might dissolve the tensions described above. Discourses may exist that motivate producers to extend their workday without increasing their wages and to distribute the resulting higher surplus to nonproducers. Done in the name of social welfare, solidarity, or other culturally sanctioned values, such behavior by the communist producers could undermine hostility or opposition to the producers' concentrated power. Nationalist discourse, for example, might successfully exhort communist workers to increase their surplus labor so more of its fruits can be distributed to, say, subsumed classes of military or party officials or production managers viewed as essential for the nation's survival or expansion. The risk that performers of nonclass processes who get smaller distributions of the surplus might no longer provide some of the conditions of existence for communist enterprises might also dissuade communist producers from using their powers in particular ways. How the contradictions unique to the coexistence of class democracy and communist enterprises change both depends on the social context.

In our third kind of power distribution, in which an oligarchy of M-N individuals wields power—or possibly only one despot does—the resulting contradictions with communist enterprises once again may but need not undermine either that power distribution or that class structure. Three linked, hypothetical examples can make the basic point. In the first, a matriarchal society organizes all communist enterprises as exclusively male, while all or some women hold exclusive power. These women do occupy communist subsumed class positions, obtaining distributed shares of surplus for providing political conditions of existence of communist class structures (writing and enforcing laws, adjudicating disputes over those laws, etc.). Our second example is a patriarchal society in which such power is vested exclusively in the hands of nonworker men who control the surpluses produced in communist enterprises in which only women produce, appropriate, and distribute surplus. Finally, consider still another form of communism in which both men and women collectively produce *and* appropriate surplus labor in communist enterprises, but only *one* gender of nonproducers exercises power over that surplus as over other relationships in the society.

Each of these power distributions can coexist with communist class structures in the society's enterprises. We can clarify this point by shifting attention momentarily away from enterprises to households where power and class processes also coexist. Production inside households (converting raw materials into family meals, repairing clothing and furniture, cleaning rooms, healing illnesses, etc.) may display communist class processes: adults collectively produce, appropriate, and distribute their surplus household labor (Fraad, Resnick, and Wolff 1994). Such communist households might contain as well a patriarchal distribution of power: father alone orders the behavior of household members in both their class and nonclass processes inside and outside the household. Mother, grandparents, children, and others perform necessary and surplus labor collectively and likewise appropriate and distribute the surplus. Yet this household communist class structure coexists with a household distribution of power concentrated solely in the father. He alone decides the sizes and dispositions of communist household surplus and most other economic, political, and cultural issues relating to household relationships. He also draws a portion of the household surplus into his own hands, partly to enable his performance of patriarchal decision making. Parents raising children, religious authorities guiding their flocks, school teachers, and others, might define gender, love, childhood, and kinship so as to naturalize and sanctify the household coexistence of patriarchy and a communist class structure. This would contribute to its continuation.

Political oligarchy can interact as well with communist class-structured enterprises. For example (see part 3 below for details), the Soviet collectivization of agriculture established collective farm enterprises that temporarily exhibited communist class structures. However, the power to decide the sizes and dispositions of their communist surpluses—and much else about collective farm life—was reserved to a small number of Soviet state and party personnel. This coexistence of oligarchic power and communist class structures in the specific context of Soviet society did not endure in many collective farms. Communist gave way to capitalist class structures inside those collective farms. Some became state capitalist farms: state officials appropriated the surplus of agricultural wage workers on state-owned land. Others became de facto private capitalist agricultural enterprises: a subset of the collective appropriated and distributed the surpluses produced by the rest of the collective on the collectively owned land. In these examples, an oligarchical power structure had coexisted with (farm) enterprises' communist class structures to define a particular form of communism. However, the contradictions of that form in the USSR of the 1930s produced transitions from communist to capitalist class structures in many cases.

Finally, as an example of a despotic form of communism, we suppose that one individual—not a communist producer/appropriator—wields total power over a vast network of communist enterprises as well as over other social sites. Cultural processes persuade the population that this despot's power secures both social cohesion and progress. By endorsing communist class structures—ordering the workers to produce, appropriate, and distribute their surpluses collectively—despotic power provides crucial conditions for their existence. A portion of the surplus that the despot orders from the communist enterprises finances the agents who manage politically and legitimate culturally this form of communism. Such agents perform military tasks of protection, perhaps crucial irrigation works, religious and artistic activities, and so forth. They interpret and disseminate the despot's grand design (or that of a God, whose chief agent is the despot), which is, in our terms, the coexistence of absolute oligarchy and communist class structures in enterprises. As Marx argued in reference to "oriental despotism," societies organized in such ways have managed to contain and so survive the contradictions between their power and class structures for centuries (Wittfogel 1963; Anderson 1975, 462–549; Turner 1978).[10]

As these examples show, communist class structures can coexist with a wide variety of social distributions of power. Each possible configuration of power and class structures—each variant form of communism—has its unique contradictions and hence its unique pattern of change. Depending on social context, such configurations will change in myriad ways. Within the changes, the communist class structures may endure or may undergo transition to some other class structures.

Forms of communism vary with the many alternative distributions of property and power than may coexist with communist class structures in production. To recognize this variability is to reject both scholarly and popular attempts to fix single and simple definitions of communism. Communisms are as variable as capitalisms. Blindness to the variant forms of both had and has serious consequences—political as well as theoretical—for efforts to understand and transform societies. This book not only challenges that blindness in the prevailing interpretations of what happened in the USSR. Part 3 below also argues that the blindness had disastrous consequences for the development and eventually the survival of the USSR. We are concerned to show how that blindness also hobbles countless efforts today to move beyond forms of capitalism to forms of communism.

It is perhaps important to restate that we focus on class not because it is the essence of society or social change. Our commitment to overdetermination precludes any such essentialism. Our focus is a response to the class blindness of other interpretations, a class blindness with negative social consequences.[11]

By examining communism in terms of surplus labor, we part company with those inside and outside Marxism who equate particular systems of property, mechanisms of distributing resources and products, or social allocations of power with communism. We likewise differ from conceptualizations of communism too narrow to grasp the variability of its forms: past, present, and future. Sketching communism's forms—a systematic task only begun here—had to precede this book's new formulation of the relationship among capitalism, communism, and the history of the USSR.

## Classless Communism and Proletarian Dictatorship

To this point we have theorized communism's varying forms as differing combinations of communist class structures and the myriad nonclass processes of social life (alternative property and power distributions, and so on). However, communism may also include yet another and different form—a "classless" communist society. The class categories of Marxian theory themselves suggest and enable the specification of a "classless" form of communism.[12] Being epistemologically self-conscious and self-reflexive, the Marxian theory we use here is driven to investigate its own conceptual limits, the boundary that defines it. This means taking a step beyond class forms of communism to consider a notion of "classless" communism.

Communism may take a particular variant form in which the necessary surplus labor distinction has disappeared and with it the Marxian theory premised and focused upon that distinction. This is, after all, as it should be. If Marxian theory is committed to the ceaseless change of human society, the forever coming into being, changing, and demise of all aspects of society, then this must apply as well to communist (as to all other) class structures and to Marxian (as to all other) theories. The argument of this chapter represents, then, more than the application to communism of certain class analytics based on a particular reading of Marx. It represents as well acknowledging the limitation of those analytics and peeking beyond them.

Marx's famous letter to Joseph Weydemeyer (5 March 1852) insists that the discovery of class and class conflict was not his but belonged rather to bourgeois historians. His new contributions, he argued, were three: a specific definition of class in terms of surplus production relations; the concept of the dictatorship of the proletariat; and lastly, the notion of such a dictatorship as transitional toward "the abolition of all classes ... a classless society" (Marx and Engels 1975, 64). While he wrote extensively on class in terms of surplus, he said little about either the dictatorship of the proletariat or classlessness. Yet Marx's work on class does provide us with some means for constructing at least an initial analysis of classlessness and taking it further than Marx or Marxists since have done.

The very phrase "classless society" remarkably defines a social arrangement in terms of what it is not. What would be missing in such a society, from our perspective, is the distinction between necessary and surplus labor, that is, the fundamental class process. By contrast, feudalism, capitalism, slavery, ancient, and still other class structures, and even the variant forms of communism sketched above, are all approached by Marxian theory in terms of their differing organizations of the division between necessary and surplus labor. That theory presumes the necessary/surplus distinction and then proceeds to work out the production, appropriation, and distribution of surplus labor in each society's unique class structure.

In a classless society no division between necessary and surplus exists. Hence the production, appropriation, and distribution of surplus labor disappear. They pass from history much as poorhouses, absolute monarchies, and religious rituals of human sacrifice largely faded from the twentieth century. The absence of class processes defines a "classless" society, given Marx's theory of class and the various forms of class societies.

That definition provokes the following sorts of questions. What social changes might enable a transition from class to classless societies—as distinct from transitions between class societies such as those from noncommunist to communist? How would labor be organized and divided among concrete production tasks in societies where class processes are absent? How are such societies different from those where some form of the class process is prevalent?

Not only can we conceptualize a society in which class disappears, we also presume that the disappearance of class would react back upon class analysis itself. Marxian theory would change, perhaps by removing its focus on class. While not forgetting the salience of class, it might focus instead on new problems, new objectives, and new social movements generated by the particular contradictions of classless societies. Marxism could thus apply its commitment to dialectics, that is, to the ceaseless transformation of all things, to envisioning the conditions of its own change as well.

The absence of the distinction between necessary and surplus labor means that all human labor applied to the production of use-values for social utilization (as means of consumption or means of production) would be understood as abstractly equivalent expenditures of brain and muscle. No portion of such labor would be "surplus." The Marxian distinction between productive and unproductive labor would disappear. All human labor—whether allocated to the production of food and cloth, or to capital goods and raw materials used up in their production, or to the production and dissemination of cultural artifacts and political laws—would, in a new and different sense, comprise necessary labor.[13]

Compared to any class-structured society, for example, a classless society would require very different kinds of organization of work tasks (what and how to produce) and allocation of products (who gets what). Who does what kind of work for how long and in what way would depend on the needs and wants of all concerned, excluding any need or want to produce or procure a surplus. No person's or group's desire for profit, rent, interest, and so on—as class categories—could be effective, could actually determine what work anyone performs or what products anyone gets. That is a condition for classlessness to continue. Another condition of existence of classlessness might be the systematic rotation of all work tasks among individuals to prevent any technical/functional divisions of labor from hardening and possibly becoming class divisions (cf. Bukharin and Preobrazhensky 1969, 115ff.) The absence of class implies as well as presupposes the liberation of all work from its historic subordination to class.

Classlessness also has its cultural conditions of existence. For example, there would have to be education of all in the multiplicity of tasks to be accomplished if rotation were to be possible. There would need to be education for all in the coordinating and designing of tasks as well as their performance. In short, the distribution of skills characteristic of class societies would have to be replaced by a distribution appropriate to classlessness: a general, mass development of the population's design, research, production, and managerial skills. Another cultural condition of existence would likely be a hegemonic ethic that places the highest priority on the equality of all in relation to production and its fruits and on classlessness as the preferred means to achieve that equality.

For classlessness to survive, still another condition is for politics to be the direct social means to decide the what, how, and for whom of production. These latter must be the direct objects of political processes without any regard to the maintenance of any class structure. Politics must at last proceed without the constraint of maintaining any existing class structure. Politics must prevent any of the rules of class maintenance—such as profit or surplus maximization—from interfering in the social decisions about economics or anything else. The absence of class implies as well as presupposes the liberation of politics from its historic interdependence with class.

Classlessness has its particular social effects. These will of course vary with the specific social contexts within which class processes cease to exist. In this tentative, partial peek into classless communism, it may be useful to mention some possible effects of long-standing concern to Marxists. A social transition to classlessness removes one factor contributing to hierarchical divisions among individuals performing various tasks in the division of labor. Workers would no longer be differentiated, consciously or unconsciously, according to whether they produce or appropriate surplus or live off surplus produced by others. Since the history of class-structured societies suggests that individuals who appropriate the surplus of others tend often to arrogate disproportionate political power and cultural benefits to themselves, classlessness can contribute toward more democratic political and cultural life.

Similarly, the absence of the necessary/surplus division of labor strengthens the scope and depth of collectivity in its gathering of all expenditures of human brain and muscle as equivalently under the continuous consideration, control, and transformation of politics. The production, distribution, and consumption of all goods and services, when classlessly organized, become more available as objects of democratic decision making. No imperatives of maintaining a given class structure block movements toward a more democratic politics associated with classlessness. In this sense, classlessness represents a social step toward the rule of "from each according to ability, and to each according to need."

For the foreseeable future, one condition for the emergence of classless communism may be the spread of Marxian theories that systematically conceptualize both the differences between communist and noncommunist class structures, and between them and classless communism. Such theories will, at the very least, considerably widen the scope of discussions as to the possible futures for contemporary societies. Alternative conceptions of communism—those never focused further than property ownership (who owns), than power (who rules), or even than surplus (who appropriates)—will likely foster different social transitions. Theories that do not recognize the varieties of class processes and the possibility of their disappearance will, in our view, likely do little to facilitate a transition to classlessness, and may do much to block it.

## Socialism and Communism

Having so far roughly equated socialism and communism, we need now to address their relationship differently. We begin by considering the many different usages of these terms. As very broad "isms," they invite commentaries that emphasize economics, politics, or culture according to the commentator's orientation (conceptual entry point). For most, the terms are passionately intertwined with utopian or dystopian visions of the future. The futures we seek and those we dread play their more or less subtle roles in influencing all interpretations of these terms.

For many on the Left, the hope for socialism and communism now rests mainly with the future because they believe that the twentieth century's experiments in constructing such social orders "failed" in the USSR, China, Cuba, and elsewhere. That failure is thought to reveal some fundamental, essential economic, cultural, or political defect that accounts for it. To "correct" that failure is then to create the conditions for that more prosperous, more humane, and freer society promised in and by the socialist and communist vision. Opposed to the Left but agreeing with the assessment of socialism and communism as failures, rightist writers locate the essential determining causes of these failures as uncorrectable flaws inherent in all forms of socialism/communism.

Most contemporary thinkers, left and right, focus on power—how it is organized and constrained, who wields it over whom, and so on. They account for the "failures" of socialism or communism in terms of the distribution of authority between state and citizen and among groups and individual citizens. Freedom, democracy, and political participation and control are the concepts that provide standards for defining the two terms, for assessing the claims of actual societies that they are socialist or communist, and for explaining their successes and failures.

For those whose focus is culture, the definitions of socialism and communism often turn on issues of consciousness and ethics: how these social arrangements are informed by distinct conceptions of humanity. Actual societies labeled socialist or communist are then evaluated in terms of whether their citizens are "new men and women" in terms of their attitudes toward life and community, their broadly defined interpersonal ethics.

For those concerned primarily with economics, socialism and communism have most often been defined in terms of collectivized property ownership in the means of production and the suppression of markets in favor of economic planning. They then analyze and assess socialist or communist experiments in terms of criteria of economic efficiency as relationships between inputs and outputs of production and/or criteria of what might be called "ethical efficiency" as expressed in the aphorism: "from each according to ability, to each according to work (socialism) or according to need (communism)."

For many who admired (and still admire) the USSR and other similarly structured countries, they did not fail because of some intrinsic flaw in Marxism or some necessarily inherent tendencies of socialism and communism. Rather, specific conjunctural events are identified that undermined what could otherwise have been a successful socialism or communism. For example, many have pointed to misallocated resources and concentrated power in the hands of a state bureaucracy, perhaps necessitated and made perverse in the USSR by the unrelenting hot and cold wars launched against it since 1917. These and/or other conditions—such as technological and cultural backwardness—are asserted to have distorted and ultimately destroyed the otherwise solid prospects socialism and communism had to be successful there.

A basic problem has afflicted such discussions of socialism and communism in the USSR and elsewhere. The various politically, culturally, and economically focused definitions of socialism and communism have not been necessarily consistent with one another. A distribution of property ownership called "socialist" often coexisted with market mechanisms, political power relations, or kinds of cultural life that were emphatically rejected as nonsocialist and noncommunist. Kinds of democracy could be achieved that some called "socialist," notwithstanding economic conditions understood as nonsocialist.

In the face of conceptual difficulties and inconsistencies, at the level of basic definitions, discussions have often taken either of two equally sterile turns. One option has been to insist on one definition as essentially correct or "ultimately decisive," thereby rendering all others as secondary or irrelevant and their proponents as wrong-headed or guided darkly by ulterior motivations. For example, the presence of political democracy (variously defined) has widely been asserted to be the central defining characteristic of genuine socialism and communism. Its absence then accounts for the failures of "actually existing" socialism or communism. For such thinkers, adding democracy to the collective property and economic planning of actual socialisms would have made them successful in the USSR and elsewhere. The other option has been to abandon the project of defining socialism and communism as intrinsically incoherent or practically inconsequential or both in an era of the "end of ideology." Those so persuaded search, instead, for absolute, universal qualities ("efficiency," "equity," etc.) of "good societies" transcending the outdated debates of capitalism versus communism.

Inconsistency, polarized contests among narrow and deterministic definitions, doubt about the terms altogether—these problems have devalued as well as plagued recent discussions of socialism and communism. Yet defining these key terms remains necessary. At the very least, such an effort at definition amounts to learning and respecting the lessons from the rich tradition of many peoples' costly and creative struggles for what they understood as socialism and communism. It is needed if we are to be clear and persuasive about the kind of future society to which we orient our current activities. The task of defining socialism and communism continues to absorb Marxian theory, much as those specters continue to haunt all social theory (especially that which most loudly declares that socialism, communism, and Marxism are all dead).

To move beyond the current unacceptable state of the definitions, we extend our specific class analysis of communisms beyond the loose conjoining of communism and socialism adequate to our argument so far. Indeed, that argument now enables us to formulate a new and different conception of the difference between communism and socialism.[14] We want to insert it into the ongoing discussions of socialism and communism because the class (in terms of surplus labor) conception is so often overlooked and because applying it in concrete analyses leads to arresting new conclusions.

Communism, for us, denotes a social formation in which communist fundamental class processes and classless production arrangements (in varying proportions) predominate in the production of goods and services. In such a social formation, noncommunist fundamental class processes do not characterize more than a small share of production activities. In contrast, socialism differs from communism in our perspective chiefly because it is not itself a class process, a distinctive form of producing, appropriating, and distributing surplus. Because the two terms are not synonymous—precisely in terms of surplus—we will henceforth stress their differences rather than conflate them.

As a label for social formations, socialism has functioned with little or no regard to their surplus labor dimensions. It has referred rather to one or more of such defining characteristics as state economic intervention, state provision of social safety nets (low or no cost housing, medical care, education, etc.), income equality, collectivized property in means of production, democratic politics, and so on. It is thus not surprising that very different social arrangements could be and have been labelled "socialist"—by advocates and enemies—across this century and across every continent. In these widely prevalent conceptions, socialism and communism differ chiefly in degree: communism being the further stage of state intervention, income equality, and so on.

From our perspective, the overwhelming majority of societies hitherto labeled socialist have been forms of capitalism. That is, they have been societies in which capitalist class structures prevail inside productive enterprises and few if any communist class structures exist anywhere. They have usually been forms of capitalism in which state activity is great (especially in the economy) and in which the basic social welfare of the general population is a high priority. Less frequently, socialism has also been defined as a transitional society lying between the capitalism it rejects and the communism it seeks to achieve.

The vast majority of supporters and detractors of Soviet society called it socialist in these traditional senses.[15] As we show below, it was actually particular forms of capitalist class structures that prevailed there, first in industry and then in agriculture. However, more than mere naming was always at stake. Calling the USSR socialist made its continuing capitalist class structure invisible as such, hence undebatable, and so off the agenda for social change. More than mere naming is likewise at stake now as new definitions of socialism and communism struggle into contention carrying their heavy implications for contemporary social change.

We can further clarify our differentiation of communism from socialism by briefly examining the thorny "dictatorship of the proletariat" that has haunted discussions of both terms. As Balibar (1977) showed so definitively, Lenin's "dictatorship of the proletariat" had little to do with the organization of state power (more or less democratic, etc.). It meant rather to distinguish between two alternative strategic commitments *regarding class structures* that a state apparatus—more or less democratic—could pursue. State supports for capitalist class structures and repression of anticapitalist impulses and movements defined a "dictatorship of the bourgeoisie." The opposite commitment—to support, strengthen, and extend socialist/communist class structures while eliminating capitalist class structures and repressing anticommunist impulses and movements—was understood as a "dictatorship of the proletariat." The terms concerned the class objectives, not the political organization, of the state.

Our class differentiation of communism from socialism implies a corresponding distinction between different dictatorships of the proletariat. A communist dictatorship of the proletariat would exist when state power builds and extends (1) communist as against noncommunist class structures and (2) classlessness as against *all* forms of class structures. Such commitments could become hegemonic within a state organized politically as a complete social democracy, a complete class democracy, various kinds of social oligarchies, or any combinations of these alternatives. A socialist dictatorship of the proletariat refers to state commitments to goals *other* than communist class and classless structures. These would be the goals traditionally associated with socialism: state management, regulation, and intervention in the economy (perhaps including nationalization of productive property, planning, and so on) to secure greater equality of incomes, a broad social welfare minimum, mass democratic political participation, and so on.

A socialist dictatorship of the proletariat would advance the socialists' nonclass goals and repress groups opposed to their achievement. A communist dictatorship of the proletariat might share many of those goals, but it would differ in adding and linking to them the particular goal of establishing and/or extending communist class structures and classlessness instead of capitalist or other noncommunist class structures. Either kind of dictatorship of the proletariat could function by means of governmental forms ranging from democratic to autocratic. The social context in each case would overdetermine which political form actually served to enable which kind of dictatorship of the proletariat.

From a class-analytical perspective, the concept of proletarian dictatorship requires adjectives: socialist or communist. These distinguish which kind of dictatorship the proletariat has achieved where and when it wrests state hegemony from dictatorships of the bourgeoisie (or possibly of still other surplus appropriators such as feudal lords). The distinguishing adjectives also draw attention to the struggles that remain even if and when "proletarian goals" and a "proletarian party" achieve hegemony within a state. Proletarian dictatorship is one thing; what kind of proletarian dictatorship is something else. Thus the necessarily two-part question to be posed about the USSR: Was a proletarian dictatorship achieved there and, if so, which kind?

Finally, our differentiation among communism, socialism, and dictatorships of the proletariat rejects any teleological notion that any one of these leads necessarily to any other. Abandoning historical inevitabilities, we presume that transitions can occur (and likely have occurred historically) in every direction among them (and indeed among other class structures as well). Thus, the notion of socialism as a period of transition from capitalism to communism can only be understood, from this perspective, as an expression of some groups' intentions for and/or interpretation of socialism. That is not our interpretation. For us, socialism is not inherently transitional in any particular way.

Our class specifications of communism and socialism can be applied to evaluate societies that were and still are labeled communist or socialist. To do that, we first determine which class processes exist within such a society—with special attention to possible communist class and classless relations of production. We explore their coexistence and contradictions within the larger social context. We look especially for evidence of movements to communist from noncommunist class processes and/or vice versa. Our results comprise a class (qua surplus) assessment of any society's relation to socialism and communism, to communist class structures and to classlessness: the foci of the particular contribution class analysis seeks to offer.

Just such class analytical questions inform the remaining chapters of this book. Our discussion of capitalism's different forms and especially our class analysis of the USSR aim to determine the Soviet system's status in terms of capitalism, socialism, and communism. Our assessment, focused on the social organization of surplus labor, will differ from those based on alternatively focused Marxian (and, a fortiori, non-Marxian) approaches and the different questions and aims of their proponents (cf. Trotsky 1961, 1972; Hilferding 1950; Rizzi 1985; Dunayevskaya 1971; Dobb 1966; Sweezy and Bettelheim 1971; Cliff 1974; Horkheimer 1978; Bellis 1979; Sweezy 1985a; Bettelheim 1975; Sweezy 1985b).

We seek to add social analysis such as ours that focuses on class—surplus labor production and distribution—to some of those listed above whose emphases fall rather upon the organization of political power, property ownership, cultural formation, planning, moral incentives, and other aspects of social structure. We appreciate that they enter into their analyses of socialism and communism by focusing upon social dimensions other than class in the surplus labor sense. We recognize as well that much of what they describe as, for example, communist or socialist democracy is as much an indispensable component of the future society we seek as is its communist class structure or its classlessness. If, in turn, their visions of true social democracy, cultural freedom, and egalitarian economic well-being were to recognize and include what we have discussed as communist class structures and classlessness as components of the future they seek, a basis for integration of our differing theoretical perspectives and for practical alliances would exist. We recognize, moreover, that the famous dichotomies that have haunted the Marxian tradition—private versus collective ownership, moral versus material incentives, planning versus market, alienation versus nonalienation, and so forth—will be radically rethought as will be our own class analysis if such an integration and alliance occurs.

Such an integration and alliance cannot and should not obscure our differences and the exploration and confrontation of them in the ongoing discussion and debate. However, based on such a mutual recognition theoretically, the discussions of socialism and communism can emerge from a long, if often brilliant and insightful, period of stalemate. That in turn might augur well for practical coalitions for socialism or communism. Steps in these directions would provide ample reward for the theoretical efforts in this and the previous chapter.

## Notes

1. A revealing example of this evolution can be found in work by the Polish theorists Kuron and Modzelewski (1972).
2. A comparable law—in a communist or capitalist society—might mandate that all adults vote in all elections regardless of their religious, financial, ethnic, or other differences.
3. In contemporary capitalism, corporate boards of directors rarely own significant proportions of the firm's outstanding stock. Nonetheless, the board still appropriates the workers' surpluses. Early capitalists not only owned and appropriated; they often also managed production. Now, capitalist boards of directors hire subordinates. Thus the appropriating capitalists neither own nor manage as they once did. These changing forms of capitalism (capitalist class structures interacting with variant nonclass processes) are comparable to the alternative forms of communism discussed in the text. See also Marx (1991, ch. 23 and 27) and Resnick and Wolff (1987, ch. 4 and especially 172-174).
4. For examples of Marx's recognition that markets (commodities) could and did occur with many different kinds of class structures, see 1990 (874) and 1991 (443); see also Wolff (1995).
5. The notion that a communist collective of workers hires its individual members raises no significant problem. It is analogous to a capitalist board of directors hiring some of its individual members as managers (who thus become, as individuals, sellers of their labor power, and, as the collective board, its buyer).
6. Determinist logics render workers' consciousness the passive effects of such ultimate determinants as markets. In the classic Marxian theory of alienation, markets determine a false consciousness in workers: the idea that market processes rather than their labor determine commodity values. The conventional Marxian solution to this false consciousness was to replace markets with planning. The latter would permit workers to gain a rational, undistorted understanding of themselves, their relationship with others and with produced wealth. Planning would end the alienation produced by markets. Rejecting determinism, we do not see workers' consciousness as (a) reducible to the effect of one or two ultimate determinants, or (b) merely passive. Worker alienation is overdetermined by many social processes. It will not likely vanish if one or two aspects of a society are

changed, even if those aspects are class structures and markets. We suppose that alienation will be different in market versus planned economies and in capitalist versus communist class-structured enterprises, and so forth. We understand preferring and struggling for one system's alienation against another's. We see no need to fantasize the elimination of alienation altogether. We find much reason to remain open to the possibilities of uniquely communist kinds of alienation whose reduction would demand corrective attention and social changes.

7. Once again we face the insoluble logical problem of measuring the positive and negative effects of any economic event to reach a conclusion as to the "net" result. Market failures surely have both positive and negative effects, benefits, and costs. The infinite effects, present and future, vastly exceed our capacity to measure them, let alone to measure them commensurately. All "cost benefit analyses" therefore select some (usually very few) costs and benefits to measure. Their results depend on their selection processes and have no general or absolute claim on our assent. Thus, celebrating market downturns as wondrous mechanisms for greater economic efficiency depends on systematically obscuring (by not acknowledging and/or not counting) their negative effects. Weighing market efficiency against that of state planning suffers from the same logical impossibility. However, logic is surely not the issue. Cost-benefit analyses unwilling to admit their partisan selectivity (and thus offered as absolute and definitive) are modern versions of what Marx called "vulgar apologetics."

8. Such a state policy would thus have an explicit class perspective. It would seek to regain or maintain full employment within a communist class structure, i.e., where workers are not exploited. In capitalist societies, conventional monetary and fiscal policies aim similarly to secure or restore job and income opportunities: by making it profitable for capitalists to provide them. When sucessful, such policies yield a labor force both fully employed and fully exploited. The class dimensions of state policy goals and state interventions in the economy would thus be different in the two societies. In both societies, contradictions and contentious trade-offs would beset state interventions. Yet what remains different are the class goals motivating and constraining each society's state interventions.

9. Many debates over whether the USSR was "really" socialist turned on whether substantive democracy had or had not actually been established there; some examples are discussed in chapter 4 below.

10. Marxists disagree about what actual class structures existed in the societies of "oriental despotism." Some argue it was a kind of feudalism; others that it was unique and distinct as a class structure; still others that it was a form of communism (Hindess and Hirst 1975; Amariglio 1984). We do not enter that debate here; we merely note that Marxists have recognized how communist class structures could coexist with despotism.

11. One brief restatement requires another. By *class* (and *class blindness*) we refer to class *in terms of surplus labor*. Other theorists, inside and outside Marxism, have produced "class analyses" but they have defined class chiefly in power and/or property terms (powerful versus powerless and rich versus poor). They minimize, marginalize, or altogether omit attention to the structures of surplus labor production, appropriation, and distribution. Hence they are class blind in our sense.

12. As is well known, communism has been widely understood precisely as classless even though the term was not uniformly defined. This alone would warrant our attention to classlessness even though we would argue, for all the reasons adduced in this book, that "classless" was, in most instances, a misnomer for what was being theorized. Our other reason for attention to classlessness follows from its definition as the "other" of class and hence entailed in (as the boundary of) any concept of class itself. A class analysis must, sooner or later, ask itself about, extend itself to, incorporate some consideration of its own, other classlessness.

13. The Marxian conception of all labor as becoming equivalently necessary under very particular, noncapitalist historical conditions should not be confused with neoclassical economic theory's

refusal to accept the necessary/surplus distinction in reference to any economic system. The latter's insistence that all labor in capitalism is equivalently necessary masks the necessary/surplus distinction that Marxists stress in their analyses of capitalism. Nor is that surprising, given the history of neoclassical economic theory's emergence after 1870. It gives ample evidence of an evolution shaped significantly by the project of theoretically negating Marxism by refusing to admit the concept of surplus (Roll 1946; Dobb 1973; Boss 1990).

14. Our work benefits significantly from that of Diskin (1990), Ruccio (1984), and Silver (1987). They used *class* and *overdetermination* critically to assess leading definitions of these terms in the literature. Diskin treated Engels, Kautsky, Bernstein, Lenin and Trotsky; Ruccio compared a number of key Soviet and non-Soviet economists and mathematicians involved in economic planning; and Silver contrasted Marx and Engels with Stalin and Bettelheim.

15. Communism as a social system (and class structure) was a future goal of Soviet socialism in most official and unofficial formulations; it was not often an accepted definition of the current Soviet Union at any given time. When the adjective *communist* was applied to Soviet society, it referred to the policies and/or political dominance of the Communist Party or to the Soviet kind of socialism: communism as the name for a further extension of what characterized Western European socialisms (*more* state intervention in the economy and society generally). Assertions since 1990 that communism collapsed in Eastern Europe are more ideological ploys of condemning by association than serious analysis.

# PART 2

## State Capitalism

CHAPTER 3

# A Class Theory of State Capitalism

Capitalism has its variant forms just as communism does. Capitalist class structures, coexisting and interacting with a wide range of nonclass processes, thereby generate those forms. In this second part of the book, we examine forms of capitalism much as we surveyed forms of communism in part 1. However, we will proceed differently. Our survey of capitalism's forms will throughout focus on one in particular, namely state capitalism. We define that form as follows: capitalist processes of producing, appropriating, and distributing surplus coexist and interact with processes that place state officials (rather than private individuals) in the class position of appropriators and distributors of the surplus.

Our stress on state capitalism so defined follows from the objective in part 3 below: to present the findings from our class analysis of the rise and fall of the USSR. The chief finding is that Soviet industry was always organized as a state capitalist class structure, while Soviet agriculture became increasingly so across its history. Hence it is important, in this chapter, to delineate state capitalism by distinguishing it from other forms generally and from the more familiar private form of capitalism in particular. Since we are hardly the first to apply the term "state capitalism" to the USSR, chapter 4 will show how our concept of state capitalism differs from all others.

## Capitalisms and Exploitation

Capitalist class processes by definition involve exploitation. Because the producers of surplus do not also appropriate it, they are exploited.[1] Capitalists and productive laborers are different persons whose relationship thus includes an exploitative dimension. In contrast, communist class processes are not exploitative: the producers of surplus are also its immediate, collective appropriators. The relationships among such communist producers/appropriators do not include an exploitative aspect.

Marx built his theory of capitalism on a familiar list of features—*in addition to exploitation*—that reflected the particular conjuncture in and for which he wrote. Hence, the opening sentences of *Capital* refer to the exchange of privately owned and produced commodities as one of those features:

> The wealth of societies in which the capitalist mode of production prevails appears as an "immense accumulation of commodities;" the individual commodity appears as its elementary form. Our investigation therefore begins with the analysis of the commodity. (1990, 125)

Marx nowhere argued that capitalist exploitation must always coexist with commodities and markets, that it must always be such a *private* capitalism. Capitalist exploitation can coexist with many different sets of social conditions; that is, capitalism can take various forms. Occasionally and without elaboration Marx touched on some of them. In *Capital,* vol. 2, for example, he wrote about "state capital, in so far as governments employ productive wage-labour in mines, railways, etc., and function as industrial capitalists" (1992, 177).

To eternalize Marx's list of the particular qualities of the private capitalism of his time amounts to reading that private capitalism as the only possible form of capitalism in human history. Theorizing in this way fixes a rather narrow definition and boundary of capitalism. It would seem to violate the dialectical method deployed by Marx.[2] Marxists have sometimes recognized this. For example, where market structures changed from competitive to monopolistic, they asked whether that altered or eliminated capitalist class structures within enterprises. Most concluded that capitalist class structures were changed but hardly eliminated. In a parallel way, we take Marxian analysis another step. We will argue that the post-1917 transformations in the USSR changed but did not eliminate capitalism. A system of state (rather than private) ownership and operation of industrial enterprises and state planning (rather than markets) amounted to a shift from a private to a state form of capitalism.

Private capitalisms actually display a wide range of different forms, beyond the combination of private capitalist enterprises with alternatively competitive, oligopolistic, and monopolistic market structures. Private capitalist class structures are sometimes highly decentralized. Surpluses are then produced, appropriated, and distributed at decentralized sites—enterprises—scattered across the social geography. Alternatively, capitalist surpluses may be produced at many sites while they are appropriated in a concentrated way: literally gathered at a few or even one corporate headquarters for distribution from there. Hence, parallel to what we argued for different forms of communism, the centralization or decentralization of surplus production, appropriation, and distribution do not signal the presence or absence of private capitalist class structures. They refer instead to different forms of private capitalism.

Another example concerns the ownership of the productive assets with which workers perform necessary and surplus labor. One private form of capitalism entails such ownership by the same individuals who also appropriate the surplus: the classic private owner and operator of a capitalist enterprise. An alternative private form, the large modern corporation, finds ownership of its productive assets in the hands of private individuals or groups who purchased shares in the stock market. In this case, the appropriators of the surplus, the board of directors, typically own few of the shares. Still other private forms of capitalism entail ownership of some or all shares by the workers themselves or even by government agencies.[3] These differing distributions of property in the means of production—to various combinations of private owners—neither necessitate nor imply that capitalist exploitation inside enterprises has disappeared. We have instead different private forms of capitalism, different arrangements of private ownership of the means of production coexisting with a capitalist class structure.

Capitalism can take still other private forms. Capitalist class structures inside private enterprises can coexist and interact with either free markets or state-regulated markets or state-mandated nonmarket allocations. These different means of distributing resources and products would comprise private forms of capitalism.[4] Still further possible variations emerge depending on whether state regulations or allocations are centralized or decentralized. That is, do local or central state agencies do the regulating or allocating? Variant private forms of capitalism emerge as well if the relevant state agencies are responsible to electorates or not, and so on.

In suggesting just this small portion of the universe of possibilities, we underscore that private capitalism—the exploitative production, appropriation, and distribution of surplus values by private capitalists—displays many forms depending on the social contexts in which it exists.[5] While other analysts may be concerned primarily with these forms—analyzing their different modes of operation, championing some and denouncing others for various reasons—our Marxian analysis focuses rather on their shared class and private dimensions. From that standpoint, they are variant private forms of capitalism.

What defines state as opposed to private forms of capitalism is the social *location* of surplus appropriating enterprises, and the *connection* of appropriating individuals to the state. In private capitalism, individuals with no formal position within the state apparatus appropriate surplus in enterprises located outside of the state. In state capitalism, individuals *with* a necessary connection to the state—employed and selected by the state—exploit labor in enterprises that occupy locations *within* the state apparatus. These two features certainly affect the particular conditions of capitalist exploitation, but we have found no reason to conclude that their presence would make capitalism disappear.

For example, if a state legislative body establishes state industrial capitalist enterprises, these may have a board of directors—surplus-labor-appropriating capitalists—appointed or elected by the legislative body. The board may acquire raw materials, means of production, and labor power via free market exchanges or exchanges that are more or less regulated by other state agencies. State capitalist enterprises may sell their products as commodities whose prices are determined in markets or in more or less state-regulated market exchanges. Or state capitalist enterprises may depend on other state agencies that physically distribute inputs and outputs instead of allowing market transactions. State capitalist enterprises may be highly centralized or decentralized, and so forth.

State capitalism can—and historically does—demonstrate many other variant forms. State capitalist enterprises may exist at the margins of or scattered within predominately private capitalist systems. A minority of state capitalist enterprises then interacts (and perhaps competes) with a majority of private capitalist enterprises. Alternatively, the private capitalist enterprises may be marginalized or delegitimated altogether, leaving most or all production to occur in state capitalist enterprises. This latter situation well describes Soviet industry after the 1920s (but not Soviet agriculture).

State capitalist enterprises can also coexist with varying distributions of property in the means of production. With only collective or state property, state agencies might allocate productive assets among state capitalist enterprises. Agency functionaries would make such allocations according to criteria established for them. Considering who might establish these criteria and how they might do so opens still more possible state forms of capitalism ranging from those whose allocational criteria emerge from a democratic determination to those that result from bureaucratic dictates. Struggles among and between state enterprises and allocating functionaries over such criteria would comprise a distinctively state capitalist, nonmarket kind of competition.

Alternatively, some or all kinds of productive assets used by state capitalist enterprises might remain privately owned.[6] Then the state capitalists, much like their private counterparts, would compete for them in markets. Such markets in productive assets might be free or subject to state regulation of such things as minimum and maximum wage, rental, dividend, and interest rates. Such state forms of capitalism would likely refocus competition among enterprises on changing the design and administration of state regulations.

The particular Soviet state form of capitalism was more or less replicated in other "socialist" countries. In them, state officials centrally appropriated the surpluses produced by industrial workers as per the classic definition of capitalist exploitation. Moreover, state administrative (command) allocation replaced markets, and state ownership replaced private ownership of industries' means of production (other than labor power) as well. The Soviet state form of capitalism was thus rather extremely statist. However, parallel to our discussion of variant forms of communism in part 1, we needed here to survey some of the many possible forms of capitalism—private forms and state forms—before focusing on the particular state form in the USSR.

### Justifying the Label "Capitalist"

We turn next to demonstrating why the USSR displays a state capitalist rather than some other kind of exploitative class structure. Marx and Marxism generally recognize three basically different kinds of exploitative class structures (where the appropriators are different people from the producers of surplus): the slave and feudal as well as the capitalist class structures.[7] To determine which kind exists in any society requires examination of how its particular nonclass processes combine to overdetermine its class structures.

Proceeding in this way to read the texts and documents on the USSR, we found no evidence that slave class structures were significant there. If a culture, politics, and economy exist that allow human beings to be property and differentiate them into slaves and masters, the possibility of a slave class structure exists. The latter is exploitative, because slaves produce a surplus immediately appropriated by others, by masters. Slave class structures often require, as conditions of their existence, hegemonic cultures that inculcate norms of subservience and mastery. They render slaves' production of surplus for masters as necessary and/or inevitable. A slave class structure may also require a political system (laws, administrations with exclusive police and military powers, etc.) to enforce a system of property in human beings and masters' rights to their slaves' surplus. A slave class structure may also be conditioned by an economic system in which masters breed slaves as they might other work animals with the costs likened to those of tools and machines.

For a slave class structure to have characterized their industries, Soviet state officials would have had to create and sustain such cultural, political, and economic processes. In that way they might have propelled Soviet laborers to perform as slaves in relation to surplus-appropriating slave-masters. The evidence that Soviet officials appropriated industrial surpluses from others who produced that surplus is, as we will show, clear enough. However, we found neither arguments nor documents indicating that a culture, politics, or economy existed in support of a class structure that differentiated (de jure or de facto) slaves and masters inside Soviet state enterprises. Hence we could not apply the label of slave to the exploitative relationship between the two classes. The hypothesis of a Soviet slave class structure warranted no further investigation.[8]

Were a different culture, politics, and economy to exist that, while rejecting human slavery, nonetheless fostered another kind of human "unfreedom," the hypothesis of a feudal exploitative class structure could be entertained. A feudal class structure involves formal relationships of interpersonal bondage ("organic" and/or "natural" and/or "religious") such that one side produces surplus for the other. Pointedly absent is any widespread notion that production entails some voluntary exchange of equivalents among "free" people. Rather, a surplus produced by some and delivered to others is thought to flow necessarily from the personal bonds between them.

For example, in feudal Europe, productive laborers were defined as bound organically to particular pieces of land and/or into personal, servile (but not slave) relationships to other individuals. Cultural norms existed—institutionalized in and enforced by church, state, and/or other organizations—that directly motivated as well as obligated individuals born and bound (as serfs) into such formalized relationships to produce surplus for other individuals (lords). Such exploitation was an intrinsic part of those relationships. In European feudalism, serfs produced surpluses appropriated by lords as customary rents either in kind or in money, or as the direct provision to lords of the serfs' surplus labor (corvée). Were similar circumstances to exist in other times or places, we would hypothesize a feudal class structure for investigation (Fraad, Resnick, and Wolff 1994).

However, our review of the literature indicated that such cultural, political and economic conditions did not generally obtain in the USSR. The mass of workers was at least nominally free in the sense of having individual rights—albeit sometimes limited—to choose how, when, and for whom they worked as well as rights to struggle over the modes and remunerations of their work. The socially sanctioned concept of labor understood employer and employee to be contractually engaged in bargained exchanges of equivalents rather than bound by interpersonal relationships as in feudalism. Where feudal lords advanced means of production—lands, water, woods—for workers to use to produce their means of subsistence, Soviet state officials advanced wages to workers who purchased their means of subsistence in state-controlled markets. Such conditions, among others, led to our rejecting the hypothesis of a Soviet feudal class structure.[9]

Our hypothesis that a capitalist class structure characterized Soviet industry did not emerge only because research eliminated the hypotheses of slave or feudal class structures. We were also persuaded that particular Soviet conditions such as a certain freedom of Soviet workers—upheld by culture, law, and politics as a constant theme—were conducive to capitalist class structures. That is, workers' "freedoms" from individual property in means of production or means of survival other than employment in state-owned enterprises under exploitative conditions led them then to "choose" to sell their own labor power. Thus they produced surplus for others, namely those who purchased their labor power. However, Soviet workers' freedoms also imposed some limits and constraints on the employment agreements arrived at and forever contested. The prevaling Soviet doctrines on labor held that the exchange of their labor power for a wage was (or could and should be) a full participation in a "socialist" economy, a kind of contribution equal to the wages obtained in return. Practices and doctrines such as these worked to preclude any recognition by Soviet industrial workers that they might be exploited within state enterprises.

Precisely this situation—a limited freedom coexisting with a structured compulsion to produce surplus for others without seeing the class process involved—resembles no other class structure so much as the condition of workers in private capitalist structures around the world. There, too, a nearly universal discourse of individual freedom, rights, and voluntary exchanges of equivalents overlays a structured compulsion to produce surplus for capitalists. There, too, the concept of surplus in production is ignored, denied, and repressed if and when dissidents advance it in political debates or academic discourses. Meanwhile the resemblance and parallel structural positions of Soviet industrial ministries, on the one hand, and corporate boards of directors of highly concentrated private capitalist enterprises, on the other, likewise suggested different forms of capitalism.[10] Hence, we proposed and proceeded to investigate the hypothesis that the kind of exploitative class structure in the USSR was capitalist.

Soviet culture and politics always stressed that workers there were now the masters of social life, free at last from centuries of feudal serfdom and from the attempt of private capitalists to replace the feudal lords. Workers were no longer tied to the land or the lord or the new private capitalists of pre-1917 Russia. The Revolution had freed them to find their own places within public systems of education and production geared above all to workers' needs, present and future. Their party and state, administering the new system for them, would arrange for all workers to have secure jobs and incomes as a matter of basic right. The discourse of socialism meant, finally, that workers could obtain a fair exchange for the labor power they provided. The feudal and capitalist classes had been overthrown because their property and their power had been seized by a workers' state. With the demise of feudalism and capitalism, all talk of exploitation, let alone vague references to surplus, seemed inapplicable to Soviet reality, absurd, or dangerous counterrevolutionary propaganda.

In such terms and tones, Soviet politics and culture successfully persuaded and pressured workers to continue to produce surpluses in state industrial enterprises (the excess of their contribution to output over what went for their consumption). They had little choice, since not working in such enterprises would have jeopardized their survival. Designated state officials—persons other than the producers themselves—appropriated the products of their labor in the form of state capitalist commodities. These commodities had values attached to them by other state officials, the economic planning personnel. The planners set these values and the values of the workers' money wages so that Soviet workers could afford to buy back a portion of the net output they had produced. In Marx's original language, this was the fruit of these workers' "necessary labor." The other portion, the fruits of the workers' surplus labor, was appropriated by the state capitalists. They then distributed this surplus for investment in infrastructure and productive capacity, for the military, the party, and so forth. State and party officials established the social priorities governing this production, appropriation, and distribution of the surplus. State administrative agencies set commodity valuations and wage levels, thereby determining the size of the surplus. The agencies also allocated inputs, outputs, and surpluses flowing into and out of state capitalist enterprises. Markets as well as private property in the means of industrial production had thereby been replaced. The goal of the state's surplus allocations was to strengthen and expand the class structure that generated the surplus.

The Soviet victories of collective over private property and of planning over markets altered how workers continued to be exploited. They did not eliminate the workers' exploitation. Successive Soviet governments, publicists, and theorists denounced capitalism—by which they meant private forms of capitalism—even as the USSR established another form of capitalism: a state form of capitalism. However, Marxists across Soviet society (and beyond) celebrated state property and centralized state planning *as negating capitalism and constituting socialism*. This obscured, to critics and supporters alike, the continuation of capitalist class processes inside state enterprises.

## Value Analysis for State Capitalism: A Technical Digression

The traditional literature in part defines capitalism as necessarily producing commodities for free markets. An implication of this definition is the argument that the USSR, having suppressed free markets, was therefore not capitalist. By contrast, this section will seek to undermine that implication and its underlying notion of necessity. We will extend the argument that in some forms of capitalism, capitalist class structures coexist and interact with non-free-market forms of distributing resources and products. This recalls our argument in chapter 2 that communist class structures can likewise coexist and interact with both market and nonmarket mechanisms for distribution. These mechanisms vary from free, competitive markets to those in which markets are restricted by monopolistic practices and/or state regulations to those in which markets disappear, replaced by decentralized or centralized plans and planners allocating resources and products.

A Soviet type of state capitalism deploys chiefly the last-mentioned mechanism for distribution. Soviet-style planning officials define, calculate, and announce the values of outputs produced in state enterprises for exchange. We will call them "administered values." Outputs are exchanged within such an "administered market" at such administered values, rather than at free market values determined by private bargaining among the exchangers. Using conventional Marxian value accounting, Soviet-style planning officials attach to each product a specific value magnitude, the "socially necessary abstract labor time" required for its production. This magnitude measures the total abstract labor time: both in the currently applied "living labor" and that embodied in the raw materials and tools produced earlier that the current laborers use up in production.[11] It becomes then a rather straightforward operation to calculate the difference between the living labor (value) added during production and the values of the commodities workers could buy with the wages allocated to them by state planners. This difference is the state-administered surplus value appropriated in state capitalist enterprises.

The planners might decide to set the actual prices at which products exchange among enterprises and citizens so that they equaled the state-administered values. Or they might establish particular differences between the state-administered values of products and the state-administered prices at which they actually exchange. This parallels Marx's famous example in the case of private capitalism when competition yields a uniform average rate of profit among private capitalists and thereby makes commodity prices diverge from their values.[12] There may well be reasons why a state capitalism's planners would likewise establish differences between output values and prices. As we show in part 3, several special considerations persuaded Soviet planners frequently to administer different prices and values for the same output.

Generally then, products produced by state enterprises for exchange—state capitalist commodities—could well have attached to them *both* state-administered values and prices. Indeed, the conventional Marxian practice of making both sets of calculations for private capitalist commodities—where markets set prices—might well be extended to state capitalist commodities where state agencies administer prices and values. In that case, state capitalist commodities would display state-administered values, prices, and profit rates. More generally, then, terms such as value, price, and profit in capitalism need qualifying adjectives (market-set vs state-administered) attached to them if we are to acknowledge and distinguish the different ways in which resources and products may be exchanged.

Because the primary purpose of Marxian theory is to direct attention to the class process in production—the distinction between necessary and surplus labor and the exploitation it can entail—Marxian *value* theory highlights how class functions as *one* determinant, among others, of the actual prices at which commodities are exchanged in free or administered markets. That class determinant is precisely what other theories of value overlook or deny.[13] Moreover, Marxian theory aims to show how the totality of social conditions overdetermines the class processes and hence, in regard to its value theory, the values of products. A secondary purpose of that value theory is then to show how other, nonclass determinants interact with the class processes to overdetermine the actual ratios in which commodities are exchanged: the prices set by market bargains or by state agencies.

Now, there would be *no* role for Marxian value theory in a capitalism (or communism) that dispensed altogether with exchange, commodities, and hence values. In a state capitalism, for example, this would be the case if the state allocated resources and products in physical quantities *without* assigning any system of numerical valuations or prices to them.[14] Marxian theory, of course, would still be an appropriate framework of analysis because that state capitalism includes class processes. Hence it would direct attention to how the class processes help to shape the state's physical allocation of resources and products. However, Marxian value theory has a place in today's analyses because most economies in modern times— including both private and state capitalisms—have relied either on markets to produce a system of prices or on state agencies to do so (or combinations of both). Marxian value theory also would have its place in analyses of communism, because of our assumption that its class structure too would rely on either state planners to administer values and prices or on markets to do so.

State-administered prices and the profit rates based upon them may or may not have far-reaching social consequences in ways quite parallel to the role played by profit rates based on market-administered prices. State planning agencies may allocate inputs and outputs among state capitalist enterprises according to their profit rates as based on the state-administered prices for their inputs and outputs. They might, for example, favor the higher-than-average-profit enterprises at the expense of the lower than average. Alternatively, such profit rate comparisons might become merely one among many other variables taken into account in determining the allocations (e.g., military survival of such a state capitalism, minimizing its ethnic and regional conflicts, attaining specific cultural goals, etc.). If the state agencies within a state capitalism view profit calculations per se in deeply negative terms, they might not respect profit very much in deciding economic matters.[15] There is a literature on where, when, how, and why profit rates are similarly set aside in favor of sales, growth or other variables as determinants of investment in private capitalist market economies; the arguments there are quite parallel.

If we presume that state enterprise profit rates, based on state-administered prices, are at least one among the criteria of those enterprises' performances and the rewards based on performance, there can and will be competition among them: so many "state capitals" competing.[16] This competition is analogous to that among private capitalist enterprises in market economies. Additionally, competitive strategies, adopted either by private capitalist enterprises reacting to market-set prices or by state capitalist enterprises confronting state-administered prices, could include a variety of other kinds of activities to enhance enterprises' success. In the Soviet state form of capitalism, for example, enterprises typically used special bonuses to statemanagers and productive workers, bribes to other state officials, hoarding of scarce inputs, overachieving state-administered quotas, and so forth to secure competitive advantages. While some of these, such as the overachieving of state-administered quotas, are likely to be found only in the Soviet form of state capitalism, others, for example, the use of bonuses, bribes, and hoarding, also might characterize competitive strategies typically deployed by private capitalist enterprises. Other kinds of private capitalist competitive strategies (such as advertising and mergers) typically would be excluded in state forms of capitalism such as the USSR.

While competition and its social consequences will differ in state versus private capitalism, in market-set versus state-administered price environments, competition is not present in one and absent in the other. Parallel to what occurs in private capitalism, the contradictory effects of state capitalist enterprises' competitive strategies radiate throughout the state capitalist economy impacting enterprises, households, and state agencies. An endless swirl of multiple effects is set in motion by such strategies as differently impacted institutions react in different ways and thereby set in motion still new complex effects. Hence it is never possible to isolate and count the infinity of resulting consequences, the benefits and costs of such strategies over all the impacted institutions and over all the relevant time periods. Because such a closure is not possible, there is no way to reach an unambiguous final judgment on the net results of any particular competitive strategy or act.

Hence there can be no unambiguous basis to rank the "efficiency" or net social effects of one strategy versus another or of market-set versus state-administered price systems or of private versus state capitalisms. Different theories select and count different subsets of the infinity of effects to reach their judgments of "efficiency"—judgments inescapably partial and relative to each theory's selected subsets. The choice between state and private capitalism or between either and forms of communism cannot logically rest on some universal efficiency standard. Appeals to such a standard may be effective rhetorically as slogans, but they are epistemological nonsense.

## Capitalisms, Communisms, and Socialisms

Capitalism can exist in an array of variant forms mixing state and private enterprises; state and private ownership of means of production; markets and planning; centralized and decentralized planning, and much else besides. The capitalist class structures common to all those forms entail a likewise shared exploitation, although it will differ quantitatively and qualitatively with each distinct form. The quality of life for inhabitants of capitalist economies depends in part on the particular forms of capitalism that emerge from each of the possibilities sketched above.

However, differences *among* forms of capitalism should not be confused with the differences *between* capitalist and communist class structures. To help avoid such confusion, we have systematically separated the differences between private and state enterprises, between private and collective ownership, and between market and nonmarket exchanges from the difference between capitalist and communist class structures. Toward the same end, we now extend the argument to other nonclass differences that have also been confused with the communist/capitalist difference.

Consider a state form of capitalism in which one group of state functionaries functions as a single board of directors for all state-enterprises. Another state agency allocates to the board raw materials, means of production, and labor power; it also attaches values to these inputs as well as to the outputs. Board members consume the labor power of allocated workers by setting them to work with means of production and raw materials. The board (and not the collectivity of workers) is in the (class) position to receive workers' labor including their surplus labor. A portion of the workers' total output is returned to them as a value sum they can use to buy means to reproduce their labor power.

This board now makes the following subsumed class distributions of the surplus. One portion finances the state agency charged with allocating resources to the board and calculating values. Another portion funds another state agency that makes payments to workers on the basis of their varying needs (relating to family size, health, etc.). Such payments enable some workers to receive incomes that exceed their wages. *Hence a distribution of produced wealth on the basis of workers' needs is not inconsistent with class exploitation of those same workers.* Indeed, many private and state forms of capitalism have learned to adopt such distribution policies to soften workers' discontent when changing needs exceed incomes.

Other portions of the surplus can be distribted to state officials to establish another fund paying a social dividend to workers who collectively own enterprises' means of production. Such dividends make it possible for all workers to receive incomes that supplement their wages. Still other portions of the surplus could be distributed to state officials charged with (1) ensuring that all citizens have equal access, irrespective of their race, gender, or ethnicity, to gainful employment, schools, or any other sanctioned undertaking in society including equal access to the board and/or any of the other state agencies, and (2) creating and disseminating a set of ideas and images that define all such state-distributions as the final achievement of a true utopian society.

Thus, this set of state capitalist subsumed class distributions of the surplus may have helped to establish a set of incomes, laws, rules, norms, and attitudes such that workers exploited by state capitalists believe themselves to have achieved utopia. The workers favor the board continuing its appropriating and distributing functions as state capitalist. Of course, the contradictory consequences of the processes fostered by these diverse funds may undermine and weaken the state capitalist class structure. Workers, for example, may extend their sense of utopian life to include participating in the appropriation of the surpluses they have produced. They might then replace the state board with a new collectivity: themselves. A transition from capitalism to communism would then have occurred. However, no inevitability is attached to this step. And if it does not occur, we would be left with what one might call a "good form of capitalism" or "capitalism with a human face"—preferable to other forms of capitalism without one or more of these desired features. Yet, a choice among forms of capitalism is still radically different from—and not to be confused with—a choice between forms of capitalism and communism.

Like needs-based distributions of surplus, worker self-management has also often gotten confused with forms of communism as if the two were virtually synonymous. To argue otherwise, we need first to explore briefly just what managerial supervision entails. In both state and private capitalist enterprises, exploitation usually requires hiring supervisory managers. They occupy subsumed class positions (obtaining distributed shares of the capitalist surpluses) to ensure that workers provide the maximum possible surplus. In private forms of capitalism, such subsumed class managerial positions are usually located within enterprises. In state forms of capitalism, such as the USSR, they exist not only at the enterprise level but also at the centralized state level. In class terms, Soviet state capitalism displayed a vast subsumed class bureaucratic system of supervisors from heads of industrial ministries to on-site enterprise managers.

Among other activities, managers exert power over productive laborers to press them to maximize surpluses. Given the strong workerist themes in Soviet culture and politics, managers were resisted and sometimes condemned as undemocratic, antithetical to socialism, and as ultimately counterproductive because manager/worker conflicts undermined productivity. Arguments and social movements for worker self-management or worker control characterized Soviet state capitalism since its inception (Sirianni 1982). In class terms, however, they rarely if ever were directed at the fundamental class issue of who in the USSR produced and who appropriated surplus labor. Their focus was rather on the related but different nonclass issues of who was to exert power over workers and how this was to be done.

Enterprise management and control are matters of power and its distribution among individuals. Because workers always exercise *some* control over their work, supervisors are hired on the assumption that they can secure more surplus than would otherwise be appropriated. The prevailing goal of worker self-management has been that workers should largely or completely displace such supervision.[17] Movements for worker self-management have been significant in both state and private forms of capitalism.

There is no necessary contradiction between workers' self-management and a capitalist class structure, private or state. Thus, worker self-management is not the same as a communist class structure. Capitalists might yield to workers' demands to manage themselves, if the workers delivered adequate surpluses *without* supervisory managers. The capitalists would then have saved the subsumed class outlays of surplus on the salaries and budgets of supervisory managers. In this case, a capitalist subsumed class would have been eliminated, but capitalist exploitation remained. Both private and state capitalists have—on their own or under pressure from workers—varied their historical reliance on managers versus workers' self-management. State capitalism, like its private counterpart, can thus exist with or without workers' self-management.[18] Soviet state capitalism oscillated between the two kinds of management (Kuromiya 1988).

The evidence on the workers' early seizures of industrial enterprises in the USSR (Sirianni 1982; Chase 1990) suggests the following scenario: in hitherto private capitalist enterprises, they took over management functions as one of their key roles in the 1917 revolution. Their other key role was to dispossess the private owners and deliver the factories and offices to the state as collective property. Thinking that worker self-management plus state ownership of the means of production was the achievement of socialism, their subsequent attitudes toward enterprise organization were largely technical. The issue became maximizing outputs relative to inputs given "decent" workers' wages and conditions. The production, appropriation, and distribution of surplus never arose as issues central to workers' objectives. Their dominant notion of socialism—socialized property, central planning, workers' state, and sometimes self-management—left them quite content to deliver their outputs (including the surplus) to a council of ministers comprising state functionaries other than these workers.[19] Exploitation and a state capitalist, not a communist, class structure were thus installed in part by the revolutionary workers themselves—often alongside their self-management. Their class consciousness did not grasp the difference between capitalist and communist structures of surplus production, appropriation, and distribution; their actions reflected that lack.

Might workers have used their political powers inside and outside the enterprises after 1917 to demand and achieve communist class structures there? Surely, but that did not happen. They also might have used their powers to redirect distributed surpluses to themselves as new subsumed class occupants of managerial positions. That did not happen either. More generally, changes in ownership and management—even the occupation by workers of subsumed class ownership and management positions—do not necessitate a change in class structure from capitalist to communist. In fact, no such class change—in surplus labor terms—was debated among revolutionary intellectuals or policy makers. It did not appear on the Communist Party's agendas for action. No major popular movement for it ever materialized.

One lesson from Soviet history is the need clearly to distinguish the class structures of production (capitalist or communist) from (a) the distribution of property (the power to control access to objects), (b) the organization of power over resource and product distribution (market or administered price systems), and (c) the organization of enterprises' managerial powers. The class structure and these various power processes have often been conflated and confused by supporters and detractors of the Soviet experiment alike (Resnick and Wolff 1993).

Rarely, usages of the term *socialism* have equated it to communism as a negation of capitalism in favor of a system in which the producers of surplus are identically its collective appropriators. However, across the twentieth century and especially under the influence of developments in the USSR, a very different usage prevailed. In effect, socialism came to be defined instead as a kind of state capitalism. In broad outlines, socialism entailed more or less state ownership of productive assets, more or less state regulation of markets, more or less replacement of markets by state planning, more or less provision of basic welfare (education, housing, medical care, etc.) as matters of human rights, and more or less popular democratic politics. Socialism came to mean state capitalism with a human, relatively democratic face.[20]

Given the prevalence of a definition of socialism as such a state capitalism, communism came to be defined as simply a more extreme socialism. When productive property was *wholly* state owned, when markets were *completely* displaced by planning, when products were distributed according to individual "need," and above all when power was *totally* in the hands of workers (or a workers' party), then the "transitional" socialism would have eventuated in communism. Since the state capitalist version of socialism nowhere actually reached that ultimate form, communism was usually declared, as in the USSR, a goal for the future. It lay nearer or further in that future according to the optimism of the declarer.

Such formulations of both the communist future and the current institutional ("actually existing") socialism lacked any real concern with the production, appropriation, and distribution of surplus labor in production. Class, in the surplus sense, had no place in the prevailing discourses of socialism and communism. Communism too, defined as the distant, ultimate goal/stage of socialism, slipped to the margins of most discourses about economic systems, or remained as at most a footnote.[21] The only serious "other" of "capitalism" as an economic system was socialism.

This socialism was and remains a state form of capitalism. The last century's intense struggles, articulated as epic battles between capitalism and socialism, were conflicts between private and state forms of capitalism. For the enemies of state capitalism (qua socialism), capitalism's violent birth out of feudalism, articulated as the liberatory surge of individual freedom against absolute state power, has been endlessly replayed. The hallowed contest of individual and state had been made familiar and anchored deeply in their consciousness. It provided them with ready-made words, phrases, moralities, and certainties to wield for private and against state forms of capitalism—renamed as capitalism versus socialism/communism. Thus, "freedom," "liberty," "democracy," and "individualism" have opposed "dictatorship," "totalitarianism," and "collectivism." The old concepts and battle cries of capitalism's birth resurfaced to understand and fight the battles between private and state capitalism (qua socialism).

The supporters of state capitalism (qua socialism) disagreed, but their response remained on the same familiar terrain. For them, it was private capitalism that negated individual freedom in countless ways by its concentrations of economic and political power. A state that truly represented the mass of individuals could overcome that state of affairs by negating private property and private market behavior in favor of "socialization." The state as agent of society as a whole, rather than agent of the minority of private capitalists, could and would secure individual freedom. Debates centered on whether a vanguard workers party or a coalitional parliamentary majority, whether violent insurrection or education and voting, were the best or only ways to capture the state and make it "serve the people." Thus for the supporters of state capitalism (qua socialism) as for its opponents, "communists" became simply the more extreme kind of "socialists." For all sides in the capitalism versus socialism/communism debates, the class structures in surplus terms dropped out of sight and out of mind.

Marx's attempt to focus attention—and revolutionary action—on the class (qua surplus) aspects of capitalist societies was lost. Instead, Marxism became a set of doctrines affirming socialization as the solution to the ills of private capitalism. In any case, socialism (qua state capitalism) was understood to be the only possible, available alternative to private capitalism. Opponents of the latter had therefore to embrace and fight for the former. The alternative communist class structure, embodied embryonically or potentially in countless revolutionary upsurges by capitalism's victims, had been rendered visible by Marx's systematic critique. But the social conditions of the time repressed that visibility on all sides, losing Marx's surplus theory of class as a weapon for critics of all the forms of capitalism.

Nor was this limitation of vision merely a matter of consciousness shaping history. The line of causation ran the other way too. Every time private capitalism's development generated a crisis threatening its survival, the practical solution found by left, right, and center typically entailed more or less extensive experiments with state capitalism. Every time state capitalism's development generated a crisis threatening its survival, the practical solution found by left, right, and center entailed the rediscovery of and return to the virtues of private capitalism. In every country, capitalism's history of oscillations between private and state forms of capitalism encouraged supporters of each form to proclaim it as the necessary and the only alternative to the other. The few claims about a communist alternative to all forms of capitalism (including those called socialism) fell on deaf ears.

However, it may now be possible to reopen and renew the communist alternative—after the many socialisms that have been tried across the globe and especially after the demise of the longest, boldest, and in many ways most successful socialist experiment that was the USSR. The latest oscillation back to private capitalism will yield again—as it always has—too many crises, victims, and opponents. This time, however, historical memory of the insufficiency and unacceptability of past shifts to state capitalism (or socialism) may provoke different outcomes. The notion and goal of a communist alternative in surplus terms (perhaps needing and acquiring a new name to break the hold of the old specters) may finally regain a place on the agenda for social change.

That private forms of capitalism have always been prone to more or less regular cycles that sometimes become severe enough to be called crises is well known across many theoretical frameworks (Wolff and Resnick 1987, 185-192). That Keynesian and other state policies of managing crises display, at best, a mixed record and cannot guarantee success is likewise widely agreed. Nonetheless, the crises of private capitalism have, for two centuries, always called forth more or less state management policies, more or less movement to state capitalism according to the severity of each crisis and the balance of power between those favoring the one versus the other form of capitalism.

The twentieth century offers a richly illustrative display of movements to state capitalisms when private capitalisms encountered crises. World War One provoked such crises as did the Great Depression, World War Two, the decolonization processes, and so forth across all continents. However, the twentieth century also displays the reverse movements. More has given way to less state management of private capitalist economies; state capitalisms have given way to private capitalisms. Indeed, the USSR is a stunning example of the passage to state capitalism near the beginning of the century and the oscillation back near its end.

These oscillations suggest that state forms of capitalism engender crises rather like private forms. State management policies for dealing with crises in state capitalisms have shown a similar history of failure mixed with success. When their crises were severe in depth and duration or badly mismanaged or both, their victims often raised demands for a solution that entailed a reversion to private capitalism. Struggles ensued over such a reversion. The outcome each time depended on the powers wielded by both sides; powers in turn dependent on the complex of economic, political, and cultural conditions then in place.

Part 3 of this book analyzes the oscillations between private and state forms of capitalism in the USSR. The 1917 revolution effected a transition from private to state capitalism. The contradictions of "war communism"'s state capitalism provoked a shift back to a hybrid of private and state forms of capitalism over the 1920s. Crises of that hybrid then entailed the shift to Stalinism as the return to a more unalloyed state form of capitalism that lasted for the next fifty years. Eventually, the contradictions and crises of that state capitalism produced a series of reforms culminating in the oscillation back to a largely private form of capitalism in the late 1980s and still underway.

Remarkably, the rhetoric of struggles over transitions between state and private forms of capitalism have been largely the same no matter which direction was at stake. In times of crisis for private capitalism, its opponents argued that it was economically inefficient, unjust, and fundamentally undemocratic. Private capitalist depressions in the first half of the twentieth century were, after all, showcases of economic waste and unequally distributed losses across their populations. Proponents of moving to state capitalism celebrated its possibilities of coordinating production so as to eliminate the wastes and losses of private capitalism and substituting a democratic, more egalitarian distribution system.

In strikingly similar terms during the second half of the century, opponents of state capitalisms in crisis denounced their economic waste, unequally distributed losses, and lack of democracy. They anticipated the economic efficiency gains to be achieved if only private property, free markets, and minimal state activity in the economy could be returned. They celebrated the democracy that movement to a destratified, private capitalist economy would secure. The history of the USSR, as we shall argue below, is a telling case not only of the workings of a systematic state capitalism. It also exemplifies the oscillations between private and state forms of capitalism and the uniform arguments for shifts in both directions. The oscillations and the arguments reveal the limited range of alternatives that most people—both supporters and opponents of the USSR and of socialism—could conceive and struggle for.

If the socialisms of this century have been state forms of capitalism, then it is no great surprise that they have encountered cycles, crises, and failures of crisis management similar to those of private forms of capitalism. The crisis mechanisms embedded in both state and private forms provoked the historical oscillations between them. Yet the repeated oscillations across many nations also provoke a question. Under what circumstances might future crises in either kind of capitalism engender not another oscillation between them but rather a break to a different, noncapitalist class structure?

### Notes

1. In Marx's words, "The rate of surplus value is therefore an exact expression for the degree of exploitation" (1990, 326). Exploitation refers *not* to the power or domination relations between capitalists and productive laborers (important as those relations are), but rather to the *class relations*, the relations of production and appropriation of the laborer's surplus labor. Once again, class and power are interdependent but not identical.

2. Marxian theory generally affirms continuous change and hence that any capitalist class structure is *always* changing, losing some qualities and acquiring others. Depending on how "capitalist class structure" is theoretically defined and bounded, specific changes will be viewed as minor or major alterations or, at their limit, eliminations of capitalism. Since different theories define different boundaries, they assess changes differently.

3. An extreme case may illustrate the fine points of this approach. Even if state agencies owned the majority of shares of an industrial capitalist enterprise, it would still be a private form of private capitalism if the surplus appropriators—its board of directors—were individuals with no official, formal position within the state apparatus. Only if the appropriators were themselves state officials would the line between private and state forms of capitalism have been crossed.

4. Of course, it need not be the state that regulates markets. Church institutions could perform these functions as might still other social organizations given such responsibilities. Considering such possibilities would introduce yet more of the possible variations among private forms of capitalism.
5. To take another extreme case, private capitalist enterprises could exist in an environment in which markets had been totally displaced by state allocations of inputs and outputs in physical quantities. However, if such state allocations extended into the internal production activities of these enterprises, then their private status would be blurred; a borderline situation between private and state capitalism would thereby be reached.
6. This arrangement suggests another possible boundary or extreme situation for state capitalism. Suppose private individuals owned most of the shares in a state capitalist enterprise. Suppose further that such private owners became dissatisfied with dividends and with the performance of the state officials comprising the enterprise's board of directors. Suppose finally that the private owners then replaced the state-appointed board with their own, private nominees instead of state officials. That replacement crosses the border between state and private capitalism. Whether any particular state capitalism would face such a challenge from private owners, how it might respond, and what might finally result cannot be known a priori.
7. For sustained Marxian definitions of the slave and feudal class structures and their differences from capitalism, see Dobb (1963), Hindess and Hirst (1975), and Taylor (1979) and the extensive bibliographies in each of these works.
8. This does not mean that absolutely no slave class structures existed in the USSR. On the contrary, we presume that the USSR, like most societies, contained multiple, different class structures (including slave class structures). Given our effort to understand the prevalent class structures in the USSR, we found no evidence that they included slave class structures.
9. Lewin (1985, 183) and Fitzpatrick (1994b, 129) do speculate that a kind of feudalism could describe Soviet conditions. However, their notions of feudalism differ from ours, since we define a feudal class structure in terms of the production, appropriation, and distribution of surplus, whereas they do not.
10. Nove also recognized the parallelism between the structural positions occupied by Soviet industrial ministers and by private corporate board of directors. He described the role of top Soviet politicians in the economic life of the USSR: "[They] were, for most of their waking hours, the board of directors of the great firm U.S.S.R. Ltd." (1989, viii). Nove's analysis differs from ours because he does not recognize or apply a concept of class in terms of surplus to either Soviet industry or private capitalism.
11. The assumptions and operations used to arrive at these magnitudes would likely be objects of discussion, debate, struggle, and change in a society that made them. The same applies, in parallel fashion, to the assumptions and operations used in calculations of prices, profits, and so on in private market capitalisms.
12. See *Capital*, vol. 3, part 2, for Marx's discussion of the relation ("transformation") of values, profit rates, and prices. Our approach here relies also on Wolff, Callari, and Roberts (1984) who show how, for market-set prices and values in private capitalism, the price/value divergence reacts back upon values such that prices become a determinant of values as well as vice versa. Their argument could be extended for state-administered prices and values in state capitalism to show how there, too, the state-administered price-value divergences react back upon state-administered values as well as vice versa.
13. Neoclassical value theory—the main alternative to Marxian value theory over the last century—rejects any place within its framework for a notion of class as surplus appropriation and distribution. Instead, it underscores how certain essentialized properties ascribed to human nature—inherent axioms of human choice and technically given production possibilities—determine the actual commodity prices (Wolff and Resnick 1987).

14. Such a physical allocation system was significant during the short-lived "War Communism" period after the 1917 revolution. Various kinds of administered value and price accounting were the norm across most of Soviet history.
15. We cannot here engage the apologetical and dogmatic claims that purely market-based (i.e., private capitalist) allocations of inputs and outputs necessarily and always yield the greatest efficiency, growth, etc. They typically ignore the problem of "externalities" (real costs and benefits not reflected in market valuations) and the unresolved debates over just what "profit" is or means. See our related discussion in the text below and in chapter 1.
16. State capitalist enterprises have historically been allowed greater or lesser autonomy from central planning and control authorities, greater or lesser freedom to compete with one another. We do *not* make the degree of such autonomy or competitiveness or the extent of markets the indices of capitalism versus socialism as do others: see Sweezy as against Bettelheim (Sweezy and Bettelheim 1971, 34ff) and Hilferding (1950).
17. The proposed mechanisms of such a displacement could include redefining all workers' tasks to include a component of self-management, having workers rotate the specialized tasks of management among themselves, having workers elect individuals to perform management/control activities, etc. The details and many variants of such proposals do not concern our argument here.
18. We thus differ sharply from advocates of workers' control (self-management) who make its presence or absence within enterprises *the* definition (and hence criterion) of the absence or presence of capitalism. Vanek (1975, 11–36) offers a careful summary formulation of this sort, contrasting self-managed with "capital-controlled (dehumanized)" enterprises. He and his associates refuse any reference to "class" (the term does not appear in his book). Where he makes capitalism impossible with workers' self-management, our class analysis—focused on the production, appropriation, and distribution of surplus labor rather than the management of labor—rejects that impossibility.
19. While some opposed this arrangement as not socialist, their disagreements concerned chiefly the centralization of surplus appropriation (they preferred decentralization). Only extremely rarely was their dispute over the *existence* (central or local) of a separate group of persons receiving and distributing the surplus appropriated from workers.
20. In contrast, we would argue that fascism comprised, in our class terms, a state capitalism with an inhuman, undemocratic face. As with the variations among private capitalisms, the range of possible differences among state capitalisms is vast as well.
21. Where "communist" remained an important discursive adjective, it referred chiefly to political entities. The word described qualities of societies in which a communist party ruled and/or which referred to itself as communist. A "communist economy" thus came to mean the actually existing socialism (a state capitalism as we have shown) in a society governed by a communist party and/or calling itself communist.

# CHAPTER 4

# Debates over State Capitalism

Since day one of the Russian Revolution, friends, foes, and others have disputed the actual class structure of the USSR. On one point, most admirers and many detractors agreed: in terms of class, the USSR was socialism en route to communism. Among critics, some saw it as a "degenerated" or "deformed" socialism or collectivism, while others judged it to be a bureaucratic or state capitalism. Some even construed the USSR's class structure to be a merger of private and state capitalist enterprises akin to European fascisms. The groping for appropriate names to identify the USSR's class structure—and the above are but a sample—reflected both its uniqueness and disagreements over how to understand it. Intense passions, ideological commitments, and high practical stakes attached to these terms in a debate that has flared up recurringly from 1917 through the present.

A small but significant part of that debate has focused on the term "state capitalism." However, neither supporters nor opponents of using this term for the USSR's class structure ever defined it as we did in chapter 3 above. Instead, they deployed the word "capitalist" to refer to a particular distribution of ownership of means of production or, most often, to a particular distribution of political power or to combinations of both. Thus, the long-standing disagreements over the definition of class resurface again. Where we use a surplus labor concept of class to build an analysis of the USSR's class structure as largely capitalist, other references to state capitalism have marginalized or, more often, altogether ignored surplus labor. This chapter aims to demonstrate how both their analyses and conclusions consequently differ fundamentally from ours.

## Conflicting Concepts

The term "state capitalism" has a long, variegated history.[1] Previously published overviews of major portions of that history (Jerome and Buick 1967; Bettelheim 1976b, 464–476; Bellis 1979; Buick and Crump 1986, 102–125) allow us here simply to summarize the basic alternative ways in which the term has been used.[2] Early in chapter 3 we documented how Marx and Engels explicitly recognized the possibility that private capitalists could be replaced by state officials. Their comments were brief probably because state capitalism was then relatively rare. Nonetheless, they stressed that capitalist exploitation need not change significantly simply because state officials replaced private individuals as capitalists (Chattopadhyay 1994, 26–29).

Notwithstanding what Marx and Engels stressed, in the generation before the Soviet revolution most Marxists developed and used a very different concept of state capitalism. They believed that the modern European state increasingly regulated, subsidized, and coordinated private capitalist enterprises in a qualitatively new phase of capitalism's development. This had occurred to such an extent that the state interventions had transformed the logic and momentum of capitalism itself. Writing in 1916, Karl Renner argued that Marx had not quite envisioned this result,

> Organized national capital uses the state power precisely as a positive economic agency.... The state deliberately assists in the concentration of capital.... State power and the economy begin to merge.... The war... has merely accelerated an already apparent line of development.... [O]ne might say that *laissez-faire* capitalism has changed into state capitalism.... Socialization, which Marx regarded as inevitable, has thus taken a course which was not to be foreseen.[3]

The possible role of the state as itself an industrial capitalist was missed or deemphasized. State capitalism instead meant increasingly comprehensive state intervention in and control over private capitalist enterprises (with or without the presence of state capitalist enterprises). Increasingly, Marxists understood the state as *the* mechanism designed to bring "stability" to private capitalism, to prevent or offset its crises.[4]

Other Austro-Marxists such as Rudolf Hilferding, Max Adler, and Otto Bauer and German Marxists such as Karl Kautsky articulated similar arguments.[5] Lenin drew on them for his *Imperialism, the Highest Stage of Capitalism*. These Marxian theories of state capitalism as state control over private capitalist enterprises—rather than the different concepts of Marx and Engels stressing the direct state appropriation of surplus—most influenced thinking and policies in the USSR. This happened both directly and indirectly via the intense debates over the relationship between the state and socialist revolution (Lenin 1932).

One side in those debates held that state capitalism, as the epitome of rational coordination of production, distribution, and accumulation, represented the final preparation for a transition from capitalism to socialism. It was the ultimate socialization of the forces of production achievable within the shell of capitalism. This side could cite Engels concerning capitalism's final stage of state capitalism: "concealed within it [state capitalism] are the technical conditions that form the elements" of a transition to socialism (1962, 382). The next historical step, enabled by such state capitalism and provoked by its contradictions, would be the socialist revolution. The revolution would take over this state that already controlled private capitalism and then also abolish private property. The newly socialized production would serve workers' interests in a society where all were workers. A basis for genuine democracy would thereby have been established. Bukharin systematically elaborated this kind of argument in various forms.[6] Production would then soar, freed of the fetters of private profitability, business cycles, and the like, and the socialist future would unfold as poverty, exploitation, and oppression faded.

The other side in the debate over state capitalism expressed deep suspicions about merely "taking over" state capitalism. For them, socialism required and the socialist revolution meant a profound discontinuity in history: a necessarily linked destruction of both capitalist relations of production and the capitalist state. The abolition of private property was necessary but hardly sufficient to secure transition from state capitalism to socialism. A radical break and something radically new, in terms of both productive enterprises and the state, were necessary.[7] As we shall show, this side came to focus its attention on the issue of a radical break in the social distribution of power, changing *who* controlled enterprise and state before and after any revolution.

Had the workers really won power over the state? If not, might a state capitalism survive a workers' revolution that had somehow been betrayed into permitting that survival by keeping the workers (as opposed, say, to bureaucrats) from real power? Without workers' real power over the state, would the state's socialization of productive property really have transformed state capitalism into socialism (as opposed, say, to another form of state capitalism)? Power had become the central concept: power over objects (property) and power over people (politics). In contrast, the issue of how the production, appropriation, and distribution of surplus labor was organized in state versus private capitalism, in socialism versus state capitalism, and so forth drew very little attention.

The early debates about state capitalism had coalesced into opposing positions on a basically political question: How would control over the state and production be socially distributed? Before 1917 these positions shaped and were shaped by the contending strategies of anticapitalist parties and factions. After 1917, the debates congealed into major battles between supporters and enemies of the class structure actually evolving inside the USSR. One set of critics of Soviet development argued that state capitalism had never been surpassed in the USSR. Instead of completing the passage from private capitalism to state capitalism to socialism, the revolution had been aborted in the middle. The USSR was actually a state capitalism. Despite the de jure abolition of private property, ultimate de facto property and power congealed in an apparatus composed of the Communist Party and a state bureaucracy. No radical break in the power of a few over the many had been achieved. Worse still, by stressing the commanding role over the state and production wielded by the Communist Party—defined as the vanguard representative of all Soviet workers—state capitalism masqueraded as socialism. Thus, in the view of the leading Marxian Menshevik, Martov, Soviet workers were suffering all the hardships and injustices associated with capitalism inside the concentrated state capitalism of a backward society.[8]

On the other side, early defenders of the Soviet Union's development path, including Lenin, also used the term *state capitalism*, but positively. Reminiscent of Engels's remark, they saw Soviet state capitalism as a necessary stage between the overthrow of capitalism and the achievement of socialism (not to speak of communism). In Lenin's view, the unforeseeable twists and turns of social conditions forced the Soviet leadership periodically (and always conditionally) to rely on a controlled "state capitalism" as the means to their socialist ends:

> The workers ... are advancing towards socialism precisely through the capitalist management of trusts, through gigantic machine industry, through enterprises which have a turnover of several millions per year—only through such a system of production and such enterprises. The workers are not petty bourgeois. They are not afraid of large-scale 'state capitalism', they prize it as their *proletarian* weapon which *their Soviet* power will use.[9]

In effect, Lenin was arguing that state capitalism, if under the control of workers committed to the transition to socialism (i.e., Communists), was an acceptable as well as necessary stage for the USSR to pass through. The transition was ongoing so long as Soviet power was secure. Not the organization of surplus labor, but rather power relationships stood at the core of such qualified endorsements of state capitalism in the USSR.

In the years after Lenin's death in 1923, the term *state capitalism* was less frequently used by defenders of the USSR as a descriptive or analytic term for state industry. After Stalin's ascendancy in the late 1920s, it vanished (Bettelheim 1978, 371–372). Instead, those who admired or defended the USSR's actual class structure labeled it socialism. Having abolished private property in the means of production, replaced markets with state planning, and subordinated the state to the workers' power via the Communist Party, they reasoned, the USSR had thereby eliminated capitalist exploitation and classes altogether. With socialism secure and communism ahead, there was no possible object for and hence no need to undertake class analyses of Soviet society.[10] Ironically, most Marxian defenses of the USSR thus came to share with most anti-Marxian defenses of Western capitalism a strong disinclination to use any class qua surplus analysis.

The defenders' reasons for banishing class analysis in this way included the undesirable and uncomfortable connotations of phrases like *state capitalism* or *class structure*. Having achieved the USSR's survival at stupendous social costs, its defenders could not tolerate phrases that seemed to them to denigrate the achievement and render those costs in vain. They also sought to distance themselves from and to counterattack the critics who denounced state capitalism in the USSR. The defenders thus rejected the notion of state capitalism as hostile propaganda.

State capitalism evolved then as a concept used chiefly by critics to attack Soviet leaders and social development for betraying the 1917 revolution's goals. One recent example casts Lenin, Trotsky, and the Bolsheviks in toto as "capitalist revolutionaries" whose activities built state capitalism in the USSR (Buick and Crump 1986, 112). However, the earlier and later conceptions of state capitalism have a much greater importance than their hyperbolic renditions in partisan debates. They comprise the most developed of the few (and even then rarely elaborated) class analyses of Soviet society undertaken since 1917. They kept alive the idea that Marxian class analysis could and should be applied to the USSR to glean the unique insights that such analysis makes possible. While we disagree with their definition of class and hence with their interpretations of the USSR, we acknowledge their importance in enabling and providing resources for the very different class analysis developed in this book.[11]

Although suggestive and influential in terms of provoking research, controversies, or strategic rethinking, the different meanings attached to the term *state capitalism* were also mostly quite vague, general, and abstract. Barry Hindess has argued that this reflected the related imprecision in existing definitions of socialism and communism.

> [T]he absence of a rigorous definition of the *socialist mode of appropriation of surplus-labor* means that the domination of socialist relations of production tends to be identified with specific forms of domination of the workers over the means of production.... In the case of the system of state enterprises ... the dominance of socialist relations is identified with certain specific forms of the domination of workers with respect to the political apparatus of the state. *Thus an economic relation is conflated with what are thought to be its political conditions of existence.*[12]

In some arguments, state capitalism refers to ownership, to a situation in which the state owns the means of production, yet leases such means to private capitalists. In several speeches from 1921 to 1923, Lenin spoke of state capitalism in that sense (Lenin 1961, 696, 738, 770, 772, 777, and 817–819), as did Stalin in 1925.[13] Lenin explained that the strategic retreat represented by the New Economic Policy (NEP) required allowing such leasing to private capitalists and also allowing them to use their own productive assets. Such state capitalism was a political necessity dictated by circumstance, but since the proletariat and not the capitalists controlled the state, Lenin insisted that the transition to socialism remained in tact. Indeed, the capitalist enterprises, by enlarging the ranks of the proletariat, contributed to the transition.[14]

Where state capitalism referred to state-owned productive assets leased to private capitalists, socialism, in contrast, referred to state-owned means of production not leased to private capitalists, but rather used directly in state enterprises. Thus, Lenin divided the Soviet economy in 1918 into five groups: patriarchal (the most primitive forms of agriculture), small commodity producers (the majority of peasants who trade in grain), private capitalism, state capitalism, and socialism (Lenin 1961, 770). Socialism here meant specifically state-operated enterprises. *How* the production, appropriation, and distribution of surplus labor was organized inside state-owned and -operated enterprises clearly did *not* determine whether their class structures were socialist or capitalist. Socialism differed from capitalism according to whether state officials or nonstate, private persons owned and operated productive enterprises.

However, at other moments, under different pressures, Lenin and others articulated alternative definitions of state capitalism and its relation to socialism. In these definitions, the adjective *capitalist,* not *socialist,* was used to refer to large state-owned *and* state-run enterprises. What made them capitalist were their

> capitalist hierarchy of authority and of wage levels, . . . the capitalist forms of organization in the overall management, . . . and the participation of capitalists and bourgeois technicians in these forms of organization. (Bettelheim 1976b, 469)

In 1917 Lenin wrote a defense of the capitalist nature of these state-owned and state-run enterprises: "In a truly revolutionary-democratic state, state monopoly capitalism inevitably and unavoidably means progress toward socialism" (Lenin 1932, 37). Workers in the USSR understood the need for state capitalism and did not fear it because Soviet state power could and would, in Lenin's words, "hedge it about with conditions to ensure its transformation into socialism *in the near future*" (Italics in original: Bettelheim 1976b, 483). In Trotsky's words:

> The dictatorship of the proletariat is expressed in the abolition of private property in the means of production, in the supremacy over the whole Soviet mechanism of the collective will of the workers, and not at all in the form in which individual economic enterprises are administered.[15]

In and from such formulations, a remarkable evolution of Soviet thinking unfolded. First, industrial enterprises owned and operated by the state were admitted to be capitalist: the internal organizational structures of those enterprises replicated those of private capitalists. Second, such capitalist organizations of production were seen to function as temporary way stations to socialism because of the control exercised over them by the Soviet state. Finally, such state-owned and operated industries came to be seen as *already* socialist by virtue of their subordination to the power of the Soviet state. Their internal organization of production ceased being relevant to the differentiation of capitalism from socialism.

In the framework of this theoretical development, state capitalism and socialism display virtually identical functioning productive enterprises. What distinguishes the two systems are not their enterprises' production processes (not their surplus labor processes) but rather who controls these enterprises and toward what ends (in whose interests). In Lenin's trenchant summary: "Socialism is nothing but state capitalist monopoly made to benefit the whole people; by this token it *ceases* to be capitalist monopoly" (1932, 37).

Most importantly for the subsequent debates over state capitalism and socialism in the USSR, Lenin's and Trotsky's formulations placed questions of power—*who* controls or manages the economy (labor processes, wage levels, etc.) and *who* sets basic policy goals—at the center of the controversy.[16] The distribution (between the state and everyone else) of final control (power) over enterprises, not the existence of expropriation and exploitation within their productive structures, became the criterion for differentiating socialism from capitalism.

Trotsky's power focus led him to oppose the concept of state capitalism as inapplicable to the USSR (1972, 245–246). He viewed the substitution of state for private ownership of means of production—state rather than private control of enterprises—as absolutely incompatible with capitalism. When such substitution had been attempted historically, private capitalists necessarily and always tried to stop or limit it *to maintain their control.* For Trotsky, a move from limited to full state capitalism would necessarily risk more than the loss of private capitalists' final control; such state capitalism would be "too tempting an object for social revolution" (1972, 246). Hence, the USSR's *total* expropriation of private capital, precisely because it was not limited and did deprive private capitalists of their former control, proved to Trotsky that the term *state capitalism* was inappropriate and misleading.[17] The distribution of power over productive assets—property—functioned in Trotsky's view to determine whether the class nature of the USSR was capitalist or not.

Not state capitalism, but rather the Soviet bureaucracy's political misdeeds distorted the achievements of 1917 and suspended the transition to socialism in Trotsky's judgment. That bureaucracy's operations risked an eventual regression to capitalism, but that would necessarily be a *private* capitalism.[18] Trotsky thus defined capitalism in terms of private property ownership, dismissing the notion of state capitalism as irrelevant to the USSR because of the extent of state ownership and control there. He concluded by focusing analytical attention exclusively on the distribution of power inside the USSR as the key variable determining the USSR's future. Albeit in different ways, both Trotsky's and Lenin's writings guided discussions of the USSR as a kind of social system. For many of their readers, those writings legitimized analyzing the USSR with the focus not on exploitation (not on the organization of surplus labor), but above all upon the distribution of power.[19]

The following sorts of questions became central: Were Soviet workers (whose power over production inside state enterprises was subordinated to state officials) nonetheless ultimately dominant via their control, through the Party, of the state? Or had groups other than workers—state bureaucrats, party officials—gained control of the state and thereby control over production (in state enterprises) and over distribution (displacing markets by means of planning)? Had they pursued their interests against the workers' interests? Had those groups congealed into new exploiting classes? How had Soviet history reflected struggles and shifts among workers, state bureaucrats, and party personnel?

The focus on power has characterized most writers in the debates over state capitalism (and, indeed, over most other aspects of Soviet society). The particular conditions that provoked Lenin's changing formulations (and those of his opponents) faded from memory, leaving the formulations themselves for subsequent debaters to develop. Thus, the issue of the workers' power in industry and their power in the state took center stage in the ongoing struggles to define and situate state capitalism and its possible relationship to socialism in the USSR.

## Power as the Theoretical Key

One large group of arguments advanced variations on the theme that socialism or the project to create socialism had been defeated in a complex power struggle after the revolution between workers and capitalists (or their agents or proponents of capitalism). Capitalism triumphed in the form of state enterprises which, while thoroughly capitalist, were disguised as "socialism" to provide ideological cover in the face of Soviet workers' expectations and aspirations.

Thus, for example, Raya Dunayevskaya often argued that there were two antagonistic planning principles struggling for dominance in the USSR: the workers' plan versus the capitalists' plan (1971, 214–240). The workers' plan aimed to raise consumption while the capitalists' plan emphasized accumulation. The latter plan prevailed. Because it focused above all else on expanding means of production rather than means of consumption, it kept workers' wages to a minimum and maximized the resources devoted to capital accumulation. Stalin and his successors, betraying the revolution, substituted a "fetishism of (capitalist) planning" for the "fetishism of commodities" that had characterized private capitalism. They thereby imposed and developed state capitalism in the USSR rather than socialism. While Dunayevskaya made state capitalism a centerpiece of her analyses and referred tangentially to surplus, she differentiated state capitalism from socialism chiefly according to which planning principle prevailed.

Dunayevskaya thus constructed definitions of state capitalism and socialism in terms of power. The distribution of social power determined which planning principle prevailed; that, in turn, determined whether a state capitalism or a socialism existed.[20] In arguments similarly focused on who held effective economic power, the international group Socialism or Barbarism wrote "the means of production will never be genuinely collective property as long as the workers . . . do not directly and totally manage production, determining both its methods and its objectives" (Bellis 1979, 214).[21] Written in the 1950s and 1960s respectively, Dunayevskaya's and the Socialism or Barbarism arguments echoed earlier statements by Bolsheviks. In 1918, the "Left Communists" had declared:

> We stand for the construction of the proletarian society by the class creativity of the workers themselves, not by the ukases of the captains of industry. . . . Socialism and socialist organization will be set up by the proletariat itself, or they will not be set up at all: something else will be set up—state capitalism. (Brinton 1970, 64)

In 1925, Zinoviev published a book entitled *Leninism* that concluded that the NEP had ceded so much power that the USSR had "abandoned socialist economic forms for 'state capitalism in a proletarian state'" (Bettelheim 1978, 370).

The consistently central issue for all these writers was who wields power, not how surplus labor was produced, appropriated, and distributed. If the proletariat wielded effective power in the USSR, its "class creativity" would ipso facto construct socialism. If power were wielded instead by state and party functionaries, state capitalism would result. Nor were such power-based definitions of capitalism and socialism restricted to proponents of the thesis that state capitalism existed in the USSR. Bukharin rebutted the thesis bluntly: "There can be no talk of 'State Capitalism' under the dictatorship of the proletariat. ... State Capitalism presupposes the capitalist State."[22] Who wielded state power settled the debate for him. Since the state was not controlled by private capitalists via parliamentarism, or such, but rather by the workers via the Communist Party, the existence of state capitalism was *therefore* impossible, unthinkable. Socialism or something in transition to socialism was what actually existed.

Power operated within these debates as strictly bipolar. Either workers or nonworkers would have state power over production. In the latter case, capitalism would prevail, notwithstanding the formal ownership of means of production by society as a whole. In Bettelheim's careful articulations concerning Soviet state enterprises, he decomposed the notion of property into an issue of power—defined this time as the polarity of "separation" and "possession." He found that Soviet state enterprises displayed a de facto *"separation of workers from their means of production* (which has, as its counterpart, the possession of these means by the enterprises, that is, in fact, by their managers)" (Bettelheim 1975, 77, italics in original). Together with the separation of enterprises from one another, this effective possession by managers of only nominally nationalized productive property comprised, for Bettelheim, the "central characteristic of the capitalist mode of production" (ibid.). Not formal property relations but rather actual power distributions over production define capitalism. He concluded:

> In transitional formations, when the agents who are bearers of state property have acquired an autonomy in relation to the immediate producers, they form a *state bourgeoisie*, and the different *powers* that correspond to this state property can be dissociated among different categories of agents: directors of enterprises, directors of trusts, managers of economic administrative bodies, managers of ministries, planning agencies, etc. (ibid., 148, italics added; see also 1978, 210ff.)

The reference here to a "state bourgeoisie" implies that the distribution of power Bettelheim found in the USSR rendered it, in his eyes, a state capitalism. One of Bettelheim's associates, Paresh Chattopadhyay (1994), has usefully updated and extended his analyses both to reinforce a property-based theory of Soviet state capitalism and therewith to interpret the USSR's demise.

Still other analysts concluded that Soviet socialism was undermined in favor of capitalism because of its failure sufficiently to transform the distribution of power: "The communist revolution is not a struggle for control of the same political edifice but a struggle to replace one form of power (exploitative and oppressive) by another (popular and emancipatory)"(Corrigan, Ramsay, and Sayer 1978, 12). This remarkable sentence, by defining communism's goals as first and foremost political and by contrasting exploitative with popular, demotes the theoretical pertinence of the production, appropriation, and distribution of surplus. These processes become marginal, derivative of more important processes, or simply irrelevant to the debate over the USSR—as does the kind of class analysis undertaken in this book.

Discussions of state capitalism have sometimes been more narrowly aimed not at state power but rather at power hierarchies at production sites. Hierarchy itself is seen as power over workers; its presence then signals the presence likewise of capitalism. The alternative, presumably a nonhierarchical organization of production, is defined as socialist or communist. Thus, C.L.R. James writes about the USSR that "In state-capitalism the state becomes capitalistic in the sense of administration, supervision, control against the proletariat" (1986, 55), and about Yugoslavia that it follows

> the administrative plan of Stalinist Russia . . . consciously organiz[ing] production according to the principle of the hierarchy in production which, as we have explained, *Marx analyzed as the heart of capitalist authority*. (ibid., 83, italics added)

Note again the equation of "capitalistic" with the organization of power (authority) over production rather than with how surplus is produced, appropriated, and distributed.

Individuals identified with the "Frankfurt School" of Marxism also developed power-focused concepts of state capitalism that were sometimes applied to the USSR.[23] Although he explicitly rejected the concept's applicability to the USSR, Friedrich Pollock (1978) authored the most systematic discussion of state capitalism originally in 1941. For him, state capitalism was the logical next step after private capitalism's market phase had developed into its monopoly phase. The model was Nazi Germany, although he noted the possibility of "democratic" as well as "totalitarian" forms of state capitalism. For Pollack, state capitalism left industrial property in private ownership but under more or less total state control. The market was replaced by state command (possibly including administered markets and prices) as *the* method of distributing all resources, including labor power, and all products. Profits, although private, were everywhere subordinated to the state's plans for full employment, target levels of consumption, and expansion. While not agreeing with the notion of "state capitalism" as Pollack defined it, his fellow Frankfurt School theorist, Otto Kirchheimer, summarized his similar sense of Nazi Germany in 1941 as "preserving the institution of private property . . . whilst abolishing the correlative to private property, the freedom of contract" (Jay 1973, 159–160).

Max Horkheimer's famous 1940 essay "The Authoritarian State" extended Pollock's and Kirchheimer's thinking by differentiating state capitalism from fascism and from what he termed "integral statism" (1978, 95–117). He theorized these as variant forms of the "authoritarian state"—the contemporary social distribution of power generated by the dominant political tendencies of modern history. State capitalism was its economic expression. It combined (1) monopolies and trusts replacing individual, competitive capitalist firms, and (2) state controls over these monopolies effectively displacing markets as sites of individual, private decision making. This basic kind of authoritarian state and its expression in state capitalism displayed to Horkheimer less and more extreme variations. Fascism was the less extreme, since it still allowed some private property and hence some base, in Horkheimer's view, for antistate thinking, organization, and activity. Integral statism was his term for the most extreme variation (1978, 102). There, all private capitalists were eliminated, state power then became virtually limitless, and "factory regimentation was extended to the entire society."

Horkheimer clearly meant the USSR as his model for integral statism. It was a state capitalism that "seems almost like a parody of the classless society" (1978, 114), since it so starkly displayed the oppression of the masses by the state-party bureaucracy. It was not, for him, a socialism in any of the senses that had motivated generations of workers, utopians, and Marxists to engage costly struggles. If anything, Horkheimer shared the views of other Frankfurt School theorists in seeing all the variations of authoritarian states and state capitalisms, and their associated social phenomena, as the latest stages of exploitative society, ripening through its contradictions to make visible once again the possibility of a genuinely socialist revolution, society, and future. Horkheimer even wrote pointedly that integral statism (that is, the USSR) kept the laborers "wage workers, proletarians, no matter how much is done for them" (1978, 102). These workers would eventually have to make a genuine socialist revolution.

The Frankfurt School's usages of the term "state capitalism" made virtually no references to the production and distribution of surplus labor. It used state capitalism to denote the apex of tendencies toward authoritarianism that it located deep in contemporary society, ultimately in the contradictory economic structure of capitalism. However, it was much less to that structure and much more to that authoritarianism that Frankfurt School theorists paid attention. Thus, true socialism was far from merely formal collective property ownership and state planning and even further from the contemporary authoritarian states' abuse of such ownership and planning for the benefit of the state bureaucracy. State capitalism and its extreme forms, fascism and integral statism, were the antitheses of socialism. This was the case because their distributions of power were so utterly contrary to the basis of socialism, which they located in *power* actually being wielded democratically by the mass of producers in society.

Pollack drew out the logical implications of the argument: the displacement of private capitalism by state capitalism "signifies the transition from a predominantly economic to an essentially political era" (1978, 78). That is, with state capitalism, political economy must give way to politics or political sociology as the science needed by socialists to criticize social reality: the "profit motive is superseded by the power motive" (1978, 78). In this statement, Pollack and the Frankfurt School demonstrated how they had deemphasized the political economy of the previous generation of Marxists and concentrated instead on politics and power.

Power had become the central issue and thus the conceptual framework through which to demonstrate that the USSR exhibited not socialism but a virulent state capitalism. The very rare and extremely brief mentions of surplus value and related economic concepts (such as Horkheimer's cited above) never evolved into a sustained analysis of the organization of surplus labor as a basis for deciding the question of state capitalism in the USSR. It was rather the distribution of power that Frankfurt School thinkers analyzed to decide that question. Indeed, the USSR was the ultimate state capitalism, having not only removed distribution from the market to the state, but also property, and having thereby empowered the state completely to regiment all social life. Earlier, private capitalisms had dreamed of such power but had found it impossible to achieve.

Writing more recently (about their native Poland), Kuron and Modzelewski's famous manifesto offered yet another variant of the power argument:

> State ownership of the means of production is only a property form; the property belongs to the social groups controlling the state.... One party has a monopoly.... As in any hierarchical apparatus, commands issue from an elite.... As the wielder of state power, this hierarchy has the nationalized means of production at its disposal.... Their surplus product is taken away from them [the workers] by force (they have no control over the amount or how it is allocated) and used for ends which are alien and even inimical to them. Therefore they are exploited.... (1972, 18, 19, 27)

This quotation is noteworthy for its unusual inclusion of some mention of surplus within its primary focus on power. The authors' preferred term is a "bureaucratic class system," but the referent here is not significantly different from what others called "state capitalism." While surplus is mentioned, it is rendered derivative of the social distribution of power ("control") over people and property upon which they focus.[24] Hierarchical power is *the* cause; exploitation (within a "bureaucratic class system" or a state capitalism) and not real socialism is the result.

Buick and Crump (1986) offer one of the more sophisticated power arguments that also marginally recognizes surplus labor, although, once again, as derivative from power distribution. They make the existence of wages, commodity production, and an orientation toward profits and accumulation their composite definition of capitalism. For them, since state enterprises have the power to operate exactly *as if* they were wage-paying, profit-maximizing, market-oriented, and accumulation-driven private capitalist enterprises, they must therefore also exploit workers and appropriate surpluses. Hence they are state capitalist enterprises. Soviet-type systems are state capitalist. Buick and Crump share with Wallerstein the view that so long as a state exists and functions in a world capitalist economy—defined in terms of wages, commodities, and profits—it cannot but preside over a state capitalism (Buick and Crump 1986, 15–16, 90ff.; Wallerstein 1979, 68–69). The power of the world market interwoven with the special power of a section of society—the state—combine here to yield a state form of capitalism as the necessary result.[25]

The Marxian theorist Bernard Chavance developed a concept of "socialist capital" that is very close to state capitalism (1980). He recognized the issue of surplus in his insistence that the USSR was an economy that organized the production of surplus by workers and its appropriation and distribution by the state. However, contrary to our approach, this point is asserted as logically necessary given the USSR's reliance on a wage labor system, evident pressure to accumulate capital, and disconnection of workers from any real property in the socialized means of production. It is because the state (not the collective of workers) really owns the means of production and because it pays workers wages and primarily accumulates capital that Chavance finds the Soviet system to be "socialist capital" rather than true socialism. Chavance concentrates on criticizing the official Soviet "political economy of socialism" for denying these realities.[26] He argues the need for a systematic exploration and analysis of the capitalist organization of surplus in the USSR that he asserts existed there, but he does not himself anywhere produce it. This book is an effort to do just that, although without reducing the organization of surplus to an effect merely of the existence of wages or of a particular property distribution as Chavance does. Yet at least Chavance found the social organization of surplus relevant to determine what the USSR actually was in class terms. We owe him an acknowledgment for that.

Finally, Paul Mattick's notion of state capitalism centralizes attention on power but inflects it somewhat differently.

> Though private ownership no longer exists, the means of production still have the character of capital because they are controlled by government instead of being at the disposal of the whole society (1969, 290) [and]

> the state-capitalist system may be regarded as Keynesianism in its most consistent and most developed form . . . in the projected wider sense of a "comprehensive socialization of investments" (ibid., 280–281) [and]

> the exploitation of men by men continues by way of an unequal system of distribution in both the conditions of production and the conditions of consumption. This inequality perpetuates competition as a struggle for the more lucrative positions and better-paid jobs, and carries the antagonisms of capitalism into the state capitalist system. (ibid., 290)

Noteworthy here is Mattick's move from the unequal distribution of social power ("control over means of production"), as the cause of a state capitalism system, to the unequal distribution of incomes and, more importantly, of bureaucratic status positions as that system's result. It thus follows that one can infer state capitalism from the empirical evidence of such unequal distributions. Mattick formalizes the logic implicit in so many designations (scholarly, journalistic, and artistic) of the state capitalist nature of the USSR across the last seventy-five years. That nature is inferred from the empirical existence of unequal bureaucratic status positions; it is thus the distribution of power that determines, in the last instance, the capitalist versus the socialist class structure of a society.

The conceptualizations of the USSR as a state capitalism reviewed here share certain basic features. The Soviet nationalization of productive property—or at least the "commanding heights" of its industry—is seen to have failed to erase its basic capitalist class nature. It was merely de jure and not de facto collectivization of ownership of the means of production. This view severs the logical link between the absence of private property in the means of production and the absence of capitalism. The USSR's elimination of the former did not eliminate the latter. The pre-1917 consensus that private property's demise would be capitalism's demise perished among those Marxists who criticized the Soviet Union as state capitalist. Now it was a de facto change in the social distribution of power generally (and not merely changes in the de jure and even the de facto distribution of property) that was required to achieve socialism.

Writers who shared in this analytical shift from property to power nonetheless elaborated their arguments differently. Some focused on how unequal distributions of power over the state (i.e., workers denied effective control over the state by its bureaucracy or by the Communist Party or both) reintroduced the separation of workers from the now nationalized means of production. This reestablished capitalism in a state-capitalist form rather than in the previous private form. Others centered attention rather on the productive enterprises. They stressed the workers' lack of decision-making power and/or management powers over production as reproducing the typical capitalist enterprise hierarchy. That circumstance plus state ownership and political power convinced them that a state capitalist system existed in the USSR (Lefort 1986, 65–77). Still others read the inequalities of income, prestige, and authority they found among Soviet citizens as direct signs that workers lacked power, since workers' power would necessarily have equalized all that. This lack of workers' power, given state property, was then equated to state capitalism.

Most conceptions of state capitalism thus refer to the distribution of power in society: power over state action, power over enterprise activity, power over income streams and job access, and so on. Because that distribution in the USSR (and in other societies based on nationalized, state enterprises) was demonstrably unequal despite state ownership of property, the term *state capitalism* seemed to capture the situation. The distribution of power in the USSR seemed to many to resemble more the distribution found in societies based on private capitalist enterprises than the equality they associated with socialism. They drew the conclusion that "socialist" was an unacceptable misnomer for what was better described as state capitalism (Buick and Crump 1986, 125).

On the other side, and not surprisingly, the arguments of those who saw and applauded the USSR as socialist *instead of capitalist* tended to make the term *socialist* a matter of state ownership (usually linked with planning rather than markets) versus private ownership (usually linked with markets rather than planning).[27]

Some defenders of the USSR as socialist also advanced power arguments like those favored among their adversaries. They claimed that power did in fact lie in workers' (or their representatives') hands in the USSR.[28] However, the difficulties (not to speak of derision) often encountered by such arguments made the state capitalism debate a contest that chiefly pitted property theorists defending the USSR as socialist against power theorists who criticized it as state capitalist.

The critics of the USSR as state capitalist whom we have discussed so far were all influenced by and mostly sympathetic to Marxism. In general, they opposed state capitalism as they opposed private capitalism. They criticized the USSR for failing to go beyond state capitalism in their sense of placing the real social power into the hands of the mass of workers. Their reliance on power theories paralleled the same reliance among most anti-Marxian critics and opponents of the USSR. The latter took the unequal power distributions of the USSR as intrinsic to socialism per se. They then attacked socialism for its centralized, undemocratic power distributions, which they judged inferior to private capitalism's relatively decentralized and democratic power distributions. State capitalism rarely arises as an explicit category for anti-Marxian critics of the USSR; they prefer to theorize within a dualism of private capitalism versus socialism. The refusal to think in terms of state capitalism comprises the common ground shared by the antisocialist critics and the Stalinist defenders of the USSR. Neither side, to our knowledge, ever explored what that commonality might mean.

In retrospect, it is not surprising that many socialists could find no theoretical comfort on either side of the twentieth-century contest between defenders and enemies of the USSR. These socialists opposed private capitalism but also the "actually existing socialism" of the USSR. Unable conceptually to break free of the contest's dominant terrain—capitalism versus socialism—they split over how to define their socialist positions. One group advocated private capitalisms with enough state controls to give them a human face (welfare supports, income redistribution, etc.) and enough civil liberties to limit state power. The other group advocated either state ownership with enterprises leased by worker collectives interacting within more or less state-controlled markets or else state-owned and -operated enterprises within legally and culturally secured structures of democratic rights and popular participations inside such enterprises as well as in relation to the state.[29] The first group often took the name "social democrats," while the second was called "democratic socialists." Both kinds of socialists oriented their arguments around the social distribution of power.

The same power considerations underlie the arguments of many (mostly socialist in orientation) who rejected the USSR as neither capitalist nor socialist (Chattopadhyay 1994, 101–120). Rudolf Hilferding, for example, used a power argument to denounce any notion of the USSR as capitalist. Because the state wielded the power to allocate resources and products, a free market was absent and that was "the decisive symptom of the capitalist system of production" (1950). Only if the power to allocate products and resources remained in private hands and was mediated by a free market did capitalism exist. At the same time, the USSR was not socialist, for Hilferding, because of its "unrestricted absolutism," its particular distribution of social power. He thus coined one of the many similar terms used by theorists who reject both capitalism and socialism as appropriate labels: the USSR was a "Totalitarian State Economy." As power was the defining characteristic and criterion of an economic and social system, considerations of the surplus once again vanished. In the words of Hilferding—otherwise recognized as one of the twentieth century's greatest Marxian economic theorists—"politics (i.e., the state) plays a determining and decisive role." This specialist in Marx's theories of surplus labor and surplus value nonetheless lost sight of or interest in them when the USSR's economic system was the object of debate. Instead, joining fully in the theoretical debates that essentialized power and banished surplus, he offered a power-as-essence theory of his own.

## Weaknesses of Power Theories

Serious weaknesses beset the power theories of state capitalism that have been applied to the USSR. The first concerns the basic concept of power's social distribution among individuals. To determine such distributions in any quantitative terms has proven to be notoriously difficult. Moreover, the quantitative determinations actually made have been equally notoriously difficult to sustain when subject to criticism. For example, the conventional wisdom held that under Lenin's New Economic Policy, the Soviet central state dominated the private capitalist producers and independent merchants scattered across the countryside—at least in its early years. Yet close, critical inspection yielded a much murkier picture of who held how much power in which domains under what set of constraints: Nepmen, private capitalist producers, the self-employed, local, regional, and central party authorities, and finally different state agencies at all levels (Ball 1990, 15–37).

The same dissolution of simplistic notions of the distribution of power has emerged over recent years as revisionist historians reexamined Stalin's first five-year plan for industrialization and his collectivization of agriculture. The prevalent idea—that Stalin wielded a total monopoly on power—had held these developments to be simply Stalin's "revolution from above." The revisionist literature has demonstrated that there was also a complex revolution "from below" in the precise sense of all sorts of powers wielded by diverse groups of workers, intellectuals, planners, managers, and others—powers with which Stalin had to contend and compromise (Fitzpatrick 1984; Cohen 1985; Chase 1990; Viola 1987; Kuromiya 1990; Thurston 1996; Bailes 1978; Davies 1993).

In this context, one might also mention the contemporary transformations of the USSR and all other Eastern European countries. Their speed, contentiousness, and multidirectionality strongly suggest that distributions of power in these societies not only are now but also were in the past extremely diverse, complex, and contradictory. This contrasts sharply with the simplistic images of central omnipotent state versus powerless masses in the prevalent power theorizations of those societies. For example, the history of Poland's Communist government testifies to the many social groupings wielding all sorts of power separate from and often hostile to Communist Party and state power and to one another: the Roman Catholic Church, shipworkers, intellectuals, and eventually the Solidarity organization were prominent among such groupings. Even after the state imposed martial law on December 13, 1981, partly to cope with the effects of their power, it still confronted all sorts of power-wielding groups such as the church, the formally dissolved but still active Solidarity (underground), the Association of Polish Journalists, the Union of Polish Writers, the newly organized People's Universities, and the Council of National Education (Kaminski 1991, 213–236).

To take yet another example, relevant to nearly all the Eastern European countries, national and ethnic conflicts that are now intense have forced the recognition that national and ethnic groups had wielded effective, if officially unacknowledged, power there for a long time. The image of dominating central authorities unaffected by national and ethnic power is unsustainable. The location of industry, the specifics of state spending on infrastructure, and access to prestigious positions in all aspects of social life were objects of struggle among national and ethnic groups. The struggles not only left mounting legacies of resentment and anger that are surfacing now: revealed, for example, in the 1990s wars in the Balkans. They also offer testimony to the effective power such groups wielded *throughout* the history of *all* the Communist regimes in Eastern Europe.

Social theories built upon the distribution of power in society as an essential determinant of social life confront a serious conceptual difficulty at the outset, namely the specification of how social power is distributed. The works cited above suggest that discourses on state capitalism (and much else) in the USSR have avoided this difficulty only by presuming simplistic and inadequate bipolar notions of how power was actually distributed there. These notions may have served well the needs of Cold War rhetoric, but as serious analysis they were deeply deficient. One close observer of the USSR's political history recently noted the consequences of such notions in the face of the reforms forced in part by its shifting distribution of power: "Sovietologists who denied for decades that change was possible in the system now lack useful concepts for even defining the success or failure of such reforms" (Cohen 1992, 262).

A second weakness, closely linked to the first, concerns the very meaning of the term *power*. As Steven Lukes has shown, examination of the classic definitions (by authors ranging widely from Max Weber, Bertrand Russell, and Hannah Arendt, to Talcott Parsons, Nicos Poulantzas, and Michel Foucault) yields fundamental and contradictory differences among their diverse meanings (Lukes 1986). Not the least of the problems in using the term *power* is its usually close proximity to "influence." Thus, if human relationships in general are conceived (defined) to include complex patterns of interpersonal influences (and hence interpersonally effective powers), it makes little sense to reduce *any* relationship to an absence of power on one side and its presence on the other. Rather, all participants in any relationship both exercise and have exercised over them a qualitatively diverse set of powers. To collapse these qualitative differences into some quantitative uniformity obscures far more than it illuminates. What matters are the particular patterns of who exercises what kinds of powers over whom and toward what ends.[30]

An example relevant to the discussion of state capitalism in the USSR may illustrate the definitional ambiguities intrinsic to power theories. Most journalistic and scholarly critiques of Soviet centralized economic planning and administration focused on the power at the center. The planning and management centers were asserted to "possess all the power" while the workers and local managers lacked power. Organized on this presumption, such critiques proceeded to conclude that the problems and failures of Soviet economic performance were effects of this power situation. The solution then lay logically in decentralizing power.

However, recognizing the basic problems and contradictions in the received bipolar power theories, one might equally reasonably have supposed that Soviet workers and local managers always had *some* powers of various kinds—in the sense of influences over the flow of events in production and elsewhere in Soviet society.[31] From this standpoint, a critique that presumed a flat quantitative absence of such power lost much of its sense and its punch. Instead the questions to ask would have been: What local powers (influences) existed at various moments in the USSR's history and how did they interact with one another and with the centralized state powers to shape the society's economic performance and much else besides?

We may push this example one step further. Suppose that workers were given all the self-managing powers proposed, say, in Vanek's careful work (1975, 11–36). Such workers might well have chosen to elect a board of directors to operate the enterprise in ways virtually identical with the profit-maximizing norms of a contemporary private capitalist enterprise in Western Europe. They might have considered this elective procedure and enterprise operation an example of self-management, the fruit of their power, and even socialism itself. The workers' wielding of such power made the system socialist in their power-focused conception, regardless of how the production and appropriation of surplus was organized inside their enterprises.

Alternatively, these workers might have insisted instead that all individuals rotate periodically through all enterprise functions from the board of directors through the management to the workers. The workers might have invited fellow citizens of their localities who were neither workers nor managers to occupy some seats on such a rotating board of directors. Such a board could well decide that not profit maximization but other goals would assume priority in enterprise decision making. Under still other conditions, the workers' power might have dispensed with a board of directors in favor of weekly or monthly meetings of all the workers (and perhaps others) who would then have collectively decided specific questions not only of management and laboring activity, but also and explicitly questions of the size of surplus labor and of its disposition. Socialism might then have been quite precisely understood as that arrangement wherein the collective of producers undertook collectively to appropriate and distribute its surplus labor.

Which questions would the self-managing workers address, given that they can no more address the infinity of all aspects of production than any conventional capitalist or other kind of management ever could? The effects of the power that self-managing workers wield always depend on the objects they wish or think appropriate to manage. For example, workers may focus exclusively on which products to produce and how technically to produce them. They may not think in terms of nor concern themselves with how the labor process affects workers' physical or mental health, the natural environment, or the relations between parents and children within households. Those dimensions of production and its consequences may therefore not change much with the advent of workers' self-management. When workers empowered with self-management do not know or strategize around Marxian concepts of class in terms of surplus labor, they will not likely use any self-managing powers they might obtain to transform the organization of surplus labor inside their enterprises from capitalist to communist class structures.

In that case, workers' self-management may yield minimally consequential variations on the conventional private capitalist enterprise. The only difference might then be that the board of directors—a group of nonworkers—is elected by workers rather than shareholders; otherwise the production and appropriation of surplus labor proceeds much as it did before worker self-management. Changing who elects or who serves as a (nonworker) board of directors appropriating surplus is not the same as changing the whole organization of surplus labor, for example, changing from a few nonworkers appropriating the surplus produced by the workers to the collective appropriation of the surplus by its producers. Workers' self-management, like other ways of enhancing workers' powers, may or may not provoke particular changes in class processes, workers' interpersonal relationships, environmental conditions, or anything else. There is no necessary class change consequent upon a power change.

This conclusion parallels our earlier findings in this book. For example, we noted how changes in property ownership, from private to collective, are likewise not essences that necessarily exert particular effects on other aspects of society. Similarly we noted that changes from markets to state planning and administration were consistent with a vast array of other social arrangements, thereby underscoring that planning is not some essence that always and necessarily produces a class structure change or any other particular result. Changing the distribution of power is like changing property ownership or systems for distributing resources and products; what social effects each of these changes has are not contained within them as their necessary effects. Here again, our particular argument reflects and reinforces the basic theoretical rejection of essentialism (and its correlates, determinism and reductionism) and commitment to overdetermination embodied throughout this book. To essentialize power, as most participants in the debates over the USSR have done, yields analyses that miss much of the dynamic of Soviet history including especially its class dimensions.

Several writers have recognized the absence of attention to the production, appropriation, and distribution of surplus labor in analyses of the USSR and in specifications of the differences among capitalism, socialism, and communism generally. Some, like Chavance, underscored the importance of constructing such an analysis. Yet no one has yet produced it. Barry Hindess referred to "the absence of a rigorous definition of the socialist mode of appropriation of surplus labor" (Bettelheim 1976a, 19). Bettelheim, in agreement with Hindess on this point, spoke of the importance of "analyzing the production relations" of "the immediate production process." Yet Hindess never constructed such a rigorous definition of socialism even though he and his coauthor, Paul Hirst, prepared important definitions for most of the other class structures that figure in Marxian analyses (Hindess and Hirst 1975). Bettelheim did construct what is arguably the best available class analysis of the USSR, but he organized it around a power definition of class under the headings of "forms of management, discipline, cooperation, and organization of labor" (Bettelheim 1978, 210ff.). This power theoretic approach omitted attention to the forms in which surplus labor is produced (by whom and how), immediately received (by whom and how), and distributed (by whom, to whom, how, and for what purposes). Bettelheim's was a *class* analysis in the particular sense that it defined the protagonists in a *power* struggle as classes. An individual was a member of a class according to whether he or she wielded power or had power wielded over them; classes pitted the powerful against the powerless across social sites (enterprise, state, etc.).

The definition of class in terms of power and the studied disinterest in the modalities of surplus labor that characterized Bettelheim's work warrant at least two conclusions. First, he shed extremely valuable light on the distribution of and struggles over power as constituents of Soviet development. Second, his disregard of surplus labor rendered his work unable to remedy what he had recognized, with Hindess, as so important an absence in analyses of the Soviet experience. Kuron and Modzelewski (1972) merited special consideration here because they were among the very few who did focus explicit attention on the distribution of the surplus product (the fruit of the workers' surplus labor) in a Soviet-style economy, Poland. However, that focus was inappropriately partial and basically tangential to their major concern. First, they failed to ask about the organization/form of the production and appropriation of that surplus (before it can be distributed). There is no warrant (indeed, they offered no justification) for neglecting the production and appropriation of surplus labor and addressing only its distribution. Secondly, they centered their analysis *not* on who produced, appropriated, and distributed the surplus and how these processes were socially organized and reproduced. Rather, they were interested in who "controls" the size and distribution of the surplus product (1972, 22, 26). They clearly did not understand that while particular individuals can be identified as producers, appropriators, distributors, and receivers of distributed shares of the surplus, it is a quite different matter to determine who wields power over the sizes of that surplus and its distributed shares.

That power is dispersed across many individuals and groups. For example, the private capitalist corporation's board of directors can be pinpointed as the persons who appropriate and distribute the surplus; all sorts of legal, cultural, political, and economic processes ensure this and can serve as evidence for it. However, power over the surplus (its size and distribution) is wielded not only by the board of directors, but also by trade unions, business associations, state officials (tax receivers, environmental regulators, monetary authorities, and so on), criminals, churches, and so on. Kuron and Modzelewski began with the intent of analyzing surplus labor, but their work (like so many others') never did more than analyze who wielded power over its distribution. They left untreated such questions as who produced and appropriated the surplus, in what multiple forms did this occur in their society, and how did these forms interact with one another and with the rest of the economy and society. They did not investigate who received the distributed shares and how those distributions interacted with the production and appropriations of the surplus. In short, while they recognized the importance of and promised to deliver a class analysis in the surplus labor sense of the term, the sway of power-essentialist theories proved too strong. They never fulfilled the promise.

The blindness of analysts, Marxian and otherwise, to the class (qua surplus labor) dimensions of the USSR both reflected and reinforced the same blindness of the people living the Soviet experience. Rank-and-file workers as well as Communist Party personnel, trade unionists, and state officials struggled almost continuously over the power to determine the size and some of the distributed shares of surplus labor, but they did not do so consciously, aware of the particular class structures that generated surpluses.[32] In other words, they did not struggle over the capitalist and other forms of the surplus labor's production and appropriation. In Marxian terms, they did not see, think, or contest the state capitalist form of the class structure. In effect, they accepted exploitation—the reality that the producers of the surplus were not its appropriators, that instead, state ministries occupied that class position.

Friends and foes of the USSR defined and measured socialism and capitalism overwhelmingly in terms of who exercised control over "the state" and "production." This was not Marx's method; he pointedly disaggregated his analysis of production to focus especially on the specifics of the organization of surplus labor and its social effects. In contrast, they dwelt on the aggregated generalities of "production" and "state" and there they focused their analysis especially on the distribution of power and control. As we shall show in detail below, with few exceptions, both Soviet participants and analysts of the Soviet experience accepted, took for granted, and theoretically ignored the class structures of state industrial enterprises in terms of how they organized the production, appropriation, and distribution of surplus labor. Nearly everyone accepted these class structures—which chapter 3 argued to be state capitalist—without much reflection (as "obvious" or "necessarily entailed by technology" or "natural" and therefore perfectly consistent with socialism or communism). Most participants and observers of Soviet society did not see class structures at all. Their eyes were focused elsewhere, on power. Power, not surplus labor, defined class structures for them.

Power, after all, has been the theoretical priority of the bourgeois age. Freedom and democracy have been the goals and justifications of its history. Blindness to class has been the other side of the fetishism of power. The Russian Revolution and the USSR later, despite their self-definition in Marx's language and imagery, remained deeply impressed with power as the essential object of thought and action. This condemned them to remain blind as well to the other side of that power essentialism, to class as the structure of surplus labor.

The history of discussion of state capitalism—like the history of so many other aspects of the Soviet experience—reveals the conceptual blinders of its time. The passions of the 1917 revolutionaries and their czarist and liberal enemies, of the Stalinists and Trotskyists, and of the cold warriors endlessly juxtaposing state and private property and planning and markets: most were obsessed with power. They struggled, albeit in different ways and toward different ends, to understand and transform the distribution of power in society as the key lever by which to shape history. They presumed, rarely stopping to wonder why, that power was *the* object that must be the focus of theoretical attention and political action.

Marxian class analyses thus became analyses of the distribution of power, whereas Marx had prioritized surplus labor for revolutionary attention. Marxists defined classes literally and almost exclusively in terms of who wielded power over objects and other people: capitalists or the propertyless masses. Anti-Marxian analyses likewise focused on power, equating Marxism with centralized, economically inefficient, dictatorial statism and contrasting private capitalism as equivalent to individualism, democracy, and economic efficiency.

Because power was the essence on all sides, no one felt the need to pay much attention to surplus labor. Theorists did not do so, nor did the Soviet authorities in the planning or execution of state policy. Nor did the workers and managers in enterprises. One result was theoretical and practical blindness to the enduringly capitalist form of the production, appropriation, and distribution of surplus labor inside the USSR. Another result was the inability to see, let alone address, the ways in which the maintenance of a state capitalist class structure—conceived as socialism by most supporters and enemies alike—contributed to many of the USSR's deepening nonclass problems, including those which finally provoked its collapse.

In part 3 of this book, we begin a class analysis of Soviet history in surplus labor terms. That analysis shows how the USSR's rise, evolution, and demise were shaped in part by class structures and struggles altogether absent from the power-theoretic accounts. This book thus begins the task of showing how the different processes of class intertwined with other processes to block the supersession of capitalism in the USSR.

The political and strategic implications of our analysis are likewise fundamentally different from those of the power theorizations. Altering power distributions, whatever its intrinsic merits and salutary effects may be, is not the essential solution to the problems that have beset the efforts so far to achieve socialism or communism. Abandoning the presumption of essentialism, there can be no pursuit of an essential solution since there is no essential problem. Presuming overdetermination rather than essentialism implies a comprehensive approach, one in which changed power configurations are sought in conjunction with changed cultural conditions *and in conjunction with changed organizations of surplus labor*. For such an approach to be possible, we need first to construct an analysis of surplus labor. That is the missing dimension that Marx's theory was intended and uniquely equipped to address systematically. By constructing a class analysis of communism, capitalism, and socialism and their relation to the USSR, we may remedy a flaw in the Soviet as well as the other efforts to date to supersede capitalist exploitation. Unlike the previous theorizations of state capitalism, ours is aimed at these targets: adding surplus labor to the power and other explanations of what happened in the USSR and adding it as well to the practical agendas and utopian visions of social change beyond capitalism, state or private.

## Notes

1. Periodically, debate shifted to focus on the related but different concept of state monopoly capitalism: for example, Fine and Harris (1979) and Jessop (1982). Our purposes here do not require attention to that concept.
2. Without direct access to the work on state capitalism of the Italian writers A. Bordiga, R. Tacchinardi, and A. Peregalli, we rely on Chattopadhyay's summary (1994, 155ff). Our quotations and references are selected to illustrate important arguments and approaches in the discussions. We need not attach particular individuals to particular positions, since the positions are our concern and since many individuals took different and often opposite positions at different times.
3. The quotation is taken from Renner's 1916 series of articles "Probleme des Marxismus" published in *Der Kampf* and translated in Bottomore and Goode (1978, 99–100).
4. See the discussion in Hardach, Karras, and Fine (1979, 53–56). Remarkable parallels link the work of such Marxian theorists to that of non-Marxians culminating in Keynes. Neither group studied direct state production. Both groups focused instead on the state's role as the necessary counterforce to private capitalism's instability. The parallels enabled Marxian and Keynesian theorists to communicate and collaborate in the 1930s and thereafter. This in turn provoked other Marxists to critical arguments that state-management could not succeed in preventing capitalist cycles and crises and thus transitions to socialism.
5. A summary and bibliography of the Austrian views is available in Tom Bottomore's "Introduction" to Bottomore and Goode (1978, 22–30). Kautsky's position developed earlier (1910).
6. Bukharin returned repeatedly in his writings to theorizations of state capitalism (clearly derived from the Austro-Marxists, Kautsky et al.), its relation to socialism, and his disagreements with Lenin on this issue, since he, more than Lenin, believed the USSR had gone beyond state capitalism to socialism (Cohen 1980, 75–86, 91–93, 255).
7. Thus Lenin (1932) stressed that a socialist state was sensible only insofar as a struggle against capitalism remained necessary *after* the revolution. Only when capitalism was finally defeated would socialism have no more need of a state; it would then wither away into a kind of communal administration.

8. Martov repeatedly used the term *state capitalism* in his polemics against the Bolsheviks after the Revolution; see the careful discussion on just this dimension of Martov's work in Burbank (1986, 13–65 and especially 60–64).
9. "Left-wing Childishness and the Petty-Bourgeois Mentality," published in *Pravda*, in May, 1918, and reprinted in Lenin (1965, 349). Italics in original. Bettelheim documents Lenin's shifts of strategic position in regard to state capitalism (1976b, 57–58, 144, 154–159, 375, 465ff).
10. After 1930, the USSR officially had workers, peasants, and intelligentsia, not classes. See for example, Stalin's discussion of "Some Questions of Theory" (1939, 57–61).
11. The best of these, Bettelheim (1976b, 1978) and Buick and Crump (1986), illustrate what original and profound insights could be achieved by Marxian class analyses and by attention to the notion of state capitalism. However, they also illustrate how thoroughly power displaced surplus labor in conceptions of state capitalism and of class itself across the analytical spectrum.
12. This insightful comment, by Barry Hindess, appears in Bettelheim (1976a, 19). Italics added.
13. Stalin's use was more restrictive: it was only leases of state productive property to *foreign* concessionaires that constituted state capitalism (Bettelheim 1978, 371).
14. Many of Lenin's and others' references presumed that such private capitalist enterprises would be overwhelmingly small-scale—as in Lenin's *Instructions of the Council of Labour and Defence to Local Soviet Bodies*: "The workers' state has enough resources to keep *within the proper bounds* and control these relationships, which are useful and necessary in conditions of small-scale production" (Lenin 1967, 312). However, as developed below, in other contexts Lenin applied the term *capitalist* also to large, state-owned-and-operated enterprises as well.
15. This passage appears in Trotsky's 1920 *Terrorism and Communism* (1961, 162), which attacked Karl Kautsky's book of the same title published a year earlier. The two books exemplify the different perspectives on state capitalism discussed in the text. In *The ABC of Communism*, Bukharin and Preobrazhensky identify state capitalism as the kind of state-coordinated capitalism in which the "bourgeois dictatorship attains its climax" while socialism is the utterly different situation when the state is in the hands of the proletariat (1969, 165).
16. Castoriadis recognized early (1949) and clearly how these formulations by Lenin and Trotsky articulated the dividing line between capitalism and socialism in deterministically political (rather than economic, let alone surplus labor) terms (1988, 117–119).
17. As noted above, such a focus on property is itself one kind of power theory. Property is a matter of power and its distribution, a matter of who controls (has the power to deny others) access to objects. This illuminates why theorists who stressed property in defining and analyzing socialism could and did shift later to a focus on other kinds of power (who controls behavior other than access to objects). Such shifts were *internal* to a general theoretical orientation that placed power distributions (rather than surplus organization) at the center of attention as explanatory keys.
18. Trotsky's words, written in the mid-1930s, foresee how the bureaucracy's abuses of power could produce a collapse eventuating in a return to a necessarily private capitalism:

> A collapse of the Soviet regime would lead inevitably to the collapse of the planned economy, and thus to the abolition of state property. The bond of compulsion between the trusts and the factories within them would fall away. The more successful enterprises would succeed in coming out on the road of independence. They might convert themselves into stock companies, or they might find some other transitional form of property—one, for example, in which the workers should participate in the profits. The collective farms would disintegrate at the same time, and far more easily. The fall of the present bureaucratic dictatorship, if it were not replaced by a new socialist power, would thus mean a return to capitalist relations with a catastrophic decline of industry and culture. (1972, 250–251)

19. These influences operated also on those uninterested in the notion of state capitalism. Bruno Rizzi, for example, articulated in 1939 the notion of the USSR as a new type of class society, neither capitalist nor socialist, in which, he argued, the bureaucracy is the politically dominant class (1985, 54–69). It engages, he wrote, in "exploiting proletarians" although he never explained or elaborated this in surplus terms. In another example, Milovan Djilas in 1957 saw the emergence of a new "privileged class" in communist societies (1983, 35): "Ownership is nothing other than the right of profit and control. If one defines class benefits by this right, the Communist states have seen, in the final analysis, the origin of a new form of ownership or of a new ruling and exploiting class." This sentence is striking for its conflation of the distinct processes of ownership over property, rule over people, and class exploitation into one composite definition of class. Finally, Howard Sherman (1995) is one of the few writers who explicitly asks the Marxian question of the Soviet Union: Who there produces and appropriates the surplus? Parallel to our argument in this book, he too concludes: "surplus labor was extracted through the exploitation of the Soviet working class" (202). However, unlike our approach, he prefers to see the USSR as neither capitalist nor socialist but rather as a "unique mode of production" (203). For Sherman, the enormous power of the Soviet exploiters over politics and means of production differentiated the Soviet "ruling class" from any comparable group of private capitalists. Once again, power is the ultimate standard for such differentiations.
20. Dunayevskaya's formulations sometimes focused on alienated labor (1992). The line of causation she elaborated went from (1) the power of some within a society to impose a production system aimed at unlimited quest for surplus to (2) the resulting alienation of labor and mass unfreedom to (3) the determination that this was a capitalist and not a socialist system. If the persons with the power to impose this were state officials, then state capitalism would be the appropriate term.
21. See also the work of the most famous member of Socialism or Barbarism, Cornelius Castoriadis (1988, 67, 1993, 98ff.).
22. Bukharin had supported the Left Opposition in 1918 when it advanced the thesis of state capitalism. Later he reversed himself. He theorized *both* the presence and absence of state capitalism in terms of power: who wielded it being the definitive criterion. For the Bukharin quotation and some background, see Dobb (1966, 145).
23. This application has been noted by several students of the Frankfurt School, including Jay (1973, 153) and Arato and Gebhardt (1978, 16).
24. Kuron and Modzelewski's disinterest in Marx's surplus theory of class emerges in their stress instead on force (which Marx explicitly opposed). And, like others, they conflate two different sets of social processes: the class processes concerned with actually producing, appropriating, and distributing the surplus and the power processes concerned with wielding influence over the dimensions of the class processes.
25. Buick and Crump do not shrink from taking their argument to a logical extreme. Genuine socialism, for them, requires the absence of the state, of exchange, of frontiers, of classes, and of the economy as such (1986, 126ff). Anything less is capitalism, either private or state. No possibility that capitalist class structures might coexist and interact with noncapitalist class structures (communist or other) anywhere is admitted.
26. Chavance credits Chambre (1974) for many insights that he further developed.
27. Of course, some who stressed the ownership of productive property were also among the USSR's critics. Sweezy, for example, in a published exchange with Bettelheim, agreed that a privileged state "stratum" had acquired de facto (if not de jure) ownership and hence constituted a "state bourgeoisie" that "controls the means of production and thereby decides how the fruits of production are to be utilized" (Sweezy and Bettelheim 1971, 119). The exchange included repeated statements by both men that amounted to designating state capitalism rather than socialism as what had arisen

in the USSR because of the de facto property and power situations there. They did not discuss the organization of surplus.

28. A sophisticated version of such an argument held that capitalist state planning differed from socialist state planning according to whether it is a "weapon of the bourgeoisie in the service of the maintenance of their rule" or a weapon of the "working people" in constructing socialism (Varga 1939, 141–142). Who ruled determined whether economic plans (and, indeed, the entire economy and society) were capitalist or socialist.

29. One developed line of such reasoning with special application to productive enterprises is found in the work of Jaroslav Vanek (1975) and his associates.

30. Perhaps the most famous example of this notion of relationships and their constituent patterns of interdependent powers wielded on all sides is found in Hegel's discussion of "Lordship and Bondage" (1949, 228–240). That discussion pinpoints and logically grounds a perspective fundamentally opposed to those deployed in most discussions of state capitalism. Master and slave are shown to struggle within a relationship of multiple, complex, and contradictory powers (influences, dominations, etc.) running in both directions.

31. See, for example, discussions of Soviet managers in Davies (1993) and production specialists in Bailes (1978, ch. 11).

32. In exactly this sense, their class blindness was similar to that of their counterparts in the United States. In both countries, workers' struggles occurred largely without any consciousness of the class processes themselves or of the alternative capitalist and communist forms in which class structures might be organized.

# PART 3

# The Rise and Fall of the USSR

CHAPTER 5

# Class Structures and Tensions before 1917

We propose here to sketch, with broad brush strokes, the multiple, interdependent class structures that existed in Russia before the 1917 revolution. We will explore the tensions within as well as the contradictory interactions among these systems of producing, appropriating, and distributing surpluses. By examining how these particular class structures shaped and were shaped by the individuals who lived within them, we aim to show how the multiple class dimensions of their lives contributed to the history that culminated in the revolutionary conjuncture of 1917.[1] To our knowledge, no class analysis of this kind exists for pre-1917 Russia. We acknowledge that the available primary evidence and secondary analyses enable only a rather impressionistic account of how surplus was organized and its fruits distributed before 1917. This might have troubled us more had not analysts of the period with very different conceptual approaches qualified their arguments similarly (Figes 1989).

## The Fundamentals: Feudal, Ancient, Capitalist, and Communist

Since most Russians (and others within the former USSR) lived in rural areas and performed agricultural labor, we begin with the class structures there. Feudal class structures were prevalent, as is well known, before the 1861 emancipation of the serfs. As we shall show, they remained important, albeit in different forms, thereafter. Russian feudalism before 1861 involved both large land-holdings centralized under the control of private landlords and larger, more centralized holdings by the czarist state itself. Given our earlier argument about the coexistence, tensions, and oscillations between private and state *capitalism* after 1917, we note here the comparable relations between private and state *feudalism* in Russia before 1861.[2] Over 50 percent of serfs "belonged" to the state rather than to private landlords at emancipation (Blum 1961, 475ff.; Pavlovsky 1968, 75ff.). The differences and relationship between the two kinds of feudalism were important influences shaping Russian history before 1917 (Blum 1961, 475ff.; Crisp 1976, 73–95).

In the 150 years before 1861, the czarist state pressed its own serfs to deliver ever more surpluses, expanded its claims for obligatory portions of the surpluses received from lower lords, and levied general per capita taxes to raise still more revenues. The state's expenditures built an army to protect Russian feudalism from external threats such as Napoleon, to sustain and administer the growing czarist empire, to start and expand state industries, and so forth. On the one hand, the private feudal lords welcomed the state activities that secured their conditions of existence and expansion. On the other, they resented and sometimes resisted the czar's demands for ever greater shares of the private lords' surpluses to pay for it all. Because such resistance was dangerous, the private lords tried to solve the problem instead by expanding their feudal estates and borrowing money. Their strategies mostly involved squeezing more surpluses from their serfs: to meet their rising obligations to the state, to pay interest to creditors, to expand their estates, and to enhance their conspicuous consumption as a mode of competing for favors from the czar including grants of land and serfs.

Contradictions between the private and state feudal class structures (especially struggles over political power between czar and lords) deepened the pressures upon both private and state serfs to produce more surplus. This provoked ever more and better organized resistance by serfs against the private lords and the state (Lyashchenko 1949, 270–280, 370–374). These complex class conflicts among serfs, private feudal lords, and the state contributed to the historic decision to emancipate the serfs and compensate the private lords in 1861.[3]

Before 1861, individual serf households or, more commonly, groups of serf households, organized in villages or communes, functioned within relationships of loyalty and fealty to "their" landlords, that is, the private lords or "state-lord" of the lands to which they "belonged." Religion and tradition enshrined these as fixed relationships entailing specific patterns of necessary and surplus labor performance and specific deliveries of surplus labor (or its fruits) by serfs to "their" lords. Sometimes the latter provided not only land but virtually all the other means of agricultural production as well; sometimes serfs owned and provided some of the means themselves. Either serfs delivered their surpluses individually to their landlords, or else villages delivered their individual households' surpluses collectively to the landlords.

Serfs performed necessary labor on lands allocated to them for that purpose and retained its fruits for their own reproduction. Some then performed surplus labor on that same land and delivered the fruits of that surplus labor to landlords as "rents" (*obrok*) in kind or cash. Other serfs delivered their surplus labor to their landlords as such (*barshchina*—roughly equivalent to the corvée elsewhere in European feudalism) with the landlord immediately appropriating the fruits of that surplus labor.

The feudal landlords existed in a hierarchical relation to one another, culminating in the czar, such that lower lords distributed some of the surplus they appropriated from their serfs to higher lords. These distributions secured the lower lords' social positions as landlords under the protection of the higher lords. The higher lords used these distributions partly to provide that protection. Many landlords both distributed surplus to higher lords and received surplus from lower lords. In general, each landlord distributed portions of the surpluses appropriated from his own serfs to other individuals to finance their activities if and when they were deemed necessary for his continued existence as a feudal lord. These portions of the surplus included contributions to the church, interest payments to his creditors, funding for his armed retainers and household servants, tribute to his overlord, and so on.

Alongside the feudal class processes—the lords' appropriating and distributing the serfs' surplus—various power proceses connected lords and serfs. Some landlords directly controlled how serfs and serf villages functioned economically, politically, and culturally. In other cases, villages or even individual serfs exercised considerable powers. Lord and serf wielded different, varying, and often contested powers over decisions on the feudal manors, including how large a surplus would be produced and how it would be distributed by the feudal lord. As political powers were variously distributed among lords, so too were powers among the serfs. Sometimes a few elders monopolized power vis-à-vis other heads of village households, usually men prevailed over women, and so on.[4]

The private landlord's considerable power to decide upon the size of the surplus and how to distribute it (how big a portion each recipient would receive) had also to be shared with others beside the serfs: the church, the czarist state, creditors, and still others wielded varying influences over these decisions. The czarist state, as feudal landlord, had similarly to share its decision-making powers. The powers to determine the sizes of the feudal surpluses produced for either private feudal lords or the czarist state were also dispersed in ways that varied across time and region: the church had its applicable doctrines, the serfs their modes of resistance, the czarist state its military and other imperatives, and so on. The feudal class processes connecting lords, serfs, and recipients of surplus distributions, on the one hand, and the power processes distributing influences over decision making were different but mutually dependent and mutually constitutive.

The feudal class structure that connected serfs to landlords in agricultural "enterprises" (the feudal manor as a farming unit) was highly centralized: typically many serfs produced surplus for a lord. Another, much more decentralized form of feudal class structures existed elsewhere in Russian society. Inside most rural households, another kind of feudal class structure linked its individual inhabitants as they produced household goods and services (crops and animals, clothing and furniture, cooking, cleaning, repairing, etc.).[5] The kind of feudal class structure *inside* the Russian rural household interacted in complex ways with the kind of feudal class structure *outside* on the feudal manor.[6] The migration to the cities during the century before 1917 seems simply to have moved feudal class structures so that they prevailed in both rural and urban households.

Inside the Russian household, its particular kind of feudal class structure assigned the surplus appropriator's role most often to the father. Religion and tradition enshrined him in the position of owner-provider of the house and other physical means of household production. Women—chiefly his wife but possibly also her children and/or their spouses—performed feudal necessary and surplus labor in the household (Tian-Shanskaya 1993, 3–10, 124–125). They performed some gardening, cooking, cleaning, and so forth for their own sustenance (necessary labor) but also did more (surplus labor) and delivered that to the father.

Having appropriated the household surplus, the father then distributed portions of it to secure his feudal class position there. He contributed to the church, paid household taxes, fulfilled obligations to the village, possibly paid interest on personal debt, and so forth. He directed some of the surplus to sustain the children until they could join the ranks of household serfs performing necessary and surplus labor. Depending on the relative strengths of church interventions in household affairs, interpersonal household relationships, and other aspects of the social context, the feudal father had to share with others the power to decide household affairs, including determining the size and distribution of the household surplus he appropriated. The "lord of the household" thus functioned within class and power processes that were different from but quite analogous to the functioning of the "lord of the land."

Since household feudal class structures endured long after emancipation, Russian feudalism was not actually abolished in 1861. Some kinds and social sites of feudal class structures continued while others disappeared. Indeed, a new kind of feudalism arose after 1861: "decentralized feudalism." Before 1861, a relatively small number of private lords and the state appropriated the surplus labor of the vast majority of agricultural laborers in the Russian villages. After 1861, the villages and individual laborers reorganized their system of production including its class structure—that is, its manner of producing, appropriating, and distributing the laborers' surplus labor. The former, relatively centralized feudalism was replaced by a decentralized and often contentious mixture of class structures. Individual farming units within the post-1861 villages displayed nonfeudal as well as feudal class structures connecting the individuals who cultivated those units. The household feudal class structure that survived largely intact from pre-1861 Russia often extended its reach onto the farming units; to that degree a decentralized agricultural feudalism partly replaced the former centralized agricultural feudalism.

However, the most widespread and prevalent class structure of post-1861 village farming was not feudal; it was the ancient class structure. The latter and the small but rapidly growing capitalist class structure of village farms are the objects of the next two sections of this chapter. Yet before moving on to nonfeudal class structures in Russia before 1917, it is worth mentioning the existence of still other kinds of feudal class structures located at sites of production other than manorial agricultural enterprises and individual households.

Before emancipation, nobles and the state also used their serfs as surplus labor performers inside the industrial enterprises they owned (Blum 1961, 287–320). Merchants also sometimes used their trading profits to establish industrial factories based on the labor of serfs. In this case, the merchants either leased or otherwise acquired serfs from their traditional feudal lords and then set them to factory work in a class relationship identical to the serfs' former situation on the rural manors.[7] In effect, the individual merchant thereby established himself in the class position of (industrial) feudal lord. Blum mentions that a few serfs even established feudal industrial factories based on the labor of other serfs acquired much as the merchants had done (1961, 299).[8] Such serfs thereby came to occupy both sides of the fundamental feudal class relation: producers of surplus for their lords and appropriators of surplus from other serfs.

Russian feudalism, like feudalisms elsewhere and at other times, displayed a wide variety of forms at different social sites. Such distinguishing adjectives as *state* and *private*, *urban* and *rural*, *enterprise* and *household*, *centralized* and *decentralized*, and *agricultural* and *industrial* indicate the range of different kinds of feudal class structures that comprised the totality of Russian feudalism. These differences also attest to the adaptability of feudal class structures to the diverse social and natural conditions of a vast territory across a long history. Later in this chapter, we explore some of the complex ways in which individuals in pre-1917 Russia occupied these multiple, different feudal class positions. There we consider the male feudal serf who provided surplus labor to an appropriating landlord (private or state, agricultural or industrial, etc.), while also appropriating the feudal surplus labor of women inside his household. We also consider his wife's possible occupation of multiple class positions such as feudal surplus labor provider inside the household to her husband and outside the household, alongside her husband, to the feudal appropriator of their surplus. As we show, these feudal class positions are but a few of the many possible different class positions, feudal and nonfeudal, occupied in varying patterns by most Russians in the eighteenth and nineteenth centuries. Knowing these patterns is a prerequisite for venturing some suggestions on how the class aspects of Russian society contributed to the revolutionary conjuncture of 1917 and to the complex class structure of Soviet development thereafter.

The "ancient" class structure differs markedly from the feudal. The person who performs both necessary labor and surplus labor does so individually (not as part of any group or collective). This individual—and no one else—*also appropriates his/her own surplus*. The ancient producer/appropriator of surplus labor thus also distributes his/her own surplus to others who provide the conditions enabling the ancient class structure to continue.

Ancient class structures had long existed alongside Russia's predominant feudal class structures.[9] For centuries, many Russian men and especially women, beside working as feudal serfs on the manor farms, also individually produced crafts distributed to consumers via markets or other social mechanisms. The latter included intrafamily distributions and individual distributions to another person for which the Russian language had a term, *remeslo*, that specifically differentiated such activity from production for markets, *promysel* (Matossian 1968, 11–12). This craft production often entailed an ancient class structure as individuals appropriated and distributed their own surplus labor.[10] The evidence suggests that for some time in parts of Russia before 1861, feudal class structures had been transformed into ancient class structures as lords responded to growing difficulties with rebellious serfs by, in effect, changing them into ancient tenant farmers.

In any case, after 1861, ancient class structures became much more important as they generally *replaced* the feudal class structures in nonhousehold agricultural production. Individual Russian peasants, freed from their former feudal obligations, now cultivated "on their own." They performed necessary and surplus labor on land that was theirs or had been allocated to them by the village communes. They sustained themselves with the fruits of their necessary labor, and then distributed the fruits of their surplus labor to secure the varied conditions of existence of this ancient class structure. Chief among these distributions of ancient surpluses were large state taxes (revenues used to compensate the private lords for their losses from the emancipation: the famous "redemption payments"). The 1861 emancipation sharply accelerated the transition from feudal to ancient class structures outside, although not inside, Russian households.[11]

After emancipation, the village communes became complex associations of families whose working adult members farmed the communal land chiefly as ancient producers (Vucinich 1968).[12] Each such family performed necessary and surplus labor on the strips of land allocated (and periodically reallocated) to it by the commune. The periodic reallocations accommodated changing household demographics, differential fertilities, and so on to reduce, if not eliminate, the differentiation among ancient producers. The goal was to prevent the erosion of the ancient class structures—and the communal life built upon it—that differentiation would have threatened. Some families did break away from the communal villages to varying degrees of more independent economic activity.[13] While the periodic communal reallocations of land largely succeeded in sustaining ancient class structures on the communes, individual household production (including household gardens) was not affected (Watters 1968, 143). Russian villages distinguished, albeit in terms other than ours, two social sites and two class structures: feudal households and ancient farms.

Each ancient communal farmer appropriated the fruits of his/her surplus labor and then distributed it to other persons.[14] However, the power to influence the size of the surplus and of distributed portions and who would be their recipients was shared by the ancient farmer with many others. For examples, the council of village elders (other ancients within the commune) collected a portion of the ancients' surpluses (in cash or kind) for various purposes; state officials had rights to another portion; church rules governed work time and hence the size of the surplus, while the church also tapped the surplus for contributions; and so on. The distributions of power over the ancient class structure of the Russian peasantry varied regionally and periodically after 1861.

The transition from feudal to ancient class structures, however glorified as emancipation, was no escape from poverty, pressure, and class conflicts for the rural peasantry. Many ancients discovered that, while different, the demands on their surplus labor were often greater after 1861 than before. The feudal lords were gone, their political and cultural domination reduced, and delivery of serf surpluses to them stopped. Yet the ancients now found their individually appropriated surpluses heavily taxed by a czarist state to finance redemption payments to former feudal lords and ambitious administrative, military, and modernization projects. Ancients faced the instabilities of the markets increasingly penetrating the Russian countryside. Ancients inside the village communes—and hence subject to their constraints—encountered competition from ancients not similarly constrained outside the communes and from the small but rapidly growing agricultural capitalists. Former feudal lords often retained some of their own land, which they offered for lease; they likewise retained rights to water and other necessities for farming. Ancients who required these resources as conditions of their continued existence found their surpluses heavily charged for access to them.

The class struggles that occupied the ancients differed from those that beset the feudal serfs before them. Ancients fought over how village communes would periodically redistribute their lands among the ancients. They wrangled with the czarist state over the taxes they paid and the state services they needed; they resented a state that seemed to favor instead the former feudal lords and the growing capitalist industry. The growth of the Russian empire after 1861 (with its military and administrative costs) and state subsidization of capitalist industrialization subjected the ancient class structure at the base of Russian society to incredible pressures, controls, and predations upon the ancient surplus. The peaceful "resolution" of one class crisis in 1861 prepared the ground for the violent "resolution" of a different class crisis in 1917.

Not only did ancient producers predominate within the totality of Russian agriculture after 1861, but ancient producers gained in importance in both rural and urban handicraft industries. Even in pre-1861 Russian feudalism, the seasonal nature of agricultural work, the gender division of labor, cultural traditions, and other factors overdetermined that many serfs also spent time as self-employed producers of crafts (destined for markets or other forms of distribution). Similarly, serfs who fled to the urban areas often survived there by establishing ancient craft enterprises to supply Russia's growing urban markets. Just as feudal class structures varied in kind as among private landlords' estates, state lands, and serf households, so ancient class structures varied in kind before and after 1861: in rural and urban areas, in agricultural and handicraft pursuits, and so on. Ancient class structures also occurred inside households with only one working adult—usually females because of widowhood or abandonment—where a feudal class structure was thus impossible (cf. Fraad, Resnick, and Wolff 1994).

Before concluding this overview of Russia's ancient class structures before 1917, we note that increasingly after 1861, Russian peasants combined ancient with other class positions. Some ancients periodically hired laborers and so functioned partly as capitalists. Many ancients periodically or regularly drew other household members into farm work alongside themselves. This usually meant that the feudal class structure inside the household was extended onto the farm. The usually male ancient peasant then occupied as well a feudal class position vis-à-vis his wife (and perhaps other family members) *both* inside and outside the household.

The evidence suggests that in the fifty years before 1917 Russia consisted of multiple, different class structures. As we have shown, it was largely an ancient society that retained a vast feudal class structure *inside* households as well as feudal and capitalist class structures in many agricultural, craft, and industrial enterprises (cf. Gabriel and Martin 1992). Moreover, as detailed below, individual Russians typically occupied multiple class positions within these structures.

Differing from the ancient class structures, the capitalist entails (1) the appropriation of surplus by persons other than its producers and (2) collective rather than individual labor processes within enterprises. Differing from the feudal, in capitalist class structures, laborers are not personally bound to the land or the surplus appropriator by ties of mutual obligation, loyalty, or religion. Moreover, they deliver the fruits of *both* necessary and surplus labor to the capitalists.[15] The latter must then contractually return the fruits of the necessary labor time (in cash or kind) as the quid pro quo for the laborers' work. This return by capitalists may or may not take the form of a commodity exchange: labor power for wages.[16]

In *private* industrial capitalism, the class position of surplus-appropriating capitalist is occupied by individuals with no official status within a state administration or bureaucracy. Private capitalist enterprises grew in Russia across the nineteenth century, especially in urban areas. A century of debate concerns the growth of private capitalism in agriculture after 1861 as well (Lyashchenko 1949, 445–472; Lenin 1956; Shanin 1986). Some private capitalist class structures emerged from a certain "differentiation" among ancient producers. The vagaries of climate, soil fertility, access to markets and credit, and many other conditions of production often yielded prosperity for some ancients and disaster for others. Sometimes, ancients sustained social organizations that prevented such differentiation from undermining their ancient class structure. The Russian village communes often reallocated land, subsidized individual peasants' temporary difficulties, and otherwise tried to counteract natural and social threats to Russia's ancient class structures before 1917.

However, the village communes did not always nor everywhere succeed. Some peasants left the communes or else remained but operated with decreasing respect for or relation to communal egalitarianism. Ancients who did well entered into new relations with ancients who failed. The former purchased the labor power of the latter and set it to work with other means of production to make goods increasingly destined for markets. These new capitalists returned the fruits of the new laborers' necessary labor to them and kept the surplus for themselves.

Private capitalist class relations arose in other ways as well. The feudal manors had long included some serfs with craft skills. The products of their part-time craftwork circulated inside the feudal manors and villages. Often, skilled serfs were able—or encouraged by lords anticipating enhanced feudal rents from them—to specialize fulltime in their craft and produce for ever wider markets. This was the origin of the famous *kustar* industries (Lyashchenko 1949, 478–481). Initially, these craft productions exhibited a feudal class structure located alongside the feudal class structures elsewhere on the Russian manors.

Before, but especially after emancipation, *kustar* industries grew in ways quite similar to the Western European "putting out" system. Raw materials were "put out" to the homes of part-time or full-time craftspersons by enterprising landlords, merchants, or others with sufficient wealth. These craftspeople worked on them to produce finished goods typically in exchange for a money payment. In many cases, the class process involved here was no doubt ancient: individual craftspersons did necessary and surplus labor on the materials provided to them and appropriated their own individual surplus, in value form, once the providers paid them for their product. However, capitalist class processes materialized where and when the relationships changed, however slowly and subtly, and the craftspeople became persons selling their labor power rather than their craft products. It was then a small step for the capitalist to gather such craftspersons under one roof in the manner of early European private capitalism.

Sometimes capitalist class structures emerged when "modernizing" landlords converted their estates from feudal to capitalist enterprises, ejected feudal serfs and hired agricultural wage workers instead. Other landlords, who had collected rents from ancient tenant farmers, evicted them to establish their own capitalist farms. The landlords-become-capitalists hoped to amass more surplus by exploiting hired workers than by exploiting feudal serfs or obtaining rents (surplus distributions) from ancient tenants.

The rapid growth of private capitalist industries outside Russia across the nineteenth century increased foreign demand for Russian exports and domestic demand for capitalist commodity imports. Foreign capital and technologies arrived; foreign private capitalist enterprises expanded into Russia. These sources of capitalist development were especially important in the last decades before 1917.

Finally, the czarist state also actively facilitated the emergence of capitalist class structures in pre-1917 Russia: "the state played the leading role in bringing large-scale capitalist enterprise into existence" (Riasanovsky 1984, 425). The state provided private capitalist industrial enterprises with massive, guaranteed-profit orders (for industries supplying Russian railways, the military, and telecommunications), tariff protection, foreign capital inflows, cheap credit, loan guarantees, and docile workers (Grossman 1973; von Laue 1963). At the turn of the century, the Russian state owned 3.5 billion rubles out of the entire capital of 4.7 billion rubles invested in railways (Lyashchenko 1949, 534). The Russian state owned and operated many banks. It derived very significant revenues from its vodka monopoly.

The post-1861 czarist state also promoted capitalist class structures in its own enterprises much as earlier czars had established state industries on the basis of serf labor (Grossman 1973, 488). Besides owning vast lands and mines, the czarist state enterprises hired wage labor to process their ores and produce vast quantities of alcohol (Lyashchenko 1949, 554). State coexisted with private capitalist enterprises within a context of massive state subsidies and supports chiefly for private capitalist development.

The decades preceding 1917 display sharply curtailed and decentralized feudal class structures outside households alongside an enduring feudalism within them, a sea of ancients as the prevailing class structure, and a capitalism that could reasonably be described as "the most challenging economic dynamism in view" (Shanin 1986, xiii). But that capitalism was still relatively small. The state's efforts to promote it were offset by other steps it took to secure ancients, especially in the rural areas, and still other steps it took in support of the remaining feudal elements (Lyashchenko 1949, 445–472). Similarly, struggles within the village communes in some ways enabled capitalist class structures to grow while otherwise blocking them to secure the ancient class structures. Even Lenin, arguing that capitalism was fast displacing all previous class structures, admitted that he exaggerated to make readers see capitalism as the revolutionary agency transforming Russian society (1956, 347).

The growth of capitalist class structures, rural and urban, was attracting increasing numbers of people into part-time, seasonal, or full-time wage work. Old political and cultural patterns were shaken in the countryside and even more in the urban areas. Institutions favoring the ancient class structures fought back against the capitalist tide, often successfully. The complex class structures of Russia before 1917 were experiencing momentous transitions, strains, and struggles for hegemony. These interacted in socially explosive ways with transformations in the nonclass aspects of Russian society. Waves of new and cheaper commodity imports interacted with rural migration to Russian cities, new modes of lending, new technologies, new kinds of business organization, and class conflicts to shock and rapidly transform the Russian economy. In politics, the inherited state apparatus, built upon and loyal to its feudal past, confronted the conflicting demands of rising ancient and capitalist class structures seeking returns for the surpluses they paid as taxes to the treasury. A deepening animosity between state and citizen came to pervade Russian politics. Meanwhile, the corrosive challenges of European modernisms in all the arts, sciences, religion, and so forth fertilized and empowered internal Russian movements to transform its inherited culture.

The communist class structures merit our attention because they did *not* exist significantly in pre-1917 Russia. Only some relatively small-scale and short-lived experiments with communist class structures occurred within religious movements such as the Old Believers and Sectarians (Stites 1989, 16–17). They nonetheless warrant discussion because (1) very important social movements argued that something like communism did exist before the revolution, and (2) a stated Bolshevik objective was to establish communist class structures in place of the other class structures.

While communist class structures, in our surplus sense, were never significant before 1917, many in the large populist movement claimed that the mir, the village commune prevalent across rural Russia, represented a partial or full communism. Here we encounter again the confusion or conflation of a *power* structure with a *class* structure. The evidence is quite clear that village communes were, as noted above, composites of ancient, feudal, and capitalist class structures. The power/class confusion arises when the political relations of the mir are taken for class relations. The village communes did often display more or less egalitarian participation by heads of households (mainly male). They made collective decisions, sometimes quite democratically, on vitally important issues (excluding internal household affairs): periodic land reallocations, rules governing labor and outputs, maintaining common lands, and so on. The power of the mir, however, was not absolute; powers over the same decisions were also exercised by the church, the state, and, of course, the individual surplus producers and appropriators themselves. The mir per se neither produced nor appropriated surpluses itself. Its members did so within a set of class structures that did not, as we have shown, include the communist class structure.

## The Complexities

To this point, our survey of the pre-1917 class structures existing in Russia has considered chiefly the different *fundamental* class processes: the feudal, ancient, capitalist, and communist. Our analysis focused thus on the different kinds of class positions that Russians might occupy as producers and/or appropriators of surplus labor in each of these forms. However, to earn incomes and survive, all Russians did not need to participate in one or another fundamental class process as a surplus producer, appropriator, or both. Instead of (or in addition to) these fundamental class positions, Russians could occupy what we call *subsumed and nonclass* positions. The subsumed class positions are defined as those whose incomes are distributions of portions of the surplus from its appropriators. For example, village money lenders provided credit—a condition of their existence—to feudal, ancient, and capitalist appropriators. In return such lenders got distributions from the latters' surpluses as interest payments. Similarly, governments provided police, road maintenance, and other services in return for taxes and fees paid by appropriators from their surpluses. Merchants provided feudal, ancient, and capitalist appropriators with quick and regular ways to convert their products back into money in return for a fee paid out of their surpluses.[17] In all class structures, fundamental class positions (as producers and/or appropriators) coexist with subsumed class positions (obtaining distributed shares of surplus from one or more of its appropriators). Individuals earn incomes by occupying either or both kinds of positions within the varying class structures that coexist in any society.

Finally, societies contain individuals who earn incomes in *nonclass positions*. That means they can earn incomes *without* participating in either fundamental class processes (they do not produce or appropriate surplus) or in subsumed class processes (they do not obtain a distribution of surplus from the appropriator). Individuals in nonclass positions are thus one social remove from any class structures. Individuals who earn incomes exclusively from occupying nonclass positions will, of course, interact with the existing class structures in many different ways, but they do not participate in any as producer, appropriator, or recipient of distributed surplus. Examples from pre-1917 Russia would include, for example, employees hired by moneylenders, merchants, and governments.[18] Such employees neither produce nor appropriate surplus nor are their wage payments surplus distributions by appropriators. While they are thus one remove from the class structure, they remain indirectly dependent on it (as it is indirectly dependent on them).

Since our concern here is not a comprehensive class analysis—requiring detailed examinations of the relevant subsumed and nonclass positions—we have concentrated our brief survey on the fundamental class structures in Russia from 1861 to 1917. That survey permits the conclusion that most of the Russian people occupied, outside their households, ancient fundamental or subsumed class positions or nonclass positions dependent on the ancient class structures. Inside their households, most participated in or depended upon feudal class structures; and, as noted, the latter also sometimes extended their reach onto village farms. Capitalist class structures, rapidly intruding in both urban and rural areas, were the most contentious, dynamic, and socially divisive class structures. They provoked strong feelings and expressions ranging from envy, hostility, and resentment to hope, admiration, and passionate advocacy. Communist class structures lay almost completely outside the experience of pre-1917 Russia.

Each of these class structures—ancient, feudal, and capitalist—was the site of many diverse pressures. Within them, producers and appropriators struggled over the quantities and qualities of their surpluses. In the case of the ancients, such fundamental class struggles occurred within the same person.[19] Beside fundamental class struggles (over the production and appropriation of the surplus), there were also subsumed class struggles (over what shares of appropriated surplus would be distributed to what recipients/claimants). The different class structures often threatened one another's conditions of existence (competing for laborers or other resources, supporting different state policies, and so on). Struggles among class structures thus intertwined with the class struggles within each structure to comprise the complex patterns of class struggles characterizing pre-revolutionary Russia.

We presume that individuals in any society typically occupy more than one class position within one class structure. We found this to be the case in pre-1917 Russia. They did so across different periods in their lifetimes and often across different periods of a day or week. To demonstrate how class structures shaped Russian history requires identifying how individuals were distributed across multiple class positions. On the basis of the major patterns in the Russians' multiple occupations of fundamental, subsumed, and nonclass positions, we can then begin to assess how class structures influenced the history building to the 1917 revolution.

To take some examples of Russians occupying multiple class positions, we may consider first a peasant wife. She might (1) perform feudal surplus labor inside the household and deliver its fruits to her husband, and (2) labor alongside him as an ancient partner producing and appropriating her own surplus on the land allocated to them by the village commune. Her husband might engage in (1) the seasonal sale of his labor power to a capitalist industrial enterprise, taking time from (2) his ancient class position within his village commune, and (3) his feudal class position within his household. Their adult, unmarried son might have left the village altogether to (1) spend weekdays as a surplus labor performer in an urban capitalist enterprise, and (2) work weekends as an ancient producer/seller of transport services utilizing his horse and cart there. Their adult, married son might also move to the city in order to (1) appropriate the household feudal surplus labor of his wife, and (2) appropriate the capitalist surplus labor of a few fellow villagers who had followed him to the city looking for employment in his small furniture workshop. Their adult, married daughter might (1) provide feudal surplus labor to her peasant husband, (2) produce and sell in local markets her ancient handicrafts, and (3) occasionally do part-time work in a local capitalist's textile mill.

In these examples, Russian individuals occupy various—and historically quite typical—patterns of multiple fundamental class positions. We can readily extend the argument to provide examples of patterns that include various subsumed and nonclass positions as well. A peasant's younger son and his wife may leave the village and establish a household in the city. The son may find work as a night watchman at a factory, while his wife works part-time as a clerk in a merchant's store. He and she occupy feudal class positions inside the household in relation to its production activities (cooking, cleaning, and so on). Outside, he occupies a capitalist subsumed class position: he provides a condition of existence—security—for the factory capitalist's appropriation of surplus value in return for a distributed share of that surplus as his wage. She occupies a nonclass position outside the household, since her wage is not payment for producing a surplus nor a distributed share of someone's appropriated surplus. Other similar examples drawn from pre-1917 Russia might include a feudal housewife who also works part-time as a small merchant buying farm produce from ancient peasants and reselling them in local markets. She occupies (1) a feudal fundamental class position inside the household, as well as (2) an ancient subsumed class position: she quickly and regularly converts ancient products into money in exchange for a discount on those products which she then resells. Her husband might then occupy (1) a feudal fundamental class position as lord of the household, (2) a capitalist subsumed class position as a peddler who buys socks from a capitalist factory for resale, and (3) a nonclass position as a part-time auxiliary fireman paid out of tax receipts by a state agency.

Individual Russians' standards of living—levels of goods and services actually consumed—depended on how much real income flowed from each of the multiple class and nonclass positions they occupied. How each position influenced their thinking and feelings, their ideology and politics, depended not only on how much income it generated for them, but also on how they experienced the time spent in each position: as a trauma or a privilege, as a temporary necessity or a situation to be treasured for the future. The contribution of a Marxian class analysis nuanced in this way flows from its illumination of the different, multiple class structures that individuals in pre-1917 Russia had to negotiate daily (1) in leaving and reentering their households and (2) traversing their class and nonclass positions outside the household.

The decades between emancipation and revolution were times of great changes in class structures and hence in the set of class and nonclass positions available for Russians to occupy and live from. Strains within all the contending class structures provoked intense struggles over the production and distribution of surpluses. At the same time, Russians were in conflict over which class structures should be hegemonic in society and whether and how they could coexist. A profound insecurity about class positions settled into the thinking and feelings of the Russian people. However, because of the lack of class consciousness, the strains and conflicts were not seen as class issues. Instead, they were experienced as specific interpersonal problems and/or regional, religious, and ethnic conflicts, and/or as a vague, ominous sense that Russian society was disintegrating, that "all that is solid melts into air."[20]

The cultural, political, and economic history of Russia was shaped, in part, by the specific and ever-changing patterns of class positions occupied and negotiated by its people. The broad social movements that evolved depended in part on the multiple class positions actually occupied by most Russians and in part on the intensifying contradictions among those positions. The movements also arose in relation to class positions that Russians wanted or hoped to occupy in the future within the context of a dramatically changing society, especially after 1861.

## The Contradictions and the Revolution

Contradictions between serfs and feudal landlords sharpened across the nineteenth century as the lords pressed for greater surpluses to offset their eroding conditions of existence (Lyashchenko 1949, 358–375). The serfs both resisted, increasingly in violent ways, and reacted by deserting feudal agriculture for the towns or for nonfeudal—chiefly ancient—class positions in the countryside. The feudal subsumed classes—merchants, moneylenders, the church, and others—demanded ever larger cuts of the surplus in return for continuing to provide the conditions of existence of feudal class structures. These feudal subsumed classes began to shift their activities toward those other class structures (becoming subsumed to their surplus appropriators) as the latter increasingly challenged and displaced Russian feudalism. Merchants saw better futures buying and reselling ancient and capitalist products, moneylenders switched to the same classes, and so on. The increasing pressure on feudal class structures in turn provoked lords to consider transforming estates into collections of ancient farmers paying them rents or into large capitalist farms. When this occurred, the remaining feudalism was often still further weakened, its contradictions exacerbated, and the vicious circle of its decline engaged.

Contradictions within the ancient class structures of the peasantry after 1861 have been exhaustively treated in the literature beginning with Lenin's polemics against the *narodniki* and continuing with Shanin's recent work (Lenin 1956, 11-49; Shanin 1986, 172-173 passim). On the one hand, ancient peasants had to distribute large portions of their surpluses to the state as redemption payments and taxes. Where they leased land from landowners, they had also to distribute another portion of their surplus as rental payments to those landowners. As suggested above, these outlays, when added to the other subsumed class demands on ancient producers (from the church, from the village commune, etc.), could well exhaust or even exceed ancient surpluses. When prices for marketed ancient outputs fell, the situation deteriorated even further. Borrowing to relieve such burdens added interest obligations to the already unmanageable demands on ancient surpluses. In such cases, ancient producers had to decrease their own consumption (sometimes below its levels when they were serfs) to free produce (or its cash equivalent) for distribution to subsumed classes. This explains the widespread evidence of extreme poverty, loss of land, and increasing landlessness in rural Russia before 1917. Sometimes the communal village organization could offset these problems somewhat by sharing the subsumed class burdens among the ancients in the village, by reallotting land to assist ancients in the greatest difficulties, and so on. Yet these very measures provoked debate, discord, and departures from the mir. Where the mir organization failed and among peasants outside the mir, the contradictions between successful and unsuccessful ancients mounted until their class structure gave way to rural capitalism and the emigration to urban class positions (capitalist and ancient) and nonclass positions.

The contradictions within the capitalist class structures likewise sharpened in the decades before 1917, although within the context of quite spectacular growth of their capitals and labor forces. Conflict between surplus producers and appropriators over the size of the surplus frequently erupted in violence as atrocious working conditions, extremely low wages, and dangerously poor living conditions made workers angry and volatile (Bonnell 1983). The same conditions attended the mass of workers occupying capitalist subsumed and nonclass positions in the towns. The state frequently had to act directly to contain eruptions.

On the other hand, contradictions between capitalist appropriators and their subsumed classes were systematically ameliorated by supportive state policies, especially but not only under the influence of Finance Minister Serge Witte. In effect, the state provided capitalists in industry with credit, subsidies, protection, and other conditions of their existence and rapid growth *without* demanding in return much of a cut of industrial capitalist surpluses (as taxes on capitalist profits). This enabled capitalists to devote larger portions of their surpluses, saved from taxes, to accumulation instead. Similarly, the agrarian reforms before and especially after the 1905 revolution (associated with Prime Minister Peter Stolypin) enhanced many of the conditions for small-scale rural capitalism to grow. In a sense, then, contradictions within capitalist class structures, while sharp, won the attention of the state, which acted to soften, repress, or otherwise overcome them in ways parallel to how the village commune organizations sought to overcome contradictions within their ancient class structures there.

Contradictions *among*—as opposed to within—class structures took different forms. The ancient and feudal class structures in village communes lost laborers who went to work instead for rural capitalists or emigrated to the cities to provide surplus labor to capitalists or find subsumed and nonclass positions there. Yet capitalists in the cities lost laborers to the village communes when wages and working conditions drove their employees to return to ancient class structures there. The success of capitalist class structures in manufacturing (both domestic and foreign) flooded relatively low-priced consumer goods into the countryside. They provoked problems for the ancient and remaining feudal class structures there whose outputs could not successfully compete with the capitalist commodities. Debts incurred by Russians occupying all class positions, undertaken in part to afford those commodities, added new burdens.

The feudal class structures inside Russian households experienced increasing pressures and internal strains as their members attempted to negotiate the class structures and struggles outside. Drawn increasingly to part-time or full-time positions in nonfeudal class structures outside, household members encountered new ways of working, new associations with others, and new ways of thinking. These problematized their acceptance of the inherited feudal structure of household life. To the influence of western European ideas and customs in challenging the traditions of the Russian family and household from the outside, we would add the disruptive force of an increasingly unsustainable feudal class structure within it. As feudal class conflicts inside Russian households reacted back upon the class structures outside, survival required men and women to negotiate increasingly diverse and crisis-ridden multiple class positions. It is hardly surprising that extremes of optimism and pessimism, revolutionary energies and deep resignation, hopes and fears for the future arose and raged across the minds of most Russians.

The demise of Russia's once-prevalent centralized feudal class structure ushered in a very conflictual mix of decentralized ancient and feudal class structures and a rapidly growing and centralizing capitalist class structure. This mix confronted Russian society with class contradictions and struggles that were deeply destabilizing. Feudalism inside the household confronted the end of feudalism almost everywhere else. Adults had to find positions within or relating to profoundly new and/or transitional class structures. Their children had to cope with the economic, psychological, and other effects of the new fundamental, subsumed, and nonclass positions found by the adult members of their households. How children, women, and men negotiated the complex, multiple, and contradictory class structures had much to do with how they understood and transformed society before and after the revolution.

To this point, we have sought to offer a particular, Marxian class analytical alternative to other analysts' approaches to the half-century before the Soviet revolution. We turn next to sketch some of the social consequences of the complex relation among class structures that we have identified. Our goal is to suggest how Russia's class structures helped to influence those changes that were and were not achieved across the Soviet experience.

No broad social experience of communist class structures existed to guide or orient Russians dissatisfied with the existing set of class structures: feudal, ancient, and capitalist. The virtually complete absence of a consciousness of class structures—in terms of surplus labor production and distribution—precluded any developed social awareness of the existence, let alone the social effects, of class in Russian society. Russians therefore identified those social problems they could recognize in nonclass terms. They likewise developed solutions in nonclass terms. Even those who used the word "class" in their social analyses or programs for social change did not mean "class" as a designation of systems of surplus labor production and distribution. Instead, for them, class referred chiefly to groupings defined by property (rich versus poor) or power (powerful versus powerless) or to combinations of both criteria. Not surprisingly, a basic transformation of the Russian class structures (in surplus labor terms) did not figure explicitly within the analyses, programs, or results of the 1917 revolution.

Among the most aggravated contradictions in the decades before the revolution were those within and between the private capitalist and village ancient class structures. The emancipation had displaced, or at least demoted, the social prominence of the contradictions within the feudal class structure and between it and ancient peasant class structures. Their place was taken instead by the contradictions within and between capitalist and ancient class structures. Domestic and foreign private capitalist class structures grew very rapidly in industry and in urban areas bringing capital and labor contradictions, tensions, and struggles into social prominence. At the same time, village ancient class structures confronted problems stemming from competition with both those capitalists outside and with the development of rural, agricultural capitalists inside the villages. Differentiation among ancients undermined village unity and society, dropped many into extreme and intolerable states of poverty while others accumulated wealth, and drove a growing number of former ancients into rural capitalist class structures instead. Rage, despair, emigration, envy, conflict, and violence grew.

Leading analysts of otherwise divergent persuasions all recognized certain major dimensions of these conditions (although not in surplus terms). Witte stressed the importance of private capitalism in leading manufacturing industries. Stolypin and Lenin, although in different ways and for different reasons, stressed the transformation of ancient into capitalist class structures among the peasantry. Countless commentators devoted prose and fiction to the emerging contradictions—and especially to the suffering they entailed—among both urban and rural masses. Increasingly, major social events became "crises" in the minds of contemporary observers who linked them to an underlying social disintegration, disruptive divisions, and deepening conflicts.

Anarchist movements, the Russo-Japanese War, the 1905 revolution, and defeats in the early years of World War One appeared to increasing numbers of Russians as awful signs of an impending general collapse of Russian society. The previous omnipotence widely accorded to the pinnacles of centralized feudalism—the czarist court, the church, and the great landowners—seemed to fade before the elemental force of change and collapse. Hitherto marginal social formations moved forward into the vacuum thereby opened: associations of industrial capitalists, increasingly centralized banking enterprises, and militant organizations of ancient farmers, on the one hand, and socialist industrial workers on the other. They glimpsed opportunities for social influence out of all proportion to their strengths because the confluence of changes was disorganizing all the existing patterns and networks of conservative social cohesion.

Rural and urban capitalist class structures could not absorb the emigrants from village ancient class structures. Nor did they well manage the tensions between accumulating capitalists and impoverished proletarians. The villages' ancient class structures faced the relentless erosion of their conditions of existence and mounting internal conflicts. Feudal alternatives outside households were fading and thus offered no resolution for the contradictions within and between capitalist and ancient class structures. Finally, the intensifying stresses among capitalist, ancient, and feudal class structures outside households reverberated inside them to place unbearable strains upon the traditional feudal class structures there. This cauldron of specific class contradictions and conflicts added its particular determinations to the explosions before 1917 as well as to the revolution itself.

The czarist state apparatus found itself the focus of social contradictions that it understood poorly and could not control. The contradictions within and among class structures often surfaced as intense struggles over state policies. The different appropriating classes (capitalist, ancient, and feudal) sought conflicting policies in return for the subsumed class distributions they made to the state. Each wanted the state to stabilize, advance, or protect its beleaguered class positions regardless of how that might endanger other appropriating classes.

Landlords used their special, traditional access to the czar to protect themselves in conflicts with both their ancient tenant farmers and their agricultural proletarians. Private industrial capitalists persuaded and bribed state functionaries for privileges, subsidies, purchases, and protection from foreign competition and from the demands of their workers. Large banks subsumed to these industrial capitalists wanted state guarantees of the credit they extended. The richer ancients and new village capitalists sought to use existing village government—and appeals to the central state apparatus as well—to secure their new, somewhat precarious, and deeply resented wealth and class positions from the poorer ancients and the landless agricultural proletarians. The middle and poorer village ancients used their numerical strength and aggregate wealth to press the state to support the continuation of their class structure as the "proper basis for Russian social stability."

Not only the appropriating and subsumed classes, but also the surplus-producing classes demanded state support. Urban and rural proletarians appealed to all levels of the state (also to the church and to intellectuals) to limit their exploitation and their impoverishment. Periodic uprisings, more than consideration of the taxes workers paid out of their wages, pressed the state to support and protect workers. Many Russians occupying subsumed and nonclass positions threatened by social change and conflict also looked to the state for help.

To manage these often conflicting demands, the czarist state needed to intrude upon and control daily life far more systematically than ever before. It therefore needed much more revenue. Trying to meet these needs, the state encountered massive, widespread resistance, increasingly articulated in terms of movements for liberation from czarist oppression (Galai 1973). Each of the contending classes struggled to provide the least state revenue while securing the most state aid and support. Depending on the rapidly shifting international and national conditions confronting the state, its likewise shifting policies ameliorated some class conflicts while aggravating others.

World War One arrived and exploded the already boiling internal situation. The political and cultural unity needed for a protracted war and the financial resources to pay for it were not available to the state apparatus. Indeed, the effort to secure the resources only more totally undermined the state and the fragile social peace among contending classes. A transitional social conjuncture had been reached, in class as well as nonclass terms.

The 1917 crisis and its aftermath amounted to a revolutionary response to and partial resolution of the cumulative aggregation of Russia's unresolved contradictions. The vast majority of Russians did not conceptualize those contradictions in class terms. Thus they did not consciously direct their activities toward reconfiguring the existing structures of production and distribution of surplus labor. They aimed rather at altering other, nonclass (economic, political, and cultural) dimensions of their society. In so doing, however, they unavoidably also transformed the class structures.[21] Some structures were eliminated, some new ones were inaugurated, and all the rest were changed.

The class changes occurred, so to speak, largely outside the consciousness of the revolution's protagonists and antagonists. In particular, the revolution's supporters and leaders were constrained all the more by that which they could not conceptualize.[22] The existing configuration of contradictory class structures proved resilient and deeply rooted. Not only did the ancient farms survive, but so did the feudal households with their feudal extensions onto farms. The capitalist class structures survived as well, both in private enterprises so long as they could function and in the Soviet state enterprises that replaced them.

It was inside the Soviet state enterprises that the absence of a consciousness of class in terms of the production, appropriation, and distribution of surplus made itself felt most clearly. The state enterprises reproduced the same basic structure of surplus production, appropriation, and distribution as had existed in the private capitalist enterprises before. Productive laborers delivered their product to a separate group of individuals, now state officials rather than private boards of directors. Those state officials returned to them the fruits of their necessary labor while keeping the surplus for distribution aimed at reproducing this state capitalist class structure.

The changes actually achieved by the 1917 revolution were important. The goals and methods of surplus appropriating state officials differed from those of the previous, private appropriators of capitalist surpluses; hence, they distributed those surpluses differently. For example, more went directly to the Soviet state for all sorts of public welfare purposes; none went to the expropriated former private owners and bankers. In addition, workers took or were given rights and influences within the enterprises that Russia's private capitalism had always rigidly refused. But these changes—however historically momentous—did not constitute a class revolution. Instead, a state capitalism with strong welfare and workers' rights commitments replaced a private capitalism with the opposite commitments. In class terms, this was reform, not revolution.

The absence of class consciousness—along with the euphoria over what had been achieved—enabled this change from one form of capitalism to another to be understood and celebrated instead as a revolutionary transition from capitalism to socialism. The "transition to communism" that remained in the policy debates after 1917 concerned how to complete the state ownership and control of production amid shifting circumstances, how to realize "from each according to his ability and to each according to his need." Issues of how communism entailed altogether different structures of surplus labor production and distribution could not become significant for debates or policy determinations in part because consciousness of class in such terms was and long had been almost totally absent (Diskin 1990).

The Soviet revolutionaries defined "socialism as a way station to communism" not in terms of surplus labor but rather in terms chiefly of the distribution of power. They had reorganized the distribution of power over objects—property—and the distribution of power over people—political authority. Private gave way to state property. Private markets gave way to state planning. The political authority of czar, gentry, church, and the new, largely capitalist rich, gave way to the alliance of middle and poor peasants and workers organized and expressed by "their vanguard agent," the Communist Party, and "their" workers' state. And they called these political changes a "class" revolution in which capitalism had been vanquished and eliminated.

The Bolsheviks neither destroyed ancient, feudal, and capitalist class structures nor could they recognize their failure to do so. Instead, they imagined and proclaimed themselves victorious in erecting socialism and moving, however unevenly and slowly, toward communism. They convinced themselves, several generations of their people, and millions of others around the world, friends and enemies, to think likewise. As we seek to show, what this meant was seventy-five years of "socialism" built upon the foundation of what remained ancient, feudal, and capitalist class structures, but largely invisible as such.

### Notes

1. *Other* kinds of class analysis have been published. Among them, we have benefited from Lyashchenko (1949), Lenin (1956, especially 190–195), and Shanin (1986). However, they focused on patterns of property ownership, income distribution, and the distribution of political power, whereas we focus on surplus.
2. The expansion of the empire drew ever more people into serfdom within Russian state feudalism while the state, for its own reasons, often distributed its land and serfs to private individuals (Lyaschenko 1949, 274–281). The size of state relative to private feudalism oscillated in the century before 1861.
3. Our focus on post-1917 class structures precludes treating the complex class history of the emancipation. However, much evidence suggests that after 1861, former serfs, newly become self-employed peasants (Marx's "ancient" class structure), faced even larger demands on the surpluses they generated. We return to this point below in discussing the ancient class structures before 1917.
4. Recent research on the particular social situation of the sizable population of widows among the serfs has underscored these variations as against the older stereotypes of all-powerful landlords, elders, and men (Bohac 1991).
5. For a systematic exposition of feudal class structures inside households (albeit not Russian households), see Fraad, Resnick, and Wolff (1994).
6. The Russian language recognized this difference as that between the peasant farm (*khoziaistvo*) and the "domestic family unit" (*dvor*); see Figes (1989, 10–12).
7. This example underscores the need analytically to keep separate the feudal class process from the particular site where it occurs. The traditional lord may make "his" serfs from "his" feudal manor

available in various ways for someone else to exploit in a feudal class process off the manor (usually in return for a share of the resulting surplus or perhaps a lump sum payment). The other person might be anyone else in feudal society, even another serf.

8. The examples of serfs as surplus appropriators are relatively few. Blum makes quite clear that for the vast mass of Russian serfs, private and state, their condition was more akin to outright slavery than to that of serfs in most other kinds of European feudalisms: markets in serfs existed in Russia (1961, 424–428, 468–469). Such markets raise the question of whether then a boundary between feudalism and slavery had been crossed. Our research did not answer this question. In any case, the examples of serfs exploiting other serfs illustrate a certain plasticity in how populations occupy the class structures within their societies.

9. A. V. Chayanov systematically analyzed what he termed "family farming" as (1) an economic structure distinct from capitalism or feudalism and (2) a structure of central importance to Russian and Soviet history: see the introductory essays by T. Shanin, D. Thorner, and B. Kerblay in Chayanov (1986) and also Shanin (1986). Our approach is based partly on Chayanov, but even more on the explicitly Marxian tradition of analyzing ancient class structures (Gabriel 1989).

10. Craft production did not, of course, necessarily entail the ancient class process. In Russia, many feudal lords had directed some of their serfs to switch from agricultural to craft production. Craft production was then accomplished within a feudal class structure. By contrast, ancient craft production arose more where and when agricultural serfs could undertake it as work separate from their feudal class positions, perhaps in the winter season, etc.

11. Sometimes, the now "ancient" Russian peasants leased land from landowners in addition to or instead of farming land allocated to them by the village communes. They had then to pay "rent" to the landlords, but ancient rent was very different from pre-1861 feudal rent. Here we follow Marx's *Capital* in distinguishing feudal from ancient rent (1991, 917–938). In the former, the serfs delivered all their surplus immediately and directly to the feudal lord. In the case of "ancient rent," the peasants appropriated their own surplus individually and then distributed portions of it to the owner of the farmland to secure access to it. The different class structures—hidden by the uniform term, "rent"—contributed to very different relationships in the countryside before and after 1861.

12. Since most such peasant households involved more than one adult producing and appropriating his/her surplus labor, it might follow logically to think of post-emancipation Russian peasant households as "partnerships of ancient producers" (Gabriel 1989). An alternative approach would presume that the feudal class structure of household labor (cooking, cleaning, kitchen gardening, etc.) might well have carried over to be the class structure as well of the post-emancipation Russian peasant family's working of the lands assigned by the village to them (father as feudal appropriator of other household members' surplus labor). We suppose that both kinds of class structures existed on the allocated fields of Russian villages after 1861. The literature seems to suggest, however, that the predominant form was the ancient class structure of farming even where and when the household class structure was feudal; hence we will focus on that situation in the text.

13. Independence from village communes entailed complex results for such peasant families. On the one hand, they freed themselves from the commune's controls and reduced its claims on their ancient surpluses. On the other hand, they were "on their own." If they prospered they might lease more land and perhaps even hire others (transition to a capitalist class structure). If they faltered, they could lose their land, work for capitalist peasants, and/or face extreme poverty.

14. While most ancient farmers in Russian villages after 1861 were male, widows, temporarily or permanently abandoned wives, and sometimes other women also functioned as ancient farmers and participated with their male counterparts in village commune affairs.

15. By personally bound we mean either legally, culturally, traditionally or, more typically, combinations of these: as medieval European serfs were bound to the land and their lords or as housewives are bound in marriage to husbands within feudal households.

16. When markets exist for labor power, this return of the fruits of necessary labor comprises the wage contract. In the absence of such markets, other mechanisms return the fruits of necessary labor to the laborers. In Soviet state capitalism, the state allocated portions of total output for that purpose.
17. Marx carefully explains how this merchant's fee is a direct distribution by appropriators from their surpluses (1991, 379–416). He shows how the visible form of that fee is the discount from commodity values given by appropriators to merchants who buy their commodities. The merchants then sell the commodities at their values, realizing the discounts as the differences between their costs and revenues from trading.
18. We exclude here any government employees producing surpluses in state enterprises; they would then occupy fundamental class positions.
19. To make explicit the concept of class struggle used throughout, the term refers to the *object* of the struggle, not to the individual or groups of individuals struggling. It is class struggle when the objects are the production, appropriation, and distribution of surplus labor; nonclass struggles are conflicts over other aspects of society.
20. The phrase is Marx's and, as shown in Marshall Berman's book (1983) of the same name, it summarizes the experience of capitalist modernity undermining precapitalist class structures.
21. Class consciousness is, of course, neither a necessary nor a sufficient condition for class changes to occur. The absence of a developed discourse about class in terms of surplus production, appropriation, and distribution made it unlikely that the solutions sought to Russia's social problems would include deliberate transformations of its class structures.
22. For example, the Bolsheviks failed to conceptualize *any* class structure within households. Some held that modern capitalism in Russia and elsewhere had transformed the family and household from units of production into units of mere consumption (and hence outside the realm of class analysis). Others focused on the sharing out of men's wages to other family members understood as their "exploitation" of the men. Still others eschewed analysis of the family/household in class or any other terms since capitalism had undermined it and socialism would complete that process (Goldman 1993, 25–48).

CHAPTER 6

# Revolution, War Communism, and the Aftermath

The USSR's first decade exhibits a contradictory but successful state capitalist development. In contrast, the Bolsheviks believed that they were establishing and developing a socialist society en route to communism. Actually, as we propose to show, having become the new Soviet state, the Bolsheviks installed a subset of themselves as the appropriators and distributors of the surplus produced by workers in Soviet industry. They did not do the same in agriculture. There Soviet policies enabled a vast and growing mass of private ancient producers to prevail, although they were soon joined by limited numbers of small private capitalist farmers. Finally, Bolshevik plans to socialize housework (and thereby eliminate production inside individual households) were never realized. Hence the Soviet state did little to disturb the dominance of the feudal and ancient household class structures (we discuss the limited experiments with communist class structures inside a few household "communes" in chapter 7).

Our analysis of early Soviet history examines the USSR's different class structures—state capitalist in industry, private ancient and small capitalist in agriculture, and feudal and ancient inside households. It will specify their internal contradictions and how they simultaneously secured and undermined one another's conditions of existence. Soviet society exhibited a rapidly developing state capitalism, yet one fraught with particular class contradictions, tensions, and conflicts. These interacted with the nonclass processes around them to build toward a social crisis and rupture as the decade of the 1920s closed.

As argued earlier, the appropriators of surplus in Soviet industry were, from the beginning, state officials and not the collective of surplus-producing workers. While produced in many industrial enterprises, the surplus was appropriated centrally by a few top state officials. First called Vesenkha, these Soviet state capitalists were soon renamed the Council of Ministers. The council distributed the industrial surplus to secure the specific politics, economy, and culture that would, they hoped, reproduce this state capitalist class structure. However, neither the production, nor the appropriation, nor the distribution of this state capitalist surplus proceeded smoothly. Difficulties, setbacks, and crises continually haunted them.

Nothing better illustrates the complexities and evolution of Soviet state capitalist industry than its ever-changing relationship with the multiple class structures in agriculture. The chaotic movement of the industry/agriculture terms of trade—the ratio of the prices at which the two kinds of output exchanged—partly reflected the uneven development of the different class structures, even as it contributed to that unevenness. On balance, the chaotic terms of trade hastened state capitalist expansion at the expense of the USSR's other class structures. Within a few decades after 1917, state capitalism was hegemonic among the society's multiple class structures. Yet alongside that hegemony—and impressive economic development generally—major social discontent and turmoil arose.

One aspect of that discontent runs as a theme through the analysis to follow: the exploitation of workers prevailed across the entire history of the USSR. When one kind of exploitative class structure was overthrown, another soon took its place (with the few exceptions noted below). The 1917 revolution displaced private capitalism in industry but established an enduring state capitalism there instead. In agriculture, the 1917 revolution virtually eliminated private capitalism and established instead a vast number of relatively small ancient farmers. However, almost immediately thereafter, the NEP reforms enabled exploitative capitalist farms to reemerge. With the important exception of the communist class structures generated by collectivization in the late 1920s, exploitation was always a significant reality of Soviet agriculture too. Finally, Soviet households, long bastions of mostly feudal but also significant ancient class structures, retained these arrangements despite some very few, very limited attempts at communist class structures there in the 1920s. Soviet workers in the factories, on the farms, and at home did not free themselves from class exploitation at all these social sites. The USSR never achieved nor even approached the social hegemony of what chapter 1 above defined as communist class structures.[1]

Between 1917 and 1940, the Soviet state and the Party established and expanded state capitalism as the only class structure of industrial enterprises. After 1917, industrial growth—usually measured in quantities of industrial outputs—quickly rose to the rank of top economic priority. Funds for this growth would not suffice if drawn only from the surpluses produced inside state capitalist industries. The latter had to be supplemented by net inflows of value from the ancient and capitalist class structures in agriculture. This chapter begins this history of the interaction among industrial expansion, multiple class structures in industry and agriculture, and the transfers of value from agriculture for industrial expansion.

## Changing the State and Class Structures

Our class analysis of events after 1917 begins with a consideration of the new Soviet state. We begin there because the state has been central to so many other understandings of the USSR. However, since we neither presume nor have found the Soviet state to have been the essential determinant of Soviet history, our discussion of the state will shift quickly from the state to classes as the dimension of that history needing attention.[2]

In our approach, state activities were but one among many factors overdetermining the Soviet system. Nor do we conceive the state to be merely the instrument of one particular class, party, or group. We think that the state always exists in contradiction, shaped by conflicting and continually changing class and nonclass influences that complexly constitute what it is and does (Resnick and Wolff 1987, ch. 5). No individual (such as Lenin, Stalin, Khrushchev, Brezhnev, or Gorbachev), no grouping of individuals (such as state bureaucrats, ministry or party officials, or factory and farm workers), nor any particular social structure (such as markets, planning, single party politics, or multiparty politics) was the essential determinant of the Soviet state. Instead, all of them—and much else—combined to overdetermine the structure and functioning of the state across the history of the USSR. The state, much like any other site in society (whether an individual, a group, an institution, and so on), was caught in a web of contradictory influences from the other sites even as it also exerted such influences upon them.

The flows of value linking the new Soviet state with other sites in Soviet society provide a useful entry point for the class analysis of post-1917 society. We first compare the czarist state's revenues and expenditures—its budget—with those of the new Soviet state after 1917. The means for this comparison will be a budget equation in class terms. We define each flow of value in terms of whether it is an appropriation or a distribution of surplus (fundamental or subsumed class flow) or whether it is neither (a nonclass flow).[3] After we briefly explain each of the terms in this equation, we will use it to trace and analyze some major class changes accomplished first by the 1917 revolution and then by war communism.

The left side of the equation below summarizes the total revenues collected by the czarist state from differing social sites. The right side indicates the state expenditures made to secure these revenues. Taken together, the two sides of this equation present the flows of revenues into and expenditures out of the czarist state in class terms, in short its budget:

$$SV(C) + SSCR(C+A+F) + NCR = SSCP(C) + X(C+A+F) + Y$$

The first revenue flow, $SV(C)$, existed because the state itself was one site of a capitalist class structure. Personifying the state before 1917, the czar occupied the capitalist fundamental class position of appropriating surplus value from productive laborers employed in state capitalist enterprises (for example, those producing vodka).

To help reproduce this state revenue, capitalist subsumed class payments [SSCP(C)] were made out of the appropriated surplus value to secure an array of nonclass processes necessary for this form of state capitalism to exist. Such subsumed class payments—distributions of appropriated surplus—included, for example, the salaries and budgets for the czarist state bureaucrats who functioned as managers of such state capitalist enterprises.[4] Other subsumed class payments (components of SSCP(C) as well) included contributions to the church (to secure its legitimation of the czar's position); wages to security personnel (to protect the czar); fees to merchants (to buy state capitalist commodity outputs quickly and thereby convert their value back into money); wages and salaries to still other state bureaucratic officials (to produce and disseminate the laws and culture that compelled or persuaded laborers to perform surplus labor for the czar); and funds for the czar's luxury consumption (to display him regally and awesomely as the venerated father/protector/sovereign deserving respect, love, and the workers' surplus as well).[5]

The czarist state's second revenue flow—the SSCR(C+A+F) on the left side of the equation—refers to income it obtained in return for providing conditions of existence for surplus production elsewhere in society (at sites other than the czarist state itself). For example, the czar received tax revenues from and fees levied upon private capitalist enterprises, the SSCR(C). The taxes and fees were portions of those enterprises' surpluses that they distributed to the czar. In return, the czarist state provided crucial conditions enabling such private capitalism. The czarist military and police apparatuses secured private capitalists from enemies both domestic and foreign. The czarist state designed and enforced tariff laws to protect private Russian capitalists from foreign competition, labor laws to prevent unionization, various regulations facilitating capital accumulation and investment, and so on. The czar promoted ideologies upholding the sanctity of private property, private enterprise, and market contracts. The state also made massive purchases of the commodities produced by private capitalists.

All these state activities required expenditures of state funds: the X(C) term on the right side of the equation. The X(C) expenditures enabled the revenues SSCR(C) and vice versa. Another example further illustrates such links between the left and right sides of the equation. The czarist state extended massive credits to private capitalist enterprises in pre-1917 Russia and received relatively low interest payments from them. The credits comprised another part of the X(C) term on the right side of the equation, while the interest receipts are included in the SSCR(C) term on the left side.

The czarist state also provided conditions of existence for noncapitalist class processes that existed at various sites in Russian society. It likewise received in return subsumed class payments from their individual surplus appropriators as taxes and fees—SSCR(A)—to the czarist state. For its part, the state undertook (expended revenues for) legislation enabling such self-employment, road construction to enable the marketing of ancient produce, provision of water, police security, and so on. Such state expenditures to fund these conditions of existence of ancient enterprises appear as X(A) on the right side of the equation.[6]

The czarist state obtained still other subsumed class distributions—SSCR(F)—from feudal class structures such as those inside many Russian households (Fraad, Resnick, and Wolff 1994). Taxes and fees levied on households could be paid from the surpluses extracted by Russian husbands from their wives' household labors.[7] In return, the czarist state endorsed and enforced marriage laws and traditions crucial for the reproduction of the feudal class structures of Russian households. The costs of such state activities comprise the X(F) term on the right side of the equation.

The last revenue item on the left side of the equation—NCR—represents nonclass revenues. This residual category includes all state revenues derived neither from the state's appropriation of its own capitalist surplus nor from subsumed class distributions made to the state by private capitalist, ancient, or feudal appropriators. Taxes on wage earners, for example, who cannot pay such taxes out of any surplus since they appropriate none, comprise one kind of NCR. State expenditures to secure such nonclass revenues are included in the Y term on the right side of the equation. Examples include state provision of educational, housing, medical, or recreational facilities for wage earners. We may now deploy this state equation to analyze the class history of the revolution and its aftermath.

In the decades before 1917, the czarist state favored chiefly private capitalist and secondarily ancient fundamental class processes in enterprises outside the state and also favored feudal class structures inside Russian households. On the one hand, this meant that state expenditures favored the X(C+A+F) term in the equation: providing conditions of existence to those class structures. It also meant that the state limited the taxes and fees it targeted at private capitalists, ancients, and heads of households. An imbalance in the state's budget arose out of this particular class bias. To offset it, the state operated a reverse imbalance in its nonclass relation to individuals: it taxed them more than it expended on services for them.

This effective class bias generated all sorts of problems for the state's budgets. The poverty of the mass of individuals in czarist Russia limited such nonclass state revenues and provoked efforts to resist taxation. At the same time, the low levels of state expenditures on public services for individuals led to demands for more. The czarist state's class bias and popular resistance thereto sometimes yielded total state revenues that fell short of total intended expenditures. If the state responded by raising taxes and fees on privately appropriated surpluses, it risked provoking resistance from those surplus appropriators, usually the most organized and hence powerful groups in czarist Russia. To raise more nonclass revenues from the desperately poor mass of individuals risked their uprisings and, more dangerous still, their potential organization. To cut state expenditures on any groups would raise parallel risks. Then too, bringing expenditures down to revenues might depress those revenues still further and prompt a disastrous spiral downward.

Such dilemmas led the czarist state in its last decades to rely increasingly on another kind of nonclass revenue (NCR), namely, state loans. These provided new revenue flows enabling the state to bridge the otherwise intractable gaps between its other expenditures and revenues (Lyashchenko 1949, 554–557).[8] State loans, of course, required state expenditures for interest payments on the equation's right side (included in the "Y" term). For a while, the greater size of the loans' principal as against the annual interest charges "solved" the budget problems of the state's relation to the society's multiple class structures. Eventually, the czarist state's rising interest expenditures and limited further borrowing capacities added a new burden on the state budget in addition to the other demands placed on the state by the different class structures in Russian society.

These diverse revenue and expenditure flows reveal a czarist state facing multiple and often contradictory claims. As the flows changed, the identity of the state shifted as the different class and nonclass processes in Russian society overdetermined which persons, coalitions, and interests prevailed in complex struggles to shape that identity. Among the class contradictions engaged by the czarist state, one concerned the conflict between using state policy—including revenue and expenditure decisions—to promote state versus private capitalist enterprises. Another reflected the use of state policies to promote private capitalist versus private ancient class structures, especially in agriculture. Still another contradiction surfaced in struggles over the allocation of expenditures and revenue demands between capitalist and ancient class structures, on the one hand, and feudal households on the other. Since the growth or even the very survival of individuals, groups, and class structures were often at stake, the struggles to shape the state's activities and its very identity were intense.

Of course, state policy struggles over class issues were not understood in class terms. Russia's "economic development," "military security," or "national prestige" functioned as the explicit goals of state policy. The socially dominant discourses raised the czarist state above all social divisions; it represented Russia as a whole. Thus the devotees of alternative class structures understood and fought their battles over the state's identities and policies through discourses that were systematically class blind. Instead of class, the contested issues included the sanctity of marriage, the integrity of the Russian nation, and the salvation of Russian souls alongside military security, economic development, and national prestige.

The combatants, with very few exceptions, missed the class dimensions of their conflicts because they lacked the surplus concepts at work in this book. Nor do we dispute that many nonclass issues were genuine objects of struggle then—matters of religion, politics, and culture generally. We seek to add and make explicit the heretofore overlooked dimension of class (in the surplus sense) as part of the struggles over the state. Elaborating these class dimensions yields conclusions that are often both new and politically provocative.

One such conclusion extends the view that the czarist state was less controlling than controlled by Russian society as a whole. The czarist state was deeply and problematically entwined in Russia's multiple, interacting class structures—both as an appropriator of surplus itself and also as subsumed to different class structures outside the state. Its contradictions emanated from the shifting class (as well as nonclass) processes of Russian society. Its policies changed and thereby often further agitated those contradictions. The czarist state was more caught up in an evolving social formation of contesting class structures than it was in control of them. We will make a similar argument below about the post-1917 Soviet state and the altered set of interacting class structures that it engaged.

The 1917 revolution inaugurated a different set of connections between the new Soviet state and the different class and nonclass structures of the new USSR. All the revenue and expenditure flows of the state changed as well. For example, the Bolshevik drive to abolish *private* capitalism meant that the state would make few or no expenditures—X(C) on the right side of the equation—to provide conditions of existence for private capitalists. Eliminating or sharply decreasing private capitalist industrial enterprises and farms also meant foregoing state revenues from them. That is, the SSCR(C) term on the left side of the equation shrank drastically.

To take another example, we consider a slightly expanded, post-1917 version of our state equation as follows:

$$SV(C+Co) + SSCR(Co+A+F) + NCR = SSCP(C+Co) + X(Co+A+F) + Y$$

As noted, two of the former *capitalist* terms largely disappeared as a result of Bolshevik policies, namely SSCR(C) and X(C). Given Bolshevik goals, four new *communist* value categories *might* have replaced them: two revenues—SV(Co) and SSCR(Co)—and two associated expenditures—SSCP(Co) and X(Co). These terms represent the *possible* establishment of communist class structured enterprises both within the state itself—entailing SV(Co) and SSCP(Co)—and outside the state, in the "private" sector—entailing SSCR(Co) and X(Co). We may label the former "state communism" and the latter "private communism," a locational differentiation parallel to that separating state and private capitalist enterprises. We may then ask whether, when, and how these four possible communist class terms became part of the new Soviet state equation.

The new Soviet state took over the ownership and management of what had been private capitalist industrial enterprises. It changed their functioning in many ways. *But it did not transform the way those enterprises organized the production, appropriation, and distribution of their surplus labor.* The Soviet state—in the name of the working class—delegated state officials to replace both private individual capitalists and private corporate boards of directors. The personnel changed (no doubt a significant event), but the exploitative juxtaposition of producers vis-à-vis appropriators of surplus labor did not.

We found very little evidence to support the existence of communist class structures within state enterprises: structures in which the productive laborers collectively appropriated and likewise distributed all the surplus they produced. Thus, no SV(Co) term entered the Soviet state equation, because no communist class-structured enterprises were developed or operated within the state. Correspondingly, no distributions of state communist enterprises' surpluses could occur to secure their existence—no SSCP(Co). State communism might have but did not in fact occur in the USSR as a consequence of the 1917 revolution.

We did find the evidence, discussed in chapters 7 and 9, of the limited but nonetheless significant establishment after 1917 of certain forms of communist class structures outside the state. These occurred at two different social sites: inside the "communal" household class structures encouraged by state policies until 1928 (chapter 7) and inside many of the collective farms established in the late 1920s and early 1930s (chapter 9). The existence of some communistically class-structured households and collective farms means that private communism did appear in the USSR as a result of its revolution. The new history sketched in this and subsequent chapters includes an examination of these new sites of private communist class structure and their relationships with the state by focusing on the corresponding terms of the Soviet state equation—SSCR(Co) and X(Co).

Finally, certain other terms of the Russian state equation survived the 1917 revolution with little change. The Soviet state, like its czarist predecessor, appropriated surplus directly from productive laborers within state enterprises, but now there were many more of them. Since these were state capitalist enterprises, the SV(C) term remained in the equation after 1917 as did the distribution of state capitalist surpluses—SSCP(C). The Soviet state also continued to obtain distributions of surplus from private ancient enterprises (especially the individual peasant farms whose numbers the revolution had vastly increased) and from the feudal surpluses appropriated inside Soviet households. These revenues were represented, before and after 1917, by the same term—SSCR(A+F). And they necessitated corresponding state expenditures as before—X(A+F). Beside these fundamental and subsumed class inflows, the Soviet state obtained additional revenues via the prices mandated by state planners for the commodity exchanges among enterprises and individuals. These additional revenues appeared as part of NCR and SSCR and they too, as we shall see, required corresponding state expenditures.

Neither the 1917 revolution nor Soviet state policies eliminated state capitalist, private ancient, and private feudal class structures from the USSR. While the czar was eliminated as the appropriating capitalist within state enterprises, the capitalist class structures within them were not. The latter remained and indeed grew dramatically after 1917. What replaced the czar as appropriating state capitalist was a collective of state officials eventually called the Soviet Council of Ministers. The council appropriated and distributed the surpluses produced by Soviet productive workers in state enterprises. The form of producing, appropriating, and distributing those surpluses remained decidedly capitalist. The new Soviet state capitalism interacted with continuing and pervasive private ancient, feudal, capitalist, and over the 1930s even communist class structures at different social sites. This new configuration of class structures entailed a new set of class contradictions overdetermining the state's policies and its identity as a Soviet institution. As we shall show, those class contradictions during war communism and then the NEP years contributed very significantly to shaping Soviet history.

### Organizing the New Class Structures

"War communism" became the name applied to the first phase of the Soviet economy. It fits the new Soviet state's drastic steps immediately after 1917 to defeat a foreign military invasion and to win a civil war. The state moved on many fronts: to nationalize the means of production used in industrial enterprises; to abolish or sharply curtail private markets, merchants, and the use of money; and to allocate directly industrial workers' labor power, other resources, and outputs. The Soviet state also began to centralize industrial production in newly established state enterprises, to foster an agricultural surplus and acquire it to finance rapid industrial development, and to establish a state bureaucracy to manage and coordinate this drastic economic reorganization. We propose here to analyze this short period's class dimensions.

War communism had little if anything to do with communism as a class structure.[9] Rather, war communism showed that capitalism, like other class structures, can operate and prosper in the context of a very diverse set of nonclass processes. In other words, capitalism exhibits different forms depending on its variable social contexts. War communism, we believe, was actually an unusual kind of capitalism. Private property in means of production, free markets, and money itself had virtually disappeared, while nearly total state control (often coercive) of economic activities prevailed. Yet, notwithstanding such emergency social conditions, the class structure within which most industrial production occurred remained capitalist. The workers produced surpluses appropriated by others, state officials, who likewise distributed those surpluses; the workers neither collectively appropriated nor distributed the surpluses they produced.[10] War communism thus designates a time when the Soviet state, fighting to survive, quickly accomplished an emergency kind of state capitalism. To focus upon markets, ownership, and money during the war communism period—rather than the social organization of surplus labor—misses the survival and development of capitalist class structures.

The new regime's experiments with actual communist class structures (in the surplus sense) were very limited. As we will discuss further in the next chapter, relatively few households established communes and only some of them involved actual communist class structures of household work. By the late 1920s, as state support for communes vanished, most of the communist households did too. In contrast, the new regime's experiments with what it (and most supporters) meant by communism were not limited and, indeed, bold. A workers' vanguard party had seized state power from the former ruling groups, socialized much productive wealth, displaced or controlled markets via planning, and generally reoriented state policy toward the interests of workers and peasants as the revolutionary alliance understood them. New cultural forms celebrating workers and denouncing nonworkers—in school curricula, movies, newspapers, government pronouncements, and so on—dramatically altered the feelings and self-consciousness of Soviet society from what had existed before.[11]

No doubt these actions helped to win the civil war and enable the new Soviet system to survive. War communism did comprise much of what revolutionaries—and especially Marxists—had long envisioned as communism. Yet, since war communism paid little attention to the organization of surplus in production, it is hardly surprising that pre-1917 forms of surplus organization survived through the period. Especially within industry, by changing *who* appropriated the surplus (the workers' state officials rather than private capitalists), the issue of how the industrial class processes were organized (*what* the class structure should be) escaped any basic transition.

Lest we be misunderstood, we are not arguing that some conspiracy or conscious betrayal blocked the workers from achieving a different, noncapitalist class structure after 1917. The socially prevalent discourses of class revolution at the time focused on property and power distributions. The workers thus largely concurred in celebrating as a transition from capitalism to communism, done in their name, what was actually a transition from private to state capitalism. They did not clearly see, any more than their leaders or their enemies did, that the two transitions—from private to state capitalism and from capitalism to communism—were radically different.

The major changes in Russia's nonclass structure (culture, politics, ownership, economic planning, and so on) did not include the new laws, rules, consciouness, or economics that would have positioned the productive workers in enterprises as collectively the first receivers and distributors of the surpluses that they produced. Despite the official celebration and dissemination of Marxism, those of its arguments focused on class in surplus terms, already faded from pre-1917 Russian Marxism, virtually disappeared thereafter. Instead, Soviet discourse held the presence or absence of markets, the social distribution of power, and, above all, private versus state property to define socialism and its boundary from capitalism. Even Lenin's explicit recognition of the "state capitalist" limits that the revolution had reached did not enable him to lead beyond those limits.[12] Communist fundamental class processes were not established in state enterprises: no $SV(Co)$ term ever appeared in the Soviet state equation. Rather, the state rapidly expanded its state enterprises embodying capitalist class processes alongside its multiple actions concerning military, cultural, political, and economic nonclass processes. Thus, the $SV(C)$ term in the state equation inherited from pre-revolutionary Russia grew dramatically.

To the ensemble of social processes found in the post-1917 USSR, we posed the Marxian questions raised in our theoretical exploration of communism in chapters 1 and 2 above. First, how did the actual Soviet state industrial enterprises organize the production, appropriation, and distribution of the surpluses produced there? Secondly, once we determined that the productive workers did not appropriate and distribute those surpluses collectively, who did? Our examination of laws, planning arrangements, bureaucratic lines of authority, documents, speeches, and various works of other authors led to a specific small number of appointed officials. They occupied positions at the top of a state agency established soon after the revolution, the Supreme Council of National Economy, or Vesenkha. That agency was soon reorganized as the Council of Ministers. Soviet laws, economic arrangements, power configurations, and cultural practices combined to make the top members of this council the first receivers and distributors of the surpluses produced by industrial laborers.[13]

The state bureaucrats leading this council functioned similarly to a centralized board of directors of a private capitalist industrial combine. Initially centered in transport, oil, munitions, and heavy industry generally, the council expanded to include most industrial production. Under Stalin it expanded once more to include the state capitalist farms and, thereby, a significant portion of agricultural production as well. As many observers have noted, the Soviet industrial economy approximated one giant enterprise whose board of directors comprised the leadership of Vesenkha and later the Council of Ministers.[14] Most of the historians of the period that we reviewed admit that the council functioned like a private capitalist board of directors but stress two key differences. First, council members were appointed state officials. Second, they operated in a workers' state-planned/command (rather than a free market) economy marked by collective (rather than private) ownership of the means of production. For most historians, these two differences suffice to determine the board's noncapitalist nature and hence the USSR as socialist.

Here we encounter again the theoretical framework that distinguishes capitalism from socialism and communism by reference to which group wields power over productive enterprises: private corporations interacting in free markets or state enterprises interacting under state plans. Such power-focused analyses undervalue the empirical parallels between state capitalist enterprises and private capitalist enterprises. The Council of Ministers, like any private capitalist board of directors, appropriated (gained first access to) and distributed the surplus labor extracted from productive laborers. From a Marxian perspective, this appropriation of the surplus is precisely the class aspect of the Soviet council's economic functioning.[15]

The particular configuration of all the nonclass processes during war communism overdetermined the specific class processes of that time. In other words, the social context produced the state capitalist class structure of industrial enterprises. The dramatic and diverse social changes over the next several decades of Soviet history altered the forms of state capitalism in industry. For example, as we show below, Soviet state industries oscillated between centralized and decentralized forms of capitalist appropriation across their entire history. However, none of the alterations sufficed to take state enterprises beyond one or another form of a capitalist class structure.

In the new history we propose to sketch here, we will simplify by referring to Vesenkha or the Council of Ministers as the capitalist industrial appropriator throughout (even though each institution went through changes and reorganizations). Under the NEP reforms, Vesenkha's centralized appropriation of industrial surpluses was challenged for a time by a decentralized appropriation located in the boards of various trusts and syndicates. The end of the NEP saw state capitalist appropriation return to a centralized form in which the Council of Ministers became the first appropriator and distributor of both industrial surpluses and agricultural surpluses in the newly established state capitalist farms.

A last prefatory caution: just as the class processes of Soviet society depended on (were overdetermined by) its nonclass processes, so the nonclass processes depended upon (were overdetermined by) the surpluses distributed to sustain them. Our approach can enter the mutual dependence of production and distribution of surplus from either end, so long as the mutual dependence is integrated into the analysis. Our history begins with distributions of the USSR's state capitalist industrial surplus and then proceeds to its prior production and appropriation inside state enterprises. In discussing those who appropriated surplus labor, we shall generally refer to them as the Council of Ministers, the state agency charged with that function across most of Soviet history. However, in our class analysis of the particular histories of war communism and the NEP, we shall refer to Vesenkha (predecessor to the Council of Ministers) when considering centralized appropriation and to "trusts and syndicates" when discussing decentralized appropriation.

The Council of Ministers distributed some portions of the surplus it appropriated to its own regional and industrial subagencies. It also distributed portions to such other state agencies as the state planning apparatus (eventually called Gosplan), the military, the educational system, and so on. It made further distributions to the Communist Party. All such distributions—included in the SSCP(C) term on the expenditure side of our state equation—aimed to finance their recipients' activities: political, cultural, and economic processes needed for the council to continue to appropriate industrial surpluses. Because these recipients produced such nonclass processes and received distributions of the surplus for doing so, they occupied state capitalist subsumed class positions. Only members of the Council of Ministers occupied the fundamental state capitalist class position of surplus appropriators.

To investigate the distribution of state capitalist surpluses more closely, we may consider the portion paid to Soviet legislative and judicial institutions. They designed laws and administered courts in ways that helped to place the Council of Ministers in its state capitalist class position.[16] Thus, Vesenkha and then the Council of Ministers, as the legal personifications of state industrial enterprises, legally possessed and used the state-owned means of production that Gosplan allocated to it. Soviet laws and courts confirmed the council's productive consumption of the labor power allocated to it by Gosplan. In effect, the laws and courts made Vesenkha and then the Council of Ministers the Soviet equivalent of the set of corporate boards of directors legitimized by the different laws and courts in countries where private capitalism prevailed.

The council distributed another portion of its appropriated surplus as salaries and operating budgets to the state's economic planning apparatus, Gosplan. Its directors thus occupied capitalist subsumed class positions and were responsible for performing various economic, cultural, and political processes crucial to sustain the Council of Ministers in its fundamental state capitalist class position. Gosplan allocated means of production and labor power to the council. Gosplan bureaucrats also performed the accounting processes that assigned the state-administered values, surplus values, and prices to all produced outputs and thereby organized their social allocation.

Gosplan's provision of these and other, related processes (such as publishing and disseminating economic plans with their justifications) enabled the Council of Ministers to equip Soviet industrial workers with means of production in more or less appropriate quantities at more or less appropriate times. Using the state calculated values assigned to outputs by these same bureaucrats, the council could calculate the surplus values it was appropriating and distribute them according to its objectives. In sum, Gosplan's activities directly sustained the Council of Ministers—*not* the workers collectively—in the position of appropriator and distributor of surplus values.

Enterprise managers on local and regional levels received distributions of yet another portion of surplus from the council to supervise production and the labor process within each state capitalist enterprise. These managers too occupied capitalist subsumed class positions. From Lenin to Stalin to Gorbachev, priority for rapid industrial growth required intense work discipline to maximize surpluses as a key source for capital accumulation. To this end, the council distributed a portion of the surpluses it received to enterprise managers for accumulation that would, in turn, yield additional surpluses that the council would appropriate and so on.

The council distributed portions of the surplus as well to the Communist Party and the police apparatus. They performed the political and cultural processes designed to pressure and/or persuade workers to perform surplus labor in state capitalist industrial enterprises. Workers should fear the consequences of not working according to plan, believe that their labor contributed to a socialist future, equate labor with patriotism, or feel it to be a patriotic duty—or internalize all these motivations.[17] Theorizations of the USSR as a class society with exploited industrial workers—let alone as a state industrial capitalism—would only have made the persuasion of workers to produce surpluses more difficult.

Military and police forces protected the council's class position from perceived threats, domestic and foreign. The Communist Party and other state ideological apparatuses designed and disseminated the concept of the USSR as socialism. This precluded or undermined notions of the USSR as a state capitalism in favor of viewing it as a workers' state free of exploitation. To assert, expose, or struggle against exploitation (or its social conditions of existence) inside the USSR became equivalent to being an enemy of Soviet socialism. Producing and disseminating specific meanings (interpretations) of Soviet life provided key cultural conditions of existence for the Council of Minister's continued appropriation of surplus values from state capitalist industrial laborers.

State efforts to establish and/or sustain all these political, economic, and cultural processes—the nonclass structure underpinning the Council of Minister's state capitalist class position—yielded contradictory effects. The state's successes always also produced contradictions, tensions, strains, and at times active struggles within Soviet society. Sometimes those struggles rose to the level of challenging the very hegemony of the kind of state capitalism developing in the USSR. As we show in chapter 10, the class contradictions, struggles, and challenges first encountered during war communism prefigured those that contributed to the crisis of the 1980s and to the subsequent oscillation in Russia from state back to private capitalism.

## A Class and Value Analysis of War Communism

To defeat foreign invasions and win the civil war, the Soviet state moved quickly to eliminate, subordinate, and/or transform a disparate grouping of class structures (Carr 1985, 73–100; Sirianni 1982). These class structures were viewed as inimical to maximizing production and hence to the war effort, socialism, or to both. They included (1) some pre-revolutionary and post-revolutionary Soviets (likely communist class structures tentatively and fleetingly established by workers committees in the private industrial enterprises that they had taken over early in the revolution), (2) industrial enterprises returned to private owners after the revolution, (3) enterprises and industries taken over by trade unions, and (4) various kinds of regional and central state committees operating industrial enterprises. The Soviet state eventually succeeded in replacing them all with a uniform, centralized state industrial capitalism with Vesenkha as the surplus appropriator. This success created, however, new kinds of contradictions. Among them, the class contradictions remained largely invisible to the Soviet leadership (and to most Soviet cadres as well) because their theoretical frameworks precluded recognizing their existence and social effects. However, one nonclass contradiction—between state and industry, on the one hand, and the peasantry, on the other—did become centrally important in the debates, practical policies, and successive crises of Soviet history.

The Soviet leadership depended on an underdeveloped industrial state capitalism, and vice versa. Both were interdependent with the noncapitalist class structures that existed outside industry and the state. Most important among the latter were the mass of individual peasant producers. In their ancient kind of class structure, these peasants produced, appropriated, and distributed their own surplus labor individually. They did so privately, not as state officials or employees. Their numbers, already large, had grown dramatically because of Bolshevik land grants to returning soldiers, former feudal tenant farmers, and former agicultural wage earners. These Bolshevik policies thus replaced private capitalist (and remnants of private feudal) with private ancient class-structured farming units.

To develop successfully, state industrial capitalism needed to draw increasing food and raw material products from private ancient farmers. Yet, if the ancient farmers sold such products to state industry and thereby enriched and strengthened their noncapitalist class structures, that might potentially challenge or threaten state capitalism and Soviet political hegemony. It was hardly difficult to envision conflict between state capitalist enterprises and private ancient farmers over, for example, state-set prices, state subsidies, favorable state policies and expenditure patterns, new laws, and so on. The possibility loomed that state capitalists and private ancients might well construct and pursue their political, cultural, and economic interests in contradictory ways. The Bolsheviks partially recognized and increasingly agonized over some of the contradictions among the multiple class structures they were trying to manage. Of course, they did not conceptualize these in the surplus terms used here. Rather, they feared a politically and economically strengthened "nonsocialist" peasant sector, especially as they noticed the small capitalist class structures emerging there across the 1920s. This nonsocialist sector might, they thought, eventually retard, undermine, or even overthrow socialism (i.e., in our terms, industrial state capitalism) or even the Soviet regime itself.

Managing the contradiction between supporting private ancient and small capitalist farmers while constricting the unwanted consequences of their productivity occupied much of the attention, time, and effort of the Bolshevik leadership during and after war communism. The Bolshevik debates and struggles—for example, over whether to use markets or state allocation or requisitioning to secure rural products—have received considerable attention from historians (Carr 1954, 89–92). However, neither the Bolsheviks nor the historians worked with the class analysis we use below. Had they done so, their conclusions would have been different.

Soviet state industrial capitalists had first to acquire labor power if they were, as Marx wrote, then to "consume" it in the fundamental class process of producing the surplus they appropriated. Newly centralized under Vesenkha, state capitalists acquired labor power in part by paying wages to laborers for it. Those wages equalled the specific values assigned to labor power by a state planning bureaucracy using the classic Marxian accounting system. First, it determined the kinds and amounts of commodities that workers should be able to purchase to reproduce their labor power at "an acceptable socialist level." Then it estimated the number of "socially necessary abstract labor hours" needed, given the technology in place, to produce those commodities: this determined their values. Finally, the bureaucracy assigned a value to workers' wages that roughly equalled the values of the bundle of commodities they should be able to buy. In this way, state bureaucrats set state-administered values for all produced inputs, all produced outputs, and for the value of the labor power sold by workers (i.e., their wages).

The difference between, on the one hand, the state-administered values of labor power plus the inputs used up in production and, on the other hand, the state-administered values of state capitalist industrial outputs, represented the state-administered surplus value in Soviet industry. The productive laborers inside state capitalist industries produced it. Vesenkha first appropriated and then distributed it.

The Marxian class equation for capitalist production, $c+v+s=w$ (where c was the value of input commodities used up in the production process, v the value of labor power, w the value of output, and s the residual surplus value), applied perfectly. Marx had devised this value calculation to understand the private capitalism of his time and to inform political efforts to overcome it. The Soviets had used a very similar value calculation to manage their state industrial capitalism. This included negotiating, consciously or otherwise, its internal class contradictions (between and among the producers and appropriators of capitalist surpluses and the receivers of its distributions). It also entailed managing the contradictory relations, including market exchanges, between state capitalist and private noncapitalist class structures coexisting in Soviet society. This latter management involved setting state market *prices*—the prices of actual commodity exchanges—that deviated from the state's own *value* calculations. This price-value difference became, as we shall show, a key part of the class contradictions and class history of the decade after war communism.

Returning to the basic state equation of this chapter, namely $SV(C) + SSCR(C+A+F) + NCR = SSCP(C) + X(C+A+F) + Y$, Vesenkha appropriated state industrial enterprises' capitalist surplus value—$SV(C)$—as a state revenue. Vesenkha also distributed that surplus value in subsumed class payments—$SSCP(C)$—to finance the various nonclass processes that it deemed necessary to sustain that state capitalism. The vast Soviet bureaucracies who provided these nonclass processes (the Communist Party, local enterprise managers, the Red army, and so on) depended for their survival on the surplus that Vesenkha appropriated and distributed to them. Likewise, Soviet state capitalism depended on the bureaucracies' performance of such nonclass processes.

During war communism, a large portion of $SSCP(C)$ paid for prioritized military expenditures to fight the civil war. Victory required maximizing the $SV(C)$ so as to maximize the $SSCP(C)$ available for the war effort. War communism thus entailed intensified exploitation of industrial workers. That exploitation in turn depended upon securing food and raw materials for urban industrial workers from private ancient farmers. Not only the quality and quantity of those inputs but also their values would help determine how much surplus value state enterprises could yield and so make available for the war effort. In an ironic contradiction, the new

Soviet state defended its revolution against private capitalist exploitation by intensifying its own state capitalist exploitation.

An analysis of war communism in Marxian value terms can clarify the new Soviet state's dilemmas in relation to both industrial and agricultural production. We begin with some basic definitions. Let V(C) represent the state-administered value (the average money wages) of the labor power purchased from industrial laborers and consumed by state capitalists in their industrial enterprises. Let C(C) represent the state-administered value of all the produced tools, equipment, and raw materials used up in industrial production. Let UV represent the different individual physical commodities ("use-values") produced by state capitalist industries. Finally, we may designate as EVs the values attached to each UV by the state bureaucrats charged with that task. Those bureaucrats calculated the value of labor power, V(C), by setting it equal to the following: the bundle of produced goods—UVs—to be consumed by the laborers (their real wages) multiplied by the values—EVs—assigned to each UV in that bundle.

To simplify, we shall assume that laborers consumed only ancient-grown food, a set of use-values that we shall label $UV_F$. Then V(C)—the value of productive labor power—equaled the number of items in the workers' food bundle—$UV_F$—multiplied by the value per unit of those items ($EV/UV_F$). Thus, V(C) = $EV/UV_F \times UV_F$.[18] These laborers worked with and used up tools, buildings, and other commodity inputs—C(C)—whose values were similarly calculated as $EV/UV_C$ multiplied by $UV_C$. Thus, C(C) = $EV/UV_C \times UV_C$.

Lastly, we need to specify the values of raw materials supplied by private ancient farmers to state capitalist industry. To do this, we divide C(C) into two components. $C_{RM}(C)$ stands for the value of agricultural raw materials (cotton, sugar beets, tobacco, etc.) used up to produce industrial commodities. $C_{IND}(C)$ represents the value of nonagricultural—that is, industrial—input commodities used up in the process of producing state capitalist industrial outputs. Thus, $C_{RM}(C) = EV/UV_{RM} \times UV_{RM}$; the value of agricultural inputs is the product of the state-set values of raw material inputs multiplied by the physical number of such raw materials used up to produce industrial commodities.

Having specified these value relations, we can continue our class analysis of the food and raw material problems of Soviet state capitalism first under war communism and then under the NEP. It is important to keep in mind that few if any private markets existed (legally) under war communism, whereas private markets and hence private prices were reestablished under the NEP alongside and interacting with state markets and prices.

Given the relatively low productivity of ancient farmers, the new state capitalist industries' war-driven demand for food and raw materials exceeded what the farmers could supply. Desperate to solve this problem, the Soviet state faced alternative price strategies. It could have assigned prices to raw materials and food higher than their actual costs (set by state officials and based on the average labor hours needed to produce them).[19] That strategy might have stimulated greater agricultural supplies by rewarding the ancient farmers who reaped this excess of prices over costs. However, that strategy would also have forced the state, given its budget limits, to reduce its purchases of food and raw materials, thereby slowing the prioritized industrial growth.

While that strategy would have eliminated the excess demand for food and raw materials, it was initially rejected because of its negative impact on industrial growth and thus upon the war effort. The state adopted instead an extreme strategy of *reducing* state-administered prices of the desperately needed food and raw materials almost to zero. It compelled ancient farmers to deliver them for little or no value in return. War communism amounted to a state-administered seizure of—the official term was "requisitioning"—rather than trade for food and raw materials.

Over time, Soviet officials actually oscillated between these two price strategies because of the different contradictions each set in motion. To analyze these contradictions, we begin with a counterfactual question. What might have happened had the Soviet state chosen to wage civil war and repel the invasions by deploying the first price strategy: raising state-set prices of food and raw materials above their values per unit? Our answer will help to explain why this policy was not adopted under war communism but was adopted, in part, during the subsequent NEP period.

Had Soviet state officials raised the prices of foods, the impact on industrial workers would have depended on what else state officials did. If, for example, they also increased the price of labor power (money wages) an equal amount, then industrial workers would have been able to maintain their food consumption standards. Because of the ideological and political role of industrial workers in the Bolshevik view of socialism, this kind of wage policy might have been likely. In Marxian value terms, this wage policy would have raised the price of labor power above its value, $P_{LP}(C) > V(C)$, to match the raising of food prices above their values.

Paying productive workers wages above the values of their labor power would necessarily have come from the surpluses appropriated by state capitalist enterprises. In effect, these workers would thereby have come to occupy a subsumed class position in relation to state industrial capitalists; the latter would have had to add a new subsumed class payment $[SSCP(C)_{Workers}] = [P_{LP}(C) - V(C)]$ to the others already straining the surplus value available for such payments.[20] While such a policy might have bought labor peace by sustaining the workers' real wages, it would have equivalently reduced the surplus value left for distribution to secure the other conditions of existence of state capitalist industry. In the first years of the USSR this would have meant reducing the surplus distributions for the war effort, for rebuilding from war damage, and for developing industry. It would have jeopardized the new society's survival. The solution to one set of problems would have provoked another set.

The state might have tried to resolve this latter set of problems without reducing surplus distributions for the revolutionary regime's survival. For example, it might have tried to get more surplus from the industrial workers (by intensifying the work effort, lengthening the work day, or both). State industrial capitalists could then have returned this extra surplus to the workers as the higher wages needed to afford the higher-priced food. Yet such an increase in exploitation risked provoking the workers' anger: just what the state sought to avoid in the first instance by raising the price of labor power.

To avoid such threats, Soviet state policy under war communism did *not* raise the price of labor power above its value. This policy alone, of course, would have placed the burden of higher food prices entirely onto workers, whose consequent reduction in food consumption would have been intolerable given their already very low standards of consumption. Nor could Soviet leaders risk a variation on this policy: (1) make state capitalist industries pay higher prices for food but purchase less of it, and (2) pay workers the higher wages needed to afford the food *but hire fewer workers*. Reduced industrial employment and ouput would have resulted, contradicting both socialist survival and socialist industrial growth priorities.

Comparable contradictions beset policy aimed to secure more deliveries of raw materials to state capitalist industry. To set their prices higher than their unit values would have required state industrial capitalists to pay for that increment. To do so, they would have had to distribute a share of their surplus to private ancients farmers (a new subsumed class payment): $SSCP(C)_{Ancients} = (P_{RM} - EV/UV_{RM}) \times UV_{RM}$.[21] As with subsumed class payments to workers if their wages rose above the value of their labor power, the diversion of state capitalist surpluses to ancient farmers for raw materials jeopardized the other distributions on which Soviet socialism's survival was thought to depend. The web of contradictions in this case was just as daunting and dangerous. Considering the contradictory consequences of higher state-set food or raw materials prices, the Bolsheviks' reluctance to pursue that price strategy becomes clear.

Beyond winning the wars they faced and achieving basic survival, the Bolsheviks also sought to achieve a successful socialism. Three indices of success dominated their thinking: real consumption per worker, the capital labor ratio, and the absolute number of productive state workers in industry. The last was the most important sign of successful growth of socialism. A rising capital labor ratio (proportion of machinery to laborer) enabling growing labor productivity (unleashing the forces of production that had been fettered by capitalism) was another success indicator. Lastly, as a fruit of rising industrial productivity, a slow but steady rise in the real wages of industrial workers was still another standard by which a successful socialism could be identified. These three indices informed much of the thinking and strategies deployed by the state in regard to state capitalist industry and its relationship to the class structures that evolved in Soviet agriculture over the ensuing decades. Thus, it became next to impossible for the Bolsheviks to purchase less of food and raw materials for state capitalist industry. To have done so would have compromised one or more of their socialist success indices: decreasing the number of industrial workers, the use of raw materials per industrial worker (in this context a proxy for the capital labor ratio), or the real wages of workers.[22]

## Class Contradictions after War Communism

War communism had displayed one strategy for state management of the class contradictions within industrial state capitalism and between it and the class structures of post-revolutionary agriculture. Requisitioning food and raw materials (effectively setting their prices far below their values) avoided the dilemmas of many of those contradictions even as it produced new ones. Moreover, war communism's class contradictions and policy options remained central issues for the USSR after war communism stopped and after many Soviet social conditions changed.

Through the 1920s and beyond, the sorts of class contradictions and policy options discussed above in relation to war communism returned anew under the heading of the "scissors crisis." Whenever prices for ancient agricultural commodities rose relative to industrial prices, the state capitalist industrial enterprises found their funds available for industrial expansion cut. A price "scissors" was thus undercutting the top priority of the state and the Party. Given Soviet leaders' concepts of succesful socialist development, as noted, the state policy response was to close the scissors again by raising industrial relative to agricultural prices. Through twists and turns of circumstance and of policy, the state always returned to its basic goal: maximize the flows of food, raw materials, and ex-farm workers into industry while minimizing the reverse flow of industrial output to agriculture. To this end, as we shall see, the state used its power during the NEP to ensure favorable terms of trade (price ratios) for state capitalist industry. The contradiction between capitalist industry and ancient agriculture was resolved by choosing for the former and against the latter as a matter of Soviet principle.

The milder form of this Soviet policy would entail persuading or minimally coercing private ancient farmers to supply state capitalist industry with increasing quantities of food and raw materials at stable prices. Under such circumstances Vesenkha could reasonably expect to expand the capitalist industrial labor force (assuming a roughly constant value of industrial labor power). Vesenkha could reasonably plan to equip the additional labor force with additional plants and equipment—all rising roughly at the same rate as agricultural deliveries to state industry rose.[23]

In a more agressive form of the policy—reminiscent of war communism's requisitioning—the state turns the terms of trade against farmers. If food and raw materials prices were officially reduced below their unit values and if industrial workers' money wages were correspondingly reduced (affording them the same quantity of food as before since food prices had fallen), state capitalist industry would gain. More surplus value would be appropriated from state industrial laborers than before since they could now be paid less. More surplus would enable more accumulation of means of industrial production by state capitalist enterprises. More raw materials could be purchased by state industry than before since their prices had dropped. An aggressive policy of turning the terms of trade against ancient farmers would allow more growth—more socialist successes—in state industry than before.

The ancient farmers' losses from such state-imposed unfavorable terms of trade in the 1920s threatened their survival, albeit less quickly and drastically than the earlier requisitioning had done. This had the potential to drive many farmers out of agriculture into urban industry even when wages there were still low. The resulting economic landscape would display ever more industrial workers, working with more machines (because of high investment) at steady wages; but it would also display an atrophying agriculture. The great risk to an aggressive Soviet industrialization policy was that private ancient farmers might respond in ways other than emigrating to state industrial jobs. They might challenge the Soviet development strategy and system in serious ways, perhaps even withdrawing from the worker-peasant alliance politically undergirding the Soviet regime.

Lenin had sought to cope with just such risks (provoked by war communism's requisitioning) when he inaugurated the New Economic Policy in 1921. Yet the same basic challenges and strategic options remained after requisitioning ceased. Insofar as industrial growth remained the top priority, the state would have to replace requisitioning with manipulations of the terms of trade between state capitalist industry and private ancient agriculture. As this replacement strategy unfolded, agriculture underwent a class change. As many private ancient farms failed, in part because of the state's pricing policies, some farmers survived by selling their land and then their labor power to those few ancients who succeeded and could buy them. A small-scale private capitalist class structure grew in Soviet agriculture.

Not surprisingly, the state's NEP pricing policies soon provoked negative reactions from both private ancient and the increasing number of small private capitalist farmers. These reactions eventually proved as counterproductive and dangerous to the state's industrialization strategy as the earlier reactions to requisitioning had been. Hence, yet another variation of the state's basic strategy had to be devised. It turned out to be the collectivization of agriculture. And when collectivization reached its limits, a renewed policy of price and value manipulations before and after World War Two shaped yet another phase of the enduring Soviet basic strategy. This sought to manage the basic contradictions within state capitalist industry and between it and the more complex class structures in agriculture so as to maximize the growth of industrial capacity and output.

Soviet debates over economic strategy neither recognized nor made distinctions in terms of class structures in the surplus sense of our approach. While invisible to the debaters, the class effects of their proposals were nonetheless significant. Quantitatively, each particular policy or strategy proposed would uniquely influence the sizes of surpluses appropriated within the different class structures comprising Soviet society. It would also uniquely shape the sizes of the distributions of those surpluses to subsumed classes. Each strategy or policy entailed a particular alteration of the relative balance and social position of the different class structures coexisting in the USSR. Qualitatively, the contesting policies sometimes also entailed transformations of the class structures (e.g., from ancient to capitalist, and so on) existing at the different sites of Soviet production (state, private, industrial, agricultural, and household).

Given our concern with class conditions and effects, we may also consider class contradictions and changes involved in particular policies that might have been, but were not, pursued after the October Revolution. For example, suppose that the new Soviet regime had established some combination of private and state communist farms instead of ancient farms right after the revolution.[24] Then the new Soviet state would have confronted not ancient food and raw material commodities but rather their communist counterparts. In that event, the USSR's basic class structure would have combined state capitalism in industry with private and/or state communism in agriculture. The prioritizing of industrial expansion would then have had to cope with the different contradictions of that complex class structure. A different Soviet history would have emerged. However, with very few exceptions, what actually occurred under war communism and the NEP was the Soviet state's commitment instead to ancient class structures in agriculture (and tolerance for small private capitalist class structures to develop there as well).

So long as Soviet industry could obtain the rising quantity of food and raw materials and favorable terms of trade that its prioritized growth required, the contradictions between state capitalist and private ancient class structures persisted. Soviet policy did not seek to resolve the contradictions by an explicit policy of altering either class structure. However, war communism's requisitioning and then the NEP's scissors crises and responses thereto sharpened and aggravated class contradictions. Tensions between state capitalist industry and private ancient and small capitalist agriculture rose ominously, as the tempo and tenor of scissors debates across the 1920s revealed. Integrating rural immigrants into Soviet industry likewise produced all sorts of class tensions inside state capitalism. At the same time, the developing small private capitalists in agriculture (revealingly called *kulaks* or "fists") experienced intense conflicts with their employees (often former ancients). Finally, the tensions that flared repeatedly within and between the feudal and ancient class structures of Soviet households interacted in complex ways with class contradictions everywhere else in Soviet society.

These class tensions and conflicts contributed significantly (alongside international political isolation and other nonclass problems) to raising increasingly acute questions about Soviet society. Could the state manage its contradictions in the 1920s to achieve what Soviet leaders defined as economic indices of "socialist" success? Might not basic changes be needed to address the seemingly intractable, recurring "crises" across the 1920s? The questioners' theoretical assumptions and frameworks precluded their admitting, let alone considering, the USSR's complex, multiple, and contradictory class structures. They rather sought essential causes for the crises elsewhere (e.g., the revolution's particular land reform, private and state price changes, speculation, foreign intrigue, cultural underdevelopment, insufficiently democratic institutions, and so on). Many saw only one remaining class conflict, that asserted to exist between "socialist" industry and "capitalist" agriculture, and which was perceived to be the essential cause of economic problems in the 1920s. Such formulations captured first Trotsky and then others, including Stalin, and underlay the strategic shift decided toward the end of the 1920s.

Given their indices of success, Soviet leaders tended to reduce all social problems to effects of insufficient industrialization funds. That insufficiency resulted from the inadequate quantities and excessive prices of food and raw materials supplied to industry. They rarely blamed workers inside state industries for the insufficiency. Such an argument, intimating criticism of industrial workers, their employers, or the relationship between the two, was then politically as well as ideologically inappropriate, if not dangerous.[25] The consensus settled on the rural capitalists and richer ancients (the "rich peasants") as the ultimate problem and culprit. Their greed, hostility to socialism, and desire to secure their own nonsocialist future threatened Soviet survival.

What was to be done? Requisitioning had necessarily been abandoned by Lenin at the beginning of the decade. Under the NEP, recurrent scissors crises interrupted and threatened the effectivity of state manipulations of industrial relative to agricultural prices in securing adequate quantities and prices of agricultural inputs. By the end of the 1920s, a new strategy had to be found. Not surprisingly, given the prevailing thinking that had no place for notions of society as configurations of multiple class structures, the new strategy came to be conceived as "finishing the anticapitalist revolution."

The new strategy in fact rapidly transformed Soviet agriculture's class structures. The elimination of both its ancient and small capitalist class structures proceeded under the slogan of abolishing rural capitalism. In their place, the Soviet state did *not* establish state communism. Instead it herded most peasants into private "collective farms"—private since the farmers held no positions within any state apparatus. A minority of peasants were drawn into state farm enterprises where they became productive laborers producing surpluses for state officials functioning as surplus appropriators (replicating the state capitalist class structures of Soviet industry). Inside many (not all) collective farms, the mass organization of communist class structures actually occurred as state policy: the first and only large-scale establishment of communism in Soviet history.

Collectivization found little difficulty in destroying the relatively few rural capitalists, albeit at heavy and enduring social costs. The mass of ancient peasants were not managed so easily. The state did collectivize most of them, but their deep attachments to ancient class structures persisted, fueled their resisitance, and threatened Soviet power. The collective farmers' attachment to the ancient class structure simply had to be accommodated. For the rest of the USSR's history, that accommodation entailed the allocation of the famous "private plots" to collective farmers who there pursued ancient class structures of production alongside (and often at the expense of) their collective farm labors.

The interactions between the USSR's actual class contradictions and perceived policy options across the 1920s not only provoked collectivization and its contradictory coexistence with ancient class structures on farmers' private plots. From our standpoint, those interactions and their results also yield overlapping ironies. The USSR's "socialist" industry remained consistently state capitalist in its actual class structure. In contrast, the newly "socialized" agriculture at the decade's end actually encompassed four contending class structures: state capitalist on the state farms, private communist and private capitalist on the collective farms, and ancient on the collective farmers' private plots.[26] Both urban and rural households remained feudal and ancient from 1917 to the present. Applying the terms "socialist" or "communist" in any general, aggregate way to the USSR in war communism, in the 1920s (or indeed at any other time), hides rather than reveals the class structures, conflicts, and dynamic of that society.

## Notes

1. Since the social distributions of property and power were greatly changed by the 1917 revolution, labeling those changes "socialism" and "communism" makes sense in and for theories that marginalize, disregard, or deny the relevance of the production, appropriation, and distribution of surplus.
2. A further difference between our theory and those of others concerns essentialism. Where they tend to make the state an essential cause of Soviet development, we make neither the state nor class an essential cause. We focus on class because it is largely absent from the existing literature, not because it is any sort of essential historical determinant. Class processes in the USSR were as much effects of other, nonclass social processes as they were causes helping to constitute them (Resnick and Wolff 1987, ch. 1 and 2).
3. The word "equation" does not signal any necessity that state revenues equal expenditures. The equation merely highlights the elements that will determine whether an inequality or an equality exists between left and right sides. As we will show, equalities will have different consequences from inequalities.
4. They provided all sorts of managerial activities—political (e.g., discipline), economic (e.g., purchasing inputs and selling outputs), and cultural (e.g., persuading productive laborers that their wages were appropriate). Managers did not themselves either produce or appropriate surplus labor. They provided conditions of existence for the capitalist fundamental class process occurring inside state enterprises and involving productive labor there by others. To secure such management, the czar allocated one portion of the surplus appropriated in those enterprises to pay the managers' salaries and provide their budgets for managing.
5. Alternatively, the czar's subsumed class distributions out of his appropriated surplus might fund a repressive apparatus that coerced—rather than persuaded—state employees to perform surplus labor. Of course, both kinds of distributions could and often did occur together.
6. Detailed investigations could disaggregate categories of state expenditure such as, say, law enforcement, to determine how much should be allocated to sustaining capitalist—X(C)—and how much to other class structures coexisting in Russia—X(A), X(F), and so on. Given the larger historical focus of this book, such investigations were not undertaken.
7. If these were cash levies, the household would have to transform its feudal surplus labor (or surplus product) into money. For example, the surplus labor of the feudal wife/serf could be embodied in

products to be sold in local markets. Alternatively, the wife's surplus labor time might provide products directly consumed by the feudal husband in the reproduction of the labor power that he sold to his employer. This would free an equivalent portion of his wages—now no longer needed to purchase such products—to be used to pay the tax on the household.

8. A state deficit is depicted by the following inequality between revenues and expenditures:

$$SV(C) + SSCR(C+A+F) + NCR_1 < SSCP(C) + X(C+A+F) + Y_1$$

Two new terms ($NCR_1$ and $Y_1$) stand, respectively, for the nonclass revenues derived from taxes placed on individuals who are not surplus appropriators and for the expenditures directed to sustain such revenues. Introducing a second kind of state nonclass revenue—$NCR_{debt}$ as the state's borrowings—and a term for state interest payments on that debt—$Y_{int}$—allows us to specify a balanced state budget:

$$SV(C) + SSCR(C+A+F) + NCR_1 + NCR_{debt} = SSCP(C) + X(C+A+F) + Y_1 + Y_{int}$$

9. Carr (1985, vol. 2, 274-279) and especially Dobb (1966, 121-124), writers sympathetic to Bolshevism, also deny that "war communism" was communism, but their reasons differ from ours. For them, it marks a time when civil war necessitated extremely unusual, unsustainable emergency policies (state requisitioning of resources and products, absence of money in many transactions, etc.) in a poor nation emerging from the massive destruction of a world war. The organization of the production, appropriation, and distribution of surplus is not cited when they reject the label "communist" for this period. For us, how surplus was organized is key to determining a class label. Thus, we differ also from anti-Bolshevik writers such as Nove (1989) who see in war communism—its collectivization of productive property and its abolition of markets and money—the essence of communism per se.

10. The state officials who appropriated the productive laborers' surpluses in large and small enterprises sometimes returned portions of them to the managers and/or laborers for their use. But a distribution of surpluses back to laborers only underscores that it was state officials, not the laborers themselves, who appropriated and distributed the surpluses. Communist class structures did not exist in these state enterprises.

11. Hill (1971, 170) cites the contemporary report of a commissar sent to a rural area: "There was general excitement. Everybody talked, and I could see that they thought something new had happened, from which they would live better." In Hill's words: "This is what the revolution meant."

12. Lenin's speeches and articles after 1917 argued that to establish socialism in Russia required two revolutions: one political and the other economic. The Bolsheviks had achieved the first by establishing a dictatorship of the proletariat. The second revolution required them " ... to study the state capitalism of the Germans, to spare *no effort* in copying it and not shrink from adopting *dictatorial* methods to hasten the copying of it" Lenin (1964, 145). See also Carr (1985, vol. 2, 93). Lenin both recognized the USSR's goals as state capitalism and yet offered no clear specification of the latter's insufficiency vis-a-vis communism in terms of the organization of surplus.

13. Allan MacNeill provided valuable research assistance in this examination. We also found the following useful: Bettelheim (1976b, 1978), Gregory (1990), Lane (1978, 1985a, 1985b), Hough and Fainsod (1979), Millar (1981, 1990), Conyngham (1973), Granick (1954, 1960), Spulber (1969), Berliner (1957, 1976), Gorlin (1985), and Richman (1965). While we found no evidence to support the hypothesis of communist class structures, there is much evidence concerning issues of power rather than class. Workers evidently lacked control over their work lives and sometimes made heroic efforts to change their relatively powerless position (Bettelheim 1978, 210-266; Carr: 1985, 317-331; 1954, 39-85; 1958, 363-419; Carr and Davies 1969, vol. 1, part 2, 453-623; Chase 1990, 38-43; and Siegelbaum and Suny 1994). In various ways (politically, via trade unions, etc.) industrial workers contested their power positions inside Soviet factories. They sought more

control over their work conditions, wages, and so on. But they did not contest their class positions as producers of surplus for state officials.

14. See Nove (1989, viii and 77) and Gregory (1990, 26) for similar analogies between the Soviet council and a private industrial "board of director's role." While Lane (1978, 298–300) generally concurs regarding the analogy, he and the others do not extend the point, as we do, to an argument about different (state versus private) capitalist class structures in the United States and USSR.

15. Interestingly, Lane (1978) also recognizes that a government ministry is the buyer of labor power in the USSR. As per Marx's logic, such a ministry—similar to private capitalist boards—consumes labor power and in the process appropriates surplus labor. However, Lane refuses to conclude that it also appropriates and distributes the surplus because of, in his words, "different structural conditions" than those of capitalism (180). He identifies the latter as "public ownership and a process of planning based on administrative control" (179) and so concludes that the USSR was socialist, not capitalist. Bettelheim (1976b), from the left, also essentializes political processes: for him too what matters most is who wields political power over (rather than how the surplus is appropriated and distributed within) industrial enterprises. He concludes his power-focused analysis by arguing that because the Council of Ministers wielded power instead of the workers, it was therefore a "state bourgeoisie" (166). The USSR was state capitalist, not socialist, for him, because of how power, not surplus labor, was distributed. Zimbalist and Sherman (1984, 281–283) and Sherman (1995, 200–205) explicitly recognize class exploitation "by a ruling class" in Soviet state enterprises. Isaac Deutscher is another: "their incomes are at least partially derived from the 'surplus value' (or profit) produced by the workers" (quoted by Zimbalist and Sherman 1984, 283). However, unlike both Lane and Bettelheim, Sherman concludes in his recent book (1995) that the USSR was neither socialist nor capitalist. The reason is that the "surplus labor extraction depended on ruling-class control of the Soviet political process and political control of the means of production" (203). For Sherman too, power is the ultimate determinant. Interestingly enough, despite these theorists' embrace of political determinism, they draw from that common perspective radically different conclusions as to the class nature of Soviet society.

16. For Carr (1985, vol. 2, 75): "Vesenkha was evidently conceived as the central planning and directing organ of the economic life of the country." Reorganized as the Council of Ministers, the Soviet Constitution recognized it as the top economic arm of the state. "The USSR Council of Ministers (Soviet Ministrov SSSR) is the highest oversight and executive committee of the Soviet economic bureaucracy . . . responsible for the enactment of the economic policies . . . " (Gregory 1990, 25).

17. The *power* of the Communist Party apparatus to influence the magnitude and distribution of the surplus differs from the *class position* of actually appropriating and distributing that surplus itself. In the USSR, the latter position was occupied by the Council of Ministers, not the Party. This is especially important in relation to this book's differentiation of state from private capitalism. The USSR differed from the West more in its power distribution than in its class structure.

18. We use the term productive here in the Marxian sense of "productive of surplus value." Hence we exclude the unproductive laborers—those not producing a surplus—working in Soviet state capitalist enterprises. As per the definition of unproductive laborers (Resnick and Wolff 1987, ch. 3), their wages are paid as distributions of the surplus to them by its appropriators.

19. Bettelheim (1978, 139) describes prices set by the state as "fixed administratively." Preobrazhensky provides the example of railway equipment in the 1920s: "The prices are formed by definite planned calculation, they are adjusted to the level of cost of production in the works of Glavmetall, either with calculation of a certain profit for the customer, or without any profit, or even with a foreseen loss in those cases where the state consciously fixes prices below costs of production and gives the factories a subsidy from the budget" (1966, 163). Preobrazhensky's chief concern in this seminal work was to show how the Soviet state could develop specific price policies aimed to benefit the "socialized" over the "nonsocialized" sectors. We discuss these price policies and their consequences below.

20. The logic here is straightforward. This pricing strategy would have confronted state industrial capitalists with a new and costly condition of their existence. Where before, state industrial capitalists could have secured labor power via purchase at its value, the new price strategy would require paying a premium in addition to that value. In other words, for state industrial capitalists to continue to purchase labor power at its value (and so appropriate the surplus value it produces), they would now have to commit a portion of that surplus value to pay for a new cost—the excess of labor power's price over its value. This new cost would accrue to the laborers as raised wages. The workers would then occupy not only the fundamental class position as producers of surplus value, but also the subsumed class position of receivers of a distributed share of that surplus.

21. A state policy raising raw materials prices above their values placed the ancient farmers who produced them in a subsumed class position. To gain access to the raw materials, state industrial capitalists would have to pay their values plus a special premium—a kind of access fee equivalent to the excess of price over value. Since access was a condition of existence for industrial capitalists' continued appropriation of surplus value, the fee would have to be defrayed by a distributed share of state capitalists' surplus.

22. To see this, we rewrite the text's two subsumed class distributions to farmers and workers respectively:

$$SSCP(C)_{Workers} = [P_F - EV/UV_F] \times UV_F/L \times L$$
$$SSCP(C)_{Ancients} = [P_{RM} - EV/UV_{RM}] \times UV_{RM}/L \times L$$

where the only new categories introduced are the state-set price of food—$P_F$—and the number of workers in state industry—L. State officials refrained from actions that would reduce industrial employment, L, the use of raw materials per industrial worker, $UV_{RM}/L$, and real wages per industrial worker, $UV_F/L$.

23. Expanding productive employment at the same growth rate as that of the food supply, while holding constant the real wage for those same workers, is equivalent to maintaining an unchanged rate of capitalist exploitation for industrial workers. Because the terms of trade and the real wage remain unchanged over time, surplus value (and hence the total of subsumed class distributions) expands at the same growth rate as does the value of labor power. The growth rate of the latter, under these assumptions, must be equal to the growth in the mass of productive employment.

24. The state might have organized farm enterprises in which members of the state collectively produced and appropriated their own surplus labor: state communist farms. Or the the state might have allowed groups that were not state members—had no position inside the state apparatus—to operate private communist class-structured farms in which they collectively produced and appropriated their surplus labor. Chapters 1 and 2 above offer the basis for such posibilities.

25. Stalin's purge of Bukharin showed the risks of conceiving Soviet industrialization in terms other than as a successfully developing socialism. Bukharin's analytic focus on power (above all state power) had led him to see NEP development as, "in the economic sphere, state capitalism, the prosperous muzhik individual, the curtailment of the collective farms, foreign concessions, surrender of the monopoly of foreign trade and as a result—the restoration of capitalism in the country" (quoted in Cohen 1980, 379).

26. On some collective farms capitalist class structures prevailed from the beginning. There the collective of farmers chose a leadership (more or less controlled by state and Party officials) to which they effectively delivered their surpluses, which the leadership then distributed, partly to secure their own exclusive surplus-appropriating positions. The languages, laws, and customs governing collective farms often supported such capitalist class structures as well as communist class structures. Over time, we believe that such capitalist class structures often replaced the communist for reasons we detail below.

CHAPTER 7

# Revolution, Class, and the Soviet Household

Class or other kinds of analyses of societies rarely include households within their purview. This chapter offers the outline of a class analysis of Soviet households across the nation's history. We will then refer back to (and sometimes further elaborate) this chapter's arguments as needed in our chronological sequence of class analyses of Soviet society as a whole in the final three chapters.

The importance of including household class structures in social histories—especially when, as in the USSR, that history involves explicit movements to alter class structures generally—lies in three basic considerations.[1] First, most individuals live much of their lives inside households where production of goods and services occurs. That production typically entails a surplus and hence a class structure. The USSR exhibits distinct household class structures. Second, the class structures existing inside Soviet households likely interacted in significant ways with class structures outside to help shape all aspects of social life. Third, Soviet adults likely became predisposed toward some and against other particular class structures (outside as well as inside households) in part as results of their childhood experience of class inside their households.

The household class structures inherited from pre-revolutionary Russia changed in some ways and remained the same in others. We propose to show how both the changes and the constancy worked to sustain Soviet state capitalism in industry while also creating certain problems for it. Further, we will argue that the possibility of introducing and sustaining communist class structures in Soviet industrial and agricultural enterprises depended in part on how Soviet society dealt with the class structures of household production.[2] Throughout, we demonstrate how Soviet policies only inadvertently affected households' internal class structures, since the Marxian theories informing those policies had no concept of class inside households and hence no plan to change them. Bolshevik household policies reveal a blindness to class in its surplus sense parallel to what we have already encountered in relation to communism and state capitalism.

The departures from the countryside of 14 million Russian men mobilized for World War One changed the class structures inside many agricultural households.[3] The men's absence left their wives in a new situation. They no longer performed household surplus labor—cooking, cleaning, making and repairing clothing, childcare, and so on—and delivered its fruits to a husband within the feudal class structure typical of Russian households. With husbands gone to war, Russian wives had two main options. They could replace the departed men by becoming heads of feudal households themselves (if, for example, younger women and/or children worked as household serfs delivering their surplus to these women). Otherwise, they could alone perform and appropriate their own household surplus labor. In short, the war imposed sudden and radical changes in many Russian household class structures.[4] Women either became feudal surplus appropriators inside households or else the household experienced a transition from feudal to ancient class structures. Those were the class implications of what a delegate told the 1916 womens congress in Moscow: "once the men are gone, peasant women have no other recourse except to do the men's work" (Meyer 1991, 217).

If the 1917 revolution raised issues of class transformation for Russian enterprises, for millions of Russian housewives class transformations were already underway inside their households. These class changes were not, however, altogether new, since they replicated the history of Russian widows (Bohac 1991). High death rates especially among rural Russian males in the centuries before 1917 had raised the problem of how to organize household production as well as farm production in their absence.[5] Not all widows remarried or returned to their original families, despite heavy social pressure to do so; some became heads of households (Bohac 1991, 109–112). They headed either ancient class households (individual widows with children) or feudal class households where such widows (or still others) replaced their deceased former husbands as feudal lords within extended, multigenerational family units. World War One produced widowhood on a massively intensified scale. Millions of wives of dead or incapacitated soldiers either experienced household transitions to ancient class structures or else became the feudal lords of their households.[6] For most women in the countryside, these transformations were as traumatic as, for example, the changes experienced by women newly drawn into industrial wage labor to replace men there (Meyer 1991, 213–214).

That Russian women worked hard inside households because of wartime deprivations was not the major change; they had always done most of the housework by all accounts. It was how the work was organized—in particular, its class organization—that had changed.[7] Many women newly experienced being a direct, feudal appropriator of the household surplus of others or being the appropriator of her own individual household surplus. However strong their hopes for the war to end and the men to return, conscious and unconscious resistances to resuming their serf positions within the old feudal households were also products of the war. As we shall see, these resistances influenced the class evolution of the USSR after the 1917 revolution.

Millions of husbands never returned from the war to resume their feudal household class positions. Many of their wives had also died, returned to their original families, or become part of a large mass of vagabonds roaming the country. For the husbands who did return, most resumed their old feudal household class structures in both the towns and the countryside. However, many widows retained their feudal surplus appropriator positions within households, and millions of women settled ever more deeply into ancient class households (where war-scarred, nonworking husbands, brothers, and sons often depended totally on them).[8] New tensions beset this postwar social combination of male-headed and female-headed feudal and female-headed ancient class structured households. Women surplus appropriators often became less willing to accept the political and cultural subordination typical of pre-revolutionary Russia inside the household and beyond. With many men newly dependent on surplus distributions from newly independent, surplus appropriating women, both genders increasingly resisted and resented all the ensuing adjustments in thought and feeling. Even where traditional feudal households continued, the class transformations of women elsewhere in society had profound effects. More or less, depending on time and place, the image of the male as dominating household feudal lord shifted to an image rather of dominant household leech.

Tensions between men and women, emerging in part from this class history of Russian households, continued as enduring features of Soviet society. The widespread image of husbands as more or less bitterly tolerated burdens on women inside feudal and ancient households took root in Soviet culture. Many Soviet women have tried to understand how this image worked its way so deeply into Soviet culture. For one, "With emancipation we not only freed ourselves, we created a generation in which too many women tried to be the heads of families"; while another believed in the 1980s that Soviet society had finally to awaken "the individualism in our men so that they cease feeling superfluous, . . . [to create] less aggressive females who can at last regain their womanliness."[9] A major recent history of women in the USSR refers to the "deep fount of bitterness" between Soviet men and women by the mid-1930s (Goldman 1993, 336).

## Bolshevik Class Blindness

Feudal and ancient class structures were the prevailing but not the only household class structures after 1917. There were also communist class structures in which residents collectively produced and appropriated their own household surplus. These emerged within the revolutionary experiments in household reorganization after 1917 (Stites 1989, 205–222). Among the movements for household "communes," a few organized actual communist class structures of household production.[10]

It was chiefly revolutionary militants in both rural and urban areas who established household communes. Partly they drew inspiration from the history of socialism and Marxism. However, they were also reviving old Russian traditions, religious and secular, favoring collective living arrangements. The militants' efforts also attracted widows, orphans, vagabonds, returned soldiers without families, and rural emigrants arriving in cities. Extreme postwar shortages of housing, jobs, and food also propelled many who found communes an affordable household option.

The euphorias and dangers of the years immediately after 1917 prompted the establishment of all sorts of communes across the USSR. Many included households within the realm of what was to be communized.[11] However, "commune" received differing interpretations. Sometimes it meant shared housing, dining, or childcare where families collectively owned the household's productive assets or pooled individual resources to hire someone outside the commune to clean, cook, and so forth. Sometimes it referred chiefly to collective decision making regarding political or ideological activities of the group. Sometimes interpersonal relations were the focus of collective decision and activity, especially sexual and parenting policies and behaviors.

Household communes did not necessarily entail or include a communist class structure of household production. While the evidence suggests that most did not, in those that did all adult members collectively produced, appropriated, and distributed their household surpluses to reproduce its communist class structure. They did not discuss their households in those class terms, since such terms did not exist in acceptable public discourse. They believed that the collectivized property and power of the militants' household communes entitled them to the term "communist." For nearly all of them, how they organized household surplus labor was not pertinent to communism. Even those that actually established household communist class structures did so as derivative extensions of their collectivization of property and power. That class structure was not a central objective of their politics per se.

Since communist class structures never characterized Soviet industry, their only urban sites were a small subset of these household communes. From 1918 to 1931–32, the Soviet Union officially supported and even subsidized many household communes—and hence their experiments in communist class structures (Lenin 1959, 335, 388; Stites 1989, 222). The transition to a communism defined in terms of social justice, equality, democracy, and solidarity seemed to warrant such households too. The immensely popular Vladimir Mayakovsky offered this poetry (Stites 1989, 205):

Communism: it's not only on the land,
in the mill, in the sweat of your toil.
It's at home, at table, in family life and daily round.

The years of war, revolution, and war communism thus yielded a traumatized and a transformed household in the early years of the USSR. Feudal households underwent major changes. Sudden and difficult transitions to ancient households were imposed on millions of others. Radically different communist class structures in household communes appeared and won praise and support from the new state and Party powers. Soviet households were caught up in a class conjuncture of genuine transitional possibilities—at once disorienting, troubling, yet also full of promise. The class dimensions, however, went unseen.

The Soviet state could have tried to weaken the conditions of existence of feudal and ancient household class structures while strengthening the conditions of existence for communist households. To that end, taxes on noncommunist class-structured households might have exceeded those on communist class-structured households. Greater subsidies and better services might have favored communist over noncommunist households. The state might have launched educational campaigns to persuade households to institute internal communist class structures as part of the revolutionary goals and strategy of the new society.[12] None of these policies fostering communist class structures inside households was ever debated, adopted, or even unofficially pursued by the Soviet state.

Early Soviet discussion did debate the need to eradicate "purely feudal marriage law" (Goldman 1993, 192). Yet despite the reference to "feudal," no participants in these debates formulated any notion of a "feudal" household class structure formed by such marriage laws. A more suggestive theorization in a 1922 Soviet Supreme Court decision declared women's household work "productive labor" (Goldman 1993, 194–196). Now, Marxists had long stressed the distinction between productive labor (whose work yields a surplus) and unproductive labor (which yields no surplus). Yet, neither the court nor anyone else pursued the point to determine which particular mode of producing and distributing surplus (i.e., class structure in our terms) existed within households where such "productive" labor occurred. The court's remark could not be pursued because the theoretical context needed to make that reasonable was absent.

The Communist Party might have organized campaigns in opposition to some and in support of other household class structures. It might have argued that the revolution's success depended on establishing communist class-structured households no less than collectivizing industrial property or substituting state planning for markets. Lenin, Bukharin, Trotsky, and other major leaders might have become famous for their statements on household class structures.[13] However, the Party, like the state, never made class transitions inside Soviet households a matter of debate or policy decision, neither during the revolution nor later in the USSR's history.

The absence of a class theory of households and the lack of interest in them among state and party leaders contributed to keeping Soviet households overwhelmingly feudal and ancient. Household communes and communist class structures inside some of them never became more than very limited movements marginal to the mainstreams of Soviet society. By the early 1930s, even that marginal status was eliminated leaving the household realm of Soviet life to the contradictions and tensions of feudal and ancient class structures. Class exploitation thus continued throughout Soviet society—not only in its state enterprises but also in most households.

After the early 1930s, the feudal and the ancient were the only household class structures into which Soviet citizens were born, where they matured, and where they formed their first understandings and loyalties vis-à-vis class (both unconscious and conscious). Before then, Soviet citizens had occasionally heard about, been provoked to conceive of, or perhaps personally encountered household class structures other than the feudal and the ancient that had prevailed through centuries of czarist society. The communes that arose after 1917 had likely struck many as more compatible with the revolutionary new regime.[14] To borrow from Mayakovsky's poetry, there were at least some places for Soviet citizens to see or at least to imagine communism *at home.*

The ironies, tragedies, and social consequences of this class history of Soviet households invite attention to its diverse causes. No doubt, early Soviet society displayed widespread pockets of social conservatism (Massell 1974). Successive Soviet regimes worried lest their uncertain peasant supporters be alienated by too much change too soon and too close to home. A certain "productivist" bias prevalent in Soviet thought considered social development dependent on the course of production in factories and on farms. Hence, developments inside households mattered far less and/or were also thought to be dependent on factory and farm conditions (Goldman 1993, 132-133).

Another cause helped to explain the class history of Soviet households. We refer here to the particular way in which leading state and party figures theorized household production and the proper way for the new Soviet regime to deal with it.[15] They occasionally glimpsed and denounced household "production relations" in a general way. Yet they saw the appropriate response as the elimination of all production (and hence class) from the household. They did not pose, let alone answer, questions about the alternative possible class structures of households. They thus could form no explicit policy about such structures.

Feminist critics have denounced the successive Soviet leaderships' "single-minded focus on production" and consequent betrayal of their promises "to socialize household labor and to foster freer, more equal relations between men and women" (Goldman 1993, 343). Much feminist literature sees Soviet experience as but one instance of a broader Marxian theory and practice that is "sex blind." In their view, Marxism marginalizes gender relations in favor of positioning production relations as the determinants of all social structures and histories, including those of men and women in families and households (Barrett 1980, 24).[16] While such feminist perspectives capture some of the overdeterminants of the Soviet experience, they also miss others that we believe worthy of emphasis.

The problem and the irony is that Marxian class analysis of production was *not* applied to the Soviet household. Soviet policy proceeded precisely *without* reference to the direct and often antagonistic class relations between men and women in relation to household production. The USSR thus achieved improvements in several aspects of womens' lives (education, medical care, formal equality, etc.) but not a basic alteration in their household class positions and all the consequences thereof. In short, some kinds of Marxism were utilized by Soviet leaders in ways that "blinded" them to the class relations inside households. However, other kinds of Marxism offer theories of household class structures whose use by Soviet leaders might have altered Soviet history in fundamental ways. Not Marxism in general but rather some particular Marxian tendencies dominated the thinking of Soviet leaderships. Those tendencies blinded them to the capitalist class structures of state industrial enterprises, the feudal and ancient class structures of Soviet households, and even to the communist class structure of household communes. As we argue in later chapters, this conceptual blindness contributed as well to the collapse of the Soviet Union's original revolutionary goals and eventually of the USSR itself.

The early Soviet goal was to eliminate the individual household itself as a social site. The reasoning held first that women's oppressed status inside households (overwork, lack of education, sexual servitude, etc.) required its elimination as a central goal of socialist policy. Secondly, since building the socialist economic base needed women's as well as men's labor outside the household, women had to be freed from housework. The Bolsheviks drew on a few basic axioms about households taken from prestigious authorities to express these ideas.[17] From Engels's *Origin of the Family, Private Property, and the State (1969B)*, "The modern individual family is founded on the open or concealed domestic slavery of the wife" and "Within the family he is the bourgeois and the wife represents the proletarian" (*The Woman Question* 1951, 39). Notably, Engels here borrows Marx's language ("bourgeois" and "proletarian") for class exploitation. Yet he never proceeds with his metaphor to inquire systematically into class structures inside households. Lenin's pamphlet *Women and Society* speaks of capitalism having "placed the toilers in conditions of poverty and wage slavery, and women in a position of double slavery" (*The Woman Question* 1951, 50). For Trotsky, "forty million Soviet families remain in their overwhelming majority nests of medievalism, female slavery . . . " (1970, 61–62). Both Bolshevik leaders glimpsed the class dimensions of households, but the glimpses remained extremely undeveloped. They seemed incapable of imagining alternative household class structures.

The Bolsheviks responded to households as they understood them with plans to eradicate the individual household as a social site of production—as in Engels's "abolition of the monogamous family as the economic unit of society" (*The Woman Question* 1951, 40). Lenin insisted that "The real *emancipation of women*, real communism, will begin only when a mass struggle . . . is started against this petty domestic economy [the household], or rather when it is *transformed on a mass scale* into large-scale socialist economy" (*The Woman Question* 1951, 56, italics in original). Two leading women theorists added another ingredient that became central to Bolshevik thinking. Clara Zetkin had argued historically that "Machine production has killed the economic activities of women within families, . . . productive activity within the family became economic nonsense, . . . the domestic activity of women [became] meaningless" (Foner 1984, 46–47.) Alexandra Kollontai developed this idea to reach the following conclusion that proved to be key for Soviet policy: "The family no longer produces, it only consumes" (1977, 117, 254; also Bukharin 1925, 156, and Goldman 1993, 43–48).

Arguments that production conditions inside households were utterly intolerable—a "humiliating yoke" (Stites 1978, 258–269)—were inconsistent with arguments that production had ceased there and left only consumption. Partly to resolve the inconsistency, the Bosheviks believed that capitalism had gone *part* of the way toward dismantling the family and individual household as sites of production. This partial process left women and children still engaged in marginal household work under the worst conditions, while the men worked in the socialized and modernized spheres of production outside the household.

The Bolsheviks planned radically to complete what capitalism had left incomplete, to liberate women and children from household drudgery and slavery. The individual household was to be dismantled: neither production nor consumption should occur there. The goals of women's equality and expanding industrial production would thereby be achieved simultaneously. The state should "socialize" housework by removing it from households and reorganizing it into state industrial enterprises alongside the others in the developing Soviet economy. Such enterprises would produce meals, clean clothes and living spaces, care for children, and so on. All consumption of these enterprises' products would occur collectively (dining halls, dormitories, creches, and so on), not in individual households (Kollontai 1977, 255ff.).

In Bolshevik thinking, such a socialization of housework would eradicate the domestic slavery of women and move them into work lives similar to those of the men. Genuine equality of the sexes would ensue (freedom for both men and women to divorce; equal educational and job opportunities; full civil rights; free access to abortion; and equal wages for women). Only by eradicating traditional families and households could couples form, change, and unform as "free unions" of equally productive and truly free adults working in socialist enterprises (Goldman 1993, 101–118). Only then might children be assured of loving care, since state-run enterprises producing child care and education would be given the highest priority in state support. Interaction between parents and children would then—and for the first time—emerge from what both freely desired. From 1917 through the early 1920s, most Bolshevik commentators argued that socialism and the transition to communism required the total disappearance of individual households.

The cumulative exigencies (famine, economic collapse, destroyed housing, etc.) of the world war, revolution, the military invasion by hostile governments, and the civil war confronted the Soviet state with emergency conditions. Among Bolshevik policy responses was the mass provision of collectively consumed meals and housing (Chase 1990, 173–213). Suddenly, what Kollontai called "the withering away" of the household (1977, 257–258) seemed a practical policy already underway. Bolshevik theories of family and household appeared to dovetail with emergency realities and policies.

Serious attention did not extend to examining what Bolshevik policy ought to be if individual household units similar to those existing before 1917 survived into or redeveloped during the 1920s.[18] Initially, few worried that Soviet state resources might not suffice to sustain mass collective dining, housing, and child-care service enterprises beyond the emergency circumstances. No officials designed or planned a fallback Bolshevik policy on individual households if state socialized housework could not be maintained. No debates over alternative class structures inside households occurred before or after 1917.

Having developed no theory/policy to distinguish/favor communist as against other household class structures, Bolshevik analysts and policy makers had no strategy—revolutionary or otherwise—once individual households proved their mass durability across the 1920s. Trotsky complained in 1924 that the USSR had achieved economic transformations "without touching on the forms of domestic traditions inherited from the past." Yet he repeated no more than the vague proposal that individual families "group themselves . . . into collective housekeeping units" (Trotsky 1924, 47, 59). No Bolshevik had proposals regarding the internal class organization of work either inside the individual households that remained the Soviet norm or inside any "collective housekeeping units" that the state might support or establish.

Theoretical blindness to the possibilities, conditions, and social effects of alternative class structures within households weighed heavily on Soviet history. It precluded any systematic state policy of favoring some kinds of household class structures against others (in contrast, for example, to the explicit Soviet policies regarding alternative class structures in industrial and agricultural enterprises: Lenin 1959). Class blindness also weakened any chance that the fledgling communist class structures in militants' household communes might become models for the USSR generally. The Bolshevik silence on alternative class structures within households had still other, lasting social effects. As we shall see, it helped to shape policy reactions to the social consequences of the New Economic Policy after 1921—including the collapse of war communism's emergency programs for mass state feeding, housing, and child care and the subsequent costs of such programs.

The eventual policy decision affirmed that the best course was to fall back upon "the family." The family would have to produce inside the household what the Soviet state could not—or not yet—socialize in state enterprises. In effect, Soviet policy thereby endorsed and reinforced the traditional household structures inherited from pre-revolutionary Russia (Farnsworth 1977). Absent the class analysis of households, Soviet leaders and thinkers could not pose, let alone answer, a key question. Might their efforts to build what they called socialism fail because they were reinforcing feudal and ancient class structures inside households?

Yet Lenin had understood that there would be great costs to leaving women in traditional households. In a 1920 conversation with Clara Zetkin he wrote:

> So few men—even among the proletariat—realize how much effort and trouble they could save women, even quite do away with, if they were to lend a hand in 'woman's work.' But no, that is contrary to the 'right and dignity of a man.' They want their peace and comfort. The home life of the woman is a daily sacrifice to a thousand unimportant trivialities. The old master right of the man still lives in secret. His slave takes her revenge, also secretly. The backwardness of women, their lack of understanding for the revolutionary ideals of the man decrease his joy and determination in fighting. (*The Woman Question* 1951, 93)

Such recognitions of the costs of the traditional, feudal household surfaced less frequently across the 1920s. The reaccommodation to traditional households and families made such sentiments of Lenin (and of others) decreasingly relevant to actual policy and troubling in their critical intimations.

## New Economic Policy/Old Household Policy

The NEP marked a major retreat in the economic aspirations, resources, and activities of the state. Meanwhile, the USSR's international isolation and recovery from the successive catastrophes of 1914–1920 put huge demands on the state. Not surprisingly, the de facto state policy toward households shifted away from the collectivization that had been envisioned in the days of revolution and war communism. Politically and economically, the costs of household collectivization were deemed too high.

One social problem linked to household and family became the topic around which debate crystallized, positions hardened, and strategic shifts can be seen. The new USSR confronted masses of children without parents or homes: "7 million waifs" by 1922, according to one recent study (Ball 1996, 1). They wandered both urban and rural areas, often became criminals to survive, and thereby threatened others. Visiting Moscow in 1926, the deeply sympathetic Walter Benjamin referred to them as "derelict, unspeakably melancholy . . . savage, mistrustful, embittered people" (1986, 103). Debates over these children highlighted the huge costs for state institutions to feed, house, clothe, and educate them versus reintegrating them into existing family/household structures at less cost to the state. The context for the debate was the national discourse then over how the state could best rebuild the nation's infrastructure, invest in industrial growth, provide consumer goods to the peasantry in exchange for agricultural goods (no longer requisitioned as in war communism), and so on. At the same time, millions of women with neither husbands nor secure land tenures pressed the state to alleviate their distress.[19] Likewise, millions of demobilized men without sufficient income or work to survive looked to the state to provide costly public services and supports for them.

Partly because these demands overwhelmed the new Soviet state after 1917 (especially while fighting foreign invasions and civil war), war communism had emerged. When it was undermined by ancients' resistance, insufficient state resources, and so on, the state retreated to the NEP. The hope was thereby better to meet the demands upon its resources. Some demands would fall as the civil war subsided and opposition from the ancients lessened. On the other hand, resources might fall if ancients, revived small capitalists, and small merchants (the famous Nepmen) used their NEP independence to withhold or divert resources from the state, legally or otherwise.[20] When Bukharin argued that "all classes and strata in Soviet society could, consciously or unconsciously, contribute to the building of socialism," he expressed a consensus that the Soviet state must carefully cultivate support among those made relatively independent by the NEP, which required "relentless opposition to those Bolsheviks whose programs produced new discord and civil strife" (Cohen 1980, 120). Advocates of "communal" households came increasingly to be viewed as Bolsheviks of that sort. Their activities, if unchecked, risked undermining crucial public support for and cooperation with the NEP.

Soviet leaders abandoned the grandiose plans for collective institutions (dining halls, creches, laundries, etc.) to replace individual households. The estimated costs of establishing and maintaining such planned institutions were too high. The state's expenditure priorities lay elsewhere in heavy industry, munitions, and infrastructure. The weight of conservative traditions bred opposition to collective households. All these factors combined to cause the state to retreat from programs and plans to eliminate individual households across the 1920s. Instead of collective dining, laundry, cleaning and child-care facilities, Soviet policy makers returned to a reliance on the individual households (dissenters from this retreat included women leaders).[21]

However, the retreat was far from total. A complete return to the households of pre-revolutionary Russia would have betrayed the revolution's commitments to women. Instead, the 1920s saw major changes in Soviet laws and social arrangements that very significantly improved women's social positions (Goldman 1993, ch. 4-7). Laws entitled women to own property (especially in land), improved access to abortion, divorce, and alimony, and moved toward equal political participation with men. The 1918 Family Code, the 1922 Land Code, and the complex, interdependent interpretations of these codes across the 1920s steadily enhanced women's roles as heads of households. For example, single-women-headed (i.e., ancient class-structured) households received formal, legal recognition for the first time. Women could also assume the position of head of a multifamily household. Women could take equal shares of household property in divorces. While enforcement of these reforms was often limited and varied widely from region to region, the changes were significant and historic. The Bolsheviks had kept several key components of the promise that the revolution would free Russia's women.[22]

Notwithstanding the abandonment of household collectivization, women's powers and rights inside Soviet households had been changed dramatically. However, their class positions—feudal and ancient—were minimally affected. The equality of women newly advanced by Soviet policies, albeit within the old class structures, produced new problems. They are revealed most clearly in the key question addressed by the 1926 Family Code that replaced the original from 1918: how to support the smaller households that had replaced the larger, pre-revolutionary households.[23]

Households in the 1920s were often barely viable. Simplified divorce and a culture of gender equality produced many split households. Men often refused to pay alimony (partly because of low wages in state enterprises). Women left in smaller feudal or ancient households faced increasingly difficult conditions for themselves, for their children, and for any other household members. "Double shifts" exhausted the women drawn into wage labor outside the household while obliged to continue surplus labor performance obligations inside (Mace and Mace 1963, 102–105; Kingsbury and Fairchild 1935, 248–251; Stites 1978, 409). Women divorced their husbands (legally or informally) on a rapidly increasing scale after 1922; criminal assaults by and on their husbands grew markedly; and abortions increased as well. The retreat from state supported collectivization of household life had left Soviet citizens with only the pre-revolutionary options in household class structures. Yet, the latter were increasingly difficult to sustain under the actual conditions of the 1920s (Chase 1990, 196–199).

Children in huge numbers abandoned nonviable and unbearable households. This only aggravated the problem of homeless children that the state had hoped to solve by its retreat to individual households. Homeless women reappeared as a social problem when the double shift proved too much of a personal strain or the elderly could no longer be supported. The individual households able to manage the difficult circumstances felt threatened by—and blamed the state for—the "social chaos" created by the homeless population.

By the end of the decade, this situation provoked a second phase of retreat. The state went beyond merely abandoning its original plans to eliminate the individual household in favor of collective institutions. It actively induced or forced Soviet citizens into traditional feudal household structures. Official doctrine portrayed such families as the Soviet ideal—with men as heads of households.[24] New policies moved to force divorced husbands to pay alimony to support children and to discourage divorce in the first place. By 1929, the leading theorist of the Soviet family, S. Vol'fson, could argue that the state had actively to support the feudal and ancient class-structured households. The state, he wrote, needs "to use this social cell" as "an auxiliary social formation" in managing the transition through socialism to communism (Goldman 1993, 310). Of course, he did not use such class analytical terms; he spoke rather in the then standard sociological terms that completely ignored surplus.

If the Soviet reversion to traditional household class structures solved certain pressing problems (freeing scarce state resources for industrial growth and avoiding confrontation with traditionalists over "family values"), it also provoked others. To survive as class structures, feudal and ancient households had to yield enough surplus to sustain their conditions of existence. For women inside feudal households, they had to produce and deliver enough household surplus to their husbands to secure their marriages. Yet they increasingly also undertook paid work outside the home, while the number of relatives living and helping to work inside the household shrank. The real incomes of the men from work outside the home were also mostly shrinking, given the state's efforts to maximize the industrial surplus it appropriated. Likewise, men's farm incomes fell under price pressures (as noted in chapters 6 and 8). In short, husbands had little in the way of incomes with which to offset the strains on their wives. The burdens on their wives reached unbearable proportions. Finally, the double shift similarly undermined the ability of women living in ancient class-structured households to perform enough surplus to enable them to sustain that class structure.

In feudal households, conflicts between producers and appropriators over the size and use of household surplus labor—that is, class conflicts—deepened. Rising rates of alcoholism and divorce and widening antipathies between men and women showed how their class conflicts could be displaced onto and aggravate confrontations around issues other than class. The comparable difficulties besetting ancient class-structured households blocked some women from leaving feudal households and likely thereby worsened tensions within them. Troubles inside Soviet households had effects outside: on workers' productivity, on citizens' civic participation, on children's education and mental health, and much else besides. Many "social problems" included, among their causes, the feudal and ancient class structures to which Soviet policy had reverted and also the unfavorable conditions with which Soviet policy surrounded them. However, the blindness of Soviet thought—both official and popular—toward household class problems contributed to the illusion that abandoning the collectivization of households and returning to a profamily orientation would solve them. As we shall show, the dilemmas of Soviet household class structures, like those of Soviet agricultural and industrial class structures, were never "solved." They remained costly, if untheorized, drains on economic and social development across Soviet history.

The role of women in Soviet technical education provides one example of how unviable household class structures contributed to undermining other Soviet development objectives. Training a new generation of engineers and technicians ranked among the top priorities after the revolution.[25] Soviet leaders tried repeatedly to recruit women into the new technical intelligentsia (Bailes 1978, 201–202). These efforts failed; even when women were enrolled, they withdrew at higher rates than men. The contradictions of Soviet household class structures surely played a part in this costly failure. Women's responsibilities for performing surplus labor inside most Soviet households interfered with their abilities and dispositions to undertake the advanced technical training necessary for rapid Soviet development. Since policy could not address alternative household class structures as possible solutions for this problem, the official response merely bemoaned women's scarcity in technical training institutes and occasionally promoted more child-care facilities.[26]

A 1928 newspaper report reveals another example of the complex impacts of traditional household class structures on Soviet society. Kiev's women, it said, shopped at private rather than state or cooperative shops, replicating women's habits across the USSR (Ball 1990, 166ff.). The first (and presumably most important) reason given was the problem of waiting in lines: the cost of shopping in terms of time. The significance of this cost was formulated by a Soviet woman worker in a 1990 interview, but her words apply as well to the 1920s:

> Our Soviet woman has a very hard life. She has to earn a wage and then run around to the shops to find something to feed her family. All her free time and days off are lost in that way. I have to stand in a different line for each product. I have to get to the store before it opens to buy milk. I have to go to another store for cereal. I have to go to Moscow for meat. (Mandel 1994, 83)

In the 1920s, bearing sole responsibility for performing household surplus labor, women patronized the Nepmen's private stores (short lines) rather than the state and cooperative stores (long lines). This enhanced private profits at the expense of state revenues on a massive scale. In short, women's particular class positions inside their households negatively affected the Soviet state's resources for its prioritized development.

As Goldman (1993) documents, many Soviet women leaders exposed the intolerable burdens faced by women in the 1920s. However, these were understood almost exclusively in terms of the quantity of labor (measured in time and intensity) demanded of them: especially the "double shift" of labor outside as well as inside households. Soviet women as well as men lacked the conceptual apparatus of class analysis that might have enabled them to identify the class structure of household work as part of the problem and hence a class change as part of the solution. Since the only alternative to the traditional feudal and ancient household class structures that they could conceive—a state-run collectivization of consumption—had been declared unaffordable by Soviet leaders, they concluded that women simply had to bear their traditional burden.[27]

A third example, the much-discussed soaring Soviet divorce rate in the 1920s, while often cited, has not yet been linked to household class structures.[28] The revolutionary euphoria of post-1917 Soviet life provoked many new aspirations and opportunities. Women's immobility within traditional household class structures likely became more difficult to bear than in pre-revolutionary times. If rooting exploitation out of Soviet society was proclaimed the highest social value, its dogged survival inside the household likely became untenable, even if the concepts and language needed to identify it explicitly as exploitation were lacking. Husbands and wives clashed not only over the quantities of housework demanded of men and women, but also, unconsciously, over the class relationships within which the work was performed. Divorce, as an increasingly frequent result of such clashes in the 1920s, prompted the growth of ancient in place of feudal household class structures. These, in turn, brought a host of problems that shaped much of the USSR's history: struggles over alimony, child support, physical and psychological damage to household members, vagabondage, public services to support single-parent households, and so on. It would be difficult to exaggerate the impacts of these problems on Soviet history. However much changes in household class structures would have altered divorce rates and/or their social effects and costs, the blockage of such changes shaped Soviet history then and since.

A more complete catalog of the social costs of maintaining traditional household class structures would have to include the effects on women's continued unequal participation in Soviet political and cultural life, on enduring patriarchal customs, on the development of children, on workers' productivity generally, and on many other determinants of Soviet development. Because the Soviet leadership and population could not recognize the existence and social consequences of class structures and conflicts inside households, they could not discuss, let alone evaluate, them. Nor could they compare the costs and benefits of strategies to transform traditional households' class structures. The USSR in the 1920s thus experienced a solidification of traditional household class structures that were hardly supportive of sustained transitions to communist class structures elsewhere in Soviet society.

A parallel with similar results may clarify the point. Studies of the Soviet blindnesses—official and unofficial—toward sexuality have reached conclusions congruous with ours regarding blindness toward class relationships within households. After some vigorous and open discussions of male and female sexuality in the 1920s,

> During the 1930s ... [s]ex surveys disappeared.... All sex education vanished from schools.... A strict puritanical morality was proclaimed for society.... [Soviet society] had restored more traditional links between sexual behavior and marital-family relations ... began consistently to root out and disparage all that was erotic in human beings. (Kon 1993, 23–24)

A doctor, directly involved, described the 1930's Soviet medical approach to female sexuality:

> [T]he notion of primordial female asexuality and non-involvement in all things carnal was implanted in the mass psyche. The education of young girls took on a

puritanical air, sexological problems were ascribed to men only, ... the sex advice bureaux being basically concerned with male sexual problems. (Shcheglov 1993, 157)

He concluded that many Soviet women with sexual problems to which their society is blind "suffer serious neurosis and depression, and even attempt suicide, yet the socially conditioned shame that women bear stops them from seeing a specialist" (Shcheglov 1933, 157). The fact that Soviet women (and men) lacked the concepts with which literally to see, let alone discuss or diagnose, female sexuality (in terms other than morally condemnatory dismissal), contributed to major personal problems on a mass scale. These problems exercised their deleterious effects, directly and indirectly, on production too. Parallel logic and conclusions apply to the Soviet blindness to household class structures and their social effects.

Goldman (1993, 296–336) has documented what in our class-analytical terms we might call the "historic compromise" reached in the 1930s between Soviet enterprises' and households' class structures. The first and second five-year plans sought and obtained a massive movement of women into wage labor. Together with the concurrent drop in real wages (enabling heavy industrialization), this movement further undercut not only the financial but also the interpersonal/emotional cohesion of the families and households of the USSR. Dramatic increases in homeless children, crime, and family breakdowns alarmed state and party officials. Some way had to be found, without additional major demands being placed on state revenues, to address family and household disintegration in the face of women entering the wage labor force and real wages falling. That way was the historic compromise.[29]

On its side, the state mandated a large scale program of day-care centers in enterprises, unions, schools, and other institutions. Soviet women in urban and industrial areas were to resume quite traditional family and household class roles alongside their wage labor positions. Rural women—once again left behind as another wave of young men left the countryside—settled more deeply into their ancient and feudal household class positions.[30] Soviet men were to stop their pursuit of divorce and their evasion of alimony obligations; they were to resume their feudal head-of-household positions. Blind to the overstressed contradictions of these revived feudal and ancient household class structures, both urban and rural, the authorities confronted the continuation of homelessness among large numbers of children as a mystery as well as a policy dilemma. The homelessness of the earlier 1920s had been theorized as a product of revolution and war, but its persistence into the 1930s required another explanation. Homeless children literally could not be thought to be products of the class contradictions specific to Soviet enterprises and households. The resolution of the mystery and dilemma lay in criminalizing the vagabond children; they were a pathological element deserving the harsh punishment and isolation they increasingly received (Ball 1996, 192–197).

Culminating in the June 1936 law that promulgated "family responsibility" (punishing evasion of alimony, virtually outlawing abortion, restricting divorce, etc.), the historic compromise solidified the basic contours of Soviet class structures in enterprises and households. In exchange for state assistance in child care, Soviet men and women were to settle into feudal and ancient household class structures of the traditional sort. Soviet men were to contribute portions of their wages to support and sustain households. Their wives would not only also contribute portions of their wages, but would also deliver their household surplus labor to the husband. He would distribute it to sustain this kind of household class structure.

Soviet industrialization would thereby secure women's labor in the present and their children's labor in the future. The state could save some of its scarce resources because it needed to provide fewer social supports for individuals once the "family" did so. Part of such savings would finance the child-care programs required to enable the women to work outside the home. The rest of the savings would become available for industrial growth.

The political and cultural envelop for the historic compromise was the much-discussed return of official ideology to the celebration of traditional family values and the bureaucratic reliance on the traditional households and their internal class structures. For example, where most Soviet citizens lived after the collectivization of agriculture—on the collective farms or kolkhozes—the reliance on the traditional household was nearly total according to the most comprehensive recent survey of Soviet peasant life in the 1930s (Fitzpatrick 1994b, 112):

> From the peasants' standpoint, however, the household remained the basic unit in the village.... Indeed, in most of the functions of everyday life ... the primacy of the household was untouched, regardless of whether or not jurists recognized it as a legal entity.

Politically, this situation reassured all who had clung to traditional households as islands of stability in a USSR that had overturned so many other aspects of the previous centuries. Culturally, it helped to divert discourse from the harsh realities of labor and income to a nobler focus on rebuilding the Soviet family and household as secure havens in a difficult world. By officially endorsing and solidifying feudal and ancient class structures in Soviet households, the historic compromise buried the remaining class impulses to transform society's intimate arenas (households) and further distanced the USSR after 1936 from its more radical Bolshevik origins. Neither socialism nor communism were ever again seriously associated in the USSR with any fundamental challenge or alternative to such household class structures—neither in practice nor in any significant theoretical debates.

This "historic compromise" on class issues mirrored other compromises reached elsewhere in Soviet society at the same time. For example, in the early 1920s, dramatic plans to transform and improve medical care in the rural areas won widespread support. The often minimally trained "feldshers" had provided most of the rural medical practice in Russia before the Revolution (other than the specialized work of rural midwives). Feldshers were to be replaced by an army of well-trained physicians bringing modern, Soviet medical practice to the countryside. Lenin personally supervised what he viewed as a crucial part of the Soviet revolutionary program and of the strategy to secure the new regime's survival (Weissman 1990). However, first the fiscal exigencies following upon the NEP and then the social consequences of the collectivization of agriculture combined to erode the early revolutionary plans. The original proposals to abolish feldshers as a category of medical practitioner could not be implemented in the 1920s, and by the 1930s they were abandoned. The Soviet state could not provide the physicians desperately needed in the countryside, given its industrial and military priorities and also the political support it sought from socially influential physicians with parochial, professional interests. Thus, "the countryside and the peasantry came to occupy a permanently second-rate position in Soviet society. The resurrection of the feldsher as a legitimate rural practitioner was but one recognition of this fact" (Ramer 1990, 139-140).[31] Alongside abandoning the class transformation of households and industries and also the collectivization of housework, the hoped-for transformation of rural medicine faded away.

As the 1930s passed into the 1940s, industrialization campaigns, five-year plans, political purges, rising expenditures on party, police, and prisons, and anti-Nazi defense campaigns absorbed most of the state's resources. The state drew those resources largely as subsumed class revenues from distributions of the collective farms' surpluses; nonclass revenues by turning the terms of trade against agricultural commodities (lowering agricultural prices relative to industrial prices); and paying low industrial real wages to increase the surplus it appropriated from state capitalist workers. These strategies relied heavily upon rural and urban households, supported by minimal state resources, to produce and sustain workers economically and culturally. For men, the status of lord of the feudal household and the possibility of securing the wife's household surplus labor would compensate for low wages. For the women, motherhood, domesticity, and the status of wage employment were to compensate for low wages and for the household surplus labor they had to perform and deliver to their husbands.

In some ways, this strategy succeeded. Soviet real wages declined over the 1930s. The increased surpluses thereby appropriated in state capitalist enterprises, added to revenues drawn as subsumed class and nonclass payments from the collective farms, enabled rapid industrialization, victory in war, superpower status thereafter, and slowly rising standards of living. On the other hand, this strategy had high costs of long duration. Family life was extremely difficult as women resented their household situations and rebelled against them in different ways. Relationships between husbands and wives became even more alienated and distant than they had been earlier.

The class exploitation of Soviet women inside their households played a role in the bitterness of their emerging attitudes toward their husbands and the family itself.

> What kind of a condition are we in when we finally get home after an hour or more of commuting from work, after another hour of being pushed around in the bus, the subway, the food queue? That's when we take it out on our husbands. . . . The man is the one we've been shopping, cooking, scrubbing, darning the socks for all week, so in our exhausted state we see him as the most immediate enemy, we start shouting, yelling, breaking up the family again. . . . (du Plessix Gray 1990, 186)

This 1980s quotation from the Soviet feminist philosopher Olga Veronina condenses our class argumnent. The anger of woman against man in the household setting, although intense and deeply disruptive of family life, is yet also accompanied by a vague and dimly glimpsed sense of something else—something absent—that is "taken out on the husband." Might that be, in part, the suffering occasioned by being entrapped within an exploitative household class structure that seems inseparable from the desired intimacies of family?

Has this experience of class taken the disguised form of such Russian proverbs as "Women can do everything; men can do the rest" (du Plessix Gray 1990, 47)? Were Soviet women, like other exploited people, both drawn into complicity with their exploitation and also rageful against it? Did rage and complicity combine to damage other aspects of Soviet life including economic growth? One answer is offered by Elvira Ossipova, a Soviet professor, in the late 1980s:

> If our men can't manage to curb the aggressive, sadistic element in their spouse's characters, women will always end up tyrannizing them, like no other women I can think of in history. (du Plessix Gray 1990, 48)

Another part of the answer is offered in a recent survey of late Soviet literature by and about women: "Gender disposition in the Soviet Union today corroborates Simone de Beauvoir's apercu that men have found more complicity in women than the oppressor usually finds in the oppressed" (Goscilo 1993, 237).

We interpret these remarks from a class-theoretic perspective. The USSR defined and celebrated itself in terms of eradicating exploitation. Yet it maintained exploitation inside its industries and its households. At both social sites, alienated, bitter, oppressive, frustrating, and mutually destructive relationships festered and spawned their costly social consequences.

The combined pressures of low wages, hard working conditions, and household class conflicts contributed to the severe problems of worker alcoholism, absenteeism, low productivity, and workplace irresponsibility that increasingly plagued Soviet industry and agriculture over the decades since World War Two. Nor did moral suasion, political pressure, and the growing provision of consumer durables succeed in resolving the long-simmering crisis of Soviet households. The class as well as nonclass conflicts besetting those households remained a major problem throughout Soviet history. That the costs to Soviet agricultural and industrial development from the official commitment to feudal and ancient class-structured households may well have exceeded the gains is obvious. That the question was never even raised is tragic.

No doubt, the resources required for the priorities of industrialization and defense would have placed heavy pressures on households with communist class structures had the Soviet state and Party fostered them. Since they did not, even marginally after 1930, it is difficult to asses how they might have functioned differently inside the USSR. However, we may reasonably suppose that the absence of significant communist class-structured households deprived generations of children of any household model of communist class relations that they might have taken with them into factories, farms, and offices. Then again, exploitation within feudal class-structured households probably conditioned Soviet children to accept exploitation in the state capitalist enterprises as adults. Perhaps the recent transition from state back to private capitalism in the former USSR owes its speed and relative smoothness in part to the ease with which feudal and ancient class households can coexist with and provide laborers for either kind of capitalism.

Alternative class scenarios were and are possible. The rapacious private capitalism now spreading in the former USSR may add burdens to feudal and ancient class-structured households that will suffice to explode them. Russians may then become as accustomed as U.S. citizens today to discourses (mostly reactionary) on the collapse of families and family values. Perhaps a new movement to rediscover communist class-structured households may emerge, or else a return to notions of eliminating individual or group households altogether as sites of production. The history of the USSR—because it remained steadfastly blind to the issue of alternative class structures of household production—bequeathed few conclusions that might have helped citizens after the USSR collapsed to cope with the household crises of their societies today. To refocus assessments of the USSR on its class processes in households as well as enterprises may yet help to yield useful lessons for their citizens and beyond. In any case, no class history of the USSR's rise and fall can legitimately ignore the class structures of household labor and their complex social effects.

## Notes

1. Since class analyses of households (as distinguished from analyses that ignore the class dimensions of household organization) are extremely rare—witness Anderson (1995, 49-67)—our inclusion of households here yields results whose implications sometimes reach beyond Soviet history.
2. Of course, the inverse holds as well. How class structures evolved inside Soviet households depended in part on how class structures evolved outside. Interactions among class structures at these different social sites are central components of the particular class history of the USSR this book seeks to unfold.

3. Meyer (1991) surveys the general impact of the war (men departing, refugees fleeing, economy disintegrating) on Russian women.
4. Further possibilities, apparently occurring rather infrequently, included other household members (e.g., grandparents or other relatives) taking the feudal appropriator position. Also, we do not here investigate the possibilities of multiple class structures existing within households, although a more detailed analysis of the USSR would require that.
5. Of course, this class-structural problem was not raised in explicitly class terms. Note also that the distinction between household and farm production was not always fixed or clear in practice; we keep it distinct here only for analytical clarity.
6. The household serfs of such women could include younger males, but more likely comprised the younger wives left behind in the household by younger males who had also been drafted for the war. Bohac (1991) describes the extended, multigenerational families that comprised the household structures of Russia before the war.
7. The different quantities of housework by men and women—measured by time—does not reveal their class relationship. A feudal housewife may work as many hours as she would within an ancient household. Yet her relationship to her children, men, her work outside the household, and so on would be quite different. Feudal serfs in many situations have struggled to become ancients whether or not their work time would be reduced. Similarly, many wage laborers in many kinds of capitalism struggle to become self-employed ancients even when no reduction of hours worked in the two different class structures is foreseeable.
8. In class terms, women as feudal lords or ancients within households had to distribute portions of their meager surpluses to sustain such men (since these men brought little or no wage or other revenue into the household). In the feudal households of the past, husbands' demands on their wives' household surplus were potentially modified by the husband's external income.
9. Du Plessix Gray (1990, 48–49) attributed these quotations to a Soviet marriage counselor and a professional editor. Her work catalogs complaints made by Soviet women about their men and vice versa, illustrating high levels of mutual hostility, distrust, and emotionally distressed gender relations.
10. Here we encounter again different definitions of key terms. "Communist" was often applied to households synonymously with "communal" or "collective." Most but not all of such households owned household property in common, nor did all make decisions collectively, and they disagreed on which decisions would be made collectively and which individually. Most importantly, for our purposes, such households only occasionally organized the production, appropriation, and distribution of household surplus in a communist class structure as here defined. We use "communist" to refer only to households' class structure (i.e., surplus organization).
11. While we focus here on communes that extended collectivization to members' households, household communes were also established outside both urban and rural communes as separate entities. There, revolutionary militants sometimes established households with communist class structures while the members worked regularly in Soviet enterprises not organized as communes in any sense of the term then in use. Frustrated revolutionary militants after 1917 likely found compensation by establishing inside households the collectivisms that it seemed too soon and too difficult to establish outside.
12. In our class analytical terms, a new set of state-expenditures—X(COM)—might have arisen to build communist households. If communist households were also taxed, a new state revenue flow—SSCR(COM)—would appear. State officials would then occupy communist subsumed class positions receiving a distributed share of the surplus appropriated collectively in each private communist household. As part of revolutionary strategy, the state might have spent more on communist than feudal and ancient households while it taxed the latter more heavily than the former.
13. Alexandra Kollontai and Inessa Armand were two Bolshevik leaders who explicitly and repeatedly

stressed the importance of communal housekeeping. Lenin's speech at the First All-Russian Congress of Women Workers in 1918 referred to passing "from small household economy to social economy." Trotsky celebrated "collective family housekeeping units" in a 1923 *Pravda* article (1970, 27). However, as Rowbotham noted, ideas of communal housing were suppressed, resisted, or rendered moot by the social crises of the times (Rowbotham 1992, 189). Nor did these ideas include references to household surplus structures.

14. The household communes that sprang up after 1917 had some partial forerunners in a few utopian "moments" of previous Russian history (Stites 1989, 17). Notwithstanding the limited scale of post-1917 experiments in housing communes, they exceeded what had been attempted before in Russian history.

15. Rowbotham, discussing the USSR in the same period, concludes that both official and popular discourse could not surpass old Marxian views of family and sexual matters as secondary, derivative, superstructural, and subjective phenomena versus the primary, basic, economic, and objective bases of society: "There was no alternative theory" (1974, 151). We argue that theoretical struggles over household production were more complex.

16. This applies also to the few feminists calling for an explicit class analysis of households. Delphy (1984, 57–77), for example, does not perform the systematic class analysis she calls for, confuses surplus labor with surplus value, finds virtually all women to be slaves within their households, and differs in many other respects from the Marxian class analysis in this book.

17. All the quotations in the text are taken from a compilation entitled *The Woman Question* (1951) that gathered selected statements from the works of Marx, Engels, Lenin, and Stalin.

18. An exception was E.O. Kabo in the 1920s. Her dissenting opinions receive a brief discussion in Goldman (1993, 46–48).

19. As Rowbotham (1974, 134–169) shows, most Soviet women, especially but not only in the rural areas, still functioned often within strict patriarchies. Even where women became feudal lords of farms and households (because husbands had died or left) or presided over ancient class structured farms and households, their success or even survival were precarious because of the powers wielded by the men in their communities.

20. In terms of chapter 6's discussion, the Soviet state confronted this dilemma: $SV(C) < SSCP(C)$. The surplus it appropriated in state capitalist industry did not suffice to fund the conditions of existence for that industry (which included its expansion). The next chapter explains why the NEP risked weakening the state's effort to offset that insufficiency, even while it helped to overcome it by turning the terms of trade against ancient and small capitalist farmers and taxing them.

21. Soviet officials calculated—as per chapter 6's state equation—that the surplus appropriated from state capitalist workers [$SV(C)$] plus whatever taxes they could raise from the public (NCR) would not suffice to allow *both* subsumed class outlays to secure and build state industry [$SSCP(C)$] and other outlays such as paying for the collectivization of households (Y). The two revenue terms on the left side of the basic state equation being too small to fund both of the expenditure terms on the right side, they chose to forego the (Y) term.

22. The evidence suggests that Bolshevik policies for women's equality aimed also to bring women out of the households to contribute their labor power to the construction of industrial socialism. In any case, the policies changed many nonclass dimensions of Soviet households as they increased women's industrial labor.

23. As many researchers have shown, Soviet household size dropped sharply across the 1920s (Goldman 1993, 164).

24. Of course the survival of women-headed ancient households—on grounds of the numerical excess of women—had to be countenanced, but ancient households were remarginalized in terms of the ideal; they became a clear second-best.

25. The engineers and technicians we refer to engaged in securing conditions of existence (maintaining machinery, research and development of both new technology and new products, etc.) of surplus-producing workers in state industrial capitalist enterprises. Engineers' and technicians' salaries and budgets were distributions to them (subsumed class payment) from the surpluses appropriated by the Soviet Council of Ministers. The latter comprised, as noted in chapter 6, the state capitalist appropriators of industrial surpluses. The engineers and technicians were thus a state capitalist subsumed class.
26. Women did enter the fields of education and medical care. But there they occupied the lowest professional levels that required the least quantities and qualities of training. Only later under the five-year plans did training opportunities for women expand dramatically, although then too at specially lowered levels thought appropriate for women's limited "capacities" (Davis 1990, 161; Lapidus 1978; Scott 1974).
27. Goldman (1993) exhaustively documents how Soviet women leaders repeatedly tried to press the state for resources to ease the labor burden, although without much success.
28. In 1918, Moscow registered 28 divorces per 100 marriages; by 1929 this number had reached 78 per 100 marriages. Goldman's discussion (1993, 297ff.) is exemplary in its detail, documentation, and discussion of the social context without any reference to class whatsoever.
29. As Goldman shows in the pages cited, this was a compromise on all sides, since the initial mass movement of women into wage labor led to a short-lived resurgence of the old revolutionary demands for socialization of households (what we prefer to call the collectivization of household consumption). Those who made those demands had to settle for little more than socialized day care while accepting in exchange the formal solidification of feudal and ancient household class structures.
30. One source estimated that during the 1930s some 18.5 million rural people, "predominantly able-bodied young men," left to work in nonagricultural, urban enterprises (Merl 1993, 41).
31. Research on other aspects of Soviet medical practice and administration in rural areas confirm the general picture here of dramatic proposals, plans, and commitments in the early years after 1917 that foundered on the realities of resource limitations, more important priorities among Soviet leaders, and political compromises the latter felt compelled to reach to achieve those priorities (Davis 1990; Solomon 1990).

# CHAPTER 8

# The New Economic Policies of the 1920s

Bolshevik requisitions of food and raw materials during war communism provoked such contradictions and resistances that Lenin had to proclaim the New Economic Policy (NEP) of 1921. The NEP, while partly a solution also engendered other contradictions that prompted Stalin's strategic shift to the collectivization of agriculture in the late 1920s. The recurring difficulties emerged mostly from the ancient (and slowly emerging capitalist) farmers' efforts to improve their situation. The state sought to placate agriculture while simultaneously favoring industry at the expense of agriculture. The basic logic of the NEP paralleled that of war communism, although the mechanisms had changed significantly. Hence this chapter begins with a brief résumé of war communism's logic.

War communism's requisitions of the ancients' agricultural output were not exchanges; they involved no prices (Carr 1985, vol. 2, 150; Dobb 1966, 102–103). Little or nothing was given in return for requisitioned output. Without requisitioning, their surpluses would have remained available for farmers to secure their ancient class structures (for repairs, insurance and contingency funds, more equipment, and so on). State requisitions were thus a compulsory ancient subsumed class revenue—SSCR(A)—that ancient farmers paid to the state.[1] This payment supplemented the surplus values that the state appropriated from the productive laborers in state capitalist industrial enterprises. Taken together these two different surpluses comprised the key revenue flows enabling the state to survive militarily. However, deprived of their surplus, the farmers' ancient class structures were jeopardized as was their personal survival. Thus, while initially successful, the requisitioning strategy eventually undermined the alliance between peasants and workers that had achieved the October Revolution. Undermining this alliance constituted the "Achilles' heel of War Communism" (Dobb 1966, 103).

Reacting to requisitioning, the ancients could attempt to increase the surplus labor they performed by working longer hours and/or reducing the portion of output they consumed (fruits of their necessary labor). Either reaction would further strain already difficult personal circumstances. They might squeeze out more surplus through partnerships—often problematic for individualist farmers—to economize on certain costs. Farmers might also pressure their wives to perform increased surplus labor inside feudal households to compensate husbands for farm surpluses lost to requisitions. Yet such reactions risked household class conflicts and interpersonal tensions that could impact badly on the viability of the ancient farm.

Caught between requisitions and the risks of all possible responses, many ancients tolerated the situation for a time after the revolution. They feared that if the Reds lost the civil war, the Whites might retake the land that the revolution had granted to them. Other ancients, often the more prosperous, expressed their opposition by producing grain for the Whites. The different reactions reflected disparities between richer and poorer farmers who all occupied the *same* ancient class position (Dobb 1966, 105–106; Nove 1989, 51).

However, to survive the requisitions, ancients increasingly hid their grain stocks and/or consumed the animals that had been means of production. The latter jeopardized the next period's harvest. By 1921, Lenin and other Soviet leaders recognized the dangers of these reactions, the building anger, and open revolts. The class crisis of the ancients threatened to turn Bolshevik victories into defeats.

Another class crisis loomed for workers inside state capitalist industrial enterprises. Mounting anger and even strikes stemmed in part from reduced real wages because of the state's increasingly difficult problems in requisitioning food. The state's effective absorption of labor unions had reduced their collective bargaining powers. Demands for increased industrial productivity combined with gross planning inefficiencies to generate great stress, overwork, and exhaustion. Workers variously directed their anger at Vesenkha, the state, the Party, or even socialism generally.

The mutually aggravating class crises in private ancient agriculture and state capitalist industry threatened to undo the new system. Further entangling these two crises and the struggles they provoked was the history of the many new industrial workers. They had only recently left the ancient class structures in agriculture. Reducing their wages, eroding their recently acquired power, and intensifying their labor might drive them to abandon factories and return to farms.

Beside these threats, another class issue (alongside the many nonclass issues that also threatened the new USSR) deserves special mention. Following the revolution, Vesenkha established a hierarchical system of subagencies (Glavki). The system centralized the appropriation of the state capitalist industrial surplus in Vesenka's hands while it centralized the management of production in the Glavki. Individuals displaced or demoted by these centralizations became oppositional. Local state officials who had appropriated surpluses in decentralized state capitalist industrial enterprises no longer did so. As surplus appropriation was centralized by Vesenkha, they lost their positions or became subordinate managers. Local managers who had received subsumed class distributions from local state surplus appropriators were replaced by fewer, much more centralized managers, or else subordinated to them. Many local appropriators and managers reacted badly to these centralizations of state capitalism.

They included a disparate grouping of Bolsheviks, former private capitalists and managers, leaders of committees of workers and trade unions, and local and regional state officials from before and just after the revolution. For them, the Bolshevik nationalization of enterprises was much less contentious than the different matter of who would manage them and how: centralization versus decentralization (sometimes articulated as "socialist" versus "independent" industrial organization). Thus Carr concludes: "The real issue in the period of war communism was not the nationalization of industry ... but the attempt of the state to administer industry on socialist lines" (1985, 175). Dobb quotes an activist of the time: "Enterprises were deprived of economic independence in operative work and *depended on the state budget*" (1966, 110, italics added). Given all the other pressures undermining Soviet state capitalism, the internal opposition of a portion of its local managers added yet another burden that it could not afford.

The tensions and problems entailed in the transition from decentralized to centralized management of state capitalist industry did not dissipate once centralization had been achieved. Conflicts arose over the chain of command and relative status among subagencies. Their personnel occupied the *same* capitalist subsumed class position: in exchange for salaries (paid from distributions of state capitalist surpluses), they performed the management processes needed for the state to appropriate industrial surpluses. However, these managers occupied *different* nonclass positions within the distributions of power, status, and income inside the bureaucracy. Conflicts over the nonclass processes of distributing authority, status, privileges, and income among them produced complex and shifting alliances internally and sometimes also with social groups outside the bureaucracy. The formations, activities, and dissolutions of such alliances could have profound impacts upon the class structure of the USSR.

Struggles over power or status are different from struggles over class, over the production, appropriation, and distribution of surplus. However, since class and nonclass struggles interact, our class analysis of Soviet history must pay attention to both. We shall argue that the struggles over power and prestige inside the Soviet state bureaucracy interacted with its complex, multiple class structure in ways crucial to understanding the rise, development and eventual collapse of the USSR.

Under war communism, the state capitalist subsumed class of industrial managers not only had to develop new ways of relating to one another. They also needed to construct new relationships with other state officials—members of Vesenkha—who appropriated and distributed the industrial surplus. In short, the rapid transition to and then centralization of Soviet state capitalism imposed a massive task of creating effective bureaucratic organization: quickly, under wartime pressures, and with completely inexperienced personnel. Disorganization, bottlenecks, production inefficiencies, and conflicts between and among different bureaucratic levels proliferated (Dobb 1966, 109–116). A central problem was the recurring inadequacy of inputs made available to industrial enterprises that were nevertheless pressed by the state to meet output quotas.

The war communism period degenerated into the war communism crisis. Ancient class structures clashed with state industrial capitalism over requisitioning ancient surpluses; state capitalist appropriators clashed with capitalist subsumed classes (over centralization and related issues); factory workers clashed with managers and with Vesenkha over the pressures for surplus production and the chaotic conditions of state industry; and so on. When struggles over nonclass processes (over allocating power and prestige across bureaucratic levels, over the distribution of power among different ethnic, religious, and regional populations, etc.) were mixed into the contemporaneous class struggles, a potentially explosive conjuncture materialized. Lenin answered his perennial question, "What is to be done?" with a major shift in both class and nonclass tactics, the NEP.

## Relations between Agriculture and Industry: An Overview

The NEP aimed to diffuse the explosive situation. The new, more supportive agrarian policy helped to end the near revolt of the ancient farmers. The new industrial policy helped to alleviate tensions among the USSR's workers, surplus appropriators, and managers, and among its different bureaucratic layers. Yet despite achieving palpable relief from approaching disaster, the NEP also set in motion social changes that provoked new contradictions and tensions. Conflicts evolved over those changes and what they portended for the goals and the future of Soviet society. At issue were different interpretations of the effects wrought by the NEP and different notions of what the state should do next in terms of its agricultural and industrialization strategies.

Questions that rose to the fore included: Was the NEP reviving and encouraging an agricultural capitalist class? If so, should the NEP nevertheless be continued or even strengthened to encourage the supply of food and raw materials by ancient and emerging capitalist farmers that was so badly needed for industrialization? Or should the NEP be disbanded in favor of a different strategy to accomplish rapid industrialization: direct state pressure and demands on the ancient and the emerging capitalist farms? Those who supported at least a short-run allowance of rural capitalism came to be known as the "right-wing opposition," while opponents comprised the "left-wing opposition" (Dobb, 1966, 199 and 183).[2]

The ideological and organizational struggles between these opponents—in the realms of culture and politics—were conflicts among occupants of the same few state capitalist fundamental and subsumed class positions (within Vesenkha, the party, and the Glavki). They all agreed on the goals of securing and expanding what we understand as state industrial capitalism. In their different theory and language, the shared goal was "building socialism and thereby the transition to communism" (a goal often missed by non-Marxian economists who examine this debate as if some abstract and absolute standard of "efficiency" had been everyone's goal).[3]

Our class analysis of the NEP begins with the problem that it inherited from war communism: how to secure desired flows of food, raw materials, and new industrial workers from agriculture, but now without requisitions. The state's imposition of grain taxes to obtain a portion of the ancient farmers' surpluses provoked such opposition that Lenin both lowered and converted them to money taxes (Dobb, 1966, 130). NEP allowed ancient farmers to sell grain in private markets for money. Private and state markets, money, and private merchanting enterprises—largely eliminated under war communism—were reintroduced.[4]

Under these conditions, the old contradiction between state capitalist industry, on the one hand, and private ancient and emerging small capitalist agriculture, on the other, reappeared. Now, however, the old contradiction changed because it was mediated by a combination of state *and* private market institutions. The central question now became: would that combination work to enable or hobble the expansion of state capitalist industry that remained not only the Soviet priority but the very definition of a successful socialism? Would this mixed system of state and private markets and merchants yield sufficient food and raw materials at prices favorable to industrial growth? Would the needed immigration of laborers from the farms to the factories continue?

To answer these questions, we return to the Soviet state equation depicting its revenues and expenditures in class terms:

$$SV(C) + SSCR(C+A+F) + NCR = SSCP(C) + X(A+C+F) + Y$$

Let us recall the basic class problem of the new Soviet regime. State industrial capitalism could not appropriate enough surplus value—$SV(C)$—from its own workers to achieve its priorities of military security and industrial growth—the key components of $SSCP(C)$. In terms of the equation above, $SV(C) < SSCP(C)$. After war communism, the new NEP solution was a combination of agricultural taxes and state and private market exchanges between state industrial and private farm products. If the NEP solution failed to supplement state capitalist industry's own surplus with sufficient subsumed class distributions from farmers, the state would face a crisis yet again. Its desire to expand $SSCP(C)$ for industrial growth would again be blocked. Party and state leaders hesitated to pursue the alternative strategy of increasing the exploitation of state industrial workers.

Our class equation of the state budget allows us to show how the Soviet leadership tried, throughout the NEP, to adjust all of the equation's revenue and expenditure variables so as to maximize its outlays on industrial growth. New or increased excise taxes and fees raised its subsumed class revenues from all the class structures within Soviet society—SSCR(C+A+F). Comparable levies upon individuals raised its nonclass revenues—NCR. At the same time, the state also reduced most of its other expenditures—X(A+C+F) + Y—to maximize instead the subsumed class outlays for industrial expansion—SSCP(C). There was one exception; certain outlays to provide conditions of existence for ancient farmers—X(A)—aimed to secure their tax payments to the state—SSCR(A). While effective, these budget adjustments did not suffice to overcome the gap between the surplus appropriated from the industrial laborers and what the state deemed to be essential industrial investment. Nor could the gap be breached by that other kind of nonclass revenue, state borrowing. Foreign states and banks would not extend much credit to the pariah "communist regime," and the possibilities of domestic credit were far too small.[5]

In relation to agriculture, the NEP strategy of industrial growth came to depend not only on the new grain tax but also—and crucially—on how the state administered the newly reintroduced state and private markets for agricultural products. As we shall show, the state could and did set prices (deviating from values) in the state markets, attempting via this unequal exchange to siphon an added value flow into state capitalist industry. Yet success in state markets now depended also on the private markets and on the prices emerging there from bargains among farmers, private merchants (the Nepmen), and individual consumers of agricultural products. In any case, a successful NEP required a thriving agriculture. To this end, soon after the NEP's inauguration, new decrees further empowered the ancients to hire labor power and lease new lands. Allowing small-scale private capitalism thereby to return and grow in the countryside had become an acceptable price to pay for building Soviet socialism.

NEP's impact on ancient farmers had complex consequences. Freed from the constraints of war communism, ancient farmers could distribute portions of their own surpluses to expand their own ancient farm production. They leased more land and rented and purchased more animals and farming equipment.[6] Some hired laborers and thus become small capitalist farmers. With a fixed rate of taxation, rising ancient and capitalist farm outputs brought rising state revenues—SSCR(A+C). Moreover, the ancient and capitalist farms could still further expand outputs whenever the state's procurement prices and/or private market prices for food and raw materials rose.[7]

Such improved circumstances for ancient farmers had other positive consequences. They had far less reason to consume their means of production or otherwise reduce production as had been their bitter responses to war communism's requisitioning. The pressures on women to produce feudal household surpluses fell, since such offsets to farm losses from requisitioning were no longer necessary. However, while rising state and private prices for agricultural products improved conditions for ancient and small capitalist farmers, they also faced prices for the industrial products they purchased that exceeded those products' values. On balance, farmers' exchanges with state industries still remained unequal and unfavorable. They gave more value than they received in return. Especially the poorer and middle-level ancient farmers remained mired in very precarious economic conditions.

The coexistence of state and private markets and merchants kept the state from ever fully controlling the terms of trade between agriculture and industry. The exchanges between commodities produced in the different class structures of industry and agriculture depended on ever-changing state *and* private decisions. For example, competition from private markets in grain pushed reluctant state officials to raise state procurement prices to avoid the risk of reduced state grain purchases. Such reactions affected not only the class structures in agriculture, but state industrial capitalism as well. Further state price (and nonprice) actions followed and provoked private responses in the ceaseless interaction of private and state decisions that marked the NEP. To take another example, the private merchants (Nepmen) often charged relatively high prices for the manufactures they sold to farmers. This not only adversely affected class structures in agriculture. It also meant that the gains from this trade accrued to Nepmen's profits rather than to the state as a resource for industral growth. One reaction of Soviet leaders was to constrict or even replace private merchants in favor of state merchants.

Over the entire NEP period, the so-called price scissors (the ratio of agricultural to industrial prices) remained open—now more, now less—against the class structures in agriculture. In 1923–24, an index of that ratio stood at 34 (based on a prewar price ratio of 100). This produced a crisis in agriculture whose likely consequences frightened Soviet leaders; hence by the end of the decade (1928–29), the index had risen to 90. This closing of the scissors dramatically improved conditions for class structures in agriculture. However, despite its rise, that index never returned to 100 during the decade. The scissors never closed fully. Market exchanges continually transferred value from private class structures in agriculture to state capitalist industry—although the scissors' gradual closing did shrink the size of the transfers across the 1920s.[8]

The terms-of-trade transfers allowed more investment in state capitalist industry than would have been possible using only the surplus appropriated from industrial workers plus the taxes on farmers, individuals, and feudal households. However, the farmers' improving terms of trade diminished the transfers across the 1920s decade. Because this threatened the pace of industrial growth—the standard of socialist success and Soviet security—Stalin responded with agricultural collectivization. State industrial capitalist surplus appropriation, taxes on farms and households, and price manipulations simply did not suffice to meet the threat. A radically new policy emerged: a change in the class structure in agriculture. That might finally enable state policies to secure the increased transfers of agricultural surpluses required for rapid industrialization.

## The NEP in Class and Value Terms

We examine the contradictions of the terms of trade policy—crucial across the NEP period—by using Marxian concepts of value, surplus value, and market price. The gains and losses to industry and agriculture depended on the relationship between prices and values for each sector of the economy. Because there were now two sets of markets and prices, private and state-administered, we must adjust our equations to include both prices. This will allow us to pinpoint the mechanisms and problems of the NEP's terms-of-trade policies and their impacts on class structures in both sectors.

First, we need to acknowledge an assumption we make to simplify the analysis of value/price relations. The NEP period was generally inflationary for all commodities. Since all prices rose, the terms of trade between industry and agriculture depended on which sector's prices rose more. Our approach connects the terms of trade to a net value transferred from agriculture to industry via unequal exchanges between the sectors: unequal precisely because the price/value disparity was different in industry than in agriculture. As we shall show, the prices of state capitalist industrial products tended to exceed their values (yielding extra income to industry) *more* than the comparable excess of prices over values of agricultural products. To focus on the unequal exchange mechanism of this net value transfer, we will make the simplifying assumption that the values of industrial and agricultural products remained the same throughout NEP. If, as is likely, labor productivity rose faster in industry than agriculture, our argument below would only be strengthened.[9]

Our analysis includes the emerging small capitalist farmers (kulaks) as well as the ancient farmers. The former were especially important because they supplied a disproportional share of total marketed food and raw materials. We also include the complexity of both state and private merchants because they played different roles in mediating among different class structures.

To offer farmers new incentives to expand marketed supplies of grains and raw materials, the NEP reestablished private markets and prices while it also raised the state-administered prices paid by state merchants for those farm products. This dual market structure, especially for grain, produced a unique set of contradictions for the state and for its capitalist industry. The state wanted grain prices high enough to induce more marketed output, yet low enough to keep food cheap and hence industrial workers' wages low. Had there been no private market, the state's grain price policy would still have been beset by opposing forces and tendencies. With a private market and merchants, the state faced insurmountable obstacles in trying to manage its internal terms of trade.

As noted earlier, when state procurement prices and private market prices for raw materials and grains exceeded their values, private ancient and small capitalist farmers enjoyed a nonclass flow of revenue (NCR) in addition to the surpluses they appropriated within their respective class structures.[10] This excess of price over value—an unequal exchange—accrued to farmers at the expense of both the state and private merchants who bought their products. Early in the NEP period, farmers enjoyed this favorable exchange position. Moreover, when the state-set prices were lower than private market prices, farmers could shift supplies to private from state merchants or speculate by retaining inventories in the hope that the state might raise prices to secure supplies.

To maximize profits in its industrial enterprises, the Soviet state sought to keep wages down by keeping food cheap. To that end its state procurement prices for grain were lower than private market prices for most of the NEP period. The farmers' reactions repeatedly forced the state reluctantly to raise its prices. In contrast, the state did not set its procurement prices for agricultural raw materials much below private market prices. Thus, where possible, Soviet farmers reallocated their production to raw materials from grain. This aggravated the overall grain supply situation and thereby contributed eventually to undermining the NEP itself.

The higher the state or private prices paid to farmers, the greater the costs for the state or private merchants who handled this trade. These merchants' profits would be squeezed or erased unless they could lower their other costs (expenses of handling goods, bookkeeping, and so forth) and/or increase the resale prices of agricultural products to their final consumers: state capitalist industries and individual wage earners.[11] The state merchants were charged with the basic task of grain collection, to be purchased at the least possible cost, for all the state's needs. Yet, they had to compete with private merchants. While Nepmen could hire and fire their employees and otherwise keep merchanting costs down, the state's merchanting bureaucracy coupled with socialist notions of job security hobbled its competitive status. The Nepmen prospered accordingly. Their wealth and ostentation, contrasting sharply with the economic hardship all around them, became a growing problem for and reproach to the egalitarian socialist image projected as the Soviet regime's fundamental commitment. State merchants had difficulty matching the Nepmen's higher prices paid to farmers because that would raise food costs and hence industrial workers' wages. State officials pressed the state merchants not to do this since it would reduce the surpluses appropriated from the productive workers in state capitalist industry.

The problems posed by the Nepmen went well beyond their competition with state grain merchants and their ostentatious new wealth. After all, most grain and raw materials purchasing remained in the state procurement system, not with private merchants.[12] In contrast, Nepmen prevailed in the markets where farmers purchased industrial products as either farming inputs or consumer goods. They were the primary retail sellers of industrial goods in rural areas for most of the NEP period.[13] This asymmetry—state merchants dominated wholesale markets as buyers of agricultural products while private merchants dominated retail markets as sellers of industrial goods—created severe problems for the state's overall economic development strategy. Eventually they provoked the state to take over retail marketing along with its collectivization of agriculture.

Nepmen purchased industrial goods from state capitalist industry at state-administered (wholesale) prices that were always set to exceed their values per unit. Especially in the NEP's early years, Nepmen, far more than state merchants, occupied this role of merchants for state capitalist industry. The Nepmen had little choice but to engage in such an unequal exchange benefiting state capitalist enterprises. Given their other merchanting costs, Nepmen's profits then depended on reselling these state capitalist industrial products to ancient and capitalist farmers and wage workers at private-market (retail) prices well above the wholesale prices that the Nepmen had paid.[14]

The role of Nepmen in retail trade, especially in rural areas, posed a new and risky dilemma for the state. For example, suppose the state further raised the wholesale prices of its industrial commodities above their values, thereby generating added revenues in its (unequal) exchanges with the Nepmen. Suppose further that the state increased these prices *faster* than the prices that state merchants paid to farmers for grain and raw materials. By so turning the terms of trade against agriculture, the state could transfer added values to the strategic priority of industrial growth. However, Nepmen could and did act in ways that frustrated the state's strategy. They did this by raising their retail prices to farmers at an even more rapid rate than the state had raised the wholesale prices charged to the Nepmen. In other words, Nepmen could widen the private retail-wholesale price difference in their own favor.[15]

Such higher private prices charged to farmers eroded, erased, or sometimes reversed incentives to produce and bring more grain and raw materials to market. Thus, even when state procurement prices for the latter were raised to stimulate the farmers' production, the Nepmen's price increases could and did undermine the state's stimulus. The Nepmen undercut the state's strategy by their actions' impact on the terms of trade—the scissors—that actually confronted the farmers. The Soviet leader Kamenev recognized "the new scissors which cut into pieces both our industry and our good relations with the peasantry" (Carr 1958, 438).[16]

The Soviet state reacted more than once by constraining the Nepmen's freedom of operation in private markets. However, this risked worsening the already limited flow of manufactures to farmers: another disincentive for farmers to market agricultural goods. Nonetheless, throughout the NEP period, but especially after 1925, the state extended its own retail operations and its controls over private retail trade in manufactures. It gradually replaced the dominance of private merchants and prices with state merchants and state-set prices in the retail markets for industrial goods. However, the state simultaneously constricted the production of light industrial goods destined for rural markets and for individual consumption (preferring, as always, to use them for heavy industrial growth). The resulting shortages of industrial inputs for agriculture and of consumer goods, especially in rural areas, kept retail prices on what remained of free markets significantly above state-set retail prices (Nove 1989, 147; Bettelheim 1978, 152). Because the state did not raise its retail prices of manufactures and in fact perversely lowered them, the excess demand (long lines) for manufactures was aptly described as a "goods famine" (Nove 1989, 129–131). The resulting disincentive impact on farmers to supply more grain and raw material was then no great surprise.

We may now summarize the NEP's complex impacts on the class structures in agriculture. Both ancient and small capitalist farmers gained nonclass revenues (NCR) because they received rising state-set and private prices higher than the values of their products. But both also had to pay out rising shares of their surpluses (SSCP) to cover the more rapidly rising prices of manufactured agricultural equipment and other inputs such as fuel and fertilizers that they purchased from state merchants and Nepmen. The likewise more rapidly rising retail prices of manufactured consumer goods also absorbed more of individual farmers' personal incomes, which added to the pressures on ancient and small capitalist farmers.

Because the terms of trade favored state capitalist industry over the NEP period taken as a whole, the overall net effect was, with relatively few exceptions, to place both agricultural class structures and the mass of agricultural population under severe strain. The farmers' ancient and small capitalist class structures gained less from high selling prices than they lost from the combination of taxes and high buying prices. Thus, they lacked sufficient revenues to secure their conditions of existence. In the terms of our equations:

$$\text{ancient farmers: } SV(A) + NCR < SSCP(A)$$
$$\text{capitalist farmers: } SV(C) + NCR < SSCP(C)$$

A similar set of debilitating inequalities beset the rural population in their capacity as consumers.[17] Their incomes fell short of their necessarily higher expenditures to purchase industrial wage goods at rising retail prices:

$$\text{ancient farmers: } V(A) < P_M \times UV_M$$
$$\text{workers for capitalist farmers: } V(C) < P_M \times UV_M$$

What agricultural class structures and rural consumers lost, the Soviet state, its state capitalist industry, and state merchants gained. Here we consider first state capitalist enterprises alone, then in combination with state merchants, and finally we present the *net* state gains from taxes and from the terms of trade between industry and agriculture (after eliminating the internal transfers—value flows—between state enterprises and state merchants). Receiving state-set wholesale prices above unit values for their manufactured goods provided industrial enterprises with additional nonclass revenues from selling those goods to state and private merchants.[18] State-set prices of raw materials above their values imposed on state capitalist industry correspondingly higher outlays to state and private merchants to pay for these raw materials. Recall that unless merchants reduced their own profits or costs, their need to pay farmers higher raw materials prices translated into the higher prices they charged to state capitalist industry. Such higher prices for inputs necessitated increased subsumed class distributions by state capitalist industries to the merchants. The state's manipulation of both their industrial goods' and raw materials' prices enabled the net flow of value to benefit state capitalist industry: $SV(C) + NCR > SSCP(C)$.[19] Over the entire NEP period state capitalist industry gained at the expense of the ancient and capitalist class structures in agriculture.[20]

A more complete, albeit more complex, picture of state revenues and expenditures under the NEP requires including the value flows of state merchants alongside those of state industrial enterprises. To focus only on the terms of trade, the following version of our state equation omits consideration of new taxes and new debt (on the revenue side) and of state disbursements other than those associated with industrial enterprises and merchants (on the expenditure side).

$$[SV(C)+NCR]_{St.\,Ent.} + [NCR+SSCR(C)+SSCR(A+C)]_{St.\,Mer.} >$$
$$[SSCP(C)+SSCP(C)_{RM}]_{St.\,Ent.} + [\,Y + X\,]_{St.\,Mer.}$$

The first bracketed category labeled "St. Ent." represents the flows of value received by state capitalists from two sources: exploiting industrial workers, $SV(C)$, and unequal exchanges, $NCR$, with state and private merchants. The second bracketed category labeled "St. Mer." represents the three sources of state merchant revenues. Included there are the three value flows received by state merchants. First, $NCR$ refers to their sales of industrial consumer goods and grains (bread) to final buyers at state-set retail prices above their values. Second, $SSCR(C)$ refers to their sales of raw materials to state capitalist industry at state-set prices above their values. Lastly, $SSCR(A+C)$ refers to their sales of manufactured inputs to ancient and small capitalist farmers at state-set prices that also exceeded their values.

On the expenditure side of the state equation, the first bracket contains two components. The first—$SSCP(C)$—refers to all but one of the disbursements of state capitalist industrial surpluses made to secure the growth of state capitalist industry. The second component is that one other subsumed class disbursement, the $SSCP(C)_{RM}$. Singling out this one subsumed class payment highlights the relationship of state capitalist industries with the merchants from whom they purchased raw materials. Since the industries had to pay those merchants prices greater than the values of the raw materials, that difference comprised another claim against and hence distribution from state capitalist industrial surpluses. The second bracketed term on the right-hand side of the state equation above, Y, represents state merchants' total expenditures to secure their nonclass revenue flows, NCR. Included there are the costs of merchanting as an activity plus the costs of acquiring two kinds of commodities: (1) state capitalist industrial products at the state-set wholesale prices greater than their values and (2) ancient and capitalist grains at state-set procurement prices greater than their values. The second category, X, stands for total expenditures to reproduce state merchants' subsumed class revenues. Included there are once again the costs of merchanting as an activity plus the costs of acquiring raw materials from ancient and capitalist farmers and capital goods from state capitalist industry at wholesale prices above their values.

We mean the inequality sign in the equation to suggest that during the 1920s, the Soviet state's administered prices achieved a *net* inflow of revenue from its entire economic apparatus (from both production and merchanting). It was this net inflow that enabled the rapid economic recovery from the war and especially the growth of state capitalist industry at the expense of ancient and capitalist class structures in agriculture. While our equation describes the overall direction and impact of price changes on value flows affecting the USSR's multiple class structures, it does not distinguish between flows within and without the state. For example, state industrial enterprises purchased most of their raw materials from state rather than private merchants. Hence a rise in industrial enterprises' $SSCP(C)_{RM}$ on the equation's expenditure side (a payment to state merchants) was offset by a rise in state merchants' $SSCR(C)$ on the revenue side. In parallel fashion, a rise in NCR on the part of industrial enterprises when their manufactures were sold to state merchants at prices that exceeded values per unit was matched by state merchants' Y disbursements on the expenditure side. These two examples illustrate a transfer of value from one part of the state to another. The first enhances the revenue position of state merchants at the expense of state industrial enterprises, while the second does the reverse. Such transfers of value may well have been important determinants of struggles within the state between, say, industrial capitalists and merchants there. However, they distract from our chief concern here, namely the relation of the state to industrial state capitalism vis-à-vis ancient and capitalist farmers and Nepmen.

Revising our equation to remove intrastate value flows, we can concentrate on explaining why (1) that relation reached a critical conjuncture marking the end of the NEP period, and (2) the Soviet state replaced private with state merchants. Moreover, every category in the following equation has been introduced previously:[21]

$$[SV(C)+\{P_{SWV}-EV/UV_V\}UV_V+\{P_{SWC}-EV/UV_C\}UV_C]_{St.\,Ent.} +$$
$$[\{P_{SRV}-EV/UV_V\}UV_V+\{P_{SRC}-EV/UV_C\}UV_C+\{P_{GSR}-P_{GSW}\}UV_G]_{St.\,Mer.} >$$
$$[SSCP(C)+\{P_{SWRM}-EV/UV_{RM}\}UV_{RM}]_{St.\,Ent.} +$$
$$[\{P_{SWRM}-EV/UV_{RM}\}UV_{RM}+Y'+X']_{St.\,Mer.}$$

Beginning with the revenue side, the first bracketed term labeled "St. Ent.," includes both surplus value appropriated from workers in state enterprises *and* the revenues gained from unequal exchange with Nepmen. These latter revenues refer to the excess of prices over values paid by Nepmen for both wage goods ($P_{SWV}$) and for capital goods ($P_{SWC}$). At least to 1925, these inflows were important sources of additional revenues for state capitalist enterprises (beyond the surpluses appropriated from state industrial workers). Thereafter, state actions constricting Nepmen's activities and the establishment of a state trading network at the retail level (in addition to the state's existing wholesale trade system) reduced these inflows. Although diminished, unequal exchange revenues from Nepmen continued to the end of the NEP.[22]

The equation's second bracketed revenue term, labeled "St. Mer.," highlights the shift across the 1920s from private to state retail enterprises. This shift gave the state a new capacity directly to control and manipulate retail prices. Thus, while state industrial enterprises lost revenues inflows as unequal exchanges with Nepmen diminished, the state retail merchants who displaced them gained new revenues by setting retail prices above values to consumers. The limited data preclude our comparing the new state retail merchants' gains with the revenue losses to the state capitalist industries who could no longer sell so advantageously to Nepmen.

In the case of wage goods, when state merchants charged state-set retail prices greater than their values, they gained a net value flow from consumers: chiefly industrial and agricultural wage workers and ancient farmers. Consequently, the real personal incomes of the latter fell. In the years after 1925, it was decreasingly Nepmen and increasingly state merchants who presided over that fall. A similar process occurred in the sale of capital goods to farmers. Thus, the workers and farmers directed their anger about the high retail prices and/or the insufficient quantities of manufactured goods less at the fading Nepmen and more against the state apparatus itself. Since the latter used "socialist" and "communist" labels to identify and justify such policies, it made those terms objects of the farmers' growing hostility. Lewin (1975, 185) revealed this process in quoting the remark of peasants then that they would no longer trade with the state "in order to teach the communists a lesson."

The final revenue category in the second bracketed term refers to the state's net gains in its vast administered grain market. As already noted, state merchants played the major role in buying whatever grain farmers marketed. Of much concern to the state were its state-set procurement (wholesale) prices ($P_{GSW}$) to farmers and its retail prices ($P_{GSR}$) to consumers. The state could derive unequal exchange revenues from the state merchants' payments of prices less than values for the farmers' grain; and it could derive still more unequal exchange revenues from those merchants' resale of the grain (bread) to consumers as prices above their values. Of course, such maneuvers were limited by the fact that state procurement prices for grain suffered upward pressure across the NEP period because of competition from rising private market prices. They were also limited, as always, by the impact on real wages of rising bread prices. The contradiction that recurringly plagued the Soviet economy surfaced again: their socialism was advanced and secured by rising wages and also by rising industrial capital accumulation, yet these often contradicted and precluded one another.

Turning now to the expenditure side of the equation, the first term—SSCP(C)—refers to state capitalist enterprises' subsumed class expenditures to secure their conditions of existence. The next term is those enterprises' payments to Nepmen for raw materials priced above their values. However, because state rather than private merchants dominated the raw material market, this outflow was never very significant. Far more significant was the spending of state merchants to acquire raw materials from farmers at state-set prices that exceeded values per unit—$P_{SWRM}$—the first category contained within the second bracketed term. Because Soviet officials equated socialist success with industrial expansion that required ever increased purchases of raw materials by state capitalist merchants, the state raised raw materials prices as an incentive to boost their supply. Thus state capitalist industries had to pay raw materials prices above their values—a net outflow of value to ancient and capitalist farmers. The final two categories of Y' and X' reflect only the other merchanting costs (net of the costs of acquiring goods) of state merchants to reproduce, respectively, their nonclass and subsumed class revenue positions. These two expenditures grew over the NEP period reflecting the state's strategy not only to replace private with state merchants, but to expand the activities of the latter as well.

Considering the NEP period as a totality, our equation's inequality suggests that state capitalist industry *and* state merchants were the net gainers from the unequal exchanges entailed by the state-set *retail* prices of manufactures rising faster than state-set *wholesale* raw material and grain prices paid to farmers. As the state squeezed the Nepmen out of retail trade, state industrial enterprises no longer gained added revenues by unequal exchanges with them. On the other hand, their absence meant that they and their private markets could no longer interfere—at least legally—with the state's gaining revenues from manipulating state-set retail prices to consumers.

Our equation's inequality offers a rough index of how the Soviet state used unequal exchange favoring state industrial and merchanting enterprises to secure needed flows of value beyond the surplus values that could be appropriated from the workers in state capitalist industries. Only with those added revenues could the USSR's "socialist program" be achieved: growing state industry, comprehensive planning, state domination of markets, and so on. What the Soviets discovered about managing their internal trade in the 1920s paralleled what Raul Prebisch and other leftist "economic development" experts would rediscover after World War Two in the different context of international trade and imperialism. In both cases, a turning of the terms of trade in favor of capitalist industry enabled a net inflow of value to occur that enhanced its development at the cost of noncapitalist agriculture.[23] The Soviet state used that added value inflow for state capitalist industrial development (their "socialism") and at the deliberate expense of Nepmen and ancient and small capitalist farmers (their "nonsocialist elements"). With these value flows, the USSR could progress toward the official vision of socialism without raising new domestic tax revenues or seeking foreign inflows of capital.

Yet this progress was never smooth or secure. Because the terms of trade shifted unevenly, they yielded uneven flows of value into state capitalism, thereby hampering its development. Additionally, while the scissors remained open against the nonsocialist sectors over the NEP, their gradual closing between 1923 and 1929 diminished the net gain in value flows to state capitalist industry. Perhaps most importantly, Soviet leaders worried that their price manipulations could drive farmers to legal or illegal private markets (thereby lifting grain prices, food prices, and wage levels) or, worse, to organized opposition to the Soviet system.

Many debates in the 1920s concerned whether industry was growing too fast in relation to what "peasant agriculture" could possibly support. If so and if this was politically dangerous, should industrial growth be slowed or could agriculture somehow be changed to accommodate industrial growth? While the dominant view of "industry first" was challenged repeatedly, especially by Bukharin, it never lost its privileged place in Soviet thinking and strategy. A growing industrial proletariat was an absolute priority and required ever more raw materials and grain for food unless the already low wage levels could be reduced still further. Yet such reduction not only violated the revolution's promise; it also alienated the rapidly growing wage-earning population from the state and the party.

The problem of more wage earners was intensified by a particularly important class consequence of the NEP reforms. Most of the ancient farmers created by the revolution's land distributions produced little if any marketable surplus. When the NEP reforms allowed the return of agricultural wage labor, those farmers supplemented low incomes from their ancient farms by occupying an additional class position: hired worker on a capitalist farm. Soviet agriculture increasingly split into a large population of ancient subsistence farmers who also sold labor power and a much smaller population of capitalist grain and raw material farmers (the kulaks) who bought that labor power and produced most of the marketable farm output. A rural, agricultural proletariat arose alongside the urban industrial proletariat in state enterprises.

All wage earners' real wages declined if and when grain prices rose. If the state lowered grain prices, wage earners would benefit. If it raised grain prices to stimulate agricultural production, that "nonsocialist" sector would strengthen. Agrarian crises followed as prices and quantities of marketed agricultural products oscillated around the clashing interests of private and state merchants, state capitalist enterprises, ancient and small capitalist farmers, and consumers generally. Some Soviet leaders believed that only a sustained catering to farmers' needs would secure adequate prices and supplies of grain and raw materials. Others denounced such beliefs as both politically risky and too high a price to pay. Even if higher farm prices induced greater supplies of agricultural goods, they argued, higher farm profits (and expectations of still higher prices) would only encourage farmers and Nepmen to speculate by withholding inventories from the market. Even without speculation, rising "nonsocialist" incomes would draw scarce resources away from investment in heavy industry, destined for the socialist sector, and toward investment in light industry and farm equipment to satisfy a growing nonsocialist demand.

In the ebb and flow of such debates, amid many fears and urgencies, and with the desire above all to encourage what they understood as socialist growth, state officials made their interventions. They adjusted and readjusted farm and industrial prices in frustrating attempts to manage the recurrent swings in prices and flows of value between nonsocialist agriculture and socialist industry. Yet their interventions often had unwanted and unintended effects. They certainly brought no closure to the recurring scissors crises of the 1920s. The terms of trade were shaped by innumerable interacting forces. State interventions were only one factor, and their impacts always depended on those other forces. The frustrations, adjustments, compromises, and tensions within and among the different groups of individuals positioned across the USSR's multiple class structures exemplified the contradictory effects set in motion by the NEP.

## A History of NEP Contradictions

The NEP's contradictions became apparent soon after war communism ended. First, the terms of trade moved in favor of agriculture, reaching a peak in the spring of 1922.[24] A desperate need for "working capital" had forced state capitalist enterprises to raise cash by selling industrial commodities at reduced wholesale prices to private merchants, the Nepmen.[25] This cut the state enterprises' nonclass revenues gained from unequal exchange. The Nepmen then resold these cheapened industrial goods at much higher retail prices to final consumers. Their trading profits consequently expanded. In contrast, agricultural goods prices rose as ancient farmers faced rising state capitalist demand for output that they could not or would not increase.[26] Higher grain prices paid to farmers ($P_{GSW}$ in the previous equation) reduced the state's revenues, while higher raw material prices paid to them ($P_{SWRM}$ in that same equation) increased state enterprises' expenditures. The lifting of war communism's controls on prices also encouraged ancient and emerging small capitalist farmers to direct their supplies to whichever market—private or state—offered the higher price: "peasants were conscious of their strength" (Carr 1985, vol. 2, 312).

The renewed development of state capitalist industry after war communism had thus contributed to producing a crisis for itself. The terms of trade moved against industry. These developments spelled reduced state revenues, greater expenditures on raw materials, and the risk that rising food prices would raise wages and so reduce the surpluses appropriated from state capitalist workers. This was an inauspicious start for the state and state capitalist industry in the first years of the NEP.

Not surprisingly, Vesenkha reacted strongly to this movement of the scissors against state capitalist industry, or as it was then described, "against socialism." Vesenkha's new policy radically altered the industry's structure and developed a new merchanting organization owned and operated by the state. State capitalist enterprises were encouraged to form relatively autonomous state-industrial trusts among themselves, and such trusts could form "commercial syndicates" with one another. Vesenkha granted them the authority to set their own state-administered prices.[27] When the trusts or syndicates raised wholesale prices to Nepmen, trusts re-turned the terms of trade even more against the Nepmen and the farmers. The trusts could then enjoy higher revenues, profits, and thus growth.[28] The more that Nepmen could respond to these higher prices by raising retail prices, the greater the fall in the real incomes of ancient consumers and capitalist workers. Carr maintains that this "new scissors" widened throughout 1923 (1954, 12; 1958, vol. 1, 422). This suggests that Nepmen expanded their trading profits at the expense of declining real incomes of workers and ancients as consumers: also an inauspicious development.

The terms of trade in 1923 were also affected by how the ancients and small capitalist farmers had responded when the terms of trade had moved in their favor in 1921 and 1922. Encouraged by higher private and state-set procurement prices then, they had expanded cultivation and brought more product to market. This also helped to turn the terms of trade against them. These forces turned the 1922 crisis for industry into the well-known 1923 scissors crisis for agriculture.

Once again the Soviet state intervened. It feared that the movement of the scissors against ancient and capitalist farmers would lead to rural unrest and an eventual decrease in the marketable supplies of food and raw materials sold. Despite opposition, a number of policies were developed to attack the rise in industrial prices (Dobb 1966, 173; Carr 1954, 86-149). First, the state reduced loans—another form of nonclass revenues—to state capitalist enterprises, forcing them again to unload inventories to raise working capital. Second, limits were placed on the ability of syndicates to raise industrial wholesale prices.[29] Third, selected manufactures were imported to increase their supply in the domestic market. Finally, the state established a new commission to increase the efficiency of industry (Dobb, 1966, 174-175). Its aim was to raise industrial productivity via the elimination of inefficient factories in various industries. Increasing overall productivity of labor meant reducing the value per unit of industrial goods. Then, if the state decreased these goods' wholesale prices—but not as much as their values had been decreased through productivity—the state capitalist industries would still earn revenues from unequal exchanges with Nepmen (Preobrazhensky 1966, 111).

Apparently, the state lowered wholesale prices for industrial goods further than productivity increases had reduced their values. The result was decreased industrial profits of trusts and syndicates (Dobb 1966, 176). At the same time, to mollify agriculture still more, the state intervened to raise its procurement prices of agricultural goods. In 1925 it also improved the conditions for private capitalism to prosper in agriculture: land could be leased for longer periods of time and wage labor could be hired on a regular basis rather than just at harvest time.

Thus, the scissors began to move back again against state industry and state merchants in 1924. Industry's nonclass revenues fell while state merchants' subsumed class payments to farmers rose. Higher grain prices to farmers again threatened higher retail prices for food with their unwanted pressures on wages and industrial surpluses. And again, partly in response to the 1923 scissors crisis for agriculture, the grain harvest for 1924 was poor and raised grain prices especially in the officially sanctioned private markets. This time, the Soviet state reacted by setting its procurement price at a lower and fixed level compared to the higher and rising private prices. Ancient and capitalist farmers then sold their grain at much higher prices to private rather than state merchants. In this "battle of grain" the state was soon defeated and so forced to raise its procurement prices.

The next few years repeated this oscillating pattern together with the contradictions, debates, and fears that it provoked. So long as private grain markets and merchants offered alternatives to state markets and state merchants, the state's grain strategy, and hence its strategy for industry and for socialism, would depend on ancient farmers, capitalist farmers (kulaks), and Nepmen. Adding to this concern over the forces that ultimately controlled socialist development was an emerging crisis in the size of the marketable surplus of grain. Despite the farmers' victory in 1924, and the relatively good harvests in 1925 and 1926, the grain surplus delivered to the market was not growing as fast as most Soviet leaders expected and thought necessary for industrial growth. This inadequacy, added to all the other problems of the difficult relationship between industry and agriculture, proved to be the catalyst undermining the NEP and provoking the emergence of new class structures in agriculture.

The incessant oscillation in the terms of trade continued, although gradually the exchanges between agriculture and industry became less unequal. The virtual closing of the price scissors in 1928–29 had class and more general economic development implications that provoked high official anxiety. Absent unequal exchanges, state capitalist industrial growth would depend solely on the surpluses appropriated from industrial workers, taxes, and foreign inflows of capital—all sources that were either already very strained or extremely limited. Soviet leaders faced the worrisome prospect of slower "socialist growth" with the evaporation of unequal exchanges benefiting industry at agriculture's expense. All the more troubling, then, was the slow growth in the quantities of grain marketed in the second half of the 1920s, despite growing grain production and improving terms of trade for the growers.[30]

Shortfalls in marketed grain required the state not only to match rising private grain prices, but also to raise wages so workers could afford the higher prices. Increased labor costs for state capitalist industry combined with the loss of gains from unequal exchanges to put heavy pressure on the state. It sought to prevent these burdens from undermining the state's priority of industrial growth (Gregory and Stuart 1990, 64–65). Yet it could not safely press industrial employees to work more or harder or raise their taxes or keep wages down as food prices rose: the risks of worker hostility and reaction were simply too high. The possibility of grain requisitions resurfaced to perhaps solve this renewal of a central predicament faced by Soviet state capitalism. Yet its risks too were obvious.

Mounting tensions in Soviet life toward the end of the 1920s focused increasingly on a marketed grain supply growing too slowly to sustain the desired socialist (industrial) growth. A vicious circle frustrated the state's efforts to deal with this basic problem. To build socialism it stressed investment in heavy industry to expand means of industrial production. Thus light industry grew far more slowly, as did its outputs of consumer goods and agricultural implements (Baykov 1947,

122–123; Volin 1970, 187). Shortages of such goods provoked farmers to respond by not marketing grain. When grain prices then rose and the state raised wages so workers could buy grain, the workers often used the wage increases to buy industrial consumer goods. Since the state did not raise its prices on industrial consumer goods (to avoid problems from the farmers), the excess of demand over their supply generated, in a familiar phrase from 1926, a "goods famine" in the state stores. Nepmen responded predictably. They raised their private prices for manufactured consumer goods and agricultural equipment. Once more, the aggravated response of the farmers was to constrict further their marketed grain supplies and thus propel the vicious circle (Bettelheim 1978, 98, 102).

This excess demand also meant that some buyers got scarce goods while others were denied. The "well-connected" individuals found ways to purchase scarce light industrial products at their relatively low state-set prices. Others—mainly ancient and small capitalist farmers—went without or were forced to purchase them at the Nepmen's much higher private prices (Nove, 1989, 130–131). Obvious to all, these disparities undermined the social solidarity the state otherwise sought to build.

The private farmers consumed more, fed more to animals, and held more in reserves. The shortages and poor qualities of industrial consumer goods and manufactured agricultural inputs constrained both the incentives and the physical capacities for expanded grain production. Toward the decade's end, the problem of grain deliveries for Soviet industrialization loomed as the key blockage to socialism's growth and perhaps even its survival.

The class effects of Soviet policy went beyond the realms of state industry, rural agriculture, and the markets between them. Soviet farmers often could buy cheaper rural-produced industrial goods of equal or better quality than urban-produced state capitalist commodities. Locally produced industrial goods were apparently plentiful in rural areas (Bettelheim 1978, 142–145; Harrison 1991, 121–123; Chayanov 1966, 106–107 and passim). Especially those produced within rural households by women were viewed as comparable or even superior to relatively poor quality state-capitalist consumer goods: "The demand of the Russian peasantry for industrial goods was very elastic, as they could have recourse to handicraft production of certain necessities such as linen, woolen textiles, home-made leather boots or bast-shoes instead of leather boots, home-made soap, candles, and utensils made of wood and glazed clay ... " (Baykov 1947, 56).

The rural industrial producers included, in class terms, ancients, small capitalists, and the women (and children) working within the mostly feudal class structures of rural households. In the feudal household, mother (and children) produced meals, clothing, leather boots, soap, bread, repairs, and so on, not only for their own needs but also for the household patriarch—the father—as a feudal surplus. The father often directed his wife and children *not* to devote surplus labor time to the fields and thus to grain output. Rather, he directed them to produce rural handicrafts for his use and/or for markets where they might well exchange for others' grain. Rather than paying high prices to Nepmen for industrial goods of poor quality, these fathers turned to the alternative of customary craft goods and services produced within households. Not only did rural handicraft production thus curtail total grain production, it also served to keep more grain in rural areas and away from delivery to state capitalist industry (Harrison 1991, 116).

Unlike the cultural and quality advantages of rural handicrafts over urban industrial consumer goods, the rural alternatives to industrially produced farm equipment were much less conducive to raising agricultural productivity: draft animals were poor substitutes for tractors. By producing little farm machinery and equipment, state capitalist industry only added to the grain supply problem it faced. As in the decades before 1917, farmers allocated their labor time as ancients to produce equipment for themselves, rented it from kulaks—that is, other, richer ancients and capitalist farmers—or purchased it from village producers. While rural production of mostly ancient and feudal crafts offset the NEP's scarcity of industrial goods, it proved a costly diversion of rural labor from grain production (Chayanov 1966, 107, 180).[31]

In 1928 Stalin explained the continuing imbalance between the demand for and supply of grain as the result of the revolution's egalitarian land distribution. It had destroyed relatively large and efficient capitalist estates that had marketed most if not all of their produced grains before the war. Instead, a mass of small ancient farmers under the NEP consumed most of what they produced.[32] Stalin's argument was starkly determinist: (1) small private individual farms were inevitably inefficient and (2) small private capitalist farms, while more efficient and richer, inevitably withheld grain from the market. Stalin concluded that small size and private ownership of farms in the USSR—what he defined as their "nonsocialist" qualities—were the essential determinants of the grain crisis facing Soviet socialism.

In contrast, our approach has not reduced the problem of grain supplies to farms' sizes and their private ownership. That problem was overdetermined by many other factors as well. We have been most interested in the role played by the interactions between the NEP and the multiple, different class structures of Soviet industry, agriculture, and households. Others have shown how such diverse social processes as market incentives, weather, and livestock participated in also overdetermining the proportion of grain marketed by the USSR's farmers across the NEP period (Wheatcroft 1991, 98–103).[33] Stalin and other state officials, however, did not see, examine, or address the complex class structures of Soviet society. They could neither ask how the class structure of state industry contributed to Soviet problems nor consider how changing that class structure might have contributed to solutions. Instead, they presumed, searched for, and found one key determinant of the grain problem: the "nonsocialist" farmers—and especially a wealthier minority among them. The Soviet state and party therefore focused their policies, angers, and insecurities on them.

The collectivization of agriculture followed. It eliminated the small, private individual farm as well as the small capitalist kulaks. Stalin's "nonsocialism" was defeated. Soviet farmers were gathered instead into much larger collective and state farms much more subordinated to state influence and control than farms had been under the NEP. As we show in the next chapter, agricultural collectivization produced results both contradictory and ironic. While it gave the state much more control, it still could not solve the problem of the relationship between industry and agriculture. While it was celebrated as the "completion" of the revolution (extending it from industry to agriculture), it actually extended state capitalism from industry to the new state farms. While it actually established communist class structures on many collective farms—the first and only mass experiment in communism in Soviet history—it also proceeded to undermine those structures from the outset. In sum, the collectivization of agriculture in the name of socialism made the class transition from state capitalism to communism only more elusive and distant for the Soviet people.

## Adjusting State Industrial Capitalism

While the Soviet state struggled with the problem of private agriculture and its complex relations with state capitalist industry, the NEP simultaneously reorganized that industry. New laws and decrees decentralized the appropriation of state capitalist surpluses. Vesenkha did not continue in its role as the highly centralized appropriator and distributor of surplus values produced in state capitalist enterprises. Instead, the NEP designated localized state capitalist boards of directors as the appropriators and distributors of industrial surpluses. They were allowed to form trusts among themselves that could sell their products in state and private markets and also exchange directly with one another at mutually agreed-upon prices.

While the decentralized boards of directors and trusts appropriated and distributed their industrial surpluses, Vesenkha still had an important role to play. While it no longer appropriated and distributed the industrial surplus itself, it retained considerable power over those who did. It appointed the members of those boards and trusts as state officials. The appointees, as the actual surplus appropriators and distributors, were the industrial capitalists "not as owners of property but as trustees of the state with terminable powers by the state in the form of a charter" (Dobb, 1966, 136). The appointees were state rather than private and decentralized rather than centralized industrial capitalists operating state-owned means of industrial production. Under the NEP, new laws designated the boards and trusts as legal entities free to operate on their *own account* and *independent* of the state budget. They were directed to pay wages to their own hired labor power. Vesenkha no longer purchased and consumed its own productive labor power. Likewise, the boards and trustees purchased material inputs, sold their outputs for their own accounts, and thereby also realized the surplus value embodied in those commodities for their own accounts. The state directed them to make their own profits.[34] Beyond its power to appoint boards and trustees, Vesenkha also exercised power over how they distributed their decentrally appropriated surpluses.[35] For example,

Vesenkha influenced the percentages of the appropriated surplus (termed "profits") to be distributed for depreciation of fixed capital, for bonuses to managers and others, for welfare to workers, for payments to the state treasury, and for funds to be retained by the board members or trustees.

The NEP did not return private industrial capitalism to the USSR. It simply adjusted the extent of centralization of surplus appropriation within an enduring state industrial capitalism. Moreover, it made repeated readjustments. After the NEP initially moved to decentralize boards of directors, the latter often grouped themselves into larger trusts. This returned a considerable degree of centralization to surplus appropriation. The oscillations from centralized appropriation during war communism to decentralization under early NEP to partial recentralization later in the 1920s established a pattern of periodic readjustments of—shifting distributions of power within—Soviet state capitalism. For example, centralization under Stalin's five-year plans preceded postwar shifts toward decentralization. When, periodically, sufficiently serious difficulties arose in the operation of state capitalist industry to build a consensus for policy change, the resulting "reforms" chiefly entailed shifts from more to less centralization or vice versa. The proponents of such reforms (whether for more centralization or more decentralization) invariably trumpeted their ability thereby to solve industrial problems.

Proponents and opponents of each such reform did not question the kind of class structure that existed in Soviet industry (as distinguished from the degree of its centralization). Hence they did not debate whether solving industrial or economy-wide problems might require a different kind of class structure. The nearly universal view was this: because the workers controlled the state and the state owned and operated industrial enterprises, Soviet industry was socialist, whereas the private nature of farms rendered them nonsocialist. How surplus labor was produced, appropriated, and distributed did not matter in Soviet analyses. Extending this logic, the launching of *state* farms under the first five-year plan would replace nonsocialist with socialist agriculture. Collective farms—while not as socialist as state farms—would at least represent a step in the right direction.

Oscillating between centralized and decentralized forms of state capitalism, the NEP's industrial reforms solved some problems but aggravated others. Depending on the ever-shifting political, cultural, and economic context, decentralization of state capitalism might have evolved at some point into a movement beyond mere decentralization. The directors of trusts or individual enterprises might have sought to sever their official connections to the state. They might have argued that "saving" Soviet industry required not merely more decentralization but also a transition from state to private capitalism. Whereas social conditions did not permit such a movement to grow successfully out of the moments of decentralization in the 1920s, they did during and after the 1970s.

Under the NEP, the state did begin to denationalize small industries or workshops—enterprises that employed less than twenty workers. They could break completely from the state, becoming new rural and urban private sites of commodity production displaying ancient or capitalist class structures (Carr 1985, 300). In addition to the decentralization of state capitalist industry and support for private ancient and small capitalist class structures in agriculture and industry, the NEP also fostered a private market among these class structures. It functioned alongside the state markets. The Nepmen who handled private market exchanges not only accumulated sizable, liquid, and provocatively visible masses of merchant capital. Their buying and selling also connected the different class structures inside the USSR to one another in particular ways. Extravagant styles of personal consumption, bribery of officials and producers, market manipulations of various kinds, and related processes began to influence the actions taken by both state officials and state and private producers working within the USSR's different class structures. Their actions (e.g., official changes in state-administered prices) reacted back upon private markets and prices and Nepmen, changing their behaviors, which further altered state officials' and producers' circumstances, and so on. These interactions ramified throughout the Soviet economy, creating in their wake, for both state and private sectors, the instabilities typically associated with markets. The NEP's particular circumstances generated the complex cyclical interaction between production and circulation (among and between state and private producers, state and private merchants, state and private markets) that eventuated in the scissors crises. When the latter culminated in the grain crisis of 1928, that proved to be a turning point: the successes of the NEP had been overtaken by the new contradictions and problems they provoked.

## Revolution and NEP as a Transition to State Capitalism

We agree with the widespread view that capitalism took root in Russia and developed rapidly under the last czars. Our analysis permits a further conclusion: the 1917 revolution did not end that capitalism. The Bolsheviks did not launch instead a non-capitalist society. The new Soviet regime transformed private into state capitalism. Under war communism and the NEP, the new state and the Communist Party succeeded in developing that state capitalism: more industrial output, workers, and capacity. They achieved that development by managing some of the major contradictions within state industry and in its relations with both the other class structures and the nonclass processes (political, cultural, and so on) of Soviet society. Moreover, this impressive accomplishment was defined by participants, supporters, and critics alike as the building of a socialism that would progress to communism.

Preobrazhensky was right that primary accumulation of capital did take place in the USSR of the 1920s. He was wrong to call it "socialist." It was rather an accumulation of capital primary (or preliminary) to a state capitalism. The extraction of surpluses from noncapitalist class structures (and sometimes their destruction) to benefit the development of capitalist class structures—classically depicted in Marx's *Capital,* vol. 1, section 8—occurred in the USSR of the 1920s as well. It resembles the transitions from noncapitalist to capitalist class structures that occurred in England, Germany, the United States, and many other countries. While those transitions required centuries, in the USSR, the transition took merely a few decades. In most of these transitions, capitalist class structures grew out of, were in frequent conflict with, and yet both strongly depended on and supported noncapitalist class structures. The USSR's contradictory transition, as detailed in these chapters, parallels most others.

When war communism's contradictions overwhelmed its benefits in accumulating capital for state capitalist industry and for the USSR's survival, NEP arrived. When the NEP's contradictions overwhelmed its benefits for the same goals, the collectivization of agriculture arrived. Collectivization largely eliminated recalcitrant private capitalist and ancient farmers. It "eliminated domestic class enemies" in agriculture by replacing them with collective and state farms. The Soviet state's takeover of retail trade—begun after 1925 and completed under Stalin—eliminated the Nepmen. The state thus gained control over the key prices (and the scissors) whose often uncontrolled and unwanted movements had repeatedly frustrated the accumulation of capital for state capitalist industrial growth. Collectivization and a nationally planned economy would, it was hoped, secure the resources to enable state capitalist industry to resume rapid growth. However, as we shall see in the next chapter, the new answer of collectivization produced its new contradictions, crises, and dangers for state capitalist development.

Our depictions of war communism and the NEP have charted a dizzying array of the different forms of state capitalist industry. As the nonclass conditions (political, cultural, and so on) changed, they overdetermined changes in the USSR's class structures as well. While state capitalism—capitalist class structures inside state industrial enterprises—endured, those capitalist class structures interacted with changing political, cultural, and economic conditions to generate different forms of state capitalism. The absence of markets under war communism, then the varying sizes and kinds of state and private markets, and finally the elimination of all but very limited private markets were changes in the nonclass processes of exchange that interacted with (and so changed the forms of) Soviet state capitalism. The same applies to changes in such nonclass processes as distributing political power among levels of the state bureaucracy and the Party and debates over concepts such as primary accumulation, state-controlled markets, individual income inequality, and socialist development. Likewise, the changes in other, noncapitalist class structures that coexisted with Soviet state capitalist industry influenced changes in its form. Despite these changes in various forms of state capitalism, they never amounted to a change from either state to private capitalism or from a capitalist to another class structure in industry.

## Notes

1. From the standpoint of ancient class-structured farms, the situation may be summarized by means of this equation: $W(A) = C(A) + V(A) + SV(A)$. The $W(A)$ term represents the total value of ancient farm output; $C(A)$ is the value of means of farm production used up; $V(A)$ is the value of the labor power contributed by the ancient farmer; and $SV(A)$ is the surplus value the latter produces. The A term denotes that this equation refers to an ancient class farm. [The value of ancients' labor power is only nominal, useful for value accounting purposes, since ancients did not, of course, sell their labor power as a commodity.] It follows that war communism effectively requisitioned the surplus product from each ancient farm: $SV(A)$ in the equation above.
2. These "industrialization debates" of the 1920s are well summarized by Gregory and Stuart (1990, ch. 4), Carr (1954, 88–92), and Dobb (1966, ch. 8). Perhaps the most famous discussions of this industrialization debate can be found in Spulber (1964) and Erlich (1960). In this chapter, we again refer often to Dobb's work. Not only its enduring insights, but especially its sensitivity to the class dimensions of Soviet history—almost unique in the large literature—rendered an invaluable resource.
3. We criticized this absolute concept of efficiency earlier in chapter 2. No economist can ever know or count the infinite chain of interacting consequences and their associated losses and gains that are set in motion from any initial action. Efficiency-based comparisons of alternative positions in the Soviet industrialization debates are thus inevitably partial and partisan.
4. War communism eliminated private markets and merchants officially, but both continued to operate illegally. Many transactions in kind and/or by bookkeeping entries resulted from the state's destruction of the worth of money. While not officially destroyed, state policies undermined the use of money as an equivalent for commodities.
5. Dobb (1966, 150, 180) points out the burden to the USSR of unavailable foreign credit—as compared with the experience of many developing countries confronting similar crises. For developing countries, the gap between $SV(C)$ and $SSCP(C)$ often gets financed, at least partially, by foreign loans. The private nature of the latter's capitalist development likely generates the different lending response. Exceptionally, the famine of 1921 enabled the USSR to obtain a one time NCR in the form of U.S. grain assistance.
6. Poorer ancient farmers often rented equipment, draft animals, and land and also borrowed money from richer, ancient farmers. In so doing, the richer ancient farmers occupied subsumed class positions, receiving distributed shares of poor ancient farmers' surpluses. These arrangements grew under the NEP and thereby deepened the differentiation among ancient farmers. Bettelheim (1978, 85–98) claims that inadequate state provision of means of production and credit to poor and middle-level ancient peasants forced their dependence on richer peasants and contributed to the "procurement crisis" in grain in 1927–28. Such dependence concentrated ancient farm surpluses—the main source of marketable food and raw materials—in ever fewer hands.
7. When state-set or private market prices rose above the values of farm products, the farmers gained from that unequal exchange. The gain is accounted for as a nonclass revenue (NCR) for the ancients (see note 10 below). Thus farmers added to the surplus they appropriated any NCR that the market prices allowed them to capture. Such NCR enabled even greater expansions of farm production and, potentially, greater marketable surpluses for the state. Whether such potential marketable surpluses materialized and, if they did, whether they would offset the cost to the state of the higher prices paid for them became key issues for Soviet policy across the 1920s.
8. Terms-of-trade calculations appear in, for example, Gregory and Stuart (1990, 65), Bettelheim (1978, 151), and Davies (1991, 288). Bettelheim shows that the high point for agriculture was 1928–29 when the index reached 90; by 1929–30, however, the index had fallen back to 77, only slightly higher than from 1925 to 1927. Bettelheim (152) also shows that for the crucial grain crop

alone, farmers experienced an even more severe deterioration in the terms of trade compared to 1913—the grain index stood at 29 in 1923–24 and rose only to 77 in 1929–30. While these indexes show improvement across the decade, they do not take into account the fact that shortages of industrial goods available from state stores/merchants forced farmers to buy them from private merchants at much higher private prices. Nove (1989, 147) documents the widening gap between state and private industrial prices after 1925. Baykov (1947, 67) dramatically compares the farmers' situation in 1927 and 1913. They received significantly fewer industrial products in exchange for one unit of rye regardless of the seller: state or private Nepman.

9. The actual NEP rise in labor productivity likely intensified the value transfers discussed in the text. Productivity in capitalist industry rose steadily, reaching its 1913 level by 1925 (Baykov 1947, 147). In contrast, agricultural productivity never reached its prewar level, although it likely rose (Davies, 1991, 272). This productivity difference implied that values per unit fell more rapidly in industry than in agriculture. Given that industrial prices rose more than agricultural prices, the resulting deviation between prices and values was far greater for industry than for agriculture. Some Russian writers claimed that prices received by farmers did not cover production costs per unit (Lewin, 1975, 184). All such possibilities would only strengthen our argument that a net value transferred aided state capitalist industry at the expense of ancient/private capitalist agriculture.

10. Farmers earned nonclass revenues—NCR—by selling agricultural goods—raw materials and grain—to state or private merchants at respectively state or private prices that exceeded their values: NCR = $(P_{AG} - EV/UV_{AG}) \times UV_{AG}$, where $P_{AG}$, $EV/UV_{AG}$, and $UV_{AG}$ stand, respectively, for the prices, unit values, and quantities of agricultural goods. Selling these goods to merchants at prices above values yielded farmers a nonclass rather than a subsumed class revenue flow because merchants are not surplus appropriators. NCR represents an unequal exchange benefit to farmers at the direct expense of merchants.

11. To simplify our analysis, we assume that the grain sold to wage earners is equivalent to the sale of bread to them. We thus omit the step of processing grain into bread.

12. While published estimates vary, they uniformly suggest that the major portion (over 50 percent in 1925–26 to 70 percent by 1929) of grains marketed were taken by state procurements: see Lewin (1975, 184; 1985, 144), Nove (1989, 102), Volin (1970, 184–185), and Karcz (1971, 44). The percentages were even higher for industrial raw materials crops.

13. Carr (1954, 11) cites a report claiming that 83.3 percent of retail trade in 1924 was in the hands of Nepmen.

14. Generally, capitalist industrial enterprises utilize merchants as market intermediaries. They buy manufactures more or less immediately as they emerge from production, thereby relieving capitalists of the costs and risks of finding final buyers themselves. In return, merchants obtain distributed shares of the capitalist industries' surpluses, usually in the form of discounted prices for their products. When merchants resell these commodities at or above their values, they thereby realize the distributed share of the surplus—the subsumed class payment—passed to them via the producers' discounts (Resnick and Wolff 1987, ch. 4). In the Soviet case, state capitalist industrial enterprises utilized at first mostly Nepmen and then increasingly state merchants as such intermediaries. However, unlike the general case, Nepmen purchased goods from state capitalist enterprises at wholesale prices that already *exceeded* their unit values. They thereby incurred a *negative* nonclass revenue (equal to the positive nonclass revenue received by state industrial enterprises). Nepmen then resold such goods at much higher private retail prices earning *positive* (subsumed and nonclass) revenues: subsumed if they sold inputs to ancients and capitalist farmers and nonclass if they sold consumer goods to final buyers. The difference between these two value flows covered Nepmen's trading profits plus other merchanting costs:

$$\text{Profits + Other Costs} = [P_R - EV/UV]UV - [P_W - EV/UV]UV$$

The first bracketed term represents the inflow of value gained by the *sale* of a quantity (UV) of commodities to final buyers at private retail prices ($P_R$) that exceeded unit values (EV/UV); and the second term represents the outflow of value incurred by the *purchase* of the same number of commodities (UV) at enterprises' wholesale prices ($P_W$) that also exceeded unit values (EV/UV).

The more Nepmen could turn the retail-wholesale terms of trade ($P_R/P_W$) in their favor, the more their trading profits could expand.

15. Turning the terms of retail trade in favor of Nepmen impacts class structures in agriculture. It increases subsumed class expenditures by ancient and capitalist farmers and reduces real incomes of ancient consumers and wage workers there. It also reduces the real incomes of urban industrial workers, and state officials too. Carr (1954, 111-112) discusses Soviet officials' gradual recognition that state control over retail trade and prices would be necessary to avoid these adverse consequences. Interestingly enough, he quotes Larin, a Soviet economist of the day, who sees in the state's control over retail trade "the transition from 'state capitalism' to 'state socialism'" (112).

16. We can show in value terms what Kamenev recognized as the "new scissors." Consider the total population of rural and urban final consumers of industrial products who had to pay prices above their values. Nepmen and state capitalist enterprises benefited from this unequal exchange. The following equation shows the gains from this unequal exchange as distributed between state-capitalist enterprises (St Ent) and Nepmen (Nepmen):

$$[(P_R - EV/UV) \times UV]_{\text{Fnl Cnsmr}} = [(P_W - EV/UV) \times UV]_{\text{St Ent}} + [(P_R - EV/UV) \times UV - (P_W - EV/UV) \times UV]_{\text{Nepmen}}$$

The left side shows the loss in value by the final consuming population. The two terms on the right side show how that value was received by state enterprises and Nepmen. When the "new scissors" ($P_R/P_W$) moved in favor of Nepmen, the second of these value terms expanded at the cost of industry and the peasantry. Further, the equation makes clear how reduced wholesale prices (see the text below) merely serves to reduce industrial and expand Nepmen's profits (Bettelheim, 1978, 198). Such effects gradually pushed the state to replace private with state retail merchants.

17. To focus the analysis, we assume that ancient farmers and agricultural workers purchase only manufactured consumer goods from merchants. Since prices for these goods on the private market exceeded those on the state market, the excess demand in the state market was met by the queuing of buyers there.

18. State capitalist enterprises earn nonclass revenues—NCR—by selling industrial commodities to state or private merchants at wholesale prices—$P_W$—above their values per unit—EV/UV: NCR = ($P_W$ - EV/UV) × UV.

19. As noted previously, state-set procurement prices for raw materials more or less matched private prices.

20. In discussing Preobrazhensky's theory of "primitive socialist accumulation," Dobb wrote: "The growth in State industry depended upon the accumulation of capital in the hands of the state; and apart from loans from abroad, the only two sources from which such accumulations could be derived were the surplus production of state industry itself, due to its own inherent productivity (i.e., the difference between the value of its production and what it paid out in wages and salaries), and what it could derive from the 'exploitation' of small-scale private economy by extracting from the latter a greater sum in values than what was given to it of industrial products in exchange" (1966, 184). Our text's equation translates Dobb into the class analytical terms of Soviet state capitalism. To complete Dobb's exposition, we need to subtract state capitalist industry's subsumed class payments for raw materials supplied by the "small scale private economy" at prices greater than their values. We thus rewrite our text's equation as follows: SV + [NCR - SSCP(C)$_{\text{RM}}$], which shows Dobb's "two sources" of value available for capital accumulation in state industry.

21. For convenience, we include here the definitions of all of these variable as they appear in the equation:

| | |
|---|---|
| SV(C) | surplus value in state capitalist enterprises |
| $P_{SWV}$ | state wholesale price for wage goods |
| $EV/UV_V$ | per unit value of wage goods |
| $UV_V$ | quantity of wage goods |
| $P_{SWC}$ | state wholesale price for capital goods |
| $EV/UV_C$ | per unit value of capital goods |
| $UV_C$ | quantity of capital goods |
| $P_{SRV}$ | state retail price of wage goods |
| $P_{SRC}$ | state retail price of capital goods |
| $P_{GSR}$ | state retail price of grain |
| $P_{GSW}$ | state wholesale price of grain |
| $UV_G$ | quantity of grain |
| SSCP(C) | enterprises' subsumed class expenditures |
| $P_{SWRM}$ | state wholesale price for raw materials |
| $EV/UV_{RM}$ | per unit value of raw materials |
| $UV_{RM}$ | quantity of raw materials |
| Y' | other merchanting costs to establish NCR |
| X' | other merchanting costs to establish SSCR |

22. According to Carr and Davies (1969, vol. 1, part 2, 962), private as a percentage of total retail trade fell steadily over the NEP from 57.7 percent in 1923–24 to 42.3 percent in 1925–26 to only 13.5 percent in 1929.
23. See also Dobb's (1966, 184–185) discussion of Preobrazhensky's parallel use of terms such as "metropolis" and "colonies" to describe the unequal relationship benefiting "socialist" industry at the expense of "nonsocialist" agriculture.
24. This short-run movement punctuated but did not reverse the basic trend of the NEP's terms of trade. Relative prices always favored the state capitalist class structure in industry over the ancient and capitalist class structures in agriculture.
25. See Carr (1985, vol. 2, 312–313) and Dobb (1966, 156–158); however, they give no definition of working capital. Common accounting conventions suggest a measure of the excess of current assets over current liabilities. A need for working capital thus suggests that state capitalist enterprises were then having difficulty meeting their current liabilities. Facing insolvency, they tried desperately to raise funds quickly by dumping manufactures at relatively cheap wholesale prices.
26. Dobb (1966, 208–216) cites two important factors constraining the supply elasticity. First, the previous Bolshevik land reform replaced larger-sized capitalist estates under the czar with numerous, much smaller ancient farms that generally sold a significantly lower proportion of their output than the previous capitalist estates had done. Secondly, ancient farmers' fewer horses and ploughs constrained their productivity.
27. Vesenkha, however, retained the power to limit the maximum price that trusts could set (and hence to limit the maximum size of enterprises' NCR). Additionally, it did not allow enterprises, trusts, or commercial syndicates to form cartel arrangements to limit output (Dobb, 1966, 159) These constraints proved important; private retail prices for manufactures resold by Nepmen could far exceed the maximum administered wholesale prices that Vesenkha allowed trusts to set. Nepmen's trading profits could expand. While a complete analysis would have to take into account a new category, "decentralized-state-trust prices," we have avoided that complication by considering only the centralized "state-set prices" which were the norm for most of the period.
28. Higher nonclass revenues enabled industrial enterprises to expand what we have called their "complex profit rate," namely (SV+NCR)/(C+V): Resnick and Wolff (1978).

29. Limiting wholesale prices, however, did not directly confront the rising margin between such prices and retail prices charged by Nepmen. Continued widening of this different form of the scissors (against the real incomes of consumers) moved the state to extend its control over retail prices of certain commodities and its own merchanting operations into the retail arena.

30. The value of the marketable surplus of grain equals the difference between the value of the total grain produced by farmers and the value they kept for their own consumption purposes, feed for animals, seed, and reserves. To avoid confusion, we underscore the difference between this *grain surplus* and the very different category of *surplus value* in grain production. For example, consider ancient farmers who sold grains at procurement prices set by state merchants. For simplicity, assume these prices equaled their values. Their trading equation can be written as:

$$[P_F \times UV_F] - [P_F \times UV_{FC}] = (P_{MC} \times UV_{MC} + P_{MK} \times UV_{MK}) + SSCP(A)$$

The value of their grain surplus (the difference between the value of what they produce, $[P_F \times UV_F]$, and what they kept for themselves, $[P_F \times UV_{FC}]$, equals two kinds of expenditures: one, $P_{MC} \times UV_{MC} + P_{MK} \times UV_{MK}$, is the value of their total purchases of industrial consumer and capital goods (capital to replace that used up in grain production), and the other, SSCP(A), is the total value of their subsumed class payments. Changes in the *grain surplus* are one thing; changes in the the *surplus value* are another. Suppose, for example, taxes levied on ancient farmers rose (a higher SSCP(A) paid to the state). Ancients could respond by reducing their necessary labor to increase surplus labor out of which they will pay the additional taxes to the state. If we assume that ancients' reduced necessary labor takes the form of reduced purchases of industrial consumer goods (a decline in $P_{MC} \times UV_{MC}$ in the above equation), then their self-exploitation rate would have risen (a higher surplus value) without any change taking place in their grain surplus.

31. On the one hand, improved terms of trade encourage ancient and capitalist farmers to substitute state-capitalist commodities for household produced goods in their consumption bundles. On the other hand, the resulting rise in farmers' incomes (the rise in NCR received by farmers due to prices paid to them greater than values) could imply fewer state-capitalist commodities purchased to the degree that these capitalist commodities were considered inferior in quality to household-based goods. If this perception of and hence bias to such household goods were strong enough, then a rise in the terms of trade favoring ancient and capitalist farmers might well be accompanied by a *lowering* of their marketable surplus. In the value terms defined in note 30, a reduced marketable surplus—$[P_F \times UV_F] - [P_F \times UV_{FC}]$—equals a reduced purchase of state capitalist commodities—$(P_{MC} \times UV_{MC} + P_{MK} \times UV_{MK})$. In this case, farmers might take their higher incomes from a rising NCR to expand their feudal households in which women and children produced these valued goods and services.

32. Dobb (1966, 208–217) provides an excellent explanation of how this so-called leveling effect produced by the 1917 land reform contributed to the problem of a slow-growing and even reduced marketable surplus of grain.

33. To summarize a number of these contradictory forces, first let (a) refer simply to the proportion of grain produced and retained by farmers, and (1–a) for the proportion of grain produced that was marketed. The size of the grain surplus becomes a product of (1–a) and agricultural productivity. Stalin attributed its decline, as compared to the prewar level, to what the October Revolution had produced in agriculture, namely a legacy of smaller-sized and subsistence farming. In a word, the Bolshevik revolution had created its own food problem by reducing (1–a) and productivity.

However, other forces also were at work overdetermining (1–a) and productivity. Generally, the NEP reforms worked to raise (1–a) and encourage productivity gains. The incentive effects were especially powerful for richer ancient and small capitalist farmers who together accounted for a significant share of the grains and raw materials brought to market. On the other hand, those same NEP reforms (the retail trading power in the hands of Nepmen; the particular kind of uncertainty always accompanying markets and if anything compounded by introducing a dual market system system) along with other state capitalist policies (wage and price strategies including higher prices paid to farmers for raw materials than for grains; industrial shortages, and relatively poor quality of such goods; a lowering of grain prices between 1926 and 1927) and revolutions that never were accomplished (the maintaining of feudal households and rural industry there) combined in one way or another to constrain and reduce both (1-a) and productivity. Hence the combined impact of these different class and nonclass forces created a marketable surplus of grain always developing in an uneven, contradictory way. A change in any one of them could have produced a different result than that faced by the Soviets in the late 1920s.

34. See the discussion of trusts in Carr (1985, vol. 2, 303–309), Dobb (1966, 136–137), and Bettelheim (1978, 268–272). In describing their status and operation, Carr (1985, vol. 2, 309) quotes the following 1923 decree:

> State trusts [ran article 1 of the decree] are state industrial enterprises, to which the state accords independence in the conduct of their operations in accordance with the statue laid down for each enterprise, and which operate on principles of commercial accounting with the object of earning a profit.

35. Vesenkha did not exercise such power alone. It had to share the power, in complex and shifting ways, with Communist Party officials, regional economic councils, and other state officials.

CHAPTER 9

# The Transformations of the 1930s

Over the 1930s, the state capitalist class structure of industry returned to a more centralized form, resembling its initial appearance under war communism. Instead of numerous state capitalist surplus appropriators located in the decentralized industrial trusts of the NEP period, a relatively small number of officials appropriated the industrial surplus. The Council of Ministers centralized appropriation at the highest level of the state bureaucracy. The size of the surplus that the Council appropriated and distributed expanded greatly over the decade. More than ever before, capitalist surpluses appropriated in state industrial enterprises became the key revenue source for the Soviet state's expenditures. While class structures in agriculture still continued to finance (i.e., shift portions of their surpluses to) the state's seemingly insatiable appetite for revenues, agriculture's relative importance diminished in proportion to state capitalist industry's internally generated surplus value.[1]

First, industrial employment rose rapidly in the 1930s, fueled by a sustained burst of capital accumulation rarely equaled in the history of state or private capitalism. Secondly, managerial pressures raised the intensity of industrial labor. Finally, downward pressure on industrial workers' real wages combined with their rising productivity to reduce the value of their labor power. The dramatically enhanced surplus appropriated from workers in state capitalist industries opened new opportunities for the Council of Ministers to pursue its priority objectives. The centralization of appropriation and the rapid growth of industrial surpluses were the key changes within the enduring state capitalist class structures of Soviet industry across the 1930s.

Agricultural changes during this decade were, in Marxian class terms, much more revolutionary. State intervention transformed the mass of private ancient and small capitalist farmers into members of private collective farms. Most of such farmers were persuaded or coerced to join these collective farms. A small number became wage laborers on state farms organized in the manner of state industrial enterprises—in short, as state capitalist farms. Millions who resisted these class transformations were imprisoned, killed, or otherwise damaged in the process.

Many of those organized into collective farms began to appropriate and distribute collectively the surpluses they likewise produced as a collective. Thus, a form of the communist class structure made its first and only mass appearance in the Soviet Union.[2] It occurred in agriculture, not industry, and in the 1930s, not during the revolutionary decade after 1917.

## New Complexities and Contradictions

Despite generating greatly increased surpluses in its industrial enterprises during the 1930s, the state's industrial growth plan required still more revenues. Once again, state industrial capitalism turned to agriculture to secure the extra resources for its expansion. However, collectivization meant that the Soviet state had to tap surpluses produced by a largely communist agriculture. If the state were again to manipulate the terms of trade against agriculture, the victims would no longer be ancient and capitalist farmers. Instead it would be the great "socialist" achievement of Soviet agricultural policy, the collective farms, that would lose a part of their surpluses, which they needed urgently to survive. Distributions out of these surpluses secured the conditions of existence—the survival—of communist class structures in agriculture. As we explain below, an unfavorable movement in communism's terms of trade threatened these distributions and, hence, the securing of communism's conditions of existence. In class terms, if the state manipulated the terms of trade in this way, it would secure a rapidly growing industrial state capitalism, but at the cost of undercutting collective farms: thereby undermining (shortly after establishing) the only widespread communist class structures in Soviet history.

While state pricing policies in the 1930s weakened agricultural communism, other state policies helped to strengthen it, and still other policies did both. The effects of three particular state policies can illustrate the complexities and contradictions. First, shortly after collectivization, the state allowed collective farmers also to work individual "private plots" assigned to them on the collective farms. The state thereby enabled the partial return of the ancient class structures that collectivization had aimed to destroy. Beside their collective farm duties, individual farmers could expend time and energy on private plots. Secondly, in 1932 the state also allowed local private markets to resume, although under certain restrictions. Thirdly, the state established a new tractor industry to raise agricultural productivity.

By allowing collective farmers also to work as ancients on their private plots and to sell the products in local private markets, the state eased the burden of the low prices it set for collective farm outputs. Collective farmers used their private plots to earn extra revenues beyond their earnings as members of the collective farms. The extra revenues could strengthen the ancient class structures on their private plots or increase family consumption or both. Additionally, once communist collectives supplied the state's quotas at its set prices, they too could sell what remained in private markets, often at much higher prices. Such additional revenues could help sustain the communist collective farms.

In these ways, the ancient private plots and the private markets not only facilitated the state's transfer of revenues from the agricultural communist to the industrial state capitalist class structure. They also reinforced the former. In other ways, despite the state's constraints on private plots, their ancient class structures threatened, economically and culturally, the communist class structures on the collective farms. In simplest terms, the collective farmers had to divide their time, energy, and productivity between the two class structures in which they worked. The contradictions and tensions between the communist and ancient class structures of Soviet agriculture continued throughout the 1930s and into the postwar years as well.

Newly mass-produced tractors successfully offset an early decline in collective farm productivity. The former ancient and capitalist farmers had resisted or reacted against collectivization by destroying livestock. As the state's restoration of ancient farming and local private produce markets had helped to secure certain conditions of communist farming, the state's supply of tractors (partly to replace animals) did likewise. Yet here again the result was contradictory. The state established machine tractor stations (MTS) that typically rented tractors to collective farms. The latter thus paid for their productivity gains by delivering to the state another portion of their surpluses (in tractor rental fees)—a portion therefore unavailable to meet their other expenses.

The rise in the rate of surplus value appropriation (exploitation) inside state capitalist industry and the siphoning of surpluses from communist agriculture pressured other sites in Soviet society to relieve the burdens thus placed on industrial workers and collective farmers. Women inside Soviet feudal households, urban and rural, were pressed to produce more surpluses for their appropriating husbands. The household use-values thereby received compensated husbands, at least in part, for reduced wages or squeezed collective farm incomes. The state compensated the burdens of state workers by providing some meals at factories, subsidizing apartments, and dispensing medical care.

However, such household adjustments and state services provoked or aggravated still other social problems. Women comprised a rapidly increasing portion of both factory and farm labor forces. When they simultaneously faced growing surplus labor demands on them inside households, tensions there intensified and eventually undermined both men's and women's productivities outside their households. Similarly, the provision of state welfare programs took some state resources away from the priority of expanding state industries.

A vastly increased industrial complex centered mostly on capital goods began construction in 1929 with the first of several five-year plans. Well developed by the outbreak of World War Two, the complex required all manner of social supports, coordination of decisions, and, as always, adequate transfers of agricultural surpluses to supply an ever expanding factory labor force. A sizable state bureaucracy was quickly formed to undertake all these required tasks. The Council of Ministers distributed a portion of the surplus it appropriated from industrial workers to pay for the salaries and operating budgets of this bureaucracy (a portion thus unavailable for other uses).

Comprised of managers of both state enterprises and collective farms, technicians, and planners, the bureaucracy organized and directed the decade's vast changes in industry and agriculture. By virtue of its policies on industrial and agricultural prices, rental fees for the state-owned tractors, and so on, the bureaucracy also drew into its hands a portion of the surplus produced inside the collective farms. Thus the Soviet bureaucracy comprised a subsumed class that received both capitalist and communist surplus distributions while in turn providing both class structures with some of their conditions of existence. In Marxian language, the bureaucrats were unproductive laborers. They produced no surplus themselves but rather provided conditions of existence for productive laborers and lived off a portion (received a subsumed class distribution) from the latters' produced surplus.

Equally noteworthy was the 1930s growth of other groups of unproductive workers in Soviet society. Chief among these were the Communist Party, police, and military establishments. Also important was a new apparatus of cultural institutions, mechanisms, and programs that (1) produced new forms of art, education, and popular discourses, and (2) disseminated them widely to influence individuals' behaviors at all work sites and throughout the social formation.

Alongside the remarkable economic growth achieved in the 1930s and its equally remarkable political and cultural transformations, Soviet society retained or perhaps deepened its fragility. New contradictions threatened its survival. For example, household strife, associated with a strained feudal class structure, weakened the class structures outside the households where harried husbands and wives worked. Collective farmers oriented ever greater attention and energy to the ancient class structures of their private plots rather than to collective farm work. Producing ever more capital goods at the expense of fewer consumer goods aggravated popular discontent, household tension, and so on. The drain on state resources to sustain rapidly growing bureaucratic, party, police, and military apparatuses was both unavoidable given Soviet policy yet also costly in multiple ways.

When these contradictions interacted with others of the time (ever rising intensity of labor in industry, rising demands on the collectives' surpluses, fall in the real individual wage, and official restrictions on the grudgingly allowed ancient farming and private trade), the result was a fragile social formation. A rapidly growing state capitalist industry and a fully employed labor force coexisted with simmering social tensions approaching crisis proportions. Moreover, enough potentially critical voices were present throughout Soviet society to articulate and thereby agitate the contradictions. Ever since the October Revolution, the Bolsheviks, including Stalin, had questioned and sharply debated Soviet development. There was every reason to expect that they could and would do so again, especially given the raw dilemmas of the 1930s.

For some critics, legalizing the private plots and private trade—however constrained by the state—aborted the socialist advance embodied in collectivization. The intractable question and explosive debates of the 1920s resurfaced. Would Stalin's retreat in legalizing the ancient plots suffice or would the state also have to produce more consumer (instead of heavy industrial) goods to exchange for the farmers' foods and raw materials? Would industrial growth slow and thereby endanger socialism's survival? Other critics focused on the growing and ever more powerful state bureaucracy. Often making the social distribution of power into the essential definition and criterion of socialism, these critics saw the rise of concentrated state bureaucratic power over workers as coterminous with the erosion of a true workers' socialism.

While neither inevitable nor laudable, it is also not surprising that the state and Communist Party under Stalin intervened excessively to maintain a fragile society increasingly at risk of disintegration. The complex contradictions provoked tensions and the tensions provoked criticisms. The state and the Party then reacted, first to the criticisms, then to the intimations of criticism and finally to the potential for criticisms. By not basically changing their policies, the state and the Party not only reproduced the conditions for their social interventions, but also for the escalation of their interventions in ever more dangerous circumstances.

State and party interventions mounted from propaganda barrages to political threats to force in campaigns to suppress what they perceived as actual or potential conflicts threatening Soviet socialism. These included class conflicts (although not conceived in surplus terms): between surplus-appropriating capitalists and surplus-producing workers inside state enterprises and between state agencies and the collective farms from which they drew communist subsumed class payments. The state and the Party also moved to stop criticism of their policies by repressing theoretical differences among bureaucrats and party members. They soon began to demonize (as anti-Soviet, foreign agents, etc.) all who were or potentially might become internal critics of official policies, of the actual practices in industry and agriculture, or of the accompanying repressive roles adopted by the state and the Party across Soviet culture, politics, and economics.

This Soviet combination of repression and demonization evolved into a cultural norm. Not only class conflicts, but countless other political, economic, personal, religious, ethnic, regional, and cultural conflicts were defined instead as contests pitting Soviet loyalists against demonized "others." Accusations ever more dire choked the space of public discourse. The terrors now known as Stalinism engulfed the USSR. However, despite the threats, terror, trials, and the gulag, they never fully silenced the longstanding Bolshevik tradition of questioning, criticizing, and even debating alternative policies and strategies. This was especially the case in regard to the pace of industrialization and the proper relationship or balance between industry and agriculture or, in more passionate language, "modern socialist industry and retrograde nonsocialist agriculture."[3]

Besides repression, state and party interventions also created a new culture. Bureaucrats, party members, and, through their agency, surplus-producing workers in state capitalist enterprises and on collective farms were to be instilled with a central idea. Embellished in various ways, this idea held that all current sacrifices were the unavoidable price all citizens had to pay to build a modern socialist and industrial USSR. The promise of and pride in that modern USSR were soon symbolized and celebrated in the ubiquitous construction sites, factories, and industrial jobs that grew apace. Further, by expanding the bureaucracy while purging critics within it, Stalin provided privileged careers to selected individuals removed from industry and agriculture. The bureaucratic profile changed from older to younger, from more to less experienced, and from less to more loyal to Stalin and Stalinism.[4]

After Lenin, Stalin assumed the mantle as father of socialism. He would fulfill the Bolshevik promise of socialism: a rapidly growing modern industry, collective farming, rational state planning, and increasing collective consumption for a fully employed work force. Stalin heavily promoted the idea that socialism—definitionally reduced to collectivization in agriculture and five-year plans in industry—was actually being achieved. His commitment to "socialism in one country" differed from Trotsky's view (Deutscher 1968, 281-293). With Stalin's dominance at Trotsky's expense, the official view held that no longer would Soviet socialism be delayed until socialist revolutions occurred in the West. Quite the proud opposite: socialism in the USSR would prepare the way for other capitalist countries' revolutions to follow. As Deutscher puts it so well: "It is her destiny to become the centre of a new civilization" (1968, 293).

This notion of an actualizing socialism in the USSR helped to solidify Stalin's position. To the extent that Soviet citizens accepted the notion, it became a core part of the national ethic.[5] Opponents (or merely critics) of collectivization, the five-year plans, or the means for their achievement found themselves charged with being antisocialist and against the emerging "new civilization." Such "bad elements" were then rooted out of collectives, factories, the arts, the state apparatus, and the Party. In a war against those defined as internal enemies of the nation, producing and disseminating nationalism covered the suppression of divisive class and nonclass differences. Stalinism's national ethic enabled the state to create an ethos of collectivity and pride in Soviet modernism that often motivationally inspired workers, collective farmers, newly arrived bureaucrats, and party members. The nationalism legitimated the state's suppression of oppositional views and conflicts that nonetheless kept arising. The bureaucrats were pushed to secure the array of processes necessary for the different class structures to play their planned roles, while the workers in those class structures were pushed to maximize the agricultural and industrial surpluses. Their collective and often heroic efforts would later enable the USSR and General Stalin to emerge victorious in "The Great Patriotic [sic] War." In class terms, the cultural milieu constructed in the 1930s helped to secure a key condition for the state's incessant drive to raise the exploitation rate of industrial workers and squeeze ever more flows of value from communist collective farmers.

Despite its industrial successes, rising grain and raw material surpluses, effective nationalist appeal, and the purges of real and imagined critics, Stalin's state never could control the contradictions and tensions of the radical changes it worked in agriculture and industry. As this chapter shows, each attempt at such control, whether successful or not, provoked new contradictions and tensions in the social formation. Yet, the inability to control the consequences it set in motion, however worrisome to the regime and threatening to its policies, also worked in their favor.

For example, by centralizing the appropriation and distribution of the industrial surplus value in the Council of Ministers, Stalin opened the way for local subsumed class managers to wield some control over the operation of collective farms, industrial enterprises, and even state retail stores. Stalin's centralization required a vast planning bureaucracy as the institutional mechanism to execute the Council's decisions. However, centralized economic planning produced certain misallocations, wastes of resources, and inefficiencies.[6] The resulting frustrations provoked local communist and capitalist managers to use secret deals, bribes, and barter to acquire from one another the required raw materials, machines, and consumer goods, promised but often unavailable on time if at all via the plan.[7] Acting on their own in these decentralized ways, managers were able to operate and expand the USSR's communist and capitalist class structures, even while they circumvented central planning in ways that undermined those same structures.

Still another example of complexity and contradiction lay in the state's successful campaign to raise industrial workers' productivity by means of increased labor intensity. Industrial workers responded by demanding and, to a degree, gaining increased control over aspects of their factory life. This was the parallel accommodation within industry to the restoration of the ancient private plots and private markets in collectivized agriculture. Newly empowered factory workers sometimes made the mandated production goals of managers more difficult to achieve. Thus, the state's pressures on and controls of industrial labor, however successful, also required their partial empowerment, possibly threatening their productivity. It is quite possible that the state's failures ever fully to control the workers benefited industrial capital accumulation insofar as workers produced more surplus while compensating themselves with more workplace power.

## Communism in Agriculture

While we found no analysis of Soviet collective farming that treated its class structures in surplus terms, there are many other analyses. Typically, they focus attention on one or both of two particular political processes. The first refers to the distribution of power between central and local state officials over the work and political lives of collective farmers. The second refers to the distribution of ownership rights (among the state, the collective, and the individual farm family) over the means of production used on collective farms.

Such political rather than surplus focused theorizations prevail within Soviet Marxism itself. For example, many official and unofficial formulations defined collectives chiefly according to the extent of collective ownership ("socialization") of the means of production and secondarily according to the presence of collective consumption of meals and housing (Davies 1980, 68; Lewin 1975, 110–111; Dobb 1966, 223). Thus they differentiated the three main types of collective farms—communes, artels, and *toz*—by their ownership rules. The *toz*—"fellowship for joint cultivation"—was considered to be the least socialized because most implements and animals remained privately owned and only the land was collectively farmed (Wesson 1963, 7–8). The eventual Soviet choice of the artel to be the main organizational form in their collectivization drive reflected how ownership (socialization) of land, implements, and draft animals had become the defining concept of what socialism meant in agriculture.

Consider, for example, Stalin's speech delivered at a conference on agrarian policy in 1929: "The collective farm as a *type* of economy, is one of the forms of socialist economy. There can be no doubt whatever about that" (Stalin 1952, 404). The collective farms "function on land which belongs to the state, in a country where the means of production belong to the state;" (ibid., 406). Interestingly, Stalin's speech responded directly and critically to Larin, an economist of the day, who saw much less socialism in the newly formed collectives. For Larin, they were transitional structures because the means of production belonged, not to the state, but rather to a collectivity of *private* farmers (Davies 1980, 85–86). Full socialization would arrive only when collectives became state enterprises, for at that critical point the means finally would belong to the state. Despite their sharp differences, both Larin and Stalin made particular distributions of ownership their definitions of socialism. Similarly, the critic Moshe Lewin saw in collectivization the return of serfdom because of the state's power over the collective farms: "Shadows of the past could be seen in this situation, ever more reminiscent of what was abolished in 1861" (Lewin 1985, 183).[8] While this claim may be more rhetorical than precise—underscoring Stalin's despotism—it nonetheless reveals yet again the ubiquitous power-focused definitions of collectives, socialism, and much else besides.[9]

Unlike these power approaches focused on who possesses the means of production or orders farmers' behavior, our inquiry stresses different questions. Who produced, appropriated, and distributed the surpluses produced in the collectives and how were these class processes organized? To whom and for what purposes were those distributions made? Our research found that the working members of the collective often functioned as the appropriators and hence the distributors of the surpluses that they collectively had produced. These farms' working members—not any centralized agency such as a Council of Ministers, nor any local Soviet officials—comprised the officially designated collective entity that appropriated and distributed its produced surpluses. From a class-theoretical perspective focused on how surplus labor is organized, we conclude that many collective farms were communist. Their communist class structure was thus very different from the class structures that our research found prevalent in state industries (capitalist) and households (feudal and ancient).

Likely for the first time in history, collectivization freed masses of farmers from exploitation and bare subsistence and organized them instead to participate in a communist class structure: to receive as a collectivity the fruits of their collective efforts. That such a basic change in a class structure was not understood or recognized in its surplus dimensions undermined its durability (as we shall show) and its potential appeal to others. That it was accompanied by so much political abuse, violence, and suffering had the same effects.

To be sure, the evidence also suggests that many collective farms sooner or later lost (and perhaps some never had) communist class structures. In them, a subgroup of members—as opposed to the collectivity as a whole—appropriated the collective farm's surplus. Perhaps they maneuvered an initially elected, temporary, or rotational position as managers into a self-perpetuating position akin to that of a board of directors of a modern private capitalist corporation. Perhaps local officials or party members usurped the position of surplus appropriators in place of the collective of farmers. Perhaps the collectivity, not interested in or conscious of class processes per se, simply gave the appropriator position to a subgroup of its members. Because the available empirical evidence on the internal workings of the collective farms was rarely gathered with any sensitivity to class in surplus labor terms, distinguishing the communist from other class structures on collective farms is often difficult. However, because the evidence we consulted suggested the prevalence of the communist class structures on the collective farms and because of our special interest in communist class structures and their relation to the history of the USSR, our discussion focuses chiefly on the collective farms with communist class structures.

In asking our class theoretical questions of the collective farms, we used the existing literature in which different theories treated them. We also examined the laws, contemporary speeches and debates about collective farms, and letters by collective members as reported in the press. We looked for information on the farms' internal functioning that might enable a specification of their organization of surplus labor (its production, appropriation, and distribution). Our distilled results gather around two points. First, the proceeds of the collective farm's crop, whether sold at compulsory prices to the state or on the private markets for higher prices, belonged first to (were appropriated by) the members as a collective. Secondly, the collective also distributed the surplus portion of those proceeds, although it was influenced in its distributions of the surplus by orders from both local and distant Soviet officials. Davies's research led to this conclusion: "In the kolkhozy, peasant families had no personal connections with a particular piece of land, plough, or horse, but the means of production *and farm output* belonged to them collectively as a 'group of private persons'" (Davies 1980, 86, italics added). Emphasizing that the output belonged to the local collectivity rather than to the state suggests that the former, therefore, also received first the surplus embodied in that output. Davies makes a similar point in noting that each collective farm—*not* any individual farmer, centralized ministry, or decentralized trust or syndicate—was designated socially (whether by law or custom) to receive the revenues upon sale of the crops.[10] Those revenues belonged to the collective and served as the financial base for its expenditures. A significant part of the revenues "went into a kolkhoz saving account" from which the collective eventually distributed portions to secure various conditions necessary to reproduce the collective (Fitzpatrick 1994b, 192).

Such communist class structures confronted state officials with a problem, but it was not the problem of who ultimately owned the collective farm's means of production. Rather the state had to deal with a class of communist surplus appropriators. The collective farm had its own goals, necessities, and rights—however contradictory and contested—in determining the size and distribution of its surpluses, that is, the surpluses it owned. The Soviet state's primary commitment to expanding state capitalist industry now encountered a very particular class problem, one defined by the specific structure and dynamic of a private (i.e., nonstate) communist agriculture.

Evidence of communist class structures on many collective farms also appears in personal reports on collective farm operations. Belov (1955) worked on a collective farm (reorganized in 1930 as an artel), became chairman of a collective in his own village, and eventually published a book based on his diaries. In explaining the structure of a collective, he writes: " . . . during and immediately after the harvest, before the deliveries to the state have been made (the 'First Commandment') and before the seed, insurance and fodder funds have been replenished (the 'Second Commandment'), all the crops are kolkhoz property, and woe betide the peasant who is caught making off with a kilogram of grain . . . " (Belov 1955, 32). Belov here captures the importance of state pressures ("Commandments") on farm collectives. The state applied pressure because the entire crop belonged first to the collective that produced it, not to any subset of its members nor to any set of state officials. This precisely differentiated collective farmers from state industrial workers (and from state farm workers). Having supported and even organized farmers into communist class structures on many collective farms, the state then found itself compelled to use pressure and eventually force to acquire the surplus distributions it wanted from the communist surplus that the collective itself appropriated. The Soviet state intervened to order the collective farm to distribute some of its surplus in certain ways, but ordering how others distribute their surplus is different from appropriating and distributing surplus. The state exerted power, while the collective produced, appropriated, and distributed a surplus.[11]

Notwithstanding state power exerted on communist collective farms and problems for their reproduction that flowed from state-mandated surplus distributions, the state also supported private communist collective farms in many ways. For example, it legislated and enforced a sequence of statutes governing the collective farms' functions and assets (Hubbard 1939, 125–147; Davies 1980, ch. 5; Jasny 1967, 338–362). Particularly relevant were the decrees establishing periodic meetings to decide upon major economic decisions relating to the management and overall functioning of the collective (Davies 1980, 57; Belov 1955, 30–52; Hindus 1988, 211–212). Yet the Soviet laws that empowered collective farmers to establish functioning communist class structures also had contradictory effects. While collectivization secured farmers' access to means of production they had lacked before, it also largely eliminated (except for the private plots) the potential of private gain. Private individuals on collective farms could not use means of production to appropriate surplus labor from others. Additionally, the productivity benefits flowing from the collective use of such means too often disappeared into the hands of the state via its mandatory procurements, price manipulations, tractor rents, and taxes. Hence the communist collectivity was restrained from benefiting from its own achievements in productivity gains.

Given such state-imposed constraints, it is hardly surprising that many farmers resisted the state's collectivization program, passively or actively, at its outset and thereafter (Fitzpatrick 1994b, 5–7). For many members, their collective farms seemed little more than forced deprivations of their private property and simple mechanisms for the state to take large portions of their output. The state and party called this socialism—because private property was gone and because they controlled the state that controlled the economy. Evidently, many collective farmers found little in such a socialism to celebrate.

Neither Soviet officials nor collective farmers recognized how processes of producing, appropriating, and distributing surplus labor defined communism's difference from any kind of exploitation. Consequently, whatever potential economic, cultural, and political benefits might have accrued from a consciousness of communism in surplus terms were lost. Unable to conceptualize, let alone disseminate, the class (qua surplus labor) issue, Soviet political, economic, and cultural leaders were unable to take advantage of the truly revolutionary change they had actually created in their own society. On the class issue, they were as theoretically underdeveloped as the supposedly backward farmers they sought to manage. Neither they nor the farmers could ask how Soviet individuals and institutions might have altered their behaviors in economically productive ways if such class consciousness had been widely developed.[12]

The history of the "25,000ers" illustrates the contradictions faced by communist class structures in the collective farms. These thousands of young, dedicated, and skilled cadres went to the collective farms charged by the party with bringing the idea of communism to the peasants (Viola 1987). On the farms they conveyed utopian dreams of a better life, images of the social ascendancy of all workers, and notions of the impending arrival of social democracy and equality. They imported a kind of cultural revolution of communism into the countryside. Their passion and enthusiasm, alongside the applicable statutes, helped in some ways to foster communist class structure in many collective farms.[13]

However, the cadres' theories and actions also undermined that same class structure. They believed, as the party taught, that agricultural communism meant extending the socialism already established in industry (Viola 1987, 4, 153–154). They foresaw organizations of surplus labor in collective farms parallel to that in Soviet factories: in effect, an exploitative class structure in which some collective farm members would appropriate the surpluses produced by the other members. They strove also to reproduce the successes of the Soviets' industrial revolution on the collective farms: above all increased intensity and productivity of labor. Thus the 25,000ers worked contradictory class pressures on the collective farms, simultaneously (albeit unknowingly) supporting communist and capitalist class structures there.

Two different communal traditions also influenced collective farms. One emerged from the older institution of the mir and the other from the agrarian communes established after the 1917 revolution. They shaped the farms' communist class structures in contradictory ways. From the mir came ideas of self-governing peasants periodically redistributing land among their households. This tradition seemed to be embodied in and thereby to legitimize the powers vested in the local collectives. In this way, the memory of the mir helped to support the communist class structure. Yet, in other ways, associating the collectives with the mir also worked against communist class structures since, after all, the mir's main function had been to provide each peasant with his own (ancient or capitalist) farm (Lewin, 1975, 27). Collectivization broke with that function, as it eliminated or constricted the private individual farm.

Although the artel replaced the commune as the preferred organizational form of Soviet collectivization, the ideology of the commune largely continued, especially in regard to supporting collective surplus appropriation. In shifting to artels, what the collective farms discarded were the communal ideas of collective housing and dining arrangements and totally socialized ownership of means of production. The practice of collective members participating fully in the receipt and disposal of the produce of their collective labor remained central to communist culture on many collective farms (Wesson 1963, 8, 130; Belov 1955, 7).

The survival of communist class structures on collective farms also depended on improving their productivity. By integrating and consolidating the formerly ancient and capitalist farmers' individually owned lands, animals, and implements, and by massively introducing rented tractors (via the MTS), the collective farms eventually (after 1934) raised their productivity of labor (Moorsteen and Powell 1966, 370). Larger than their predecessor ancient and capitalist farms, the collective farms enabled a new cooperation and division of agricultural labor, which also helped to raise productivity. New, state-trained managers, located strategically inside each collective and in the local MTS, oversaw and orchestrated collective farm development and intensified the pace of work. The effects on productivity were positive. Finally, by officially sanctioning the return of ancient household plots and private markets, the regime relieved some of the pressures associated with the state's drive to make collective farms more productive.

By enabling the collective farms to become more productive, state policies supported the many communist class structures established in them. Yet other state policies, such as the pricing strategies (discussed further below), gave a distinct advantage to the ancient class structures on the private plots over and against the collectives' communist class structure. As with the pricing policy under the NEP, farmers faced an incentive to produce for and sell on the private market, even though the state also restricted and constrained that incentive and market. Unlike the NEP situation of the 1920s, in the 1930s few if any private merchants functioned as middlemen. Ancient farmers had thus to take on the additional task of being their own merchant in local private markets.

Most importantly, the 1930s Soviet farmer was internally conflicted as two radically different farming personalities warred inside him/her: the worker/member in the collective farm's communist class structure and the worker/individual in the private plot's ancient class structure. Farmers only recently assembled into collective farms labored, appropriated, distributed, voted, and thought about their lives there while simultaneously engaged in and influenced by these two different class structures. However, the contradictions and struggles that arose in Soviet agriculture were never recognized nor confronted as class conflicts: conflicts precisely over the social organization of surplus labor. The leaders and the led did not think in such class terms; their theories of Soviet socialism ignored the specifics of how surplus labor was produced, appropriated, and distributed. Thus the class contradictions could and did deepen with relatively little hindrance from state policy. Eventually, as we will show, this would help to undermine both goals of collectivization: establishing communism in agriculture and sustaining rapid state industrialization.

Parallel to our previous analyses of ancient and capitalist farming, we can use simple value equations to highlight key aspects of the 1930s Soviet social formation. We will focus upon (1) the communist class structure on collective farms, (2) how the state tapped communist agriculture for revenues to supplement the surpluses that it appropriated from state capitalist industries, and (3) how the ancient interacted with the communist class structures on the collective farms.

We return to our earlier notation for the value flows of a communist class structure: $C(Co) + V(Co) + SV(Co) = W(Co)$. The $C(Co)$ term stands for the means of production used up to produce the crop. The $V(Co)$ term represents the value of labor power, the value of what collective farm workers got for their individual consumption. The $SV(Co)$ term is the surplus value received collectively by the farmers who produced it.[14] These three value terms comprise the total value of the produced crop, $W(Co)$. This total value was also understood as the "cost of production" of the collective farm output.

The Soviet state intervened in such communist class structures on collective farms chiefly in two ways. First, it mandated the portions of the harvest to be sold to state procurement agencies at state-administered prices. Second, the state pressured the general meeting (everyone aged sixteen years or older) to distribute their appropriated surplus, SV(Co), to replenish specific collective farm funds. The state's initial demands for portions of collective farm harvests differed from the requisitions of war communism because the obligatory deliveries to state merchants (procurement agents) were paid for at state-set prices. The difference widened early in 1932 when the collective farms, after completing obligatory deliveries to the state, could legally sell some or all of the remaining harvest on local private markets. For a more complete statement of the value equation for the collective farms, see appendix A of this chapter.

A key issue concerns the price paid by state merchants for the obligatory collective farm deliveries. Some observers claim that these prices were below the collective's production costs (Lewin 1985, 169–170; Volin 1970, 251; Fitzpatrick 1994b, 72 and 129). If correct—and remembering that "production costs" equal the total values of marketed collective farm products—it follows that the Soviet state forced an unequal exchange upon the collective farms. The communist class structures on collective farms thus received less from the state in money than the worth, in value terms, of the products they sold to state merchants. Such action by the state would have significantly damaged those communist class structures. On the other hand, other evidence suggests that state procurement prices for obligatory agricultural deliveries rose in the early 1930s and perhaps later as well, possibly even exceeding their values.[15] Had this been the case, such state pricing policies would have, in effect, subsidized the communist class structures by an unequal exchange in their favor. Unfortunately, no conclusive evaluation of these claims is possible.

However, two other contemporary realities overwhelmed the exchanges between state merchants and collective farms. First, the prices of industrial goods that collective farms purchased from the state rose very quickly. Because few consumer goods manufactured by state industries were available to farmers from the state merchants (in state stores) at their regulated prices, the so-called goods famine of the 1920s had reappeared in the rural areas in the 1930s. Not surprisingly, the price of manufactures—even in state stores as well as the uncontrolled or private "commercial stores" and markets—rose dramatically.[16] The collective farms' terms of trade (the ratio of the state procurement prices they received to the high prices of the scarce manufactures they could find chiefly in the "commercial" stores) moved decidedly against them. Thus their communist class structures suffered a severe financial squeeze whether or not they may have enjoyed a slightly favorable unequal exchange for their products. For a more complete statement of the value crisis faced by the collective farms in this pricing situation, see appendix B of this chapter.

The second important reality impinging on the communist class structures in the collective farms were the much more favorable prices facing the ancient class structures on the private plots. Unlike the collective farm products sold to state merchants at state-set prices, the products of the private plots sold in uncontrolled, private markets. There they fetched prices that rose far faster across the 1930s than the state's procurement prices (Dobb 1966, 285; Baykov 1947, 240–241).[17] Thus, communist class structures found themselves damaged financially by a pricing system that simultaneously rewarded the ancient class structures on the private plots. It is reasonable to suppose that collective farmers adjusted their hopes, energies, attitudes, and labor commitments toward the one and away from the other class structure available to them on the farms.

The communist class structures on the collective farms soon found themselves in a critical situation. Unable to alter the prices that effectively deprived them of a significant portion of the value they produced, they accommodated their losses by cutting collective farm expenditures. They could not safely choose to forego replacing the means of production used up: the requisite quantities of seed, fodder, implements, and fertilizer needed at least to maintain collective farm operations. When that was nonetheless done, as in the desperate circumstances of 1932, it contributed to famine the following year.

Equally risky were reductions of certain expenditures that state officials pressured the collective farms to maintain. These were expenditures from the collective farm's surpluses (what remained of the harvest after state-mandated deliveries, the replacement of used-up means of production, and distributions for the members' own consumption.) Such expenditures—communist subsumed class payments—included providing salaries and operating budgets to collective farm personnel for supervision, bookkeeping, planning, insurance, cultural activities, child-rearing, and some collective-farm capital accumulation.[18] The state also demanded another such expenditure in the form of rental payments (typically in kind) for tractors leased by the state's MTS.[19] Finally, the state pressed still more of such subsumed class payments on the collective farm: for example, taxes, fees for specific state services, and interest on loans from the state. All of these expenditures aimed to secure crucial conditions of existence for the collective farms. To lessen or refuse such expenditures jeopardized that existence.

Not surprisingly, the collective farms, therefore, often accommodated their price-induced crises by cutting their members' consumption (of manufactures and retained food). In class terms, this meant raising the ratio of surplus to necessary labor within the collective farms' communist class structures. In the very different Soviet conception prevalent then, collective farmers' net personal incomes and, hence, consumption were viewed as a "residual or dividend" left to members after all the other, necessary expenditures in money and kind had been satisfied (Davies 1980, 175).[20] Of course, such consumption expenditures—however conceived as "residual"—were at least as necessary as all the others to reproduce the communist class structure of the collective farms. In constricting consumption, the state weakened the communist class structures of the collective farms.

The continued movement of the terms of trade against the collective farms across the 1930s threatened to keep depressing consumption unless the collective farms found offsetting opportunities. These included (1) raising their productivity, (2) marketing more of their retained crop (what remained after meeting state procurement requirements) at the higher prices on the uncontrolled markets, or (3) turning to noncommunist sources of income to supplement their members' collective farm earnings. How collective farms variously pursued each of these three opportunities shaped the changing agrarian scene across the 1930s.

The history of agricultural labor productivity during the 1930s appears to be U-shaped, falling from 1930 to 1934 and rising thereafter. For the decade as a whole, no perceptible change emerged.[21] The initial fall likely reflected opposition to collectivization as farmers reduced their activity and ate their animals (Fitzpatrick 1994b, passim; Dobb 1966, 246–247). Reduced draft animals and manure lowered agricultural productivity. The upturn after 1934 reflected an increased supply of tractors, shrinking opposition to collectivization, and probably more efficient use of land, labor, and implements. However, the evidence suggests to us that rising productivity did not suffice to offset the depressing effect of unfavorable terms of trade on collective farmers' consumption levels.

On the other hand, destroying livestock likely benefited communist farmers' consumption immediately after collectivization: extra meat and the grain no longer needed to feed reduced herds. Lower fodder needs enabled them to satisfy the state's supply quotas more easily. Early in the first five-year plan, this phenomenon temporarily offset otherwise squeezed consumption levels. But the falling productivity consequent upon eating animals then contributed to the extreme famine of 1933 and the urgent problems it posed.

The Soviet state, continually forced to react to threats emanating from its own policies, shifted its positions. From Stalin's well-known admonition to party zealots in his 1930 "Dizzy With Success" letter, policy lurched to the reluctant raising of procurement prices for collective farm outputs. In 1932, private trading was again allowed, and the state fixed supply quotas *in advance of the actual output*. In 1935 the state officially accepted ancient household plots and eliminated rationing. These policies relaxed the pressures that other state policies had placed on collectives, and especially on their consumption levels.

State policies were not consistent. For example, farmers' resentments and resistance led the state in 1932 to change how it assessed the collective farms' supply quotas. Prior to the harvest, it fixed the amount of produce to be delivered, and local authorities could not demand more if the harvest proved abundant. The state also permitted collective farms to sell produce beyond the state's quotas in local, uncontrolled markets. Yet these concessions seemed to make matters worse. Even when reduced, the fixed supply quotas for grains were not met. Instead, crops were not produced or consumed on the farms or shifted from state deliveries to sales on the uncontrolled markets. Unfulfilled procurement plans threatened the state's industrialization program. Stalin reacted strongly. Increased procurement quotas were reimposed and strictly enforced.

Such state oscillations set in motion still new contradictions. Collecting more grain for the state reduced what farmers could sell on the uncontrolled markets and/or keep for their own consumption, fodder, seed, and reserves. The pricing environment they faced deteriorated in 1932 as planned procurement prices fell. At the same time, the costs of grain production rose: the delayed effect of the previous reduction of the animal population, itself a reaction to collectivization. In Marxian terms, the value (cost) of grain rose just as the state's prices for it fell. Ever rising prices of manufactures, available only in the uncontrolled markets, completed the economic depression of the collective farms, setting the stage for the 1933 famine. Once again the state had to react. It shifted industrial production from consumer goods to tractors to raise farm productivity. The 1935 Articles of Association granted communist farmers, among other freedoms, the right to participate in ancient class structures on private plots.

The changing, often chaotic and contradictory policies of the 1930s resembled those of the 1920s. Common to both decades was the impossibility of the state foreseeing or monitoring—much less controlling—the infinite set of contradictory consequences set in motion by its own actions. Despite differences between the two decades' specific class structures and policy mixes, in both periods the combination of state planning and markets failed to prevent profound economic instability. In that sense, the USSR's social formation—its socialism—remained as much at risk in the 1930s as under the NEP.

The collective farms suffered persistent, debilitating disadvantages as their exchange relations with the state forced a net outflow of value from their communist class structure to the state industries' capitalist class structure. Added to this outflow were substantial subsumed class rents paid for state-owned tractors. That the communist class structures on the collective farms could survive and keep funding state capitalist industrial growth depended chiefly on the official support of private plots and private trade. By so compensating for the squeezing of the collective farms' communist class structure, Stalin's policies helped the latter to endure, even while compromising their future.

The fragility of the communist class structure on the collective farms emerges further if we distinguish male from female farmers. For the male heads of traditional (married adults) households, personal revenues had three main sources: (1) income from the communist class structure in the form of "collective labor day dividends," (2) income from their labor within the ancient class structure of the private plot, and (3) income in the form of feudal surplus labor appropriated from their wives.[22] Occasional extra revenues depended on selling farm or private plot produce at prices above their values (costs) on uncontrolled markets. When such males found their collective labor day dividends squeezed for the reasons discussed in this chapter, they responded by obtaining more income from their other two sources.

Their wives faced the other side of these conditions. In addition to labor within the collective farms' communist class structures, they worked long hours on the private plots with their ancient class structures as well as providing surplus labor to their husbands within the feudal class structures of those households.[23] Where male collective farmers generally spent much more time working within the farm's communist class structure than within the ancient class structure of the private plot, their wives displayed the reverse allocation of their labor time.[24] Within the traditional households, the female farmers performed necessary labor (whose fruits they consumed) and surplus labor (whose fruits the husband appropriated and consumed or distributed) in the feudal class structure. Thus, female collective farmers received personal incomes from (1) their labor within the communist class structure of the collective farm, the "collective labor-day dividends," (2) their work on the ancient class structure of the private plot, and (3) the necessary labor they performed in the feudal class structure of the traditional household. Like their male counterparts, they too could benefit occasionally from opportunities to sell produce at prices in excess of their values or to sell their labor power. But where the traditional household was a source of surplus for the husband, it was the site of additional surplus labor for the wife. In contrast, for the collective farm women who lived in single adult households, their revenue sources there substituted an ancient for a feudal class structure. Unlike their married collective farm colleagues, they neither exploited a spouse nor were they exploited by one inside their households.[25]

Stalin's revolution in agriculture liberated the majority of women as well as men from being exploited within capitalist class structures there. On the other hand, collectivization did not liberate most women from continued feudal exploitation within collective farm households. Women's arduous household labors producing surpluses there added to their work burdens on the communist and ancient class structures of the collective farms. In contrast, husbands appropriated their wives' feudal household surplus (and, when possible, increased it), as a kind of compensation for the husbands' labor burdens within the other class structures of the collective farms. Such different experiences of men and women collective farmers—and especially their different vulnerabilities to pressures on the collective farms—aggravated gender inequalities and tensions. As we shall show, the tensions eventually weakened not only the collective farms but the Soviet social formation generally.

The survival of the communist class structures on collective farms came to depend on the private plots. In the view of one farm chairman, "it was the plots which saved the majority of households from starvation" (Belov 1955, 179). Lewin made a similar point: "[the small plot] was also, as Soviet writers agree today, a factor sustaining not only the country but the whole kolkhoz system as well" (Lewin 1985, 180). Hubbard's limited sample of collective farms showed that in 1934, 97 percent of their grain consumption came from their labor dividends, but ancient plots provided most of their other food needs. The latter supplied 87 percent of their potatoes, 78 percent of their vegetables, and 100 percent of their milk and meat (Hubbard 1939, 173). In examining another study done in 1934, Hubbard found that 37.7 percent of the farmers' total incomes derived from collective farming, 56.6 percent from the household plots, and 6.4 percent from occasionally sold labor power (1939, 177). These and still other studies attest to the ancient private plots' contribution to the survival of the collective farmer then and later.[26]

The importance of the private plots in sustaining the collective farms' communist class structures emerges as well from the market conditions of the 1930s. Stalin's industrialization engaged ever more laborers. The resulting demand for more food, whose production, transport, and storage would have diverted scarce resources from industrial growth, led Stalin to impose food rationing to 1935. This drove up food prices on the uncontrolled markets (Baykov 1947, 241). Both grain (produced by the communist class structures on the collective farms) and other foods (largely produced by the ancient class structures on the private plots) enjoyed these higher prices.

However, ancient class structures benefited much more from these price increases than communist class structures, because procurement quotas and other state pressures limited what collective farms actually could sell there.[27] Whatever grain supplies collective farms retained after meeting state demands were sold to state merchants and other enterprises under "decentralized purchases," to local industrial enterprises under barter arrangements, or to workers in local private markets. In contrast, private plot produce (animal products, vegetables, and so forth) could be entirely sold in uncontrolled markets at high prices to industrial workers (who were unable to buy them at state stores at official prices). The entire collective farm system—and especially the communist class structure at its core—was enabled to continue because of the incomes farm members could derive from their private plots. When collective farmers confronted the high prices for manufactures in both official and uncontrolled markets, they again recognized the greater rewards from work on their private plots as compared to work as part of the collective.

Thus, the ancient class structures of the private plots were favored, encouraged, and strengthened—in fact if not in official rhetoric—far more than the collective farms' communist class structures. Yet the latter survived. Its members tolerated the collective farm system increasingly because of what they obtained from their private plots. They probably presumed the necessity of conjoining both class structures inside the farms. Yet they might not presume that in the future, especially if the difference in rewards from the two class structures widened. The relationship between the ancient and the communist class structures on the collective farms was thus contradictory; they simultaneously supported and undermined one another.

Per capita consumption in agriculture at the end of the 1930s seemed to have improved from the 1930–33 decline. Yet, it had not recovered to the level of the late 1920s (Harrison 1994, 52). This suggests that while private plots and private trade improved living standards, their benefits did not offset the state's pressures on the collective farms. Delivery quotas, unfavorable terms of trade, tractor rentals, and other taxes and fees bled the communist class structures Stalin had established on the collective farms. The beneficiary was state capitalist industrial growth. Yet this overall judgment too needs to be tempered by other considerations.

First, collective farms received benefits (as did their individual members) in return for sending the state so much of the surplus produced in their communist class structures. From the mid-1920s to the end of the 1930s, the state supplied collective farms with many more agronomists, veterinarians, and research scientists; with more libraries, newspapers, cinemas, and medical services; and with a vast expansion in educational opportunities (Baykov 1947, 328; Hubbard 1939, 238). Such benefits supported communist class structures in collective farms.

Second, the collective farms displayed marked differences in soil conditions, size, efficiency and honesty of local officials, commitment and productivity of collective workers, size and wealth of farm households, efficiency of private plot production, and so forth. Such differences produced disparities in income and wealth among collective farms that shared the same class structures: "Instead of poverty being eliminated from the countryside and a better and more equal distribution of agricultural income brought about, collectivization shows relative wealth alongside great poverty no less than the old system of independent peasant enterprise" (Hubbard, 1939, 237). As argued in our first two chapters, communist class structures can occur with or without equalization of wealth and incomes; Soviet collective farms illustrate the latter possibility. However, most Soviet citizens saw matters in the light of different theories. They often attributed the greater wealth of some collective farms to their greater collectivity of ownership, commitment, or effort. Without a class (qua surplus) analysis of collective farms, their alternative perspective would have functioned socially as a support for the communist class structures of the farms.

While collectivization established communist class structures widely in the USSR, the state's subsequent policies did much to undermine them. On the one hand, collective farmers were legally, officially, and popularly differentiated from the farmers under the NEP, from workers in state enterprises, and from women working inside households. They owned their farms and their farms' outputs. On the other hand, precisely because collective farm members occupied that social position, the state had to intervene *from the outside*, to influence how the collective farm, as a separate, nonstate institution, functioned. State officials did not appropriate the surpluses produced on collective farms as they did, by contrast, on the state farms and in the state industries. Instead, in Lewin's apt description, the state engaged in "taking grain" from collective farmers (Lewin 1985, 142–177). It manipulated terms of trade, tractor rents, and taxes and fees to extract distributed portions of the communist surplus first appropriated by the collective farmers. The Soviet state supported and undermined the communist class structures on the collective farms simultaneously across the 1930s. Likewise simultaneously, the collective farmers supported, resented, and resisted the Soviet state and their own communist class structures.

Despite endless discourses about communism, state officials and party theorists lacked any class analysis of their problems in surplus labor terms. They did not think in terms of the multiple class structures of 1930s agriculture, let alone differentiate communist from capitalist or ancient class structures on the farms. Nor did they recognize the existence or social impact of the feudal and ancient class structures in traditional farm households. They could not assess—or debate alternative policy responses to—the class contradictions and struggles besetting Soviet agriculture. Instead, their discussions proceeded as if collectivization simply resolved and hence removed from consideration all class issues. The only problem was simply quantitative: how to secure sufficient grain and raw materials deliveries to fund "socialist industrialization."

The state's various agricultural policies thus followed one another without any awareness of their differential impacts on Soviet agricultural class structures. As we have shown, one result was to maintain but also progressively to undermine the communist class structures there. Another result was to support instead the ancient class structures of the private plots and the feudal class structures of households.[28] While the consumption afforded by the ancient and feudal class structures sometimes compensated farmers for the inadequate consumption levels flowing from the communist class structures on the collective farms, the complex class structure of Soviet agriculture was rendered fragile and unstable. This portended a future of agricultural problems for the USSR that contributed to endless economic difficulties and to its eventual collapse.

Lastly, one agricultural development of the 1930s best illustrates how the interaction between agricultural problems and official Marxian theory undermined the collective farms' communist class structures. Inadequate farm deliveries to state industry produced debates that concluded with a predictable state and party consensus: the problem lay in the still private—that is, not state—ownership of the collective farms. The solution was to convert collective farms into state farms. A relatively small number of these state-owned, state-capitalist alternatives to collective farms had been established during collectivization. The consensus held this conversion to be movement toward communism since it "socialized" farm property. Once again we encounter the property concept of class and hence of socialism and communism (which the consensus attributed to Marx). With a different Marxian interpretation of class, the Soviet shift from collective to state farms represents the opposite transition: away from communist to capitalist class structures. Soviet history thus displays both the establishment and the withering of agricultural communism as policies undertaken by a state and party that used Marxism to reach their conclusions.

## State Capitalism and Industry

Soviet industrial successes in the 1930s are well documented (Dobb 1966, ch. 10–12; Nove 1989, ch. 8, and 9; Harrison 1994, ch. 3; Gregory and Stuart 1998, ch. 5). The following table summarizes industrial growth over this decade:

### Average Annual Percentage Growth Rates, 1928–1940[29]

| | |
|---|---|
| Rolled metal (steel) production | 11.2 |
| Pig-iron production | 12.6 |
| Industrial capital accumulation | 12.3 |
| Industrial employment | 7.0 |
| Capital per worker in industry | 5.3 |
| Electric power | 18.9 |
| Tractor production | 30.0 |

Annual growth rates exceeding 10 percent in iron and steel production reflected the priority of heavy industry in the Soviet five-year plans begun in 1928. This remarkable industrial expansion accompanied increased mechanization: the capital labor ratio in industry rose 5 percent annually. Finally, rapid growth in electric power generation and in tractor production indicates the structural changes that transformed urban and rural lives.

However impressive, these growth rates are not the full story of successful state capitalist industrial expansion. The USSR acquired a huge capital goods sector with modern industrial complexes in chemicals, metal fabricating, and engineering (Dobb 1966, 281; Davies 1994, 143–154). For example, while heavy industry accounted for 33.1 percent of total manufacturing value added in 1928, by 1937 it was 62.7 (Gregory 1970, 29). Industry's proportion of net national product rose from 28 to 45 percent between 1928 and 1937 (Gregory and Stuart 1998, 87). Such development placed the USSR among the leading industrial capitalist nations in the world. Germany during World War Two and the United States during the Cold War encountered the achievements of Soviet industrialization.

The cost of financing this unprecedented industrialization had to be met domestically, since significant foreign aid or lending were unavailable. Moreover, the USSR's huge industrial capital accumulation accounted for only a part of its expenditures from—and hence demands upon—the surplus its economy generated. In addition to industrial growth, the state was also rapidly increasing expenditures on a state bureaucracy, the Communist Party, a modern military apparatus, and the provision of many free or subsidized collective consumption goods. The latter included public education, health facilities, transportation, and even meals for some industrial workers. The revenues enabling such state expenditures derived chiefly from (1) an increased rate of exploitation of ever more industrial workers, (2) terms of trade favoring industry against agriculture, and (3) manipulations of wholesale and retail prices.

These sources of state revenues were also indexes of what threatened Soviet society. Increasingly exploiting industrial workers while also squeezing farmers and workers (by imposing unequal exchanges upon them) produced dangerous levels of discontent in Soviet society. The state responded in part with economic interventions: providing free public goods to at least partially offset declining real individual incomes, allowing private plots and markets, offering industrial jobs to those leaving the countryside, increasing employment in the state bureaucracy, and so on. Discontent also prompted the state's political interventions—police terror and the gulag—to suppress first actual and then "potential" unrest, increasingly labeled as "anti-Soviet."

The state also intervened heavily in Soviet culture. Officials and others produced and disseminated images celebrating current economic policies as expressions of national pride. Rapid industrialization became the definitive symbol of the USSR's break with historical backwardness. Opposition to rapid industrialization or its domestic costs became synonymous with subjection to foreign jealousies and intrigues against Soviet ascendancy. Fear grew among the Soviet masses as proliferating warnings about foreign capitalist aggression escalated to hunts for its possible internal allies. All kinds of cultural production—often organized and subsidized by the state and the Party—were pressed into service. Industrial construction, nationalist pride, and fear of foreign and domestic "wreckers" intertwined as major themes of literature, films, music, and painting. They helped to rationalize and justify the necessity of workers' reduced individual incomes and consumption despite their rising productivity levels. Personal sacrifices were protecting the growing achievements of Soviet socialism.

The state's economic, political, and cultural interventions in the 1930s sought to sustain its top priority of a rapidly growing state capitalist industry, a subordinated communist and ancient agriculture, and an even more subordinated mix of feudal and ancient households. Individual citizens negotiated stressful lives among these multiple, fragile, and unstable class structures. Tensions within and among the interdependent class structures added problems for state policy since they threatened its concept of socialism. The state's responses, whether or not they solved those problems, added new contradictions, strains, and new problems in the endless dialectic that framed the class history of the 1930s.

We may begin to explore that dialectic by considering the flow of food and raw materials from the countryside into the cities. State merchants bought them from the collective farms at state-set prices roughly equal to their values (or costs) for food and sometimes exceeding their values for raw materials. Under the rationing which lasted through 1935, the merchants resold food crops to industrial workers in cities at variously higher prices. The price difference yielded the state merchants' incomes. Price policies were never altogether clear nor consistently applied. The evidence suggests that the state merchants sold many grains and even raw materials at official prices set higher than the procurement prices they paid to the collective farms. However, the merchants also sold these items often at still higher, unofficial prices (referred to as "commercial" prices) under certain demand conditions and/or when special, ad hoc circumstances (apparently politically motivated) made that possible.

Once rationing was eliminated, the price situation changed. The post-1935 official prices for the grains and raw materials resold by state merchants remained much higher than what they had paid to the collective farms. But now the price difference had two components. One part yielded income to the merchants. The second—the turnover tax—yielded income directly to the state. The turnover tax also served to soak up excess demand in the market, thereby roughly equilibrating supply and demand. In these ways, the state manipulated wholesale and retail prices in the "grain trade" to add to its resources (by taking the state merchants' profits and collecting the turnover taxes). The burden of providing these resources to the state fell ultimately on industrial workers' real wages: what their money wages could actually purchase.[30] In other words, a retail scissors (the ratio of retail to wholesale prices) remained open against workers throughout the decade.

In the controlled raw material trade, state merchants purchased them from collective farms at rising wholesale prices that sometimes exceeded unit values. From the evidence, we surmise that state merchants resold these raw materials to state capitalist industrial enterprises at little more than their wholesale prices, although at times they likely managed to sell them at even higher unofficial prices. Hence for trade in raw materials, state merchants passed on to industrial enterprises any excess of their prices over values. To that extent, the state industrial enterprises bore the ultimate burden of any excess of raw materials' prices above the values paid to the collective farms. That excess amounted to another demand/claim upon (i.e., subsumed class payment from) the surpluses generated in the state capitalist industries and so may have detracted from the funds available for industrial growth.[31]

The ancient class structures on the private plots accounted for most of the trade in uncontrolled markets. They gained both before and after the elimination of rationing because they could sell their food products at free market prices far above their unit values. Indeed, the latter were declining because of rising productivity on the private plots. Industrial workers bore most of the burden of this unequal exchange, since they purchased most of the scarce meat and dairy products, vegetables, and fruits in the uncontrolled markets. Squeezing industrial workers' real incomes provided additional support for the ancient class structures of the private plots.

State merchants and even industrial enterprises also purchased food from ancients in the uncontrolled markets, but to a far lesser extent than industrial workers did. In such cases, the unequal exchanges benefiting the ancient private plots meant corresponding losses for state merchants and state industrial capitalists. State merchants were able to pass on their losses to industrial workers by charging much higher retail prices for such food (when industrial workers could not purchase them directly from farmers). State industrial capitalist enterprises often purchased food from ancients to serve free communal meals at the factories. The enterprises were sometimes able to recoup such outlays insofar as their workers accepted lower wages when such meals were provided.

Finally, state merchants, industrial enterprises, and even industrial workers purchased relatively small quantities of food in uncontrolled markets from collective farms with produce for sale after fulfilling the state's quotas. Unequal exchanges there yielded the collective farms some extra nonclass revenues (from state merchants and industrial workers) and subsumed class revenues (from state industrial enterprises). Once again, the state merchants passed on higher free market prices by charging industrial workers even higher retail prices. To the degree enterprises provided free meals to workers, they too tried to pass on such costs to workers by reducing money wages paid. Nonetheless, in these limited ways, the communist class structures on many collective farms received some support at the expense of industrial workers and the capitalist class structure of state enterprises.

However, the dominant motif was to use production and exchange to gather revenues for the state to devote to industrialization. The sale of products manufactured by state capitalist industry yielded important additional revenues to the state beyond the surplus appropriated in their production. We infer from the evidence that state capitalist industrial enterprises sold manufactures to state merchants *near or at their values*—which likely declined at least after 1932 and particularly from 1932 to 1935. The state merchants then resold these manufactures to both urban and rural individual consumers (wage goods) and to enterprises such as the collective farms (means of production) at much higher retail prices.

Through 1935, few consumer goods were available at the official prices in the state's retail stores. The murky evidence suggests an even murkier set of conditions governing the prices charged in such state stores. There seem to have been two sorts of state stores, one of which was also sometimes referred to as "commercial." The commercial stores could sell the same consumer goods as the other, more "official" state stores but at much higher commercial prices. The evidence also indicates that the official stores could also sell some consumer goods at the commercial prices charged in the commercial stores, although the rules for why and when they could do this are unclear and apparently varied from time to time and place to place. In addition to official and commercial prices, there were also special prices set by the state for specific goods. However murky the conditions of retail selling, the frequently high prices—far above the values (costs) of manufactured consumer goods—yielded very large net revenues to the state, which gathered much of the merchants' profits into its hands.

After rationing was abolished, the supply of manufactured consumer goods still remained far below the demand. That is, had the retail price of manufactures been set equal to their values (or "costs," since Soviet calculations using Marxian value concepts effectively equated these two terms) there would have been massive excess demand for those manufactures. The state then added turnover taxes to manufactured goods' costs. Their costs plus the turnover tax yielded prices that reduced the quantity demanded (what retail buyers could afford) to the quantity that state industry supplied. When supply limitations provoked long lines of customers, the state often raised turnover taxes to erase the lines. In this way, the state earned massive revenues from the unequal exchanges imposed on the final purchasers of manufactured consumer goods. The state's organization of trade in manufactured consumer goods, like that in grain, proved to be an important source of the state's revenues.

A similar flow of resources to the state emanated from the sale of manufactured capital goods to collective farms and to the individual farmers working within the ancient class structures on their private plots. State merchants bought the capital goods at their values from state capitalist industrial enterprises. They resold them for higher retail prices to collective farms and to the individual farmers for use on their private plots. The communist and ancient class structures on the farms thus depleted their surpluses as needed to pay for the excess of price over value of the manufactured capital goods they purchased as inputs to their productions.

Across the 1930s, and despite the few ways in which some unequal exchanges favored collective farms, the state-set prices for the grain, raw materials, and manufactured consumer and capital goods handled by state merchants accomplished a massive shift of value. The collective farms lost what the state and state capitalist industry gained. The losses sapped the economic strength and viability of their communist class structures. Similarly, the ratio of retail to wholesale prices of most consumer goods imposed unequal exchanges on industrial workers. In contrast, the ancient class structures on the private plots fared much better. As far as we could determine, the free market prices they received for private plot food products exceeded their values by more than the difference between the values and prices of the manufactures bought by the ancient farmers. Thus, the price system for them yielded a net inflow of value in addition to the ancient surplus each of them produced and appropriated from his/her private plot. This inflow, however, came not from the state (and so did not thwart its promotion of industrial growth). Rather, the ancients' gains from unequal exchanges came from the losses in industrial workers' real wages as the latter paid the very high prices for private plot produce, prices made possible by the dearth of basic food products in state stores.

Weighing the different market losses and gains over the 1930s suggests that Stalin's policies placed the ultimate economic burden of rapid industrialiaztion upon workers in state capitalist industry and in private communist agriculture. What they lost, the state and the ancient producers in agriculture gained (Ellman 1984, 35; Millar 1990, 59). The communist class structures on collective farms depended increasingly on their members' work within the ancient class structure of their private plots. Yet, this crutch for communism's survival also shifted the collective farmers' energy and commitment toward the ancient class structure. This shift amounted to nothing less than a "transition from/out of communism"—although, of course, the inability to theorize agriculture's class structures as we have done here made the shift officially invisible.

## The Industrial Workers

Despite Soviet industrial workers' increased productivity, their real wages fell over the 1930s (Chapman 1963, 166).[32] The value of their labor power fell further, we believe, because wage goods became cheaper to produce (via productivity gains) alongside the fall in real wages (because of fewer commodities actually being consumed). Soviet workers thus endured a rising rate of exploitation in its precise Marxian sense of producing more surplus value for the state's appropriation relative to the value they produced for themselves (the value of their labor power). The industrial workers were thus major financiers of Soviet industrialization in the 1930s.

Industrial workers' productivity rose partly because the state successfully increased the intensity of factory labor. Pressures to that end accelerated in the late 1920s with the introduction of shock brigades and competition among workers. In the official view, the brigades "truly promote the improvement and *acceleration* of industrial processes, the reduction in costs, the *intensification* of labor, and the solution of other important economic issues" (cited in Kuromiya 1990, 120, italics added). After 1935, new state pressures included the Stakhanovite movement and the rapid spread of piece rates for workers' wages (Mandel 1968, 594; Nove 1989, 222; Lewin 1984, 62). The piece rates rarely if ever matched the increase in the value of commodities produced by the workers' intensified labor: hence rising labor productivity. Of course, the five-year plans' relentless increase of capital labor ratios in industry also raised productivity. Falling real wages combined with rising labor productivity to produce ever greater surplus values in Soviet state capitalist enterprises.

The wage and productivity changes occurred in the context of the state's rush to fashion a disciplined industrial labor force. Endless problems and tensions arose as workers moved from one class structure to another: from ancient and communist class structures on the farms to capitalist structures in industry. Workers and managers needed time to learn the new discipline and culture of state capitalist factories. Whereas similar adjustments spanned decades in private capitalist countries, the Soviet experience compressed them into ten years. Not surprisingly, rapid turnover of workers, poor job discipline, and costly conflicts among workers and managers beset Soviet factories. The ex-peasant newcomers mixed uncomfortably with an older and more privileged industrial labor force. A relentlessly inadequate housing stock and falling real wages further problematized the process. That a disciplined, skilled, and loyal industrial work force was quickly achieved measures the success of the USSR's drive to construct state industrial capitalism.

The new industrial labor force basically supported Stalin and his policies (Thurston 1996, ch. 5). It did so despite a rising rate of exploitation. Especially the newer industrial workers largely supported the shock brigades, increased competition, the Stakhanovite movement, and piece wages. With relatively few exceptions, they accepted the increase in the intensity of their labor and the fall in the value of their labor power partly because of the new role assigned to them by the state and the party. They were treated as cultural heroes, provided job security, and thus given unprecedented recognition and dignity. Moreover, the state and party offered historically unprecedented advancement opportunities to them and, via mass education, to their children. Recognized and celebrated as the progenitors of the new communist civilization soon to emerge, industrial workers seemed willing to make the necessary present sacrifices to achieve the future plenty that would soon arrive.

Women workers perhaps best exemplified the contradictions of the 1930s. Their lives changed dramatically as millions more began to sell their labor power to factories and offices. Females in the state-capitalist economy rose from 28.6 percent of total employment in 1928 to 40 percent by 1940 (Barber and Davies 1994, 88). They were officially recognized as equal partners and co-builders with men of the new communist civilization, a significant change in their social identification. Their rising participation in the industrial labor force (added to the general decrease of unemployment) enabled Soviet urban households' real consumption per capita to fall much less across the 1930s than workers' real wages (Chapman 1963, 166–167). However, women, like men, were employed in state capitalist industry at an increasing rate of exploitation. Women, more than men, confronted the full costs of unequal exchanges in the retail markets (the endless lines and daily tensions of shopping as well as the prices).

The contradictions faced by Soviet women were not restricted to the factory or office. Working outside the household in the 1930s proved no escape from the long established feudalism that continued inside it. Women still worked long hours performing their traditional household tasks (cooking, cleaning, washing, and so forth). As before, only a portion of the products of women's household labor went to sustain themselves. Their husbands appropriated the rest. Hence, during the same day urban women were exploited twice: once while working in the factories of state capitalism and another while working in the home of their feudal lord/husband. Male industrial workers could use the surplus wealth women produced inside the home to help offset the decline in their real wages. When they did, the tensions and conflicts thereby engendered within Soviet families had far-reaching, cumulative, and largely negative social consequences (to which we return in chapter 10).

Further complicating assessments of the conditions of Soviet industrial workers in the 1930s was the increasing availability of free or very-low-cost public services. Declining wages for both sexes were partly offset by state-subsidized collective consumption (sometimes called the "socialist wage"). The state provided, for example, significant quantities of the following: food at many factory canteens, nurseries and child care, medical care, and education. Aggregate real household consumption per capita showed an increase of about 10 percent between 1928 and 1937, which contrasts sharply with the decline in real consumption per capita excluding such state-provided public services (Bergson 1961, 255). No doubt, these public services mollified both male and female workers suffering falling real wages, but perhaps especially the women because of the nurseries and child care.

The Soviet state could only increase the exploitation of industrial workers while also imposing unequal exchanges upon them so long as they accepted such conditions. Mollifying men and women with public services was only part of securing their acceptance, while reinforcing household feudalism and providing women with nurseries were other parts. Just as important was a powerful optimism about the future systematically nurtured by promoting the visible successes of Soviet industrialization as proud markers of rapid modernization. The job-site empowerment of workers flowing from the severe excess demand for their labor power (itself a product of rapid industrialization) and from official ideology also encouraged such optimism. As Thurston (1996, ch. 5 and especially 169-172) shows, workers at factory meetings or caught up in the Stakhanovite movement won and used rights to participate in setting work norms including the tempo of their labor. They voiced criticisms of managers' attempts to control their labor, and even complained publicly about the shortages of consumer goods they faced.

Despite exploitation, shortages, and high prices—and all the resulting tensions—the larger social context of the USSR in the 1930s made many industrial workers strong supporters of Stalin. They embraced the "socialism" he was understood to be constructing for and with them. Not surprisingly, they never inquired about, much less protested, the production, appropriation, and distribution of industrial surpluses. They focused instead on the exciting new reality in which factory and office managers seemed obliged to listen and respond to their complaints and criticisms about managerial abuse, inefficiencies, safety and quality control within the factory, and the availability of consumer goods. The Soviet Communist Party and media proved themselves responsive, more or less, to the workers' concerns. At least formally, the "workers' state and party" championed workers' more immediate interests for the sake of national production and modernization and also to prove the importance of having the state under the workers' party's control. By focusing their activities among the workers in these ways, party and state officials reinforced the absence of all consciousness of class in surplus labor terms among themselves as well as across the population.

Soviet state capitalism in the 1930s built successfully on what the NEP had achieved. Nonetheless, however muted or invisible, dangers to the regime remained. There were growing tensions inside stressed feudal households and inside collective farms strained by the gap between the surpluses they produced and what the state took from them. The competition between ancient and communist farm class structures undermined their symbiotic connection. The stark difference between workers' value added in production and the value returned to them as their wages threatened to surface wherever conflicts arose between workers and state industrial officials. The intrigues and machinations among state and party bureaucrats from different industries and regions, battling over disposition of the state's rising revenues, persistently distorted economic planning and administration with potentially devastating social effects.

Yet the Soviet system brought to maturity in the 1930s held such dangers and threats in check for the next fifty years, even as catastrophic external risks added to the internal contradictions. Eventually, however, the Soviet state and the Party could no longer extract—from exploitation, unequal exchanges, and the other revenue measures we have surveyed—enough revenue to sustain the network of expenditures (military, cultural, political, and so on) necessary for their reproduction. The potential dangers lurking throughout the 1930s then erupted into actual crises. As chapter 10 will show, such crises in the particular global conjuncture after 1975 proved more than the Soviet state and the Party could manage. Drastic changes in politics and culture then ushered in complex class transitions, above all a major shift from state back to private capitalism in industry.

The other side of workers' decreased real wages was the state's continuing expansion of the output of means of production far faster than the growth of consumer goods production. Household consumption fell as a percentage of net national product from 82 percent in 1928 to merely 55 percent in 1937. Net investment over the same period rose from 10 percent to 23 percent of net national product (Davies, Harrison, and Wheatcroft 1994, 272). The relentless excess demand for consumer goods provoked especially dangerous daily tensions. In state stores frustrated shoppers strained a poor retail service system that deteriorated further across the 1930s. Pinched retail sales forces adopted indifference to cope with their inability even remotely to satisfy the shoppers, whose frustration worsened in a vicious cycle of resentments. The rising market prices in uncontrolled markets angered the buyers already frustrated from their experiences in the state stores. The rudeness and sarcasm of retail interactions made daily life even more difficult.

Yet, paradoxically, the consumers' malaise worked to help sustain state capitalism, even as it also undermined it. In effect, the state had displaced onto the retail distribution system many of the strains and frustrations produced by Soviet state capitalism's lowering of real wages while driving up workers' productivity. The retail store, and then the household, absorbed many of the costs and problems of a rising rate of state capitalist exploitation. Industrial workers turned their frustrations on the retail distribution system, and when that yielded little relief, the tensions spilled into their (overcrowded and undersupplied) households. While this deflected workers' attention and disaffection from their job sites and hence from their exploitation there, it made consumption the flash point of rising alienation from the Soviet system as a whole. If not checked by more individual consumer goods, expanded supplies of collective goods (especially housing), and/or effective campaigns for still more workers' sacrifices, the growing alienation could fatally erode social support for the Soviet system. And this would be yet more dangerous if Soviet citizens became aware and envious of much higher standards of individual consumption abroad.

Soviet leaders' efforts to solve the problems of unsatisfied consumers often merely compounded them, or else they capitulated, sooner or later, to other priorities. For example, paying higher money wages only added to the excess demand problem (Chapman 1963, 115). Then the second five-year plan sought to compensate somewhat for the first five-year plan's concentration on industrial expansion by emphasizing much greater consumer goods production. However, fear of war in Europe intervened to negate that emphasis and resume the expansion of means of production rather than means of consumption (Dobb 1966, 269–280).

Likewise, rising labor productivity across all industries might have yielded increased supplies of consumer goods. Instead, the state manipulated price ratios between means of production and means of consumption to prevent that. While the unit costs (i.e., value, in Marxian terms) of both kinds of goods fell, the state did not correspondingly lower the prices of means of production. This forced consumer goods enterprises to pay prices increasingly higher than the costs/values of the means of production they purchased. Simply put, consumer goods enterprises suffered from unequal exchanges with producer goods enterprises. This squeezed the resources available to consumer goods enterprises and thus depressed the growth rate of output they might otherwise have achieved.[33] The unequal exchange imposed by the state once again favored the means of production industries at the expense of the consumer goods industries.

The threat of war looming in the later 1930s only added to the discrimination against consumer goods production already embedded in policies that flowed from the dominant Soviet theory of "socialist construction." It held that after Lenin's early socialization of industrial production and Stalin's extension of socialization to agriculture (collectivization) what remained was to "unfetter" the industrial (forces of) production. This was interpreted to mean an explosion of growth in heavy industry, in the capacity to produce means of production. Once completed—hopefully in one five-year plan or two—the basis would exist for an explosion in consumer goods production capacity and output. Consumer goods would eventually be distributed according to need rather than according to work performed. The powerful Soviet state, required to reach that point, would then wither away. To achieve such a transition from socialism to communism needed several more years of workers' sacrifices accompanying massive industrial construction. International dangers added to the sacrifices and to the emphasis on nonconsumer goods production.

The continuing discrimination against consumer goods production profoundly affected Soviet state capitalism (beyond the already noted tensions and conflicts imposed on retail trade and households). Limiting investment in consumer goods production hobbled the development of new technologies and productivity gains there. It also blocked the development of new consumption goods (cars, household appliances, consumer electronics, clothing) and improvements in the quality of the old consumer goods. In short, the successes of Soviet heavy industrialization were intricately interwoven—theoretically as well as practically—with the relative underdevelopment of consumer goods production and consumption. The latter became a kind of Achilles' heel of Soviet state capitalism when it was eventually compared to the development of consumer goods in the private capitalist economies of the West and Japan.

## Stalinism and Class

This chapter has focused chiefly on the class processes of the USSR in the 1930s: how surpluses were produced, appropriated, and distributed and how those class processes influenced Soviet development generally. In contrast, others who analyzed the Soviet Union over the past fifty years rarely considered those processes, let alone examined them systematically. Instead, the dimension of Soviet development in the 1930s that drew the attention—often obsessively—of virtually all analysts, especially during the Cold War after 1945, was Stalinism. We conclude this chapter by investigating its relationship to class.

Stalinism in the 1930s refers to a certain extreme or excessive quality of the main social transformations of the time. It denotes the dictatorial coordination of the state and party apparatuses that forced through those transformations. "Stalinism" represents both the driving and the driven results. More than merely one variant of the more general notion of "totalitarianism," Stalinism in the USSR of the 1930s (and also later) became that notion's definitional incarnation.

Thus Dobb described Soviet industrial growth in the 1930s and thereafter as "very similar to military strategy . . . single-minded concentration on a strategic timing and crucial line of thrust" (1966, 244). Cohen criticized Stalinism as more than a totalitarian state, an "excess," a wildly extravagant use of state power (1977, 12). The still more critical Fitzpatrick protrayed Stalinism as a new culture established in the 1930s: "Cultural Revolution as Class War" (1984, 7–40). Such descriptions across the political spectrum reflect a shared sense of what the 1930s represented for Soviet society.

Debate over Stalinism colors studies of the USSR to this day (Cohen 1977). Many analysts conceive Stalinism as the phenomenal form of an underlying power drive that always governed the USSR. Born in the October Revolution, barely held at bay during the NEP, despotism was fully realized and embodied in Stalin and his centralized state bureaucracy, that is, in Stalinism. Others disagree; they prefer to see Stalinism as a "discontinuity" in Soviet history. Some equate Stalinism with socialism or communism, while others stress their incompatibility. Similar oppositions swirl around the relation of Stalinism to Russian history before 1917 and to global hostilities afterward.

Because we approach Stalinism as the interaction of a particular set of class and nonclass processes, we reach different conclusions. Stalinism's distinguishing class components included capitalist exploitation in state-owned-and-operated industries; a shifting mix of communist, ancient, and capitalist class structures in collective and state farms; and feudal and ancient class structures inside households. Stalinism's nonclass components included rapid economic growth, suppression of consumption, political terror and considerable workplace democracy, often chaotic and inefficient state planning, and a cultural mix of resigned pessimism and utopian hope. Our research found nothing to suggest that Stalinism's particular class and nonclass processes and contradictions were inevitable. Nor were they inscribed in some intrinsic nature attributable to Bolshevism, Marxism, Leninism, the Russian or Slavic souls, economic underdevelopment, a backward agriculture, state industrial capitalism, foreign enmity, or Soviet geography. Rather, Stalinism emerged from the specific intermingling of cultural, political, and economic circumstances, foreign as well as domestic, particular to the 1930s. Indeed, as those circumstances changed, so too did the Stalinism overdetermined by them.

The foundational commitment to build an industrial state capitalism emphasizing heavy industry provoked Stalin to replace one particular set of agricultural class structures with another. Alongside the gains from these class changes, new class contradictions appeared. They were as dangerous for the USSR, albeit in different ways, as the contradictions that led to collectivization. Stalin tried to manage them. The successes and failures of the effort to manage the new class contradictions were important aspects of Stalinism that shaped every other aspect.

Managing the contradictory and contested class structures of the 1930s led Stalin's state apparatus to perform a set of nonclass processes expanding itself into (i.e., establishing) a massive state bureaucracy. The state allocated a significant portion of its revenues to recruit, train, pay, and equip a huge bureaucratic army. The continual adjustment of that bureaucracy to rapidly changing circumstances proved to be as difficult, costly, and urgent as its establishment. Beyond its tasks of planning, monitoring, coordinating, and controlling the Soviet economy—and performing parallel tasks in relation to Soviet politics—the bureaucracy also had a top priority task in relation to culture in the USSR. The goal was a culture that celebrated or at least tolerated massive bureaucratic intervention in all aspects of life.

In coordination with a Communist Party similarly expanding, the state bureaucracy had to design, disseminate, and inculcate new (or at least significantly changed) attitudes, values, and behaviors. These cultural changes were aimed to integrate formerly ancient, agrarian masses into all levels of the industrial enterprises, into urban environments, into the altered class structures of agriculture, and into the state and party bureaucracies as well. The new culture had to justify and celebrate as "necessary and heroic sacrifices" the serious difficulties of its diverse class structures. In addition to the falling real wages and countless consumer goods shortages suffered by workers and strained households, those difficulties included the state-set prices, tractor rentals, taxes, and state fees that favored industry against agriculture. The new culture not only aimed to defuse or deflect political opposition provoked by those sacrifices; it simultaneously exhorted and tried to mobilize ever more effort by all producers of surplus. When that culture did not achieve the desired results, the directly repressive apparatuses of the bureaucracy were deployed.

Stalinism included the high financial costs (diversions of the social surplus away from industrial growth and social welfare outlays) to sustain the massive bureaucracy. It embodied the immense social and psychological consequences of bureaucratic performance of its assigned tasks. Soviet farmers found their political, cultural, and economic activities falling under deepening surveillance, their lives increasingly under state controls. Soviet industrial workers suffered increasingly intrusive measures to promote and enforce factory work discipline, often against the workers' opposition.[34] Dissent was banned or tightly circumscribed. Intellectuals and other "producers of culture" were either absorbed into the bureaucracy's mission or else demonized by those who were.

The Stalinist policies and bureaucracy quickly encountered their own contradictions. Controversies erupted within the state as it too became a site, much like households and retail stores, of struggles often displaced from the class confrontations in production. Carrying forward debates from the 1920s, some groups in the state and the Party opposed a too rapid "socialist industrialization" that would too severely restrict the USSR's "nonsocialist agriculture."[35] Even those who agreed with Stalin's official theory of socialist construction did not always agree with the means or tempo of Stalinism.[36] Stalinism thus represented precisely what those state and party officials had criticized and warned against. They feared its consequences: chaos, stagnation, a disenchanted working class, a repressive bureaucracy, a sullen and resentful population, counterrevolution.[37]

Among Stalinism's early critics were many "old Bolsheviks" with great personal prestige inside and outside the state and the party. They raised opposition to high theoretical levels questioning not only particular policies and actions but Stalinism as a whole. Their social influence confronted Stalin and the emerging Stalinism with a major struggle over which ideas, politics, and economic plans would dominate. More than a struggle over who would control the state and the party, it was also a struggle over which class processes would be promoted and which extinguished, what exploitative and nonexploitative class positions Soviet citizens would experience, what roles state and party power would play.

Stalinism was in part the response to this opposition and to all that it had represented during the NEP period and into the 1930s. Stalin's group within the state and party suppressed its critics and opponents there. It silenced their arguments, reforms, and alternative strategies to remove the political danger they represented.[38] In 1933 and then again in 1937–38, Stalin's group purged existing state and party officials, even as it created many new bureaucratic positions. Those eliminated were often older Bolsheviks, experienced veterans of the NEP struggles over economic policy. The young cadres who replaced them owed their personal rise from humble beginnings (often to powerful and well-paid bureaucratic positions) to Stalin's group. They gave theoretical and political allegiance—and often unquestioning loyalty—to Stalin and Stalinism. They worked hard to inculcate the same across Soviet society (Deutscher 1968, 339).

Over the 1930s Stalin's loyal state and party officials performed the bureaucratic processes that expanded industrial state capitalism, siphoned surpluses from the communist and ancient class structures prevailing in agriculture, and reinforced the feudal and ancient class structures of households. Thus, for example, they raised the state to be *the* engine of transition to communism. No other Marxist movement had ever before assigned such overarching importance for the achievement of communism to so absolutely powerful a state apparatus. Stalinism pronounced classes abolished. The state-owned factories and the collectivized agriculture, freed finally from class conflicts and contradictions, could now realize their productive potential under and because of the state's management and control. Communism and economic abundance would come soon if and only if Stalinism mobilized the people to repel external enemies, silence their internal counterparts, and thereby let the Soviet socialization of production work its wonders unimpeded.

The Stalinist culture thus further developed and deepened productionist attitudes and philosophies. Virtually all calculations of social issues were reduced to numbers of produced outputs and producing workers: so much grain produced, so many tons of steel forthcoming, ever more industrial workers and new factories constructed. Such measures of progress fit a conception of communism in which underdeveloped forces of production remained as the only barrier to its achievement. Previous Bolshevik debates about, references to, and concern with the USSR's "relations of production" (sometimes called class relations) all but disappeared from Stalinist discourse. Stalinism did categorize opponents and dissidents within and without the state as class (bourgeois) enemies of the now classless USSR.

Stalinism also built upon the actuality of intrigues by the USSR's foreign enemies' to magnify the image of a "socialist homeland" besieged by capitalist predators deploying agents and, when possible, armies against it. It merged that image with a rekindling of classic Russian nationalism. No longer would the USSR be backward, ever susceptible to Western economic, political, and cultural imperialism. Part of Stalinism became a nationalist cultural mandate: to ensure that workers would take pride in the building of a modern industrial socialism in their country alone, one that would develop the capacity to resist all foreign threats. Soon it even would have the capacity to export its successful socialism—by example or otherwise—to the rest of the world.

Stalinist images of a strong state mobilizing the nation in a successful socialist rush to modernization—promoted as assuring safety from foreigners as well as prosperity at home—served many functions. These images explained, justified, and encouraged the sacrifices by industrial and agricultural workers. By and large, the former seemed to tolerate low real wages, while their productivity rose. The collective farmers seemed to endure the low real incomes they received from collective farm work, while fulfilling the state's rising demand for grains. Inside households, Soviet men and women accepted, albeit no less grudgingly than elsewhere, the exploitative class structures and privations of that social site. The earlier Bolshevik notions and dreams of going beyond "feudal and bourgeois" family structures faded. The Stalinist culture of the 1930s thus helped to secure a rising rate of class exploitation in capitalist industry, a squeezing of communist agriculture, and docile households. The costly fight for that culture seemed, at least to its proponents, to have been warranted.

While crucial in these ways, Stalinist culture did not suffice. A Stalinist politics was also mounted to secure the USSR's distinctive 1930s mix of class and nonclass processes. The new entrants into the state and party bureaucracies used rules, force, and terror to manage agricultural and industrial workers, managers and planners, artists, educators, scientists, soldiers, and police officials alike. Fitzpatrick argues that the purges and trials produced an environment "of crisis . . . to justify the regime's demands for sacrifice. . . . The wreckers also served as scapegoats for economic failure, shortages of consumer goods, and a general fall in urban living standards as resources were channeled into the priority area of heavy industry" (1984, 12). Stalinist culture and politics often slid into cultural and political repression.

On the other hand, as we argued above, the Stalinist culture celebrating workers also empowered them in particular ways. Workers in factories organized meetings and aired grievances. Meetings of collective farmers were required and often raised problems of all sorts. Managers at all levels seeking inputs to meet mandatory output quotas found limited freedoms to maneuver around official plans. Women newly participating in the paid labor force found some expression for their concerns. The Stalinist society took on a curious blend of partial, carefully delimited freedoms, even as it grew more repressive: both dimensions flowed from Stalinism's function to hold together the particular Soviet social formation of the 1930s and thereafter.

Finally, Stalinist officials (in the state and the Party) directly planned, organized, and managed industrial enterprises and, via the MTS, collective farms as well. Parallel to Stalinism in the political and cultural spheres of Soviet life, a distinctively Stalinist economy emerged in the 1930s as well. Official campaigns of unprecedented intensity drove relentlessly to raise the ratio of machines to humans in production, promote Stakhanovism, tighten worker discipline, and threaten workers with myriad punishments. The glorified aim in industry was rising labor productivity. In agriculture, the goal was an equally dramatic provision of ever more food and raw materials to supply industry even as masses of peasants were pushed from the countryside into the urban industries.

The combined effects of the cultural, political, and economic processes comprising Stalinism enabled the class structures in Soviet industry and agriculture to yield industrial growth. That is why Stalin's Council of Ministers distributed so much of its surpluses to the state and party bureaucrats providing these processes. Receiving such distributed shares of the social surplus enabled industrial managers to employ more machines and workers; planners to direct the flows and exchanges among industrial and agricultural enterprises; party officials to oversee and intervene, mobilize effort, mitigate excesses, and institute reforms; the military to protect the USSR from foreign attack; police to discipline and terrorize workers; educators to train them; and artists and writers to properly motivate everyone to endorse Stalinism as *the* path to a modern communist society.

Each particular bureaucratic agency demanded its share of the surpluses appropriated and distributed by the Council of Ministers. Each contested for more and feared that its shares might flow to others. For example, the growing German threat across the 1930s prompted greater military demands on the council's distributions. Rather than reduce distributions to the other bureaucratic agencies supporting the Soviet system, the council pressed the workers to generate greater surpluses. Other bureaucrats were pressed into service to campaign anew for the workers' sacrifices needed to meet the German threat. In this and other ways, Stalinism increased industrial exploitation and the squeezing of collective farmers, even as it was also an effect of both phenomena.

Stalinism was thus neither a counterrevolution to socialism nor a continuation of it. Rather, it represented a particular phase in the development of the USSR's peculiar mix of class processes and nonclass processes. Above all Stalinism refers to the nonclass processes that Stalin's group thought necessary to secure that mix (which it defined as socialism). In Marx's sense of communism as a particular social organization of surplus labor (as argued in our first chapter), Stalinism's only connection to communism lay in its collectivization of agriculture. And, as argued above, Stalinism also undermined the communist class structures on collective farms after it had established them.

Stalinism's chief result in class terms was also its chief purpose: to solidify the overwhelming predominance of an expanding industrial state capitalism in the USSR. On that basis, Stalinism modernized its industry, organized a massive state and party bureaucracy, built an army able to stop Hitler, inaugurated an ambitious social welfare program of collective consumption, and froze its politics and culture into a rigid statism. However, to sustain the industrial growth and secure the cultural, political, and economic processes that comprised the Stalinism required expanding surpluses appropriated from state capitalist workers and expanding surpluses siphoned from collective agriculture via unequal exchanges. The next and final chapter continues the dialectics of this story, focusing on the contradictions of the postwar Stalinist period and the fading of Stalinism in subsequent reforms. It will be shown how, when, and why the Soviet state could not finally find enough surplus to sustain the state capitalism that it called socialism or even the USSR as a nation.

## Appendix A: The Value Equation for Collective Farms

Using our previous notation, let (a) stand for the proportion of the crop retained by the collective to support members' consumption in kind, fodder for animals and reserves, and allowed sales on private markets; (1 − a) stands, then, for that required proportion sold to state procurement agencies.[39] In Marxian value terms, the collective's trading equation with state capitalist merchants alone becomes:

$$EV/UV_{AG} [(1-a) \times UV_{AG}] = (EV/UV_V \times UV_V) + (EV/UV_C \times UV_C) + SSCP(Co)$$

The first term on the left-hand side of the equation is the total value (measured in Marx's labor terms) of agricultural products sold by the collective to state merchants. That value is a product of two terms: the unit value of agricultural products, $EV/UV_{AG}$, times the state mandated proportion of products produced, $(1-a) \times UV_{AG}$. The collective's marketed value equals the sum of three kinds of expenditures: the value paid to state merchants for industrial consumer goods, $(EV/UV_V \times UV_V)$; for capital goods to replace those used up in the agricultural production process, $(EV/UV_C \times UV_C)$; and for the value of communist subsumed class payments, $SSCP(Co)$. The latter sum includes tax payments to the state, rents to MTS, capital accumulation within the collective, insurance charges, interest paid on state loans, and distributions to secure various funds within the collective.

## Appendix B: The Value Crisis of Collective Farms

To show how different pricing conditions threatened communist farmers, we may recast our previous trading equation for them in three ways. First, we value the crop that farmers delivered to state merchants in procurement prices received ($P_{AG}$) and farmers' purchased consumer manufactures, including processed food, in prices paid ($P_V$) in uncontrolled markets. Second, we include and add to the procurement value of the supply quota the value (in labor terms) of the crop retained by farmers, where (a) stands for the proportion kept by them—$EV/UV_{AG}$ (a) $UV_{AG}$.[40] Third, by including this latter term, we need to account for what farmers did with their retained crops. Three new terms explain their distributions. One proportion ($a_1$) went to replace seed and fodder used up to produce the crop, another proportion ($a_2$) was retained for human consumption, and a third was distributed for reserves—$SSCP(Co)_{Res}$. Because of the pressures placed on collectives, these respective proportions often became objects of intense struggle.

The new equation's net revenues are a combination of the communist class structure's realized and produced values less the exchange values of replaced means of production. The resulting net revenues are then expended by farmers to secure, respectively, their consumption, accumulation, cultural, tax, rent, and other such needs. The equation becomes:

$$[P_{AG} (1-a) UV_{AG} + EV/UV_{AG} (a) UV_{AG}] - [EV/UV_C UV_C + EV/UV_{AG} (a_1)UV_{AG}]$$
$$< [P_V UV_V + EV/UV_{AG} (a_2) UV_{AG}] + [SSCP(Co) + SSCP(Co)_{Res}]$$

The first term in brackets on the left-hand side of the equation measures the total value of the collective farmers' crop: the value they realize in selling a portion of the output to the state at procurement prices—$[P_{AG} (1-a) UV_{AG}]$—plus the state-set value of that portion of the crop they retain for their own use—$[EV/UV_{AG} (a) UV_{AG}]$. Continuing, the second bracketed term measures the total state-set value of constant capital replaced in the process of crop production. The right side of the equation is a composite measure of market and state-set exchange values. It shows how the value added of communist farmers was used to reproduce their lives. The first bracketed term measures the amount they expended on consumption, and the second the amount the state mandated in subsumed class distributions. As we shall see, these different expenditures both sustained and undermined that class structure.[41] The equation's inequality indicates the very unfavorable movement in communism's terms of trade.

## Notes

1. Ellman reached similar conclusions using a different theoretical approach (1984, 28–53). The Soviet state's industrial surplus rose both in its mass—SV(C)—and in its rate—S/V.
2. Collective farms comprised a mass establishment of communist class structures. This differentiated them from the earlier, episodic, nonmass experiments with communist class structures elsewhere, especially inside militants' households in the first decade after 1917.
3. For evidence on the durability and diversity of criticisms—and hence of the class and nonclass problems of the USSR across the 1930s, see Fitzpatrick (1984, 18), Davies (1993, 105–123), Thurston (1996, ch. 6), and Fainsod (1989, ch. 13).
4. The view that significant segments of the Soviet population—workers, managers, state officials—supported (and feared) Stalin and his socialism can be found in Thurston (1996), Cohen (1977, 28), and Shearer (1996, 17). Fitzpatrick argues that the 1930s "cultural revolution was the vehicle for training the future Communist elite and creating the new Soviet intelligentsia" (1984, 11). In our words, it marked the elimination of an old and the emergence of a new state subsumed class of officials charged to secure the changes in state capitalism and communist agriculture that were central to Stalinism.
5. Day states: "Socialism in One Country was more than a slogan or even an economic programme: it was a psychological watershed in the history of the revolution. . . . The new doctrine helped to restore the sense of mission . . . lost in 1921" (1973, 105).
6. Our argument here is *not* any version of the simplistic essentialism dear to neoclassical theorists: that centralized decision making is intrinsically or necessarily less "efficient" than decentralized decision making. Each mode of decision making entails its unique set of costs and benefits in the present and the future. No final accounting of them all ever was or is possible. Hence no valid conclusion is available as to which system has an absolutely or ultimately greater benefit/cost ratio. Soviet centralization was a response to certain costs of decentralization, just as managers' decentralized decisions were responses to certain costs of centralization.
7. Nove argues that Soviet socialism positioned local factory managers to help shape plans, even as they were forced to comply with them (1983, 77–78). Bailes discusses alliances between factory managers and "production specialists" to meet and challenge imposed planning targets (1978, 269–279, 294). Shearer concludes that factories in the early 1930s operated "on their own devices to get supplies, secure labor, and actually produce something" (1996, 233).
8. In this regard, Lewin is not alone. Fitzpatrick entitles a chapter "A Second Serfdom?" and discusses the labor, tax, and procurement obligations that the state placed upon collective members as well as state-enforced restrictions on their movement (1994b, 128–151). State power is again central to her argument.
9. Jasny also deploys a power theorization in describing the organization of Soviet collectives (1967, 325–326). He rejects the notion that they resemble what traditionally has been understood to

be cooperatives or even collectives. Any similarity between the latter two organizations and the Soviet collective is a sham, he argues, because of the state's use of forced deliveries of grain at low state prices.
10. According to Davies, "During the NEP the individual peasant household, with help or hinderance from arrangements made by the mir, was directly responsible for its own production, and sold its own crop on the market or through an intermediary. But the collective farmer of 1930 worked on the collective lands under the instructions of the kolkhoz, *which also undertook the sale of the collective products*"(1980, 59, italics added).
11. Based on the evidence, we rejected the counterthesis that state officials were surplus appropriators on collective farms. No discourse recognized nor did existing laws empower a centralized board of ministers or decentralized local officials to allocate labor power and means of production or to appropriate the crops harvested (or the proceeds from their sale). As explained in the text, the statutes passed, the culture produced, and the local collective economy combined to create something very different. The workers of collective farms collectively possessed the means of production, set in motion their own labor power, and had the first command over the produced crops and values. They distributed their surpluses to secure the survival of the collective. Paradoxically, it was the communist fundamental class position held by these agricultural workers that necessitated the extensive power used by communist state officials to try to influence those workers' activities. State power aimed to acquire resources from a communist class structure outside the state.
12. Thus we cannot know how collective farms might have fared had they allowed, for example, private property and free markets alongside a communist class structure (defined and fostered as communist in terms of its collective production, appropriation, and distribution of the surplus). As discussed in chapter 2 above, this would have represented one particular form that a communist class structure could take. It was never possible in the USSR to consider or experiment with such a form in part because Soviet Marxism could not conceive it.
13. Viola (1987, 152–178) describes their strategies to surmount the individualist traditions of formerly ancient and capitalist farmers. They aimed for a new collective coordination and cooperation of labor, to raise the intensity of labor, and above all to impose new disciplines on the recently collectivized farmers. For example, Viola poignantly describes the cadres' efforts to achieve disciplined meetings of the collective. As occasions for the distribution of the collective's surplus, such meetings were key to the survival of its communist class structure.
14. As with our other equations, the terms of this equation for communism utilize notations derived from our understanding of Marx's discussion of capitalist enterprises. We adjust them in this case for communist enterprises. Each term represents the communist analogue to Marx's value categories for the capitalist enterprise. As in Marx, all terms specified here are counted in units of socially necessary abstract labor time.
15. Between 1928 and 1932, we computed the ratio of our estimates of the labor requirements in communist agriculture based on the reciprocal of labor productivity (Moorstein and Powell 1966, 370) to state (planned) procurement prices (Karcz 1971, 50). This ratio provides a rough measure of the spread between unit values and procurement prices. On an index based on 1928, our calculations show the ratio to have been greater than one in 1929 but less than one from 1930 to 1932. This suggests that with the exception of 1929, communist collectives gained nonclass revenues at the expense of state merchants and hence the state. For the following years, Karcz (53) states that "farm prices of food products remained—by and large—unchanged after 1932." If so and with labor productivity rising after 1934, nonclass revenues would continue to favor communist farmers at the expense of the state. Some support for this thesis can be found in slightly increasing procurement prices for grains. Between 1928–29 and 1937, Volin reported that the state's procurement prices rose by 17 percent for wheat, 25 percent for rye, 28 percent for oats, and 6 percent for

barley (1970, 251). Based on continued higher labor productivity and only these higher grain prices, our calculated ratio for 1937 is less than one.

16. Under rationing (1929–1935), uncontrolled or private markets refer to a collection of different exchanges taking place in "commercial trade," local bazaars, illegal markets, and a bewildering variety of state supported factory shops. Common to all of these were trades in which manufactures sold for prices significantly higher than the official state prices for the same (but mostly unavailable) goods in official state and cooperative trade (Baykov 1947, 233–250; Nove 1989, 194–197; Dobb 1966, 406). In "commercial trade" inside state stores, the same good unavailable at the official price was available at the higher commercial price. In "commercial stores" it sold for even higher prices. When rationing was abolished in 1935, the turnover tax, first introduced at the end of 1930, was extended to cover all commodities. Given the continued shortage of consumer goods, its imposition became the main instrument to eliminate excess demand. This tax provided a significant share of the state's revenues.

17. In the following table, we compare the terms of trade facing communist and ancient farms. The table shows clearly the dramatically different price conditions for the two class structures at least up to 1932, and after that, for wheat (W) and rye (R) in 1937 for communist farms:

|            | 1928 | 1929 | 1930 | 1931 | 1932 | 1937           |
|------------|------|------|------|------|------|----------------|
| Communist  | 100  | 72   | 53   | 30   | 13   | 19(W)<br>21(R) |
| Ancient    | 100  | 167  | 241  | 207  | 355  |                |

Between 1928 and 1932, the terms of trade for communist farms are given in Karcz as the ratio of the index of state (planned) procurement prices to the index of retail prices of manufactures in the private or uncontrolled markets (1971, 50). We calculated the terms of trade facing ancient farms over the same period from his data. For these farms, the ratio is the index of uncontrolled agricultural prices in private markets to the index of retail prices of manufactures prevailing in those same markets. We estimated the terms of trade for communist farms after 1932 as follows. In 1937, we took procurement prices for rye and wheat only (Volin 1970, 251) and deflated them by selected industrial goods typically purchased by farmers (Hubbard 1939, 214). These terms of trade for wheat (W) and rye (R) reported in the table above show a slight improvement over 1932 (although procurement prices in 1932 included all farm products). For the intervening years, if we accept Nove's reported price of wheat in the Ukraine and his claim that it remained constant from 1928 to 1934 and increased 10 percent in 1935 (1989, 199–200), our calculated terms of trade for wheat in 1935 would show only a very slight improvement over 1932. However, because this estimate is based on such limited information, we do not report it in our table. Despite these limitations, these calculations suggest the terms of trade for communist farms remained unfavorable throughout the 1930s.

18. For discussion of these distributions, see Davies (1980, 116–130) and Belov (1955, 85–86). Davies (119) reports some resentment over these expenditures.

19. Tractors were part of the state's socialized means of production. To gain access to them, collective farms had to distribute a share of their collectively appropriated surplus as rents paid to the state's machine tractor stations (Hubbard 1939, 148–159). Hence these rents were communist subsumed class payments.

20. As calculated in note 39, in 1938, 62 percent of the produced grain was kept by the collectives. The rest was delivered to the state to meet the required quotas, paid to MTS in rents, refunded to the state for seed advanced, and sold in private and state markets for higher prices. If we use Baykov's numbers (1947, 311) to calculate the allocation of the retained grain between other kinds of subsumed class payments and consumption, we see that 56.5 percent of it was distributed to secure

funds for seed and fodder, children and the aged, and other needs, and 43.5 percent went to satisfy grain consumption. Grain consumption itself amounted to 27 percent of the total grain produced in 1938.

21. The following table gives an index of agricultural labor productivity based on 1928 (Moorstein and Powell 1966, 370):

| 1928 | 1929 | 1930 | 1931 | 1932 | 1933 | 1934 | 1935 | 1936 | 1937 | 1938 | 1939 | 1940 |
|------|------|------|------|------|------|------|------|------|------|------|------|------|
| 100  | 96   | 100  | 97   | 93   | 91   | 90   | 96   | 94   | 109  | 99   | 100  | 103  |

The U-shaped curve is evident in two different productivity cycles: more or less declining to 1934, and rising irregularly afterward.

22. Collective members also sometimes added to their incomes by selling their labor power as temporary workers.

23. Belov describes women's lives on the collective farms: "The kolkhoz woman had to rise at dawn to get breakfast, feed the animals and get out to the fields. If she did not return at noon, her lunch was apt to consist of bread and onions or cold potatoes, and when she came back at night she would be faced with the tasks of cooking, washing, mending, and so on, as well as working on the homestead plot. Small wonder that the women suffered from overwork and exhaustion and that the number of invalids increased yearly. By the age of thirty-five most women were already old" (1955, 189). In arguing that the state made use of older traditions and ideas when they served its new aims, Lewin touches on the rural household: "it was clearly the large, archaic, rural family, with its high demands on the reproductive faculties of women, authoritarian structure, and apparently solid moral stability, that was presented as a model" (1977, 127).

24. To estimate women's total labor effort, we need to add the considerable labor time they spent in households producing meals, cleaning, washing, sewing, mending, and so forth to their worktime on the collective farm and the household plot. The difference between men's and women's labor times are mentioned in Hubbard (1939, 295-297), Jasny (1967, 393-394), Fitzpatrick (1994b, 146), and Wheatcroft and Davies (1994, 129). Jasny commented on Merinov's 1939 study of collective farms: "He was eyeing not only the time the kolkhoz women spent on their private farm enterprises, but also the time left to them for their really titanic housework. For what passes for liberation from the family slavery and for equal rights, the peasant woman has to pay by doing a large part of her housework on Sundays and at night" (1967, 395).

25. Belov suggests that single-headed households and especially those abandoned by husbands typically fell into the Soviet category of "below average," that is, poorer than average (1955, 177).

26. Referring to a 1938 estimate, Lewin writes, "The kolkhoz family derived from this plot half of its money income, almost all of its animal foodstuff, and most of its potatoes and vegetables, while the kolkhoz supplied them mainly with grains" (1985, 180). On collective farmers and their ancient plots, Davies says, "So even in 1930, the Indian summer of the Kolkhoz system, their efforts and enthusiasm were directed to their personal economy; their work on the collective lands were less conscientious, and undertaken only for the minimum number of days required to obtain essential supplies of grain. A substantial increase in payment for collective work could change these priorities; but for the next quarter of a century this did not take place" (1980, 169). Also see Wheatcroft and Davies (1994, 126-128).

27. For example, collectives acquired rationed industrial goods to the degree they fulfilled their quotas.

28. State policy also supported the state farms where the state owned the means of production and state officials appropriated the surplus produced by hired agricultural laborers. The capitalist class structures of state farms replicated those of state capitalist industry as a matter of policy. Finally, state policy provided some supports for the ancient class structures of single-adult households, although tension surrounded that support because of social pressures favoring feudal household class structures.

29. Steel and iron production are measured in tons (Clark 1956, 10). Capital accumulation is the growth in nonagricultural, nonresidential net capital stock measured in 1937 prices (Moorsteen and Powell 1966, 348). Employment is total nonagricultural employment adjusted for changes in hours (Moorsteen and Powell 1966, 365). Growth in the capital labor ratio in industry is calculated as the difference between the respective growth rates of industrial capital accumulation (12.3 percent) and industrial employment (7.0 percent). Electric power is measured in kilowatt-hours and tractor production in 15-horsepower units (Davies, Harrison, and Wheatcraft 1994, 296).

30. State merchants purchased grain at a wholesale price, ($P_{FW}$), paid to farmers roughly equal to its unit value, ($EV/UV_F$). Merchants then resold the grain at a higher retail price, ($P_{FR}$), to industrial workers, thereby gaining a positive nonclass revenue: $NCR_{GAIN} = (P_{FR} - EV/UV_F) \times UV_F$. Merchant gains came at the direct expense of workers in the form of their reduced real wages.

31. In paying wholesale prices for raw materials, ($P_{RMW}$), that exceeded their unit values, state merchants incurred losses: $NCR_{LOSS} = (P_{RMW} - EV/UV_{RM}) \times UV_{RM}$. These losses equalled collectives' nonclass gains. When merchants resold these goods to state industrial enterprises at roughly the same prices they paid to farmers, their subsumed class revenues [$SSCR = (P_{RMW} - EV/UV_{RM}) \times UV_{RM}$] offset these nonclass losses, $NCR_{LOSS}$. As the final retail buyers, state enterprises bore the ultimate burden of input prices that exceeded unit values. In our class terms, the collective farms' gain required subsumed class payments out of the state enterprises' surplus. When merchants charged enterprises higher official or unofficial prices, that burden increased. In these cases, merchants' positive gross profits required even higher subsumed class payments out of enterprises' surplus.

32. Chapman estimates that urban real wages fell roughly 43 percent from 1928 to 1938 (measured in 1937 prices). Real wages in 1940 remained 46 percent below the 1928 level. "Moscow workers' real wages were 52 per cent of their 1928 level in 1932, and still only 63.5 per cent in 1937. The more important consequence of their low standard of living during the years of Stalinist industrialization was that like other features of Soviet society then it was tacitly accepted as normal. The low priority accorded to satisfying the material needs of the working class would thus survive long after the initial period of rapid economic growth had passed" (Barber and Davies 1994, 103–104). Acceptance of a lower real wage "as normal" is what Marx (1990, 275) called a change in the "historical and moral element" of wages. Lowering "the average quantity of means of subsistence necessary for the labourer" lowers the value of Soviet workers' labor power.

33. The class and value concepts developed earlier can clarify the different situations faced in Marxian terms by Department One (enterprises producing means of production) and Department Two (enterprises producing means of consumption):

$$\text{Dept. 1 } SV(C) + SSCR(C)_{1,2} > SSCP(C)$$
$$\text{Dept. 2 } SV(C) < SSCP(C) + SSCP(C)_{2,1}$$

$SSCR(C)_{1,2}$ stands for the subsumed class revenues received by Department One from Two: the difference between the prices of means of production and their unit values or EV/UV. $SSCP(C)_{2,1}$ stands for the subsumed class payments made by Department Two to One. Thus, by definition, $SSCR(C)_{1,2} = SSCP(C)_{2,1} = (P_1 - EV/UV_1) \times UV_1$. The state intervened more or less to fix the price of means of production ($P_1$) despite their falling unit values. In effect, Department One enterprises earned a SSCR(C) debited against Department Two enterprises and therefore likely reducing the latter's expansion plans. Of course, to the degree that Department Two could maintain its prices while its unit costs fell, it offset its increased subsumed class payments to Department One. However, that would aggravate the already strained consumer goods distribution system. In fact, consumer goods output lagged both demand and the growth of means of production across the 1930s.

34. Workers suffered increasing penalties for absence from work over the 1930s (Nove 1989, 225). Carrere d'Encausse describes a "coercive system imposed upon a . . . working class" (1981, 24).

Baykov (1947, 361–362), Lewin (1984, 61–62), and especially Thurston (1996, ch. 6) describe both the discipline imposed on and empowerment of workers during the 1930s.

35. Accounts of this opposition can be found in: Medvedev (1973, 30–70), Deutscher (1968, 298–317, 344–385), Dobb (1966, 181–207), Cohen (1985, 71–92), Fitzpatrick (1984, 11–23), and Carrere d'Encausse (1982, 191–223; 1981, 1–53).
36. "The two men [Stalin and Bukharin] were united on the theoretical question of Socialism in One Country; but they interpreted the concept differently. Stalin believed that socialism meant industry, especially heavy industry. Bukharin assigned first importance to light industry and the peasant" (Day 1973, 111).
37. See, for example, Day's summary of Trotsky's assessment of Stalinism (1973, 187–192). However progressively silenced, Trostkyist critiques of Stalinism were widely held inside the USSR after Trotsky's own departure.
38. The perceived threat continued beyond the assassination of Kirov in December of 1934, the removal of one more opponent of and possible rival to Stalin. It also contributed to the next set of purges in 1936–39.
39. We can infer some concrete dimensions of these proportions from Baykov (1947, 311). In 1938, (1−a) equalled 15 percent for collective farms producing grains. That excluded additional portions of the crop delivered to state officials other than state procurement agents. Those portions included a relatively small refund to the state for advancing seed and a larger rent payment to the MTS. Adding these latter distributions raised the state's total grain collections to an overall percentage of 33 percent of the grain produced. This higher amount still did not count grains sold to the state at higher contract prices or to other buyers in uncontrolled markets. Adding the latter sales produced a total crop delivered to the state or marketed of 38 percent of the gross yield (the rest was retained by collectives for that year). Of that total crop delivered to the state or marketed, 87 percent comprised required deliveries to the state, rents to MTS, and repayments of advanced seed. The remaining 13 percent represented the collectives' local market sales.

Baykov indicates that much higher percentages of gross yields had to be delivered to the state by collectives producing raw materials. Compared to the 38 percent for grain collectives, sugar beet and cotton collectives delivered almost 100 percent of their gross yields to the state in 1938 (1947, 311–312).

To get some idea of the total grain deliveries to the state over the 1930s, we present the following table showing the average percentage of the gross harvest that was counted as total grain collections. As noted above, collections include required deliveries to the state, rents to MTS, returns of seed, and contract sales to the state. The table reports our computed average percentages for three periods based on data provided in Davies et al. (1994, 290):

|  | 1928–32 | 1933–36 | 1937–40 |
|---|---|---|---|
| Average percent | 29.7 | 36.0 | 41.1 |

40. Our equation assumes, for simplicity, that no portion of the retained crop was sold in the private market; that is why it is valued in labor rather than market price terms. In fact however, when permitted, collectives sold a portion of that retained crop in uncontrolled markets. They could even sell a portion to the state for a contract price that was set higher than the procurement price (for the required quota). Using data for 1938 provided in Baykov (1947, 311), these private and state sales for grain collectives amounted only to 6 percent of their total retained grain. The latter is [a $UV_{AG}$] in the equation.
41. For example, members could purchased additional manufactures by selling their retained food products on local private markets at much higher prices there.

CHAPTER 10

# Class Contradictions and the Collapse

The USSR was born out of class contradictions similar to those in which it died. In 1917, Russian private capitalism and its social context—especially the distribution of private property, markets, and the czarist state—had either collapsed or reached such extremes as to undermine confidence and support. Socialist critics of the ultimate unworkability and unacceptability of private capitalism responded vigorously to growing sympathy for their arguments and programs. The crisis of 1917 provoked the USSR's birth in a transition chiefly from private to state capitalism. In the 1980s, it was the state capitalism and its social context—especially collective property, state planning, and the Communist Party—that were in critical decay. This crisis reversed the direction of 1917: this transition went from state back to private capitalism.

In class terms, no crash happened at the end of the 1980s. It was rather certain nonclass aspects of Soviet society that changed dramatically. Their impact on Soviet class structures was marginal and limited. The demise of the USSR was not a collapse of communist class structures in favor of the capitalist alternative. The USSR as a nation and the social position of the Communist Party collapsed. In contrast, the USSR's class structures marginally adjusted.

Charles Dickens once tried to capture in a novel how one historical moment could be both "the best of times" and "the worst of times." In Marx's language, every moment is understood as the play of such contradictions. Richard B. Day identifies the contradictions in the USSR of the mid-1970s as such a best/worst historical moment (1995, 275–276). Soviet leaders and supporters then celebrated what they understood as "the best of times." They believed that the Cold War project—"containment" of the USSR and its "satellites"—had failed. The USSR had grown industrially, militarily, and in global influence. Estimates of Soviet economic growth between 1929 and 1970 and especially after 1950 (by Soviet officials, the CIA, and independent academic economists) showed stunningly rapid development: far greater than U.S. growth over the same periods (Gregory and Stuart 1998, 225–226). Reveling in global superpower status and rising domestic standards of living, Soviet spokespersons and supporters exulted.[1] The achievement of "peaceful coexistence represented the *containment of capitalism*" and "when Brezhnev launched his own adventures in Angola, Ethiopia, and Afghanistan, he acted ... in the conviction that capitalism was in historical decline" (Day 1995, 275, italics in original). The peaking of Soviet achievements and self-confidence from 1950 to 1975 confirmed the faith of Soviet leaders, while it challenged the faith of those who presumed that the Soviet system would fail.

Of course, the USSR's critics and enemies found evidence for the bad sides of Soviet life, especially in terms of civil rights and political freedoms. They repeated or reformulated long-standing critiques of the USSR as an economically inefficient and politically undemocratic political system—a coupling which they insisted would surely undermine the USSR eventually. Yet these arguments, however effective in supporting hostilities toward the Soviet system, lost persuasiveness as the USSR's economic and political situation improved steadily from the war's end to the mid-1970s. The critics offered no credible arguments as to how or why the USSR would collapse a decade later.[2]

Neither Soviet leaders nor their supporters nor their critics analyzed the class contradictions of Soviet society. As those contradictions evolved after World War Two to undermine the successes and deepen the deficiencies of Soviet society, its leaders could neither recognize nor cope with them. By the mid-1980s, a decade's sense of decline became, for both the leaders and masses of Soviet society, a shared crisis of confidence in what they understood as Soviet socialism. The leaders' failure to cope combined with this crisis to revive the faith of those, inside and outside the USSR, who believed in Soviet socialism's impracticability and in private market capitalism's superiority.

## Class Structures after World War Two

The destruction and trauma of World War Two for the USSR, arguably the worst suffered by any combattant nation (Keep 1995; Dunham 1976, 214ff.), did not basically change the prewar class structures. Industry remained state capitalist. Despite various reforms and "liberalizations" after Stalin's death, successive regimes never fundamentally challenged nor even questioned state capitalist industry as central to what they deemed "Soviet socialism." Only with Gorbachev and Yeltsin did the shift from state back to private capitalist industrial enterprises become significant (Gregory and Stuart 1998, 301–304). In agriculture, only the distribution of farms among the different kinds of coexisting class structures of production changed. The relative importance of state capitalist farms rose vis-à-vis both the collective farms and the ancient class structures on the individual private plots.[3] Some of these collective farms retained their communist class structures while others changed to swell the numbers of collective farms with capitalist class structures.[4] The argument of this chapter leads us henceforth to refer to communist and/or capitalist collective farms since the term *collective farms* abstracts from their different and shifting class structures. Lastly, households retained their mix of feudal and ancient class structures.

Alongside state capitalist industries, state capitalist farms, private capitalist and communist collective farms, and private ancient plots, a so-called second economy existed throughout Soviet history (Grossman 1977, 1989). It comprised unofficial, largely unacknowledged, and sometimes illegal enterprises of all sorts. Since the second economy grew quickly after the mid-1970s and since its enterprises were largely organized as ancient class structures, the latter thus grew relative to other class structures inside the USSR.

To supplement the surpluses it appropriated within industrial state capitalist enterprises, the state continued to gain revenues at the expense of private communist collective farms and private capitalist collective farms. As before World War Two, the means to accomplish this diversion of surpluses from private to state class structures were (1) state-set prices that turned the terms of trade between industrial and agricultural products in favor of industry and (2) state taxes and fees levied upon farm enterprises. Additionally, the state appropriated increasing surpluses directly on the ever more numerous state capitalist farms. In this case, turning the terms of trade against state capitalist farms reallocated revenues *within* the state from its state-agricultural to its state-industrial enterprises.[5] Of course, these levies upon state and nonstate agricultural enterprises made more difficult the securing of their class structures' conditions of existence. Thus the shift from collective to state farms did little to change the basic precariousness of Soviet agriculture.

Besides appropriating surpluses from industrial and farm workers and obtaining subsumed and nonclass revenues from terms of trade effects and taxes on agriculture, the state also relied on indirect taxes—turnover taxes—levied directly on the retail prices of commodities. Starting in the early 1930s, this tax eventually became (by the 1980s) the most important source of total state tax revenues. The turnover tax represented a growing source of nonclass revenues for the state at the expense of reducing workers' real personal incomes. To the degree that the state continued allocating resources to the production of capital rather than consumer goods, the result was excess demand for consumer goods, although this excess was mitigated by postwar increases in consumer goods production. The excess demand that remained was largely removed by the state using the turnover tax to raise retail prices to consumers (over and above their values per unit).[6]

The postwar Soviet economy continued to comprise an interdependent, contradictory complex of these multiple, different class structures: contradictory because they simultaneously provided and undermined one another's conditions of existence. State capitalist industrial enterprises purchased outputs from and sold key inputs to the state (capitalist) farms and the private (capitalist and communist) collective farms. These exchanges supported all the class structures engaged in them. Yet once again, the state's price and other policies directed against agriculture enabled state capitalist industry to gain (subsumed and nonclass) revenues above and beyond its surplus value. Such value inflows at the cost of class structures in agriculture permitted a more rapid industrial capital accumulation, an expanded Communist Party and state bureaucracy, and growing levels of collective consumption, even while it threatened the viability of farms. At the same time, the state (capitalist) farms and the private (capitalist and communist) collective farms provided many of the conditions of existence (equipment, storage, etc.) for family (ancient) farming plots. Yet those ancient class-structured plots took individual farmers' time and energy away from work on the state and collective farms, thereby threatening their class structures.[7]

Soviet household class structures yielded surpluses in part because industrial and agricultural class structures provided household members with personal incomes, that is, with means for household surpluses to be produced. Because such surpluses supplemented the other incomes flowing into households from outside, they served in the circumstances to compensate somewhat for low wages and high turnover taxes.[8] In value terms feudal household surpluses delivered by women to men thus lowered the value of these men's labor power (i.e., the wages they had to be paid) and thereby raised the rate of surplus value. Similarly, the production (chiefly by women) of both feudal and ancient household surpluses relieved some of the pressure on the Soviet state to devote the surpluses it gathered to the production of use-values delivered free (or subsidized) to households (as elements of collective consumption). This too freed more of the state's surpluses for use in industrial capital accumulation or for the Party and bureaucracy.

Women worked doubly as surplus producers outside as well as inside households.[9] The resulting exhaustion of women, their limited individual incomes, and the insufficient (albeit growing) state-provided public services served to exacerbate tensions within household relationships, thereby undermining their class structures and threatening the continued production of household surplus labor (Lapidus 1978).[10] Soviet households' problems reacted back upon the class structures outside households. The endless references to problematic worker discipline, morale, and productivity in Soviet industrial and agricultural enterprises suggest the contradictory relationship between class structures inside and outside households. They both supported and undermined one another. The net effect—whether the "stability" of mutual support or the "explosion" of mutual destruction—depended on the larger social context—the nonclass conditions that overdetermined the class structures.

In class terms, the postwar USSR differed only slightly from the prewar USSR. Both were fragile complexes of class structures caught up in contradictory relationships precariously balanced. For its first fifty years a remarkable set of circumstances combined to hold together the fragile Soviet class configurations as their composition changed in the ways we have sought to trace. Internal catastrophes, actual and anticipated foreign attacks, forced march preparations for and recoveries from both catastrophes and attacks, and socialist fervor combined to produce historically unprecedented social development and to prevent the contradictions of the USSR's class structures from exploding. The euphoria and consolidation of the revolution drove the first decade. Completing the revolution by spreading it from industry to agriculture—collectivization—drove the second. Forced march industrialization arose across the first two decades to become the spirit of the third. Winning and recovering from World War Two defined the fourth and fifth decades.

Soviet history includes the awesome, unprecedented fifty-year achievement of not only sustained unity but industrialization and superpower status alongside the United States. All this happened despite the devastation of two world wars, a civil war (which included foreign invasions), agricultural collectivization (almost another civil war), and continuously dangerous encirclements and containments. Yet, not the least irony of Soviet history is that this achievement proved to be as well its undoing. When finally the USSR could stalemate its enemies, arrange a detente with the United States, and open its borders toward more regular political, cultural, and economic interactions, it could not find a new driving spirit for these new circumstances that could hold together the contradictions of its ever-fragile class composition.

Beginning in the 1970s, postwar nonclass changes altered the balance among contradictory Soviet class structures: mutual support gave way to mutual weakening. Dissatisfaction, resentment, corruption, and conflict deepened. Initially Soviet leaders searched for particular solutions to what they saw then as the particular problems of state industries, state farms, collective farms, and households. As these proved ineffective, there arose instead a society-wide sense of a need for some more fundamental, sweeping reorganization of the entire system. This set the stage for the collapse of the late 1980s.

Throughout the postwar period Soviet achievements and problems received often intense debates and sustained academic and policy-oriented examinations. As conditions deteriorated across the 1970s and 1980s, the quality of debate and examination became more open and far-reaching than it had been since the 1920s. Yet at no time were Soviet analysts able to bring any sustained class analytical apparatus to bear on the central issues. An officially Marxian society could not deploy a Marxian class analysis to save itself. Partly this happened because official culture denied the possibility of a complex class structure existing inside the already "socialist" USSR. Partly the absence of a sophisticated culture of debate over the different definitions of class within Marxism deprived postwar Soviet citizens of the means to undertake class analyses. Deeply influenced (often more than they realized) by Soviet society's class blindness, both sympathizers and enemies outside the USSR offered very little class analysis—and none of the surplus labor kind— that Soviet citizens might have borrowed. Since the resources of Marxian class analytics were thus largely unavailable, they were not utilized to understand or cope with the problems of the postwar USSR.

No transcendent or intrinsic inevitability attaches to postwar Soviet history and the remarkable differences between the changes in its class and nonclass aspects. The response to social deterioration after the mid-1970s might have been different and successful in reversing the collapse. A radical change of class structures—for example, a serious, society-wide experiment with communist class structures in industry; a return to and reform of communist class structures in agriculture; a renewed interest in and experiment with communist class structures in households—is one alternative that might have been attempted. Had Marxian class consciousness and debates over the class analysis of the USSR been major features of Soviet life, that alternative might have received more attention or even become official policy.

In class terms, two basic questions confronted the postwar USSR. First, would the surpluses appropriated from state capitalist industries and farms, the value flows from terms of trade manipulations and taxes at the expense of collectives, and the turnover taxes on workers suffice for the state to fund the USSR's program of heavy industrial capital accumulation, its superpower costs (military and political), its state and party expenses, and a growing allocation to raise collective consumption (housing, medical care, etc.)?[11] Second, would the Soviet state and the Party be able to manage the economic, political, and cultural (nonclass) processes needed to allow the USSR's fragile structure of classes to survive? The next three sections of the chapter show how changes in postwar Soviet culture, politics, and economics plunged the USSR's class structures and the Soviet state into a mutually reinforcing spiral into crisis.

## Postwar Culture

Postwar changes in Soviet culture—understood in Raymond Williams's sense of "structures of feeling" (1977, 128–135)—affected its class structures in two interrelated ways. Cultural changes aggravated some class structures' problems by contributing to their difficulties in generating enough surpluses to sustain themselves. At the same time, they contributed to strengthening other class structures by facilitating their generation of more surplus and thereby their ability to survive or grow. In short, cultural changes contributed to altering the relative viabilities and hence proportions among class structures within the Soviet social formation.

As noted above, Soviet cultural changes after 1945 did not include any challenge to the inherited lack of class consciousness (in the surplus labor sense) among Soviet leaders, intellectuals, and people generally. The class structures that comprised Soviet society in the postwar years remained—even more than in the 1920s and 1930s—beyond conceptualization and hence beyond debate or explicit policy treatment. The contributions of those class structures to Soviet history likewise remained invisible, leaving supporters and critics alike with only the nonclass aspects of economy and society (e.g., distributions of political power between ruling elites and workers, effective property, and so on) to consider in their efforts to understand and shape that history.

One complex of cultural changes after the war is associated with the establishment of detente with the West, slowly and in fits and starts from the 1950s to the

1970s (Riasanovsky 1984, 558–562). The rhetoric and realities of that Cold War period coincided with (and often contradicted) the concerted Soviet effort to construct agreements and relationships around the concept of a peaceful coexistence or detente. In turn, as detente emerged, it enabled and provoked a set of significant shifts in how Soviet citizens felt about their lives. The siege mentality dissipated gradually, although occasionally revived by moments of Cold War intensification. Public and private decisions were less often reached or justified under the pressures of actual or impending social dangers or catastrophes. Finally, after so many years of forced march preparations for and recoveries from social cataclysms, individual lives could begin to be viewed as occurring in peace—not only in the sense of the absence of war but in the sense of a relatively stable normalcy of daily life. Perhaps for the first time since 1917, for many of those who more or less supported the official goals and values of the USSR, the absence of acute social crisis meant that personal needs and desires could become legitimate individual priorities.

A certain detachment from feelings of immersion in vast social projects of industrial production, collectivization, constructing a new socialist civilization, war preparation, hysterical purges, and recovery from war became widespread. Stalin's death, the ensuing weakening of Stalinism as a cultural as well as political and economic condition, and detente encouraged this shift toward the personal or "private" spheres of life.[12] These developments had practical and also symbolic consequences in addition to legitimating the relaxation of the hitherto relentless crisis environment. Detente especially promoted the shift to private life by facilitating all sorts of contacts, communications, and exchanges with Western societies. In the latter, the spheres of private life were officially much more valued than those of public life, and no comparable tradition of siege mentality existed. Soviet sociologists undertook many studies that documented their society's shift toward individual concerns, and they offered varying explanations for it (Shlapentokh 1989). There was even considerable official acceptance if not endorsement of the shift. It could be interpreted as proof that the USSR had "arrived" at the stage where citizens could finally reap those rewards of revolution deferred earlier to defeat its enemies. The officially sanctioned and heavily subsidized postwar production and nationwide dissemination of political posters (with impacts perhaps comparable to advertising in western countries) stressed "serenity and joyfulness amid abundance"—a far cry from the poster themes before and during the war (Bonnell 1997, 260).[13]

The shift of Soviet feeling and focus from the larger society to the individual concerns of relationship and personal life had several class consequences. A deepened alienation from politics spilled over into a parallel alienation from what might be termed "social" production. Even before detente, the turbulence of party struggles and the legacy of Stalin's purges had turned many Soviet citizens away from participation in or even engagement with the dangerous domain of politics. But total commitment to the urgent goals of production had been much less affected. With detente, the relaxation of Soviet citizens' public and social foci and activities withdrew energy not only from their relationships with the state and the Party, but also from their work in the enterprises identified with the state and the Party (Shlapentokh 1989, 153–163).

Reduced commitments to work in state capitalist enterprises and in private capitalist and communist collective farms took various forms. Earlier patriotic and/or party-driven surges of extra (and unpaid) labor and campaigns to reduce waste of productive resources occurred less often and less effectively. Many individual Soviet laborers worked less intensely and with less commitment. For them, work became more a job for pay than a social mission, crusade, or project of national salvation. Unlike the 1930s, work intensity and labor productivity declined. Thus, in class terms, one effect of the postwar cultural changes associated with detente entailed such workers producing less surplus labor than before.[14] Of course, this influence operated alongside all the other influences overdetermining the quantity of surplus that the Soviet state could gather into its hands and devote to its priorities. Yet, just when these priority demands on the state's available surplus were expanding with the USSR's superpower status, it did not augur well for the future that cultural changes were reducing some of the state's surpluses.[15]

While the cultural shift into private concerns thus undercut the capitalist class structures of state enterprises and the capitalist and communist class structures of collective farms, it strengthened other class structures in the USSR. Chief among these were the ancient class structures on the private farm plots of individuals and families. They were the more "private" class structures: individuals or family groups labored alone rather than collectively with many other people. The widely recognized enthusiasm of Soviet workers for their private farm plots and their remarkable productive efficiency there contrasted ever more sharply with waning labor enthusiasm and troubled labor productivity in capitalist and communist class-structured enterprises.[16]

The new Soviet constitution of 1977 officially recognized and endorsed the private plots as crucial components of Soviet productive life. Where most Bolsheviks after 1917 had considered individual or family farm units as politically necessary but hopefully temporary concessions, Stalin had later reestablished them as compensatory adjuncts to agricultural collectivization. After Stalin, Khrushchev had returned to denouncing them as counter to socialist commitment and obstacles to industrial and agricultural growth. The constitutional recognition of 1977 represented the end of such oscillations. Official policy had been forced to accommodate in this basic way the cultural shift to private, personal concerns and its class consequences. Brezhnev and Gorbachev celebrated the importance to Soviet socialism represented by private plots.

Official state policy from the mid-1970s on not only celebrated the private plots but also welcomed more or less free markets for much of the produce from them. In this way, many Soviet citizens began, more or less consciously, positively to associate private concerns, market relations, and, in our terms, ancient class structures as components of economic and social progress. A cultural shift had contributed to a class shift that reacted back upon and so further developed the cultural shift. The direction of this interaction, in subtle and different ways, undermined both capitalist and communist class structures. Nor did Soviet leaders stop this undermining; they did not think in such class terms, nor envision any practicable alternative to accommodating private plots, nor could they blame some external or internal enemy for it. Thus it proceeded relatively unchecked.

The growth of ancient class structures and markets in their products was not limited to private plot farming. There is evidence (sketchy, of course) that across the postwar period increasing numbers of Soviet citizens supplemented their state jobs with semilegal and illegal productions of service commodities. Most of these seem to have been organized in individual, ancient class structural forms. Examples include the repair of apartments, automobiles, shoes, and appliances; the provision of transportation; the manufacture of selected consumer goods such as T-shirts; the tutoring of children and adults; and the private practice of medicine and dentistry (Shlapentokh 1989, 192–196). Millions of Soviet state employees participated. They worked in such ancient class structures in addition to working within the state's capitalist class structures. This no doubt provoked them to make comparisons just at an historical moment when the latter were experiencing increasing problems and difficulties while the former found increasing acceptance and success.

The significance of these cultural changes interacting with the shifting balance of class structures within Soviet society emerged in the 1980s. Then the accumulated difficulties of state capitalism—a result in part of the growing attachments to other noncapitalist class structures—provoked a crisis mentality throughout the USSR. As problems mounted, millions of Soviet citizens began to generalize from their personal histories. As they had shifted personally from reliance chiefly on state capitalist employment to an increasing reliance as well on significant amounts of "private" ancient self-employment, they began to see or accept a parallel social solution for the USSR. However, absent the class terms deployed here, they utilized instead the dominant concepts and languages of their time and place. They reasoned and spoke about the need to solve the problems of socialism by freeing (from the state and from collective activity) private/individual initiative and private/individual labor. At first this took the modest form of advocating such new freedoms merely as accompaniments to the state capitalism they called socialism. Later, as the problems deepened, more militant arguments demanded the replacement of socialism with such "private initiatives."

Of course, this juxtaposition of private/individual versus public/social is very different, theoretically and logically, from the polarity of capitalist versus noncapitalist class structures. Soviet demands for shifts from public to private enterprise rarely addressed whether such private enterprises should have ancient, capitalist, or still other possible class structures. In fact, the private enterprises—legal, semilegal, and illegal—that had grown during the postwar period displayed different class structures. Not all were self-employed, individual ancient class structures. For example, one of the more remarkable private enterprises involved teams of freelance builders who supplemented their state jobs by using vacation and other times to engage in construction work across the USSR (Shlapentokh 1989, 193). Such building teams did not display individual ancient class structures, but it is not clear whether they organized themselves into capitalist class structures, communist class structures (akin, say, to the private communist collective farms), or still other class-structural possibilities.

In sum, the cultural turn from public, social concerns toward more private, personal foci had effects that included changing the balance among the USSR's class structures. On the one hand, the ancient class structure was favored at the expense of both the capitalist and communist class structures. On the other hand, the general turn toward things private served to legitimate a general, rising valuation of private over social organizations of production. The theoretical class blindness of virtually all observers precluded their inquiring about or debating such private enterprises' class structures. Likewise, their class blindness precluded examining how each of these would differently influence Soviet development generally, its socialist character, or its communist future in particular. Because both Soviet intellectuals and leaders wrote and spoke in terms of public versus private rather than in class-qua-surplus-labor terms, they contributed to the general invisibility of the class changes underway. Hence no policy debates or actions emerged explicitly to address those changes. In their absence, we can understand the remarkable postwar convergence in the class blindness with which both Soviet intellectuals and leaders and their western counterparts reasoned about economic and social development generally. Thus, what differentiated "capitalist thought" in the West from "socialist thought" in the East was not the absence versus the presence of class analysis in terms of surplus labor. Rather, both kinds of thought utilized the state-versus-private juxtaposition; they differed only (and decreasingly) on which was considered positive and which negative for economic and social progress.

In the realms of the "fine arts," academia, and the top echelons of the natural sciences, the connection between Soviet cultural changes and class is more difficult to delineate. However, we find such a connection in the history of Soviet state and party leaders' struggles with various representatives of "high culture." One central theme recurring (although in different ways and rhythms) was the official goal of connecting culture to "class." However, the concept of class at work in the struggles over high culture in the USSR, during and after Stalin, was not the surplus-labor concept of Marx at work in this book. Rather it was the classical dualistic differentiation of "proletarian" versus "bourgeois" chiefly in terms of rich versus poor. In its cultural expressions, this differentiation amounted to juxtapositions of positive against negative, revolutionary against reactionary, popular against elitist, poor and working against rich and idle, new against old. From the rise and fall of the "proletkult" and "socialist realism" movements after the revolution to the rise and fall of the "proletarian genetics" associated with Lysenko and Zhdanov's strictures on literature, Soviet cultural struggles were often represented as displaced forms of "the basic class struggle" between proletarian and bourgeois tendencies.[17]

Such a connection of high culture to class reduced a complexity to a dualistic simplicity. Not merely, as noted by so many critics of Soviet high culture, were all kinds of artistic autonomy and creativity lost by censoring artists allegedly linked to "bourgeois rather than socialist/proletarian" tendencies. The complex reality of the USSR's multiple, contradictory class structures was also thereby repressed from or at least marginalized within cultural expression. Because Soviet art was so heavily pressed into this proletarian-bourgeois dualism, it could only rarely explore or illuminate the complex diversity of the USSR's shifting class realities.

Official discourse (emanating from state, party, and high culture sources) defined postwar state capitalist enterprises and private capitalist and communist collective farms structures all together as proletarian or socialist. The labels applied because these structures had a "socialist class" dimension in the usual Soviet sense of "class": their means of production were socially rather than privately owned and their inputs and outputs were distributed chiefly by state planning rather than by markets. Proletarian or socialist art was thus connected to "class" through its cultural affirmation and celebration of such "socialist" structures and/or of the "socialist" labor occurring within them. Neither these "socialist" structures nor their "socialist" laboring activity were connected in any explicit way to the concrete modes of organizing the production, appropriation, and distribution of surplus labor.

Art viewed as critical, however obliquely, of those "socialist" structures or of laborers' experiences in "socialist" production, received official denunciation as non- or antisocialist art. Forms of expression troubling or strange to the prevailing tastes among workers and/or Soviet leaders likewise obtained the designation of "that other" kind of art, namely "bourgeois." It became the cultural enemy to be combated. Art that might have addressed the contradictions within and among the different, coexisting modes of producing, appropriating, and distributing surplus labor in the USSR (class contradictions in that specific sense) was systematically repressed, actively and passively, unofficially and officially.

Those relatively few critical assessments of work and life that did find artistic expression did not address the issues of who produced and appropriated surplus labor in these structures. For example, in Vladimir Dudintsev's novel *Not By Bread Alone*, Professor Busko explains to Nadia how the postwar USSR carries "the residue of capitalism" deeply inside individuals, including those with important state positions (1957, 253–257). Nadia is moved by these words as they resonate with her own vague but developing social criticism. Capitalism is here depicted as merely a residue, then not yet eliminated. It is associated with bureaucratic self-serving and not linked to class in the surplus labor sense, either tangentially or metaphorically, anywhere in the novel. In general, when serious problems of factory and collective farm work in the USSR did obtain cultural expression—increasingly after Stalin's death—they were likewise unconnected to class in the surplus labor sense. Instead the problems were conceptually categorized as workplace bureaucracy, careerism, corruption of "socialist morality," and/or insufficient (or absent) democracy.

A parallel post-Khrushchev theoretical blindness characterized the endless criticisms of Stalin and Stalinism within the USSR and beyond. These critiques blamed bureaucracy (and its ultimate "cult of personality" form), careerism, and corruptions of "socialist legality and morality" located in some deep Russian traits or else in the Bolshevik distortions of them.[18] In contrast, Louis Althusser sharply lamented the dominant critiques of Stalinism in the USSR and elsewhere precisely because even the Marxists among them did not ask how the class structures of Soviet society contributed to the rise and survival of Stalinism. He suggested forcefully that by failing to do so, the criticisms had failed to defeat Stalinism within the Marxian tradition (1976, 92). High culture in the postwar USSR, in both its social celebratory and social critical formulations, elided anything approaching a class analysis in the sense of what we have argued in this book.

The criticisms that were voiced focused especially on injustices, venalities, and inefficiencies attributed to unbridled bureaucratic power and not (even partly) to the social organization of surplus labor. Hence, the chief objects of attack were the largest and most bureaucratized social institutions: the state and the state capitalist enterprises in industry and agriculture. Their problems and failings, it was argued, flowed from their bureaucracies. Such arguments affirmed some inherent nature of bureaucracy per se (thwarting individual initiative, responsibility, and reward) and/or claimed that the still insufficiently socialized nature of the Soviet citizenry produced a largely passive general population in the face of a bureaucratic despotism (Hochschild 1994, 118).

One effect of such criticisms was a growing tendency after Stalin, sometimes conscious but usually inadvertent, to celebrate and thereby encourage transfers of admiration, loyalty, and effort to enterprises with less or no bureaucracy. These were, of course, the smaller, private enterprises whose class structures were capitalist, communist, or ancient. These enterprises came to be viewed increasingly as sites of less bureaucracy and hence less of the careerism and corruption that kept the large, bureaucratized state industries from making the Soviet economy more productive. Soviet high culture's criticisms along these lines thus contributed to the Gorbachev-Yeltsin-Putin approach to solving the USSR's perceived crisis: policies enhancing the conditions of existence of private enterprises (of whatever class structure) at the expense of the state capitalist class structures in the USSR.[19]

In still another way, postwar Soviet high culture helped to shape its class structures. To the degree that it adopted and repeated the dogma of top state and party officials that dichotomized society into a "proletarian" positivity struggling against a "bourgeois" negativity, high culture reinforced the dialectical potential of such dichotomies. If ever the vaunted positivity encountered a serious crisis that undermined popular loyalties, then people would know of nowhere else to look but to the one "other." If the Soviet people ever came to view the "proletarian way" as mired in intractable problems that could not credibly be blamed on "bourgeois" agents, foreign or domestic, the way would have been prepared for increasing numbers of people, entrapped within the dualism, to reverse its valuation. The "time" might then arrive to try the only conceivable other way (bourgeois) instead of the one in place ("proletarian") that had become exhausted and intolerable. The crescendo of economic and political problems of the 1970s and 1980s combined with detente and the nearly universal cultural dualism of proletarian versus bourgeois to produce such reverse valuations in many people. Since "proletarian" had long been associated with the supposedly socialist state and collective enterprises, collective property, and economic planning, the reverse valuation exalted instead their opposites: private enterprises, individual property, and markets.

Economic theories debated in the top echelons of the state, the Party, and academia exercised relatively direct impacts on class. For example, Marxian economic theory has a long history of debate over whether produced and sold services are commodities like physical objects and should be theorized in the same class and value terms. For a variety of reasons, the prevalent Soviet practice into the postwar years had considered only produced physical objects as commodities entailing surplus value and exploitation. This relegated most service workers, in contrast to object producers, to a different and often lower theoretical and social position.[20] However, developments in Western thinking, especially during the 1960s, provoked a switch in the official Soviet position in this old debate (Day 1995, 180–187).[21] Western economists and others had increasingly found that the production of physical goods was declining in "advanced economies" relative to service work. From this observation they inferred that proletariats (equated nearly everywhere with object-producers) and hence their theoreticians, political parties, etc., were becoming historically irrelevant in such economies. For example, many Western analysts credited service personnel (or students training to become them) and not proletarians for the powerful left movements in Europe and the United States that culminated in 1968 and 1969. Soviet writers responded in part by revaluing service work as no less productive of surplus than work producing objects. By this means, they could combine both kinds of workers inside capitalist societies into one undifferentiated mass of proletarians confronting "state-monopoly capital." On this basis they refuted claims that proletariats were shrinking anywhere in the world and that communist parties were anachronistic.

Those who crafted such refutations, however, thereby further entrapped themselves within a class-blind analytical framework. Noting that both service and goods laborers were wage earners, they made wage earning per se the standard of one's class position. Proletarians were wage earners and vice versa, whereas wage payers were capitalists or at least parts of a "capitalist ruling class." In contrast, Marx had gone to remarkable lengths in his *Capital* precisely to differentiate the wage earner in a bank or state office or retail store from the wage earner directly involved in commodity production—whether of the physical object or service sort—within a capitalist enterprise. The latter was a "productive" laborer (or wage earner), for Marx, because he/she generated a surplus value appropriated by a capitalist. The former wage earner was "unproductive" because he/she did not generate such a surplus value. Hence the receipt of wages was not the standard that distinguished productive from unproductive labor.

Unproductive workers provided the conditions of existence for productive workers to produce the surplus. Part of that surplus was then distributed to the unproductive workers as their wages and salaries. Because of these *different* relationships to the production of surplus value, the two kinds of wage earners comprised two different classes (Resnick and Wolff 1987, ch. 3).[22] The different classes and class interests within the aggregate of "wage earners" may or may not construct an effective political alliance, but Marx's theory provides no warrant to simply assume that wage earners are a unified economic or political force. Soviet theoreticians' collapse of the two different classes of wage earners into one undifferentiated "working class" identity influenced the thinking of many officials and hence state policies and enterprise practices. The mix and evolution of the USSR's class structures was thus different from what might have been the case had another conceptualization of class been widely influential.

We may suggest this influence by considering some questions logically posed by a class analysis of the USSR that focused on the production and distribution of surplus value—rather than on wages. What contradictions and tensions existed inside the USSR between productive and unproductive wage earners? What were the impacts of these contradictions and tensions on labor productivity and discipline and on workers' political attitudes toward the Soviet state and socialism? What sorts of changes in the relationship between productive and unproductive laborers might have better facilitated the achievement of Soviet economic and political objectives? Because Soviet class theory precluded such questions being asked, researched, or answered, the internal class conflicts that weakened Soviet state capitalism remained beyond the reach of policy solutions.

Similarly, Soviet social theory's largely undifferentiated focus on wage earning as the sign of membership in "the exploited working class" reinforced Soviet analysts' inability to undertake class analyses of Soviet households (partly because no wage payments occurred there). Thus they could not inquire into how Soviet citizens participated in the production, appropriation, and distribution of surplus labor inside their households. Nor could they examine how their participation in household class structures affected their participation in enterprises.[23] The class structures of households in which Soviet citizens spent half their lives could not become objects of the prevailing class analysis or of policy debates.[24] Partly because post-war Soviet theorizing secured the invisibility of the feudal and ancient household class structures inherited from before the war, those structures endured. On the possibility that those enduring household class structures may have undermined state capitalist industries or private capitalist and communist collective farms (say, in their effects on workers' productivities, interpersonal values, political loyalties, etc.), postwar Soviet economic theory had nothing to say. On the possibility that those household class structures functioned, even if only implicitly, to strengthen ancient and feudal class structures as desirable models for organizing productive work and thereby to thwart social transition toward communism, postwar Soviet economic theory was likewise silent.

In theoretical discourses on economics there was remarkable agreement between Soviet and U.S. economists despite their mutual hostilities. Socialist economists in the USSR as elsewhere had long differentiated socialism from capitalism according to whether property was collective/state or private and according to whether markets or central planning distributed resources and products. When Western economists hostile to the USSR based their arguments on the same differentiation, Soviet economists did not question whether that agreement might itself be worth investigation.

Thus, debates between Soviet and Western economists turned on whether private property and markets encouraged more "efficiency," more economic growth, and more rapidly rising standards of living than did collective property and planning. On both sides of the debate, the production, appropriation, and distribution of surplus labor was absent. As David Ruccio's important work has shown, Soviet economists and economic planners produced analyses and proposals without reference to or concern with the organization of surplus labor (Ruccio 1984). Their concerns were limited to the relation between physical inputs and outputs; they were not interested in the effects of planning on Soviet class structures.

The consequences of Soviet economic thought emerged after 1975 when a rapidly growing number of Soviet economists believed that economic decline had reached crisis proportions. Their increasingly desperate search for solutions brought to the fore the influence of their conceptual frameworks—as parts of the structures of thought and feeling that comprised Soviet high culture—on the USSR's class dimensions. Sutela has usefully distinguished these conceptual frameworks into three groups: the slavophile, the radical socialist, and the westernizing (1991, 154-167). Even after the last of these emerged victorious among policy makers in the 1990s, proponents of the two others continue to agitate significantly throughout the former USSR.

Slavophile economics responds to the economic crisis by seeking a return to some vaguely defined Russian community; its nationalism and commitment to full employment display clearly corporatist overtones of the prewar German and Italian varieties. The stress is placed on collective, nonmarket economics that would serve to reinforce state and collective enterprises and undermine private enterprises. Although no reference to class in the surplus labor sense is discernible in their arguments, the class implications of their program are quite clear. They amount to a deeply conservative commitment to expand chiefly state capitalist industry and secondarily the private capitalist and communist collective farm agriculture. They serve as well to undermine private ancient and small capitalist undertakings of the sorts mentioned earlier in this chapter. Slovophile theory likewise favors male-headed feudal over the mostly female-headed ancient households as inherent to the "Slavic family and soul."

What Sutela calls "westernizing" economics aims instead to reduce the role of the state and collective property in favor of private property and to enhance markets at the expense of planning. While it too makes no reference to class in surplus labor terms, its stress on privatization, markets, and openness to foreign trade and investments carries class implications. Since this trend emerged victorious in the 1990s, these implications became all the more clear as Yeltsin's policies proceeded to enact many of them. Privatization and markets would tend to convert state capitalist into private capitalist enterprises, to expand and strengthen private capitalist and, to a lesser extent, ancient farms (based on private property) at the expense of communist collective farms, and to maintain the ancient and feudal mix of household class structures.

Sutela's "radical socialist" economics focuses on decentralized worker self-management as the solution: the *arenda* movement. In this solution, the state would own but lease to worker collectives the means of production, which they would then collectively self-manage. This would provide workers with the requisite incentives for increasing productivity while overcoming their alienation, which was the cause of Soviet economic decline in the radical socialist view. *Arenda* would also finally establish a real, democratic socialism by devolving management down from an elite central apparatus to the workers themselves. The absence of any reference to surplus labor in the radical socialist formulations reminds us of the 1917 revolution's parallel lack of attention to class in this sense. Once again, workers are to take command of the factories and the farms but this time without ceding management to a central state apparatus.

This time, workers would self-manage state-owned factories and farms leased to them and negotiate democratically agreed deliveries of their inputs and outputs (via markets or otherwise) with one another. The idea that *management* is one thing and *class* another never arises. With no concept of surplus labor organization, the radical socialist formulations suggest nothing so much as the likelihood that self-managing workers would repeat what their revolutionary forebears did after 1917. They would organize their factories and farms to be "efficient" (a concept borrowed uncritically from Western and "westernizing" economics): most workers would produce surplus while also electing others (perhaps from among themselves) to appropriate and distribute it. This would be viewed and done as a technical matter, merely an efficiency-driven division of labor. That this model entails an exploitative class structure—whether or not the surplus appropriators were once workers themselves or are elected by the workers—is invisible theoretically and practically. That this radical socialist plan suggests a replay of 1917 follows from the absence of class theory, the prevalence of class-blind, efficiency-focused theories of the organization of production, and the 1990s imperative to revive and expand output.

A radical socialist policy of promoting *arenda* enterprises would likely enhance capitalist, not communist, class structures (albeit perhaps more humane capitalist structures than their western private capitalist counterparts). State capitalist enterprises would be transformed, via leasing, into more or less private capitalist enterprises. Collective farms would likely evolve even more rapidly from communist to private capitalist enterprises. Private ancient enterprises would decrease, if such private capitalist enterprises absorbed them, or else increase to the extent that they offered more attractive situations. The diminished prestige, power, and revenues of the state that would likely follow from establishing *arenda* would probably promote market rather than planning mechanisms of resource and product distribution. No particular change in the inherited ancient and feudal household class structures would seem likely.

As these lines are written, the westernizers (advocating privatization and marketization) prevail in the Putin regime but also confront many obstacles. State capitalist industrial enterprises and communist collective farms remain and struggle to survive. A powerful nationalist, conservative movement wins millions of supporters. Advocates of *arenda* and *arenda*-type social reorganizations take advantage of the injustices and costs of westernizing to agitate for their preferred alternative. What remains invisible to all participants in these profound historical struggles is the contradictory coexistence of structures of surplus labor performance, appropriation, and distribution and the social consequences of these class structures.

The class blindness of Soviet culture in general and of economic theories in particular meant that the basic class composition of Soviet society could not be seen or explicitly criticized in cultural forms. Again, the parallel with class blindness in the United States is remarkable. Industry remained state capitalist up to 1990 in part because Soviet culture could not challenge that class structure per se. Likewise, Soviet culture supported an agriculture becoming ever more state and private capitalist and private ancient at the expense of a shrinking private communist sector. Soviet households remained feudal and ancient partly because Soviet culture could not integrate a household class critique into its agonized depictions and dissections of deeply distressed family life.

One of the greater ironies of the twentieth century was a society that endlessly proclaimed and celebrated its communist revolutionary origins and commitments while being anything but communist revolutionary in its own class structures. The blindness of supporters and critics alike to Marxian surplus-labor concepts of class precluded their revealing and debating the USSR's fundamentally conservative stance toward class. Partly because it could not recognize the contradiction between revolutionary rhetoric and goals and the underlying conservatism of its class structures, Soviet postwar culture sank into a kind of resignation in relation to politics and economics. Progress toward communism became ever more elusive, distant, and vague. Mass mobilizations and campaigns struck ever more Soviet leaders and citizens as unnecessary or irrelevant. Actual or proposed mass mobilizations became instead objects of ridicule or jokes or else were viewed as cruel hoaxes attributed to distrusted leaders pursuing ulterior motives. The distrust further deepened a profound conservatism that many observers have noted and studied (Cohen 1985, 145–157). It also contributed to a disengagement from the entire ideological context of official Marxism-Leninism that had been so pronounced a feature of prewar thought, speech, and public action. The post-Khrushchev era, 1964 on, was widely experienced as "an ideological vacuum in the Soviet Union" (Leonhard 1984, 56).

After World War Two, much Soviet culture turned inward to private concerns and away from the storms of public (collective) life. The hope was that the storms would become fewer and shorter. Resignation to the apparent impossibility of real change settled deeply into the national psyche. At the same time, those poets, novelists, journalists, filmmakers, painters, and others who did not resign themselves and did dare social criticism lacked concepts of the class organization of surplus labor to integrate into their work. Thus they vented their critical genius only on nonclass aspects of Soviet society—the arrogance of state power, bureaucracy, economic inefficiencies, corruption, alienated intimacy, and so on. They could not link those to any imagining of a revolutionary project aimed at a communist class alternative to the present Soviet society.

Those aspects of postwar Soviet culture that we have discussed illustrate certain of its contradictions: how it partly contributed to a maintenance of the state capitalist Soviet status quo while it also reinforced or encouraged private capitalist, ancient, and feudal class structures in small enterprises and households respectively. The celebration of private life and the general conservative aversion to any more campaigns for social transformation displayed similarly contradictory class effects. In addition, the class-blind theoretical climate in which the *only* conceivable alternative economic arrangements were either state property with planning or private property with markets was pregnant with yet another eventual class effect. If and when Soviet state capitalism lost the confidence of the Soviet people, the only conceivable resolution would be more or less transition to the only conceivable alternative: the kinds of private capitalism associated with European social democracies and the United States.

## Postwar Politics

In their impacts on class structures, postwar Soviet political conditions display many parallels with its cultural conditions (with which they were closely intertwined). Political developments combined, on balance, to strengthen state capitalism to the 1970s and thereafter to undermine it in favor of private capitalism. Likewise, politics contributed—albeit not without contradictory effects—to the growth of private ancient class structures and the sustenance of the inherited feudal and ancient class structures of Soviet households.

We first consider external political conditions impinging upon the USSR in the first decade after 1945. The combination of Cold War encirclement, nuclear confrontation, and the defeat or decline of communist parties and movements in many Western countries created a new form of the siege mentality that had inspired previous surges of Soviet economic growth. Social mobilization to recover from the world war's devastation could still win popular support when combined with the simultaneous march toward the superpower status needed for defense. Maintaining the strong central state apparatus to manage all this seemed a self-evident social need. Wage increases could again be deferred while labor productivity was raised. Many argued that the third world would become the postwar scene of socialism's and communism's advances until, in partnership with the USSR, the private advanced capitalist world would become encircled and somehow eventually overwhelmed. Mao's revolution in China seemed, at least until 1960 in Soviet eyes, to prefigure this scenario. Developments as different as postwar Western rearmament and the Hungarian uprising in 1956 seemed to underscore the importance of renewed Soviet concentration on industrial growth (especially in industries linked to the military).

Such an international political climate supported the impressive, albeit uneven, growth of state capitalist industry in the USSR during the three decades after the war. The state gave first priority to that growth; technical advances in military production were sometimes diffused to enhance nonmilitary industrial expansion; and Cold War alliances sometimes provided important industrial inputs under more advantageous terms than would otherwise have been possible. On the other hand, that same international climate also posed major new problems for Soviet state capitalism. The Cold War arms race with the United States required the Soviet state to distribute to the military and to industries producing military products growing portions of the revenues gathered in its coffers (the surpluses appropriated in state capitalist enterprises, those collected by the state from other surplus appropriators, and nonsurplus sources of state revenue). This left less of the state's revenues to distribute to nonmilitary industrial expansion, agricultural growth, social infrastructure (collective consumption), and so on.

While the Cold War climate perhaps stimulated Soviet workers to labor more intensely and productively and promoted technical change, thereby yielding the state some more surpluses from its state capitalist industries, that climate simultaneously absorbed more of those surpluses into the costly production of rapidly obsolescent weapons systems (Gaddy 1996, 9–46).[25] If future developments slowed the growth of surpluses produced in state capitalist industries or the growth of state revenues from other sources while political considerations increased state expenditures on the military, a crisis of insufficient state revenues might quickly mature, unless, of course, the state could sufficiently reduce nonmilitary expenditures. However, reducing the latter undermined the survival of state capitalism's class structures as well as the private communist, capitalist, ancient, and feudal class structures outside the state (see appendix A to this chapter).

The international political climate also confronted the USSR with a single hegemonic superpower, the United States. Not only U.S. foreign policies but also its internal laws, political practices, and prevalent political theories came to define the challenging "other" against which the USSR measured as well as articulated much of its own political life. The remarkable economic prosperity of the United States after 1945, its military buildup, hegemony over its allies, and the relative ease with which all of these survived its few political reverses (especially China in 1949, Cuba in 1959, and Vietnam in 1970) steadily reinforced this situation. In the West, official pronouncements, mass media, and countless academic formulations explained these U.S. successes as consequences of private property, markets, and the political freedoms of voting, nonstate mass media, and civil liberties. The whole was summarized most often in a morally inflected celebration of "decentralized democracy" as against "totalitarianism."[26] Because of global bipolarity, U.S. political conditions and U.S. explanations of their effects wielded great power in the USSR as well. As one recent study has found,

> we need to rethink the ways in which socialist societies were shaped by the capitalist West during periods in which they seemed internally stable.... [T]he official ideology of the Cold War should not prevent us from exploring the penetration of socialist societies by local "translations" of Western-capitalist military, economic, cultural and political institutions. (Steinmetz 1997, 348)

Thus, for example, when postwar Soviet economic growth showed signs of decline, the debate over the appropriate policy responses hinged repeatedly on the relative merits of decentralized (sometimes referred to as "democratized") versus centralized management and control of industrial production sites.[27] Khrushchev's reforms in the late 1950s, Lieberman's a few years later, and then the technical proposals of Kantorovich, Nemchinov, and Novozhilov all turned on how much and what kind of decentralization would best serve Soviet economic growth (Sutela 1991, 49–73). Decentralization proposals were central to policy debates both before and after the demise of the USSR. Little was new here: from war communism and its imposed centralization to the decentralization carried through under the NEP reforms to the once-more centralized strategies under Stalinism, the state oscillated between which of the two forms of management would best enhance industrialization. The class structures of Soviet production sites did not arise in these debates, whether before or after World War Two. Reformers and their opponents both presumed that workers would produce surpluses in enterprises (increasingly referred to as "profits") and that these surpluses would be appropriated by a different group of persons. Debate centered only on whether the appropriators would be better localized or centralized, organized by industry or by geography, state appointed or otherwise selected/elected, and so on.

On one side, the more "conservative" defined the USSR over against the United States and so demanded centralized appropriation of industrial (and at least part of agricultural) surpluses in state enterprises and the distribution of resources and products by central state planning. This they identified with the socialist commitment and uniqueness of the USSR. On the other side, the "reformers" or "radicals" insisted that only decentralization to local regional or local industrial or even enterprise levels of authority offered a way forward to economic growth as central to the socialist project. Almost everyone on both sides presumed without question that industries and an increasing portion of farms would remain state capitalist enterprises. In effect, the debate turned only on how to organize the appropriation of state capitalist surpluses: should the appropriators be a Council of Ministers in Moscow or local officials at the enterprise level or other officials located at some intermediate position.

The most radical position in the debates favored the most decentralization, often described, as noted above, in terms of worker self-management. They equated this with democratization in the context of arguing that the only genuine socialism was a democratic socialism. Local enterprise managers would be state officials but also directly accountable to—and preferably elected by—enterprise workers.[28] Democratization (decentralization) would get the best results in terms of workers' productivity. Granting that such accountability might pressure local managers to devote some surpluses to supplement their workers' wages, radicals argued that that would still leave larger surpluses available to the state for industrial growth and its other priorities.

The logic of what was called "economic" reform in the USSR as elsewhere in the socialist countries was thus overwhelmingly conceived and debated in political terms. The issue was who would exercise effective power over means of production (central state officials or local state officials or possibly even some local persons with no state positions) and, likewise, who would wield power over the distribution of resources and products (property owners acting in markets or local officials or state central planners).[29] In his elaborated discussion of economic reform of the type that evolved in the postwar USSR, Janos Kornai (1992) argues that such reform amounted to political changes making Soviet-type economies more like Western and especially U.S. private capitalism. Since, for him, "Socialism differs first and foremost from capitalism in having replaced private ownership with public ownership" (1992, 87), it follows that reform amounts quite simply to the reverse movement.[30] He describes this as movement toward private property coordinated through market exchange in the context of a dominant ideology that minimizes the state's interference with private property and markets.

International politics made the United States a major touchstone for Soviet thinking about their own society. The model of the U.S. economy that systematically attributed economic and military success to its political institutions (especially laws securing private property and limiting state activity) proved subtly persuasive to supporters as well as critics of postwar Soviet society. The latter saw in Soviet economic and social problems the effects of this or that quality of U.S. society that was regrettably absent from the USSR. The former saw in the United States the great threat—militarily, politically, and economically. They aimed to learn from (and eventually outperform) the United States technically, to mobilize the world's workers so as to outmaneuver the United States politically, and to stalemate it militarily.

The political impact of the United States upon the USSR worked profoundly and on many levels. The image of the United States—as a society in which the state apparatus was far less centralized and much less socially intrusive than in the USSR—supported those inside the USSR who connected U.S. successes and Soviet failures to just that difference. Soviet citizens with all sorts of grievances against the state could and did take comfort from the United States as a model of where, more or less, to direct the political transformation of Soviet society. A general reinforcement of antistate attitudes and social theories inside the USSR flowed from the U.S.-USSR global confrontation. This happened alongside and in contradiction to the strengthening of the state required and justified as necessary to mobilize the Soviet people to defend against "U.S. imperialism" in all its manifestations. People influenced more by the antistatism than the defensism inculcated after the war might, therefore, have looked less favorably on state capitalist enterprises than on private capitalist and ancient enterprises. As we noted earlier, such shifts in attitude could have negative effects on the labor intensities and productivities of labor in state capitalist enterprises and hence on their profitability. This would further problematize the surpluses available to Soviet state planners just as increasing demands were placed upon such surpluses. In addition, growing antistatist attitudes prompted Soviet workers to devote more labor and hope to existing and prospective private capitalist and ancient enterprises.

The great U.S.-USSR detente declared by Nixon and Brezhnev in the early 1970s shifted the balance of antistate and defensist attitudes and hence their contradictory effects on surplus available to the Soviet state. On the one hand, detente, viewed as the achievement of Soviet military might, legitimated the mobilizations and sacrifices it had required. On the other hand, detente itself worked against any further mobilizations and sacrifices, legitimated the cultural turning inward toward more private concerns discussed above, and enabled more questioning of and opposition to the power of the Soviet state. The political process of detente, by reinforcing antistatist tendencies already developing inside the USSR, also further weakened the capacity of the Soviet state to appropriate surplus within its state capitalist enterprises.

Detente also accelerated the post-Stalin relaxation of political obstacles to the flows of tourism, professional and mass media exchange programs, and so on between the USSR and other countries including the United States. The consequences of this relaxation went beyond greater Soviet awareness and appreciation of the United States as a less statist society. As Soviet citizens grasped the difference between Soviet levels of individual consumption and those in the wealthy Western countries, many reacted by questioning the legitimacy of Soviet political institutions. Such questioning flowed in part from Soviet leaders' earlier statements about the virtues of those institutions. When Soviet consumption standards had seemed to be catching up with Western standards, Khrushchev had not only promised Soviet workers standards of living that would soon surpass those in the United States. He had taken the further and remarkable step of making that promise the measure of the comparative worth and success of the Soviet system vis-à-vis the West. When, soon thereafter, detente revealed that Khrushchev's promise was not materializing, the society's own measure of its comparative worth operated to deepen Soviet workers' political disaffection and further problematize their contributions to state capitalist surplus production.

It was not only a matter of comparing U.S. and Soviet consumption quantitatively but also qualitatively. Detente revealed above all the much higher levels of private or individual consumption of U.S. workers, especially their private consumption of housing, clothing, automobiles, meat, and appliances.[31] Supporters of the USSR responded by stressing the collective consumption provided by the state to Soviet workers, especially subsidized medical care, education, transport, childcare, and so on. A contestation emerged over the relative merits of private/individual versus state/collective kinds of consumption. However, such a contestation worked against the USSR, precisely because it coincided historically with the turning inward, private focus, and antistatism that were increasingly pervasive across Soviet culture. It was private consumables which just then seemed the most important. Detente allowed the United States to represent itself as the realization of a level of private consumption that Soviet citizens could only yearn for.

Moreover, in the USSR private consumption seemed closely linked to private ancient class structures. The goods most prized for private consumption (goods beyond the basics) emerged from them. In private ancient class structures the connection between personal labor effort and rewards in the form of heightened personal consumption seemed most direct. If work in and for state capitalist enterprises and private capitalist and communist collective farms could not generate the promised levels of private, individual consumption, then that work was not worthwhile. Workers would be somehow justified in either shirking labor in those enterprises and farms or else shifting their enthusiasm to private, ancient class structural production sites, or both.

Alongside the effects of international politics and especially the interactions with the United States, political changes inside the USSR also participated in the overdetermination of its class structures. Most of the "economic" reforms after Stalin were in fact political: they shifted the power to make managerial decisions to relatively more decentralized levels of the state apparatus. For the reasons discussed earlier in this chapter, postwar Soviet thinking increasingly linked decentralization of managerial power to greater economic growth and development. The reform shift culminated in the Law on State Enterprises passed in 1987. It mandated that managers and directors would be elected by workers' collectives (although they would not be workers themselves and would still be controlled by state officials). In the years leading up to passage of this law, the celebratory climate of decentralization expanded the informal, "out of plan" contacts, exchanges, and mutual assistance among local enterprise managers and directors (Ellman and Kontorovich 1998, 145–146). As a result of these political changes in the social location of effective managerial power, the central plan became less important relative to the ad hoc arrangements of local enterprise managers in shaping the Soviet economy and the broader society.[32]

In this way a step was taken that could, under certain conditions, function as an intermediate stage in moving from state to private capitalism. Some insiders in the upper reaches of the Soviet political apparatus understood the political decentralization in approximately such terms (Ellman and Kontorovich 1998, 16). The increasing managerial powers of local state officials in charge of individual enterprises or groups of enterprises brought them nearer to possibly also functioning as appropriators and distributors of the surpluses generated in those enterprises. Indeed, Soviet industrial development did evolve before 1990 from (1) centralized state capitalist appropriation of surplus and centralized management to (2) centralized state capitalist appropriation and decentralized management to (3) decentralized state capitalist appropriation and decentralized management. In the dramatically altered political landscape after 1990, the next evolutionary step, achieved with remarkably little social upheaval, entailed decentralized private capitalist appropriation with decentralized management. In the specific political conjuncture of the postwar USSR, the decentralization of managerial power did contribute to a class transition from state to private capitalism.[33]

The cultural and political changes we have discussed—associated with decentralization, de-Stalinization, and detente—were hesitantly accommodated or actively pursued by successive postwar Soviet regimes. However, these changes also appeared dangerous and threatening to many. As was endlessly reiterated by the opponents of these changes, they risked stopping Soviet progress, weakening socialism (equated with the central state guidance of social development), or even aborting the centralized march through socialism to communism that the 1917 revolution had initiated. There was thus a contradiction between the need to make these changes and the need to preserve the revolutionary heritage of Soviet society. The latter was usually depicted as state ownership and control of the economy's "commanding heights," the Communist Party's political monopoly, and the state-party hegemony over most other social institutions (such as schools, mass media, the arts, and so on). How Soviet leaderships managed this contradiction entailed further changes in political conditions that also had significant class consequences.

To manage this contradiction successive regimes combined decentralization and centralization in a particular way. On the one hand, centralized state controls over culture, politics, and economics diminished. On the other, membership and centralized social controls exercised by the Communist Party expanded, especially within the workplace.[34] In simplest terms, the Party's assignment especially during and after the 1970s was more closely than before to monitor, supervise, and manage. One goal was to offset the relaxation of centralized *state* controls over the economy, politics, and culture. The Party thereby sought to preserve the integrity, growth, and basic directions of the USSR (as well as its own position), while the Soviet state accommodated the social pressure for decentralization and the revaluation of private life.[35] As Brezhnev told the seventeenth Komsomol congress in 1974:

> If we are to single out the main thing in the Party's economic policy at the present stage of our development, then it is the sharp turn towards raising the effectiveness of the country's economy, ... improv[ing] the quality of work done ... at each place of work. The quality of work ... is composed of many production-economic factors and at the same time it embraces a broad range of moral problems. (Brezhnev 1974, 3)

Soviet development thus became dependent in part on this reconfiguration of the relationship between party politics and society. Would the contradictions of Soviet society be managed by coupling state decentralization with the Communist Party's enhanced size, power, and reach? Or instead would Soviet contradictions deepen and transform the Party, thereby undermining its ability to manage those contradictions? While the USSR's "official" base-superstructure Marxism presumed that economics always determines politics, the Communist Party's goals and activities rather presumed the reverse.

The results of the decentralization reforms of the Soviet economy undertaken periodically after Stalin's death have been summarized by Janos Kornai.[36] He believes that the "coherence" of the "classical system of socialist economy" was destroyed by the reforms (1992, 377–379). They worsened the "irrationalities" of the Soviet planning system as ministries, regions, industries, and enterprises increasingly secured their own situations by circumventing central plans. Decentralized economic planning introduced greater uncertainties (than had centralized planning) into the flows of material and financial inputs needed by enterprises to fulfill their plan targets. At the same time, decentralization further enabled enterprises—singly or in various groupings—to evade the targets or else to achieve them by hoarding inputs and/or reaching separate, "private" exchange agreements with one another outside of the central plan. As the well-being of these enterprises and enterprise groupings came increasingly to depend upon such circumventing of central plans, the effectiveness of the plans declined. For Kornai, the economic "inefficiencies" he believed to flow from one essential source—decentralized state planning—warranted only one conceivably "rational" response, namely further decentralization to an economy that was chiefly "free market coordinated."[37]

We need to add that decentralization of management need not necessarily undermine (centralized or decentralized) state capitalist appropriation of surplus labor. When confronted with the inefficiencies of centralized state planning in the 1930s, local managers had taken on a variety of schemes—outside of the central plans—to acquire needed but often delayed or never delivered promised resources, including food for workers at the local enterprise level. Such an unintended decentralization of management helped to secure Stalinism's centralized surplus appropriation of surplus labor. However, in the different context of the years after Stalin's death and very much unlike the social environment of the 1930s, such enterprising efforts of managers—whether unintended or intended under the reforms—likely undermined first centralized and then decentralized state capitalist appropriation. The difference was in the attitudes of managers who, like many others in the USSR, increasingly saw themselves coping with economic disorganization flowing from reforms, struggling to secure their own positions, and less caught up in a larger social movement or campaign.

Officially, the Party believed that its expanded social role would function as the antidote for the economic problems associated with the decentralization reforms. But that did not happen. Instead, party leaders and many members were increasingly integrated into the routines for circumventing the economic plans. Enterprises determined to operate outside of central plans had to secure the Party's approval or at least its disinterest. The party did not rise to this economic challenge. Instead, local, regional, and industrial managers (themselves often party members) persuaded party officials to condone the necessity of their semi- and illegal maneuvers in the new, reformed economic circumstances.[38] Where and when that proved difficult, the extraordinary (and "off-the-books") gains from working around economic plans enabled financial inducements (bribes) to supervising party authorities. Management "corruption" in coping with the problems of reformed economic planning spread to corruption of the Party itself. The decentralizing economy had transformed the Party more than the Party had been able to control it.[39]

Political "corruption" of the Party—in the sense of a growing, systemic dereliction of its economic control duties—evolved into the individual corruption that drew increasing popular anger and derision. Economic bureaucrats and party officers and members formed interlocking directorates that often went beyond maneuvering around central economic plans to secure privileges that elevated their individual standards of living and power positions ever further above those of average Soviet workers (Keep 1995, 212–216).[40] Their alienation from the general population thus deepened, as did popular resentment of the controls exercised by a privileged Communist Party in the name of Soviet society as a whole.

For the mass of Soviet citizens, this system provided certain benefits, notwithstanding how distasteful it became especially in the 1970s and 1980s. War seemed ever less a threat to Soviet society—a victory widely attributed, at least in part, to the state's diplomacy. Levels of mass consumption, collective and private, grew, albeit at declining rates. Cultural freedoms and the space for private, individual life expanded. And perhaps most important, a kind of entitlement to obtain and keep one's job settled in as a virtually absolute political commitment of the state and Communist Party to Soviet workers.[41] Hence the famous workers' joke aimed squarely at the post-1975 enterprise-Party directorate: "They pretend to pay us properly, and we pretend to work properly." Better than most treatises, this joke summarized many of the economic, cultural, and political dilemmas into which the postwar USSR had descended.

The growth and corruption of the Party had contradictory class consequences. On the one hand, its presence and control functions within nearly all enterprises and labor unions likely raised the intensity and productivity of labor. In this way, party activities expanded the surplus and thereby the state's revenue. However, as noted above (party facilitation of out-of-plan arrangements, corruption, etc.), its activities also likely undermined labor productivity (and hence surplus production in individual enterprises), siphoning appropriated surpluses to non-plan distributions or personal use, or both. Another contradictory effect was the Party's own costs of operation that were covered by state expenditures. A rapidly expanding Communist Party absorbed more of the state's revenues. That left less revenue for the state's other priority objectives: industrial growth, military preparedness, provision of public services for mass, collective consumption, and so on.

To maintain or, better still, to increase the surpluses that the state could appropriate in its capitalist enterprises, party policy also often aimed to justify restraints on productive workers' wages there. Party pressure worked likewise to limit the portions of state capitalist surpluses (subsumed class payments) that were spent on the unproductive laborers (the wages and budgets of clerks, managers, and so on) in those enterprises. At the same time, the unofficial activities of the Party enriched their leaders and many of their activists. Popular opinion increasingly defined them as an unjustifiably privileged group, whose intrusions into social life were then all the more unwelcome. Resisting or avoiding hard work became, in part, a form of protest against the Party's policies and pressures. This situation also fostered shifts of workers' productive efforts from state enterprises toward private ancient class structures where the Party intruded much less. Productive laborers in state capitalist enterprises worked less intensely, broke more tools, and produced low-quality outputs and/or ever fewer outputs per hour. This happened partly to vent dissatisfaction with party policies or personnel and partly because workers were tired, having spent increasing time and energy elsewhere on private plots and second-economy undertakings.

Widespread distaste for the Party combined with envy at its privileges (especially after detente revealed western standards of individual consumption) to reinforce, if not promote, apparently large and rising levels of pilfering especially in the

1980s (Shlapentokh 1989, 214–216). In class terms, if outputs were pilfered, they represented a portion of the surplus produced by productive workers but diverted from surplus appropriators (in state capitalist industries or in private capitalist and communist collective farms). If means of production were pilfered, they represented corresponding declines in labor productivity: a day's labor yielded less output and thus less surplus than would have been the case without such pilfering. Pilfering supplemented the perpetrators' incomes and so perhaps eased the tensions and contradictions of the ancient and feudal class structures of Soviet households. However, the pilfering directly and indirectly reduced the quantities of surplus appropriated in and by the USSR's state capitalist, private capitalist, and private communist enterprises.

It is impossible to quantify the enlarged Communist Party's net effects on surplus production and appropriation in the USSR during the 1970s and 1980s. However, the broad literature suggests to us that the unintended negative results outweighed—perhaps by a wide margin—the intended positive goals. To the extent that Soviet leaders had hoped to manage the postwar reform movement (decentralization of state planning and power, and reduced social intrusion by the state) by enlarging the centralized Communist Party's social role, that plan failed. The Party's evolution in the circumstances proved wholly inadequate to the task. The vast turning inward to private and individual and away from state and social concerns that characterized Soviet postwar culture came to include a turning away in resentment and anger from the Party as well as from the state. Central to this development was a growing gap between the surpluses produced and available to the state and the state expenditures necessary to sustain the multiple demands of the USSR's postwar global position.

The de facto political guarantee of nearly absolute job security helped this highly contradictory and potentially unstable social situation to survive for as long as it did. However, that guarantee also contributed to further class structural difficulties, to the class transitions underway then, and to the eventual crisis situation at the end of the 1980s. Job security in state capitalist enterprises had two problematic effects. On the one hand, automation (replacing workers with machines) was often blocked or slowed. New labor-saving technologies, if and when adopted, were often added to existing technologies rather than substituted for them. Whatever the practical difficulties planning staffs had (in finding or generating new technologies, establishing and financing facilities to retrain and relocate workers, installing new techniques, and so on), the political untouchability of job security added significantly to those difficulties. Thus, the surplus-producing capacity of Soviet productive workers grew more slowly than the state's needs for surplus.

At the same time, the number of unproductive workers (clerks, secretaries, managers, and so on) grew in the USSR, and they too enjoyed the political guarantee of job security. In Marxian class terms, the costs of their wages and their means of performing unproductive tasks represented a growing demand on the surplus produced by the productive workers. Inside state capitalist enterprises, for example, unproductive workers' job security blocked or slowed their replacement by machines (e.g., office computerization). Had state capitalist enterprises been able to economize on the portion of their surpluses paid out for unproductive work, that would have left more surplus for the state to try to tap. In this way, too, the state was thwarted in seeking to enhance the revenues it needed to finance its expenditures.

Another historical irony emerges from comparing this Soviet dilemma with the different way in which private capitalist enterprises solved parallel problems in the West at the same time (after the mid-1970s). Intensified global competition among the three blocs of private capitalism (the United States, Western Europe, and Japan) had introduced costly new demands on their surpluses. These included especially rising sales costs (especially advertising), managerial expenses, and research and development outlays to both cheapen production costs and invent new commodities from whose production surpluses could be appropriated. Private capitalists had either to appropriate more surplus from their productive workers or reduce other surplus outlays (or both) to find the resources to meet these new demands on their surpluses. The solution found more or less everywhere in the private capitalist economies was an attack on the state aimed to reduce the portion of capitalist surpluses that had to be paid out as taxes and as costly accommodations to state regulations.

Thatcher in the United Kingdom, Reagan and Bush in the United States, and later the more social democratic regimes elsewhere commenced their politics of assault against the welfare state as grossly inefficient, excessively expensive and regulatory, corrupt, and generally the major obstacle to economic and social progress (Fraad, Resnick, and Wolff 1994, 88-111). In effect, by cutting state social and regulatory programs and state employment of the unproductive laborers who staffed them, taxes on private corporations' surpluses could and did fall. At the same time, as state employment absorbed relatively fewer unproductive workers, competition among them for the remaining private sector (including the surplus-producing) jobs lowered private wages there. In Marxian terms, as workers came to accept lowered wages as a new norm, the value of their labor power fell. Since the productive workers labored at least as long and as productively as before, the difference between the value of their labor power and the value added by their labor—the surplus value appropriated by private western capitalists—rose steadily.

The strategy of state reduction thus increased private capitalist surpluses just as it lowered the portion of them that had to be paid in taxes to the state. The privatization of formerly government-provided services also offered the private capitalist sector new commodities to be produced with the now cheaper workers yielding increased surpluses on which fewer taxes had to be paid. Private capitalism "solved" its problems of financing new demands on its surpluses by appropriating more surplus from their workers and distributing less of it to the state.

In direct contrast, the state capitalism of the USSR, which also confronted new demands on its surpluses, found no equally effective solution. In Soviet conditions, productive workers became less, not more, productive of surplus value. As U.S. private capitalists achieved markedly higher rates of exploitation, Soviet state capitalism's rate of exploitation fell further behind. As private capitalism in the United States economized on unproductive laborers, Soviet state capitalism moved in the opposite direction. These divergent patterns reflected the typical longer-run cycles that similarly afflict both state and private capitalisms (as many economists have noted).[42] The cycles made their uneven appearances in the 1980s and 1990s: downturn in the USSR in the 1980s and in Japan after 1990, upturn in the United States especially in the 1990s, and a very mixed set of cyclical patterns in Western Europe.

The 1990s displayed the consequences of the diverging conditions of U.S. private capitalism and Soviet state capitalism in the 1970s and 1980s. The United States entered upon an unprecedented peacetime explosion of private corporate surplus appropriation (reflected in its stock market boom) that encouraged (and financed) a euphoric global celebration of the neoliberal "perfection" of private property and markets. The Soviet state could neither appropriate enough surplus in state capitalist enterprises nor siphon enough surplus away from other class structures nor find other revenues sufficient to secure its own survival even to the end of the 1980s. It was increasingly unable simultaneously to finance industrial expansion, military preparedness, global superpower status, and a rising standard of living for its masses. A population increasingly able and determined to compare the Soviet state's troubles with Western private capitalism's economic boom and political and cultural openness became ever more disaffected as citizens and unproductive as workers. The state and the Party collapsed.

Soviet history starkly exemplifies a global pattern of the twentieth century. The century's first half displays tendencies of transition from private to state capitalisms. The second half moves in the reverse direction. The specific problems of the private capitalisms inherited from the nineteenth century included their growing difficulties in appropriating enough surplus to secure their nonclass conditions of existence. These problems eventuated in crises that were resolved by solutions that ranged from state-regulated to state-managed to state-owned-and-operated capitalisms. The rightist versions in Nazi Germany, fascist Italy, and imperial Japan focused on military aggression. On the left, the post-1917 USSR was the longest sustained and most globally influential of these statist solutions. In the reverse movements provoked by the 1970s crises of state-regulated, state-managed and state-run capitalisms, the solutions entailed returns to various forms of more private capitalism. The post-Soviet return to private capitalism has been the starkest example.

## Postwar Economy

Beyond the many economic conditions unavoidably included in the above discussion of culture and politics, a few others deserve brief mention here. Trade relations with foreign countries changed after 1945 (Gregory and Stuart 1998, 177–194). Imports of machinery and foodstuffs rose reflecting the enhanced priority of industrial growth and the difficulties of feeding Soviet workers from the produce of Soviet agriculture. The USSR partly paid for those imports with the revenues from its major new export industry: fuels and energy (from 9.6 percent of Soviet exports in 1955 to 52.1 percent in 1982). At the same time, Soviet trade with capitalist countries rose relative to its trade with other socialist countries until they became roughly equal. Finally, the USSR depended increasingly on foreign debt to finance this trade across these years. Gross Soviet debt rose from $12.5 billion in 1975 to $47.8 billion in 1989. While there was little direct investment by foreign enterprises inside the USSR, the USSR did obtain bank loans.

On the one hand, both the trade and the borrowing supported Soviet state capitalism. Imported machinery especially facilitated technical innovation in industry and thereby surplus value accruing to the state capitalists.[43] By supplementing their own appropriated surpluses indirectly through foreign bank borrowing, state capitalist enterprises had more to distribute to secure their conditions of existence and growth. Imported grain also reduced the need for state expenditures to expand agricultural production inside the USSR; this left more for the state to use for other purposes. Lastly, grain imports also made possible an increase in the surpluses state capitalists could appropriate from their workers.[44]

On the other hand—and unavoidably—the need to repay debt and to cover the interest costs of the rapidly rising debt represented new, additional demands on surpluses. Against the gains from borrowing, the Soviet state had to weigh the costs of surpluses paid as interest to foreign lenders—surpluses that were therefore unavailable to use for capital accumulation, for the arms race, for the growing party apparatus, for meeting popular economic demands, and so on. To the extent that the costs outran the gains from borrowing, the dangerous spiral familiar among many Third World debtors surfaced for the USSR as well: increased borrowing undertaken to pay interest costs leading to ever higher interest costs. Having become increasingly dependent on borrowing, the risk that delay or nonpayment of interest might cut off future loans made this new demand on Soviet surpluses undeniable. The worsening post-1975 productivity problems of Soviet state capitalist enterprises—the chief borrowers—suggest that the balance shifted against the USSR: the gains from borrowing fell behind the costs and so constituted yet another net drain on Soviet surpluses and hence the state's ability to secure its conditions of existence.

To the net drain on surplus eventually characterizing its foreign borrowing was added the cost of the state's dependence on state capitalist enterprises' oil exports (the most rapidly rising and largest of all Soviet export commodities). When oil prices rose above their values in terms of Soviet production conditions, the difference represented a kind of windfall gain. In Marxian value terms, this favorable unequal exchange represented an additional nonclass revenue inflow to the state available for its expenditures. When world oil prices fell below their values, it meant that Soviet state capitalists producing oil could not realize a portion of the surplus values in that oil.[45] Such a reduced state capitalist surplus value reverberated through the system in negative ways. The reduction pinched state revenues generally and raised special problems for the state in securing sufficient foreign currencies to pay for imports and service its foreign debt.

From the earliest days of the USSR, a recurring debate pitted the proponents of foreign trade against its detractors over the issue of whether the gains from trade outweighed the costly risks and uncertainties of dependence upon it. In Marxian theoretical terms (different from the actual terms of debate), this amounted to weighing the value-enhancing versus the value-depleting effects of trade (see appendix B to this chapter). Some overdeterminants of the balance between positive and negative effects of international trade lay beyond Soviet control (in the political acts of foreign states and the market strategies of private foreign merchants and industrial enterprises). Other overdeterminants lay in the use that the Soviet state made of the benefits available from trade. These overdeterminants depended on the overall health and productivity of the Soviet economy. When that deteriorated during and after the 1970s, for the many reasons discussed above, the ability to gain from trade deteriorated as well, thereby raising anew the specter of a trade dependence that could become debilitating. The same logic applied to foreign borrowing.

Lastly, anecdotal evidence suggests that the postwar opening to trade had yet another effect on Soviet class structures. That trade brought scarce foreign consumer goods into the USSR, sometimes illegally. Transporting, copying, and trading in such goods enhanced the second economy. More individuals could derive more income from participation in that economy. Since, as noted earlier, the second economy displayed a likely ancient class structure, trade's stimulus thereby added its influence to the expansion of that structure.

The absolute levels of real wages and other sorts of family income comprise another economic condition that shaped Soviet class structures. Kerblay estimated the average mid-1970s monthly income per family in the USSR (combining both monetary income and a valuation of "indirect benefits") at 342 rubles (1983, 219). Given Roy Medvedev's (1975, 268) estimate at about the same time that a Soviet family of four needed 300–400 rubles per month "to sustain life," Kerblay concluded that "a great many families . . . must supplement their resources by means of produce from their family plot or by a second job." Especially if such a second job were located in the "second economy," there was a high probability that participation in ancient class processes would be involved. Since Soviet women earned, on average, significantly less in wages than men (roughly 70 percent according to Gregory and Stuart 1998, 152), their interest and participation in ancient class structures of private plot farming and/or the second economy was likely also enhanced. Thus, for example, considerable evidence suggests that prostitution had become an increasingly important source of extra income for some Russian women in the 1970s and 1980s (Kon and Riordan 1993, 71–75).

The postwar history of changing distributions of wages among Soviet citizens also participated in overdetermining class change. Kerblay (1983, 217) shows that from the 1950s through the early 1970s, the prevailing trend was toward equalization among virtually all categories of Soviet workers, including employees on state farms and collective farm workers (the sole exception seems to have been construction workers). Later studies reviewed by Gregory and Stuart confirm Kerblay's conclusions; but they also show a clear shift from declining inequality to the early 1970s, to stable inequality during the 1970s, and to growing inequality across the 1980s (1998, 155–157). If the admittedly difficult estimates of second economy participation were taken into account, as some recent researchers have attempted to do, an even greater increase of inequality among incomes is suggested for the 1980s (Gregory and Stuart 1998, 157). This is consistent with the evidence suggesting that the second economy was far less important an aspect of the Soviet economy before 1975 than after. It also suggests that worsening wage inequality within state capitalist enterprises in the 1980s may well have induced growing numbers of workers there to resort to second jobs in the second economy or even to full-time immersion in it. As argued above, this would likely have reinforced their withdrawal of time, energy, commitment, and loyalty from their state capitalist, private capitalist, and private communist jobs in the "first economy."

An historical comparison reinforces this conclusion. After NEP was introduced in 1921, a sharp increase in income inequality led to much public outcry. The dominant explanation blamed the private merchants and small private ancient and capitalist businesses that the NEP had fostered: the growing inequality derived from forces outside of and antithetical to socialism. We may compare the last few years of post-Soviet economic history. As income inequality again rose sharply and quickly, citizens across the former USSR again reacted with considerable resentment and hostility. The nationalist and communist parties made political gains by attacking Yeltsin and Putin as the causes—as antithetical or "foreign" to either the nationalist or socialist goals that those parties champion.[46]

Considering both historical moments, rising income inequality from 1975 to 1990 lacked any blameworthy "non-" or "anti-" socialist cause comparable to the Nepmen before or to Yeltsin and Putin after. No person or group, situated as somehow external to Soviet socialism, could serve as the target of resentment and anger. Yet, to have explicitly connected income inequality after 1975 to Soviet social development itself would have violated a taboo of the culture, been a personally risky action, and contradicted deeply entrenched modes of thinking. Blocked in these ways from any generally warranted object of blame for the income inequality that agitated many Soviet workers, Soviet citizens vented their resentment instead in private forms. Endless griping, ridicule, alienation, withdrawal, and hostility increasingly characterized individual workers' relations toward one another, their state capitalist employers, and the Party. This reinforced the declines in labor intensity and worker productivity that we have already noted.

The shift toward wage inequality after 1975 thus also worked to undermine the state capitalist class structures.[47] Many Soviet workers transferred their initiative and energy to the noncapitalist class structures of private and often semilegal or illegal enterprises. Nor could the Party's expanded and intrusive controls across the 1970s and 1980s prevent these developments. While state or party controls might have solved similar dilemmas in earlier periods, the changed conditions made them no longer effective. Instead, the "stagnation" associated with Brezhnev had, in Gorbachev's famous report to the twenty-seventh Communist Party congress, "begun to surface in the life of society." Gorbachev's report attributed that stagnation to "the inertia and stiffness of the forms and methods of administration, the decline of dynamism in our work, and an escalation of bureaucracy." He mentioned neither growing wage and income inequality nor their consequences on class structures. For him, they existed neither among the causes nor the effects of stagnation. For us they were both causes and effects, a downward spiraling interaction among and between the USSR's multiple class structures and its distribution of personal income as one of those class structures' economic conditions of existence.

Finally, despite the quite impressive record of industrial growth since at least the early 1930s, workers' private consumption in 1985 still remained far below that achieved in other (private) capitalist countries including even Spain, Portugal, and Turkey (Gregory and Stuart, 1998, 159). On the one hand, the state persisted in its commitment to heavy industry over the production of consumer goods and the associated heavy reliance on the turnover tax to absorb the excess demand for consumer goods. On the other hand, the inefficiencies and poor marketing skills of its underfunded retail organization further aggravated the privations of Soviet consumers. Dissatisfaction and long suppressed resentment turned to disenchantment with socialism and openly expressed anger as workers became aware of the gap between their individual consumption levels and those of workers in other countries. The state capitalist class structure—conceived to be socialist—seemed unable to secure for workers the rising standard of living it had long promised. This failure of socialism to deliver the desired appliances, television sets, and automobiles stood in sharp contrast to the stunning private consumption successes achieved by private capitalist economies with their ubiquitous private markets and property.

The economic problems of postwar Soviet agriculture also influenced its class structure. The steady transformation of collective farms into state capitalist farms coincided with (and may have contributed to) a serious problem of declining productivity. Recent studies argue that the problem was *not* a matter of land or labor productivity, but rather that "output gains were made with input gains" in the sense of grossly wasteful use of produced inputs to farming (Gregory and Stuart 1998, 164–167). If the state industrial enterprises' wasteful hoarding, misuse, and pilfering of produced inputs (partly via plan circumvention) afflicted state farms too, then their diminished growth would likely have damaged agricultural productivity as a whole.

This kind of decline in agricultural productivity influenced the class structures of Soviet society in multiple ways. In Marxian value terms, the decline would raise the value per unit of food production and hence also the value of productive labor power. Absent offsetting factors including a fall in real wages (that is, for example, a fall in the bundle of food items consumed by workers as their normal and customary diet) that would have reduced the surplus value that the state could appropriate in state capitalist industries and farms. If state capitalist farms absorbed industrial products as inputs in wasteful excess, that meant so many fewer industrial products available, say, for industrial capital accumulation. Lastly, the USSR's deepening agricultural production problems also entailed growing foreign grain imports. These required payments that either diverted scarce foreign currency resources or else incurred loans whose interest costs entailed new claims on Soviet surpluses in future years. In such ways, declining overall factor productivity in Soviet agriculture, especially after the early 1970s, undercut the ability of state capitalist class structures to generate and distribute enough surpluses to grow or, later, even to survive.

Party preferences, state policies, and other factors combined to overdetermine three important shifts in postwar Soviet agricultural development. The first two entailed movements (1) from private collective farms to state capitalist farms and (2) from communist to capitalist class structures (designating surplus-appropriating boards of directors, adopting wage systems of remuneration, etc.) within the remaining private collective farms. This double proletarianization of rural, agricultural workers subjected them to those kinds of workplace alienation that we have already analyzed among their urban, industrial counterparts. However, compared to urban, industrial workers, farm laborers could shift their labor time, energy, and hopes much more easily and readily to private family plots.[48] The third shift inside Soviet agriculture was this kind of movement to private plots.

Soviet agriculture thus provided its laborers more fluid options among class structures than industrial workers had. Low productivity state or collective farm work supplied a secure and steady, if low, wage income as a base. In addition, workers there could divert much of their time and energy (and their employers' physical resources in partly legal and partly illegal ways) to work their individual or family plots with high productivity (Kitching 1998). The symbiosis that evolved in the USSR (as in other eastern European socialist states) between the ancient and the nonancient class structures in "collectivized" agriculture helps explain why individualist and profit-maximizing convictions could remain at least as strong as collectivist ideas among rural Soviet people. That symbiosis also helps explain why the movement toward privatization and market capitalism since 1989 has nearly everywhere been much slower in agriculture than in industry (McIntyre 1992; Gregory and Stuart 1998, 426). In sum, Soviet agriculture's evolution during and after the 1970s contributed to the difficulties of state industrial capitalism and replicated those difficulties in state capitalist farms. Yet, in so doing, agricultural changes stimulated workers' interests in private, ancient class structures symbiotically connected to both capitalist and communist private collective farms. The collective farms were thus strengthened, even as they declined relative to state farms in agriculture.

## State, Enterprise, and Household Transitions

From 1945 to the mid-1970s, its nonclass changes affected but did not basically alter the USSR's class structures. In contrast, during the 1970s and 1980s, the interaction of class and nonclass aspects of Soviet life displayed a different dynamic. Cultural, political, and economic changes made it increasingly difficult after the mid-1970s for state capitalist industries and farms to appropriate enough surpluses to (1) secure the absolute social priority of rapid industrial capital accumulation, (2) enable the state to maintain Soviet superpower status and provide growing levels of collective consumption, and (3) fund the considerably enlarged party apparatus and state capitalist bureaucracy—those unproductive workers who policed and managed the mix of class structures in agriculture and industry. Nor could the state obtain adequate revenues from other sources to solve this problem. That is, it could not obtain enough additional value flows from private class structures (via taxes, terms of trade effects, fees, etc.) or income from direct levies on individuals to make up the difference. In class terms, the state confronted a growing difference between these class and nonclass revenues, on the one hand, and the expenditures needed, on the other, to sustain them:

$$SV(C) + SSCP(C+A+F+COM) + NCR < SSCP(C) + X(C+A+F+COM) + Y$$

The inequality signaled the looming crisis for the USSR.

The private capitalist and communist collective farms faced parallel if less severe problems in generating sufficient surpluses to secure their conditions of existence. By contrast, the class structures of private farm plots and the second economy—mostly ancient class structures—were able to generate and distribute surpluses adequate to their health and growth. Neither Brezhnev nor his successors found ways to reverse this pattern of change emerging from the post-1970 dynamic between the USSR's class and nonclass processes.

During the 1980s, this pattern of class problems and changes reacted back on the cultural, political, and economic processes of Soviet society to produce a social crisis. As state capitalist enterprises sought to squeeze more surplus from their workers, the already heightened disaffection of those workers boiled over in a variety of forms (job actions and strikes in addition to the earlier individual acts of resistance). As successive leaderships seemed powerless to reverse economic declines, political disaffection boiled over in demands for long-deferred civil liberties, open resentment of the Party, and demands for an end to its political monopoly. As expectations of and demands for higher levels of consumption rose ever faster than what individual wages and state-provided public services could supply, popular discontent was further aggravated. As private class structures seemed ever more attractive as income sources and work experiences than the preeminent symbols of Soviet society—state capitalist enterprises—both the viability of those enterprises and the legitimacy of those symbols plummeted. Soviet leaders could not solve the now overwhelming problems and the Soviet masses could no longer tolerate the problems or the ineffective leaders. This was the social crisis.

It became clear to some Soviet leaders during the 1980s that the crisis had reached a point requiring much more drastic changes than any hitherto contemplated in Soviet history. Gorbachev recognized this in part and made some drastic changes. Yeltsin made more and, as this is being written, Putin continues on that path. Soviet leaders unwilling to do likewise lost power. In rapid succession, the USSR abolished itself as a political entity, radically reduced its military aspirations, programs, and apparatus, deprived the Party of its political monopoly, and established a more Western-style parliamentarism. More slowly yet steadily property in means of production is being privatized in a variety of ways (Gregory and Stuart 1998, 293-462). Private markets in products and resources, a banking system, and a stock market are replacing state planning. In place of the USSR's Council of Ministers as owner, operator, and surplus appropriator in state capitalist enterprises, the emerging successor state agencies move toward becoming Western-style tax-collecting regulators, via monetary and fiscal policies, of a largely private capitalist enterprise economy.

The crisis thus provoked a radical downsizing of the state in Soviet society as well as a change in its social roles. State officials would henceforth do much less appropriating of industrial or agricultural surpluses. Private citizens and groups would take over those surplus appropriation functions. Once again the capitalist class structure of most industrial and agricultural production did not change. Rather, private capitalists replaced state officials within that same class structure.

Through the 1980s (and since), nearly all supporters as well as enemies of the USSR continued their shared tradition of theorizing its uniqueness in terms of its "socialist class structure." They continue to define the terms "socialist" and "class" as pertaining to the social distribution (state versus private) of power (over property, markets, and resources) and not to the social organization of surplus labor (which most ignored totally). What fundamentally distinguished the USSR, for them, was that the state (or collective) rather than private individuals or groups had the dominant power to own, manage, and operate most means of production. The state (via planning) rather than private individuals and groups (via private market exchanges) wielded the dominant power to determine the social distribution of resources and products. When marginal policy changes of the sorts attempted repeatedly in the postwar period seemed incapable of reversing a decline that became a crisis, a preponderance of opinion emerged that finally some more "fundamental" policy changes were needed.

By "fundamental" the Gorbachev-Yeltsin-Putin administrations meant exactly what was implied by the previous seventy-year history of shared theorizations of the USSR's socialism. Administrators, like most Soviet citizens, thought and acted in terms of those theorizations. Hence the requisite fundamental changes seemed only too clear: to change the social distribution of power; to alter radically *who* owned, managed, and operated means of production and markets. If the state was to be deprived of the powers of ownership, enterprise management and operation, and planning, the only conceivable alternative, nearly everyone agreed, was private ownership, management, and operation coupled with market exchanges among these new private owners. Disagreements swirled only around subsidiary questions. Did private owners mean only individuals or groups or both? Would any state ownership, enterprise operation, or planning remain in a privatized market economy? Would foreign capitalists be free to buy into the privatization? How far would political and cultural life be adjusted in parallel ways, removing state controls and party monopolies? Some believed in preserving the USSR; others preferred decomposing it into a Commonwealth of Independent States or further still.

For some, the goal of transition was a society they called "democratic" or "social democratic" or "democratic socialist." They envisioned the growth of a private sector characterized more by cooperatives, factories leased by workers from the state, and, in general, enterprise forms owned and operated by workers rather than by the traditional Western sorts of private corporate enterprises.[49] They remained committed to a quite interventionist state (for limited welfare and redistributive purposes). They also sought a political system entailing parliamentary politics, an independent judiciary, and so on. For them, the Soviet crisis presented a chance to combine a "democratized" economy and polity and so enable true democracy and/or true (i.e., democratic) socialism to emerge from the distorted Soviet form of socialism (Denitch 1990).[50] Others, inside and outside the USSR, championed a much more minimalist state and a capitalist corporate structure with private managements and shareholders along the lines of the British and U.S. economies. Across all these positions, the common definition of "fundamental change" was to change the social distribution of power. In one remarkably succinct statement:

> A litmus test for the completion of the transition is the emergence of an order with an autonomous economic system based on competition. There is no third way to organize a modern society. . . . The great lesson that can be drawn from the unfortunate experience with state socialism is that an institutional design of a politico-economic order that would be able to survive in a rapidly changing world should observe the autonomy of the economic system and society. (Kaminski 1991, 211)[51]

Thus, the collapse that began in the late 1980s and continues since has been, for participants and observers alike, chiefly a shift of power out of the interlocking hands of the central state apparatus and the Communist Party. A private, "autonomous" economy and a parliamentary polity are taking that power. Class structures—in the sense of the social forms in which surplus is produced, appropriated, and distributed—have been of even less concern to most participants and observers over the last decade than they were after 1917. Then, private capitalism gave way to state capitalism as part of a shift of power into state hands—just the reverse of what happened after 1989.

However, our different, Marxian analysis is more focused on specifying what happened to class structures than in delineating the power shifts across the Soviet crisis and its aftermath. In 1985, 91.1 percent of the Russian labor force was employed directly by the state. In 1990 the comparable percentage was 82.6, and in 1994 it was 44.7. Privately employed percentages went from 8.9 in 1985 to 33.0 in 1994, while employees of "mixed" state/private enterprises rose from 0 in 1985 to 21.2 percent of the Russian labor force in 1994 (Gregory and Stuart 1998, 305). Notwithstanding all the statistical problems underlying such numbers, the trend is clear. Private capitalist enterprises have been increasingly replacing state capitalist enterprises. Where before the Council of Ministers appropriated the workers' surplus labor, now that class position is increasingly occupied instead by private persons who are neither state officials nor Communist Party members and do not function as representatives of either.

The collective farms—both those that retained their communist class structures and those that shifted to a capitalist class structure—have experienced considerable difficulties. Some dissolved to be replaced by individual private ancient and capitalist class structured farm enterprises. The largely ancient class structures of private plots and second economy enterprises have sometimes survived and sometimes combined and reorganized into new private capitalist enterprises, both legal and illegal. Inside households, feudal and ancient class structures remained the unchallenged norms across the crisis. Despite the enormous stresses on family life under the economic and social conditions of the time, the class blindness that governed enterprise transitions reigned hegemonic inside households too. No explicit discussion or action aimed to alter household class structures as a way for families to cope with the crisis or its aftermath.

We can now summarize the class changes wrought by the crisis in the later 1980s. By far, the major class change was from state capitalist to private capitalist enterprises in much of industry and agriculture. No change (or revolution) from a communist to a capitalist class-structured economy occurred. Capitalist class structures were not "introduced" into the former USSR to resolve its "socialist" crisis, since capitalist class structures had already long been dominant there. The capitalist nature of the main class structures in productive enterprises was never the issue; it was only their particular form, state or private.

After 1989 the USSR's non-state-capitalist class structures in enterprises and households survived with relatively minor changes in their relative proportions. We thus conclude that the social mix of capitalist (state and private), ancient, feudal, and communist class structures characteristic of the USSR remained the social mix after the USSR dissolved. The major change lay in the proportions of state and private capitalisms; the minor change lay in some much lesser shifts in the proportions among the noncapitalist class structures.

In contrast to the USSR's social mix of class structures, its Communist Party's social position could not survive the crisis of the later 1980s. As official vanguard and manager of the USSR's overall direction, the Party could not evade the blame when that direction seemed to have become a downward spiral. As agent of the control and retrenchment associated with Brezhnev, its social prestige had suffered. By Gorbachev's time, the Party's social intrusions and special privileges made it appear to ever more Soviet citizens (including some party members themselves) as an elite securing its position in a general decline for which it was responsible (Shlapentokh 1989, 207–218).

The 1970s and 1980s saw no socially significant challenge to the class structures of Soviet households. Of course, households were no more understood or analyzed in terms of their organizations of surplus labor than were enterprises or the state. The serious debates of the 1920s, which at least had questioned the traditional household and family in the name of liberating women, had long since disappeared never to return. The postwar Soviet households reproduced their feudal and ancient class structures without sustained social criticism beyond some relatively weak feminist stirrings (which did not touch on household class structures as such).

Postwar Soviet women's virtually total engagement with wage labor alongside men imposed a "double shift" (work outside the home added to work inside) more intense than that endured by women in the West (Danes, Doudchenko, and Yasnaya 1994). Meanwhile, Soviet men remained opposed to shared housework. Thus, as the social conditions described above generated ever deeper alienation among both male and female wage earners, the men sought traditional compensations inside the household partly in the form of more household goods and services delivered to them by their wives. For the women, this meant that the strains of work outside the household were accompanied by demands, however implicit, for still more surplus labor to produce and distribute compensations to their husbands.

Yet, the surpluses that women still had the energy, time, and disposition to produce inside many households were shrinking. This meant fewer surpluses to distribute to other household members. Complex familial relationships were entwined with feudal and ancient household class structures. The relationships could not survive those class structures' incapacity any longer to produce, appropriate, and distribute sufficient surpluses in the historically familiar ways (Hill 1975, 122). The household tensions inherited from pre–World War Two conditions (as discussed in earlier chapters) exploded in a crisis roughly contemporaneous with the crisis maturing outside the households. Even when wages and state services supportive of households (subsidized child care and housing, pensions for elderly household residents, maternity leaves, and so on) were rising, for many Soviet households, such resources flowing into the household from outside could not suffice to offset the class crisis inside. During the 1970s and 1980s, for example, hostilities between young couples and their parents become an increasingly recognized and examined issue in Soviet society (Shlapentokh 1989, 168–170).

Conflicts mounting inside crisis-ridden households reacted back upon the outside world to lower productivity, exacerbate hostilities toward the state and the Party, and also to revive old patterns of national or ethnic scapegoating. The downward spiral outside the postwar Soviet household, especially after the mid-1970s, became cause and effect of that inside (du Plessix Gray 1990; Goscilo 1993).[52] The disintegration of family life and the rise of many problems familiar from "collapsing families and family values" in Western countries became issues both increasingly widespread and publicly acknowledged by the late 1980s.[53] Productivity in state capitalist enterprises, participation in civic life, and respect for the Soviet state all declined as consequences, in part, of the unbearable pressures placed upon the already fragile class structures and interpersonal relations of Soviet households, especially after the mid-1970s.

## The Collapse

The historically quite rapid economic, political, and cultural changes of the later 1970s and 1980s broke upon Soviet society (and most outside observers) as rather mysterious and overwhelming. Many ignored them in the belief they were minor or temporary. Others revived or refurbished versions of past reforms and campaigns of exhortation on the presumption that they would again reverse the flow of events. Rapidly intensifying conflicts erupted across Soviet society in which the two alternatives that the different sides could imagine were debated. At first, the old positions resurfaced: more versus less centralized "socialisms." Then debate swirled around alternative socialisms allowing more or less private property and markets, more or less political pluralism, and so on. But rather quickly this time a new willingness and even eagerness to discuss the two alternatives as "socialism" and "capitalism" overtook their designation as alternative kinds of socialism.

However, the basic polarity—common to all the different ways of describing the alternatives—was familiar because, in one form or another, it had long haunted Soviet society as its dominant conceptualization of the two alternative paths. One side tended to favor more private property, multiparty parliamentarism, cultural freedom, and private markets; the other side supported more state (or collective) property, state-administered (planned) markets, and Communist Party political and cultural hegemony. With all the positions mixing only various degrees of the classic two alternatives, the old dichotomy resurfaced repeatedly as reformers or liberals confronted bureaucrats or conservatives.

Because economic growth slowed drastically, because the Afghanistan disaster marked a decline in Soviet superpower status, because detente made the comparison of Soviet and U.S. living standards (cultural and political as well as economic) socially subversive, the early 1970s peaking of the USSR turned into a cumulative and unstoppable slide into disaster. The Soviet leaders too recognized the exhaustion of their "system" and so moved from the one polar alternative toward the other. They partly made and partly allowed a relatively bloodless transition from state property to private property, from state planning to private markets, from Communist Party monopoly to multiparty politics, from state and party cultural controls to a largely private cultural life. The Soviet system "collapsed."

What the Soviet leaders could not see—because they lacked the concepts—were the class dimensions of what had led to their impasse, what was happening to them, and what they were doing. They could not grasp that they were preserving the capitalist class structure of industry and only changing the form of capitalist exploitation from state to private. They did dimly grasp that they were undermining rural communism in collective farms (to the extent that it still existed) by fostering ancient and capitalist class structures there instead. They had neither understood nor directly treated the class crises of industrial and agricultural Soviet state capitalist enterprises; they had likewise failed in relation to the collective farms' communist and capitalist class structures. Trapped within the same paradigmatic polarity of state and private that informed their critics at home and abroad, they collapsed into the other side of that polarity. Thus, while we arrive there via a very different theoretical route, we share other commentators' rejection of "the fashionable theory that the Soviet system was toppled by the Party and state officials in order to turn their power into private wealth" (Ellman and Kontorovich 1998, 27). No doubt, such motives guided some and perhaps many officials (Kotz 1997), but our analysis has sought to explain how the class contradictions of Soviet development helped to shape such motives, swell the numbers so motivated, and enable them to prevail.

As much as the Soviet people and leadership brought down state capitalism and the Communist Party's political hegemony, they preserved and indeed strengthened capitalism as the prevalent form of surplus labor organization in both industrial and agricultural production. Gorbachev and Yeltsin saved capitalism by removing the state and the Party from their social roles, replacing a discredited state capitalism by its private counterpart. The historical parallel might be Franklin Roosevelt saving capitalism in the United States by the reverse movement, bringing the state into a much greater role as regulator, employer, and even commodity producer to correct and compensate for a discredited private capitalism. While many nonclass dimensions of life "collapsed" in and with the USSR, its capitalist class structures survived and grew in their new, private forms.

The death of the Soviet experiment thus shares something with its birth. At both points, a class-blind theory informing the agents of change combined with the social circumstances constraining them to preclude any basic class transformation beyond capitalism. In 1917 and thereafter these agents made no society-wide transition from capitalism to communism; in 1989 and thereafter they made no society-wide transition from communism to capitalism.

The Soviet revolution certainly did make momentous changes in economics, politics, and culture, but—except for some years in agriculture—not changes in the social organization of surplus labor from capitalist to communist. The Bolsheviks socialized productive property, established central planning, and deprived most private capitalists, feudal landed gentry, orthodox clergy, czarist state officials, merchants, bankers, and so on of their fundamental and subsumed class positions respectively. These latter groups lost the political, economic, and cultural hegemony they had wielded before 1917. The Bolsheviks dramatically bolstered the ancient class structure in agriculture and established a vast new state capitalist class structure in industry and then extended it to agriculture in state farms. At the end of the 1920s and over the 1930s, they also established private communist class structures in collective farms, allowed a transition of some collective farms to private capitalist class structures, and then after the war actively encouraged the growth of state capitalist farms alongside the collective farms. In this way, successive Soviet leaderships transferred political, economic, and cultural hegemony from the old fundamental and subsumed classes who had held it before 1917 to a new group. The members of this new group included the few who were members of the Council of Ministers, leaders of the Communist Party, the chief managers of state capitalist (industrial and farm) enterprises and of collective farms, and top state officials (planners, technocrats, and police enforcers), academics, journalists, and so on.[54] Since these individuals came from families that had occupied the lowest class positions before 1917, the USSR worked a genuinely remarkable transformation of life for many millions of its citizens.

Yet the Bolsheviks could not get beyond the transition from private to state capitalism. They achieved stunning economic growth, global political power, and rising standards of living despite the setbacks of two world wars, a foreign invasion, two civil wars, and nearly continuous encirclement by hostile powers. Given their class-blind social theories, they understood and celebrated those achievements as themselves signs or markers that the USSR had superseded capitalism, achieved socialism, and was progressing successfully toward communism.

Gorbachev, Yeltsin, and Putin, like the Bolsheviks from whom they descended and absorbed class-blind theory, have also made momentous changes, often precisely in directions opposite to the Bolsheviks'. Over the past twenty years, they have been dismantling the state capitalist enterprises and much of the state bureaucracy, replacing them with private capitalist enterprises and markets. Privatization and other related policies are displacing the relatively few communist class structures left in agriculture in favor of ancient and capitalist class structures. Having destroyed the Communist Party's political monopoly and cultural control apparatus, they are presiding over the rapid development of a multiparty parliamentary system, private media enterprises, universities dependent on business enterprises, and the other components of the group that typically dominates civil society in western societies. Given their class-blind social theories, the followers of Gorbachev, Yeltsin, and Putin understand and celebrate these achievements as signs or markers that the nations of the former USSR have broken fundamentally with and superseded the Soviet economic and social system.

Like most of their Bolshevik ancestors, Gorbachev, Yeltsin, and Putin cannot recognize their roles as agents of oscillations between state and private capitalism. They take themselves rather as agents of far more fundamental changes. Lenin at least glimpsed the possibility of communist class structures radically different from those of capitalism. He wanted and strived to be, even while recognizing that he could not yet be, more than an agent of an oscillation from one to another form of capitalism. With Stalin's ascendancy, what Lenin had glimpsed as a future possibility was transformed instead to something already achieved. Official Marxian theory now held that the establishment of Soviet power simply equalled the abolition of classes. The heroic sacrifices of mobilized militants that had made the revolution, won the civil war, constructed a hegemonic state industry and marketing apparatus, and established the Communist Party in full power had thereby abolished classes. It remained only to do likewise in agriculture, which collectivization did, in the official view. Thus capitalism, classes, and class struggles had been vanquished and socialism established in the USSR. Neither Stalin nor the hegemonic groups within Soviet society thereafter could admit, to themselves or anyone else, that their vast struggles, achievements, sacrifices, and losses from 1917 to 1989 could have gotten them no further—in class terms—than an oscillation from private to state capitalism.

Gorbachev, Yeltsin, and Putin likewise cannot admit (or imagine) the possibility that their social role has been no more than to enable yet another oscillation of capitalism from a state to a private form. They and their supporters worldwide need to theorize their actions as entailing rather the defeat of communism and a victory for capitalism, democracy, civil liberties, freedom, and prosperity. They strive to convince themselves that what they are establishing will look more like Sweden, Germany, or France, than Turkey, Mexico, or India. They need to believe that mass corruption is limited to a transitional "mafia" rather than becoming the normal mode of social life. In short, they strain to shape how the people of the former USSR construct their deepening disappointment with the gap between the promised benefits of their "revolution" against Soviet socialism and what the renewed private capitalism actually delivers. They lack, so far, any political organization comparable to the Communist Party to accomplish such a consciousness-shaping project. So their recourse is to media-driven persuasion, to an endless drumbeat of argument that the problems are only temporary (and the fault of the former USSR), progress is happening everywhere, the future is bright, and the return to the past unthinkable (while tarring all social critics as proponents of such a return).

Once again, no conceptualizations of classes in the surplus labor sense are current. Absent them, it takes no great foresight to suggest how post-Soviet society will likely understand and respond when the first great crisis hits its private capitalist economy. On the one hand, many will then demand a "fundamental" change of the sort that might enable a Russian FDR to lead the pendulum swing back to a liberal or leftist state-managed private capitalism or maybe even further to a state capitalism. On the other hand, many may well demand something more like a rightist state-managed or even a fascist state capitalism. Either way, a transition from private back toward state capitalism will be conceived instead as a fundamental change from one social system to another.

The USSR was not the first, nor will it be the last effort of people suffering a social crisis to find fault with and rise against the mix of class structures in which they live and especially against the capitalist class structures within that mix. This has happened and will happen whether or not class structures are explicitly theorized in surplus labor terms. For us, the abiding questions therefore are these: What will happen in future revolts against societies in which capitalist class structures (state or private) prevail? What will their people have learned from the experience of the USSR? Where those revolts occur against state capitalisms, will their thinking and strategies be limited to an oscillation back to private capitalism? Where revolts materialize against private capitalisms, will a shift to state capitalism be the limiting horizon of their activists?

Or might the sort of class analysis of the USSR undertaken here contribute to the realization that communist class structures can and should be tried and tested on a social scale as an alternative to all forms of capitalism? For us, that realization is the answer to the question: "What is to be done?"

## Appendix A: The Value Equation for Military Expenditures

To show, in value terms, how growing military expenditures could pose a crisis for Soviet state capitalism as well as other class structures outside the state, we regroup total Soviet state expenditures into two parts (departing from our earlier categories of the state's capitalist subsumed class payments—SSCP(C)—and nonclass payments of X(C+A+F+COM) and Y). The first part—E(M)—comprises expenditures destined for the military and for the accumulation of capital in state capitalist industries producing military outputs. The second part—E(NM)—includes expenditures for all other state purposes (nonmilitary industrial growth, investment in agricultural growth, provision of public services for mass consumption, Communist Party expenditures, payments to sustain the state bureaucracy, payments destined to secure other class structures, and so on). It follows that for any given total state revenues, the more expenditures on the first part, the less remained for the second: SV(C)+SSCR(C+A+F+COM)+NCR = E(M) + E(NM), where SV(C) stands for revenues derived from appropriation of surpluses in state capitalist industrial and farm enterprises; SSCR(C+A+F+COM) for revenues from subsumed class payments from other, private class structures; and NCR for revenues from turnover taxes and other levies on people who did not appropriate surpluses. Cold War growth of E(M) along with the continued necessity of a growing E(NM) put increased pressure on raising the left-hand side of the equation. However, expanding those needed revenues was made more difficult because of the text's described cultural, political, and economic conditions of postwar Soviet history. The Soviet state thus faced pressure to reduce its E(NM) expenditures, even though such an action would undermine the reproduction of class structures within and without the state.

## Appendix B: The Value Equation for International Terms of Trade

Consider the example of state capitalist industry importing machinery while exporting processed oil. To keep the example simple, we abstract from any foreign exchange considerations. To the degree industry can trade oil to merchants at world prices that are greater than domestic values, it earns a nonclass revenue flow. The latter is a measure of the USSR's value gain from its participating in international trade at favorable world export prices. The value loss of importing machinery at world prices greater than values per unit can be measured by state capitalist industry distributing an additional portion of domestic surplus value to foreign merchants in the form of a new subsumed class payment. Taking exports of oil and imports of machinery together, the impact of the international terms of trade—the ratio of export to import prices—on the USSR's state capitalist industry can be written as:

$$SV(C) + NCR(C)_{oil} = SSCP(C) + SSCP(C)_{mach}$$

where $NCR_{oil} = (P - EV/UV)_{oil} \times UV_{oil}$; $SSCP(C)_{mach} = (P - EV/UV)_{mach} \times UV_{mach}$; and the equality sign indicates an assumed balancing of the respective gains and loses from the USSR's trading at these international (world) prices. An inequality sign in the equation would reflect either trading gains or losses, depending upon whether the foreign terms of trade moved in favor of or against the USSR. If such price terms improved, $NCR_{oil}$ would be greater than $SSCP(C)_{mach}$, while worsened terms would produce the converse. The effects of such international movements in the terms of trade on state capitalist development parallel the internal movements (ratio of agricultural to industrial prices) under both the NEP and collectivization. For example, a turning of the international terms of trade in favor of the USSR would enable the state to enhance SSCP(C) and, therefore, its state capitalist development.

### Notes

1. Consumption per capita grew 4.5 percent annually from 1951 to 1955 and 4.0 percent per year from 1956 to 1960 (Gregory and Stuart 1990, 144). Thereafter, according to Gregory and Stuart (147), consumption per capita still grew although at declining rates.
2. Much criticism of Soviet economic inefficiency and political totalitarianism had by then the aura of crying wolf too many times. Those qualities had, after all, dogged Soviet society from the beginning and throughout the period of its ascendancy to the mid-1970s. Why those defects should undermine the system after 1975 when they had not done so before was rarely asked and never persuasively argued.
3. Gregory and Stuart (1998, 164–165) show the growing importance of state capitalist farms: in 1953, the 97,000 collective farms accounted for 83.9 percent of the total sown area; by 1983, there

were only 25,000 collective farms that together accounted for only 43.75 percent of total sown area. In contrast, the state farms (with their state capitalist class structures) rose across the same period from 4,900 to 22,300 in number and from 9.6 percent to 53.4 percent of the total sown area in the USSR. During these years the percentage of total sown area cultivated in the ancient class structures of the "private plots" shrank from 4.4 to 2.9 percent. Thus, state capitalist displaced both private capitalist and private noncapitalist (communist and ancient) class structures in terms of sown acres of agriculturally productive Soviet land. However, war's damage to agriculture provoked the state to allow more production on private plots (the ancient class structure), free market activity, and illegal economic activity (also involving to some degree the ancient class structure) (Barber and Harrison 1991, 99–102).

4. The specific histories and circumstances of each collective farm overdetermined their class structures. Because the kind of class differentiation we use was not used by collective farmers or by students of collective farming, they did not discuss or measure class processes as such; hence we cannot reliably determine the relative proportions of their two class structures across Soviet history. What historical records do suggest, given especially the pressures of Communist Party policies and the power of the example set by both Soviet industry and state capitalist farms, was a post-1945 transition from private communist to private capitalist collective farms. Fitzpatrick (1994b) tells of this kind of transition occurring even in the 1930s: "As collective farms grew more prosperous . . . reports multiplied of their efforts to free themselves from the cooperative framework and move towards a kind of rural capitalist market in labor" (147). Elsewhere in discussing the relationship between collectives and so-called independent peasants (some 7 percent of the peasants in 1937 who were not collectivized), she states: "When collective farms hired outside labor, as they frequently did in the latter part of the 1930s, independents were often the people that were hired" (157). Finally, she describes (193ff.) kolkhoz chairmen who kept proceeds of sales of kolkhoz produce for themselves and friends, arrogated all sorts of power to themselves, provoked complaints, and so forth. This kind of evidence suggests to us that for a number of collectives, while collective ownership remained, collective appropriation and distribution of the surplus gave way to a situation in which a small subset of collective farmers—chairmen and their friends—took over those functions.

5. This intrastate value flow differs from the previously analyzed flows from private ancient, capitalist, and communist class structures in agriculture to the state capitalist class structure in industry. For example, assuming that agricultural inputs were sold by state capitalist industry to state capitalist farms at state set prices exceeding values per unit, then industry received a subsumed class revenue equal to a higher subsumed class payment on the part of state farms. If state farms also were required to sell raw materials to state industry at prices below their values per unit, then industry gained thereby nonclass revenues offset by an equivalent revenue loss on the part of state farms. Turning the terms of trade in favor of state industry gained it an inflow of value equal to the value loss incurred by state agriculture.

6. If we recall the value theoretic equation for the Soviet state, its income included the surplus appropriated in state capitalist industrial and farm enterprises [SV(c), a fundamental class receipt] plus the receipt of subsumed class payments from other class structures plus the nonclass receipts obtained by unequal exchanges, turnover taxes on workers, and so on. The total income represented by the state's inflows of fundamental, subsumed, and nonclass receipts was the fund with which it could try to enlarge Soviet industry, sustain its superpower status, improve mass consumption of industrial commodities, and respond to whatever other claims obtained state consideration.

7. Gavin Kitching (1998) argues that the pressures of the Soviet state on agricultural class structures—state capitalist farms and private capitalist and communist collective farms—forced them into a symbiotic relationship with the private plots that functioned increasingly after the 1930s to alienate agriculture from the rest of Soviet society and the Soviet state.

8. Of course, this "compensation" did not benefit household members equally, since women did most of the households' surplus labor. Likewise, no necessity attaches to such compensation; Soviet households might have refused to permit wages to fall because of household surpluses. They might have insisted on precluding any compensatory relation between the two sites of class structures (wage work outside and nonwage work inside households). That they did not effectively do so in the USSR reflects the specific circumstances there and then.
9. Women's postwar labor force participation rate steadily matched that of Soviet men at the remarkable 88 percent level (Gregory and Stuart 1998, 152).
10. Dunham (1976, 214ff.) also shows how this postwar double labor burden for women reinforced the already extreme strains on household relationships between women and men that the war and its legacies had provoked. Soviet officials responded to some of the pressures on women by liberalizing divorce and abortion rights while tightening legal punishments for rape—including spousal rape (Clements 1991, 272–278). They did not respond to (because they could never see) the class crises of Soviet households. That is, they did not question whether changes in Soviet society were undermining the production and distribution of households' surpluses needed to sustain their feudal and ancient class structures. Nor could they confront the likely consequences for Soviet industry and agriculture of deepening strains within or collapse of the existing household class structures.
11. The urgency of postwar reconstruction combined with the focus on state industrial capital accumulation inherited from before the war to keep the state's priority on heavy industrial growth. That priority was credited with enabling the defeat of Hitler's invasion. The USSR's emergence as the Cold War nuclear archrival of the United States induced an even greater emphasis on military development that further reinforced the priority of heavy industry. The Cold War also sharpened the pressures on the Soviet state to raise workers' consumption levels—especially of industrial products—relative to those boasted by Western Europe and the United States. State capitalist industrial capital accumulation including accumulation in wage-good industries was thus the overwhelming priority.
12. Hochschild (1994, 115–127) eloquently explores how and why, despite denunciations of Stalin and Stalinism, the latter's multiple layers unevenly and yet doggedly held a grip on the consciousness of Soviet citizens throughout the postwar period.
13. That public posters became major influences on Soviet consciousness after 1917 is graphically documented in Guerman (1979).
14. Reduced work intensity meant that less value was added by a day's labor than had previously been the case. Worker's wages, in value terms, were already too low to be any further reduced; in other words, the value of wages that had to paid out to workers was fixed by the circumstances. Hence the reduction in value added by workers meant an equivalent reduction in the surplus value portion that could be appropriated. In addition, workers became less productive in the sense of generating fewer use-values of output per hour of abstract labor (i.e., each use-value therefore embodied more labor). In Marxian value theory terms, this meant that the consumer goods that workers required to reproduce their labor power embodied more labor per unit than they had before. Thus the value of their labor power had risen (assuming again no further reduction in the already meager basket of consumer goods given to workers). Given the length of the Soviet working day, if the value of labor power rises, then the remaining surplus labor portion of the working day must correspondingly fall.
15. Reduced labor intensity and productivity reduced the surplus labor the state could directly appropriate from the capitalist class structures of its industrial and farm enterprises. Likewise, the reduced surplus labor that private capitalist and communist collective farms could appropriate added to their difficulties in delivering the portions of their surplus that the state demanded from them (taxes, fees, etc.) while still retaining enough to secure their own survival.
16. Shlapentokh writes that one third of the urban Soviet population, as well as most of the rural popula-

tion, engaged in private plot (or "garden plot") farming. He also cites several reports suggesting there was far greater labor productivity on private plots than on state and collective farms (1989, 191).

17. These representations occurred despite the official and widely accepted notion that no bourgeois class as such any longer existed in the USSR after the 1930s. Before then, the bourgeois classes had been personified as remnants from before 1917, Nepmen, and kulaks: the very classes finally defeated, it was argued, under Stalin. By the postwar period, cultural struggles thus concerned class only in the metaphorical sense of pitting high culture "in tune with" Soviet classless reality versus high culture at variance with and so anathema to it.

18. Stephen Cohen has presented a critical evaluation of such critiques (1977).

19. The association of collective property ownership with "socialism" and hence with the Soviet state tarred it with bureaucracy as well. Thus, antibureaucratic social criticism tended not to support communist class structures such as those within some collective farms; this left the small private capitalist and ancient enterprises as those most free of "bureaucratic distortions."

20. Of course, that did not preclude all sorts of Soviet analyses of the differential social importance of "technical experts," academics, teachers, and so on.

21. Day's book (1995) in its entirety testifies to how Soviet economic theorizing illustrates the Hegelian maxim concerning the ineluctable unity of opposites. In this case, the cultural reinforcement of the official dichotomization of virtually all social thought settled into a postwar pattern of equating the struggle between proletarian and bourgeois to the superpower confrontation of the USSR and the United States. Soviet thinkers increasingly tended to define their society over and against that of the United States. This served, as Hegel might have enjoyed pointing out, to make Soviet economists particularly attentive and responsive to U.S. formulations (which completely dominated the postwar field of economics vis-à-vis formulations emerging from other countries). As Day shows, this became almost a dependency. An interesting task that remains would be to illustrate as well the reverse: how postwar U.S. economic theorizing functioned as a response to Soviet economics, much as neoclassical theory functioned as a response to Marxian theory in the previous century (Dobb 1938).

22. As is detailed in Resnick and Wolff (1987, 132-141), "unproductive" wage earners provide crucial conditions of existence for the productive wage-earners to generate a surplus. The unproductive laborers' wages are payments for so doing from the appropriating capitalists. The latter distribute a share of the surplus they appropriate from productive laborers to pay the wages (and salaries) of unproductive wage earners.

23. Just as Marxists and non-Marxists outside the USSR shared in the prevailing Soviet tendency after Stalin to think in terms of one undifferentiated working class, so too did they share the Soviet class blindness in theorizing households and their social effects.

24. Indeed, a widespread devaluation of women's work and household work coalesced with this kind of class analysis to make households a much less important object of social thought and policy than enterprises and the state. In this respect, Soviet and Western thought shared more than a little in common (as, for example, Western gross domestic/national product analyses omitted accounting for the labor and products of household labor). Likewise both therefore systematically neglected the interactions of class and nonclass conflicts inside households with their counterparts outside households.

25. Gaddy (1996, 44-45) stresses the immense costs of the Soviet commitment to "extensive development" in this regard. Old weapons systems and the economic resources devoted to producing them were maintained alongside the new systems and the labor and means of production allocated to them.

26. Of course, the political practices and discourses in the United States were likewise shaped by those in the USSR; the influences were dialectically interactive. Thus the prevalent forms of U.S. politics defined and justified themselves often against those asserted to prevail in the USSR.

27. Of course, it was not only international politics that shaped this form and focus of economic policy debate. The history of socialism and of economic thought generally and many other factors also contributed. The point here is to show how politics also influenced the debates and thereby the class structures of Soviet society.
28. A very few voices took the notion of decentralization to the point of arguing, in effect, for private instead of state enterprises. That is, the state might own the means of production, but the appropriators of surplus—usually called "management" in these debates—would not be state officials. The workers would instead elect persons without a position as a state official of any kind to "manage" their enterprises at the local level. This amounted to suggesting the private capitalist collective farms' class structure as the norm to replace the existing Soviet state capitalism. Only in this small minority position did the decentralization debate encounter a dissent from the otherwise nearly universal presumption of state capitalist enterprises as the basic form for Soviet production.
29. Of course, all kinds of power sharing could be and were debated: for examples, mixtures of state and private property and mixtures of private market exchanges and state-planned distributions.
30. Kornai assures readers that his analysis considers all the many aspects of reform: "To confine the analysis to some particular sphere could produce a one-sided picture" (1992, 386). Yet, like the others involved in the debates, Kornai actually limits his attention to issues of who wields the power to control rights of access to objects, namely who owns. He ignores, for example, any class analysis in the sense of how surplus labor is produced, appropriated, and distributed. In his 644-page tome entitled *The Socialist System: The Political Economy of Communism*, there is nothing about such class structures; no entry for class appears in the index. He offers no defense of such a class-blind interpretation, nor any recognition, let alone critique, of alternative interpretations (1992, 204–207, 635–638). He devotes to the family a tiny handful of pages containing this sentence with its remarkable opening phrase: "As a diversion, it is worth dealing briefly with an important sphere in the life of society: the role of the family"(1992, 455).
31. The comparisons of consumption levels stimulated by detente became weapons in official propaganda battles and in intense academic and public media debates (themselves often deeply influenced by official propaganda). Problems inherent in determining and gathering the relevant data and in its statistical organization guaranteed that all comparisons would be deeply colored by the broader interests of those offering the comparisons. However, the United States possessed far more developed industries of information dissemination—above all, advertising. Thus it could easily best the USSR, which lacked anything comparable, in spreading its spin on such comparisons across the world and into the USSR. To this day, it remains remarkable how well citizens of the former USSR grasp the existence and extent of high levels of individual consumption in the West and how poorly they recognize the extent of low levels of collective consumption there.
32. It is worth noting that decentralization of enterprise management likely operated as both effect and cause of the economic slowdown in the USSR that began in the 1970s. While the slowdown no doubt strengthened the social forces favoring decentralization, decentralization also contributed to the slowdown, as even Kornai (1992) admits. Only those committed to equating decentralization with exclusively positive economic effects regardless of context need to deny that it can ever have negative economic effects and that centralization can ever have positive economic effects.
33. We attach no historical necessity or inevitability to the stages of class transition sketched here for the postwar USSR. Only the specific, historical conditions then in place, internationally and domestically, overdetermined that political decentralization of Soviet enterprise management would serve as a step in that class transition. Had those highly unstable conditions changed or been otherwise, a different pattern of stages would have occurred.
34. In 1952, Soviet Communist Party membership stood at 5.9 million; by 1981, it had risen to 17.5 (Kerblay 1983, 246–266). A third of the 1981 membership had been recruited since 1965. By the 1960s, the average number of party members per industrial enterprise was 81 and per collective

Class Contradictions and the Collapse — 331

farm 40; 94 percent of collective farm chairmen were party members. In Kerblay's words, "96.8 per cent of the Party membership operates in the workplace, for it is in the enterprise that the primary Party cell is organized" (1983, 250). Party members also prevailed in the leadership of three of the most important mass organizations: the trade unions, youth organizations, and the local Soviets. Combined together they included the majority of all Soviet citizens. These organizations were further integrated into the Party's sphere of major influence, since they functioned as key sources for new recruits. Other writers such as Keep (1995, 205–207) have argued that the Party after the war recruited disproportionate numbers of relatively more educated managers, technicians, academics, and intellectuals who generally looked down on the less educated workers who had been the dominant group before. This, too, probably contributed to the alienation of the Party from the masses. However, we prefer to emphasize rather the alienation flowing from the contradictions of the functional relationship to class structures that was assigned to the Party.

35. Analyzing similar developments in Poland in the 1980s, Kaminski refers to a "syndrome of withdrawal" by citizens, enterprises, and even the state from participation in the overall, official socialist project when it encountered systemic difficulties (1991, 162–193).
36. Kornai claims a "positive" rather than a "normative" approach (1992, 577). This represents an epistemological naiveté (a positivism advanced as if none of the many, complex critiques of it existed and as if no defense of it was even passingly necessary). The naiveté is coupled with an absolutist apology for one set of theories (those that link private property and markets with economic "success"). Just like the Soviet theorists he abhors, Kornai believes his theoretical approach to be scientific and realistic—it gets (absolutely) at how the socialist economy really worked—while others' are wrong and/or evil. He writes without awareness let alone critique of the possibility that alternative perspectives reach alternative understandings and judgments—different understandings based on different criteria and methods of analysis: difference rather than absolutes of right and wrong.
37. A return to more centralized planning, perhaps very different from what had existed earlier, seems not to have figured even as a possibility in Kornai's work (1992).
38. Cohen has stressed in this connection the devastating effects of Stalin's late 1930s terror against the Party (1986, 63–66). The repeated decimation of the "old Bolshevik" party leaders undermined many of the qualities (independence, principled courage, etc.) that might have made the next party generation able to perform rather than betray the enhanced watchdog role assigned to it under the later reforms.
39. This conclusion is consistent with the evidence from "insiders" in the Soviet political apparatus: namely that "The withdrawal of the Party from economic management made the economy ungovernable in the old ways" (Ellman and Kontorovich 1998, 27). In our view, "the old ways" refers to party control over the Council of Ministers, Gosplan, and other central levers of surplus appropriation and economic management. The new way—the Party's assignment to more microlevel controls—could not (for the reasons listed in the text) compensate for the demise of the old control system.
40. Recent calculations suggest that when taking into account earnings outside of officially sanctioned activities (in the "second economy"), income in the USSR became more unequally distributed during the 1980s (Gregory and Stuart 1998, 157). The higher incomes were correlated with higher educational attainments and party members were increasingly better educated than the Soviet population at large (Kerblay 1983, 249). A reasonable inference is that at least after the mid-1970s, party members were located in the higher reaches of the income distribution.
41. To view the Soviet system's full employment commitments as guaranteeing each worker that he/she can keep the *same* job entails a logical error. State-planned full employment is compatible with all sorts of reallocations and retrainings of workers (from declining industries to growing industries) who remain employed throughout the process of shifting from one job to another. It was not Soviet

planning concepts or forms per se, but rather the specific conditions of postwar Soviet planning that tended toward freezing workers in particular jobs rather than facilitating their movement among and retraining for different jobs according to changes in technology, final demand, and social priorities for economic change.

42. Economists from widely divergent theoretical camps (inside and outside the USSR) have agreed both that cycles characterized the Soviet macroeconomy and that they have been very similar (other than when they occurred) to the cycles of private capitalisms (Chattopadhyay 1994, 139–140).

43. In Marxian value terms, rising productivity achieved by technical innovation via imported machines yielded declining value per unit of the expanded output from those machines (less total labor needed per unit). When such value declines occurred in wage goods production, the value of Soviet labor power fell. Assuming no change in the length of the working day, Soviet state capitalists appropriated more surplus value. In other words, the rate of exploitation of Soviet productive workers rose.

44. When state agencies priced food grain imports below domestic food grains, this also lowered the value of labor power and thereby increased the surpluses appropriated by Soviet state capitalists. This application of Marxian value theory to state-set values and prices parallels our earlier discussion of state-administered values for food grains involved in domestic Soviet exchanges.

45. Assume that produced oil is sold to foreign merchants at an international price that is greater than its domestic value per unit. In this case, the value equation for state capitalist industry becomes: $C + V + S + NCR = P \times UV$. If, however, the price deviates below the value, industry earns a smaller value: $C + V + S - NCR = P \times UV$, where $P \times UV + NCR = W$ (the total value of the oil produced). The term $(S - NCR)$ represents what the text calls a reduced surplus value when prices fall below values.

46. Indeed, political rhetoric from both parties repeatedly suggested that Yeltsin's and Putin's policies derived literally from foreign interests asserted to control them.

47. Of course, growing wage or income inequality will not necessarily undermine a set of dominant class structures. Depending on circumstances, the opposite can occur. Each historical context will overdetermine the relation between wage inequality and class structure. Because long-standing Soviet ideology stressed the moral value of movement toward wage and income equality and because the 1950s and 1960s had realized such movement, the post-1975 shift toward inequality undermined the dominant Soviet class structures.

48. Certain studies of private family plots, focused on their outputs as portions of the total Soviet output, conclude that they became less important across the later 1970s and 1980s (Hill 1975; Gregory and Stuart 1998, 163). Yet the evidence on family life in those years suggests to us rather that private plots became more significant—chiefly for rural but also for some urban workers—in terms of their labor, energy, and time. This was implicitly recognized and celebrated as a basis for economic renewal by Gorbachev at the twenty-seventh party congress.

49. A publication by Bim, Jones, and Weisskopf (1993) combines a discussion of the late Soviet legislation enabling these sorts of enterprises with an evaluation of their early post-Soviet experiences and prospects. Their article also displays precisely the sorts of hopes such observers displayed toward the possibilities for development in such "democratic" directions.

50. Denitch's book, written by a lifelong social democratic activist in both Europe and the United States, summarizes this position comprehensively. The operative definition in his references to "class" is solely in terms of power. For example, he lauds the Swedish Social Democratic Party's Meidner Plan as a "move irretrievably beyond the boundaries of capitalism" for its "collective transfer of stocks to bodies elected by unions, employees, and the local community" (1990, 77). This is what he means by "workers control." At no point does he refer to, let alone discuss, alternative organizations of the production and distribution of surplus in the USSR or in a future democratic socialism.

# Class Contradictions and the Collapse — 333

51. By "autonomous" he means "private." Kaminski's book concerns Poland. However, the quoted conclusion is worded in more general terms because, as the author argues repeatedly, he believes that it applies to all "Soviet-type" economies.
52. There is no contradiction between the privatizing turn in Soviet culture inward toward the family (as a haven from an increasingly difficult economic and social situation) and the explosion of that haven. Indeed, it is partly because of the hope that family life would compensate for life outside that the crisis of the household was so difficult for the Soviet people and affected their work and political participation so negatively.
53. The class crisis of households in the USSR parallels that in the United States at the same time, but the mechanisms were different. In the USSR, economic and political decline deepened by spreading to the households. By contrast, in the United States, the class crisis of private capitalist enterprises in the 1970s received intense state attention. By lowering state taxes on private enterprise surpluses while lowering the wages they had to pay to productive laborers, U.S. policy succeeded in reversing their crisis in the 1980s. However, the resulting pressures on households from falling wages coupled with declining state services pushed them over the edge into family and household decline (Resnick and Wolff 1994).
54. These members comprise what others often describe as a "ruling elite." In this sense, Mawdsley and White (2000) offer a history of members of the Party's Central Committee from 1917 to 1991. In our class terms, these were individuals who occupied state capitalist subsumed class positions as members of the Central Committee and in many cases also occupied state capitalist fundamental class positions as members of the Council of Ministers. Of course, in addition to one or both of these class positions, they could and did occupy still other state capitalist subsumed class positions in the military, union, police, industrial, financial, or administrative bureaucracy. Mawdsley and White provide glimpses into the multiple class positions occupied by these individuals.

# References

Althusser, Louis. 1976. *Essays in Self-Criticism*, trans. by Grahame Lock. London: New Left Books.
Amann, R., J. Cooper, and R. W. Davies. 1977. *The Technological Level of Soviet Industry*. New Haven: Yale University Press.
Amariglio, Jack. 1984. "Economic History and the Theory of Primitive Socio-Economic Development." Ph.D. diss., Dept. of Economics, University of Massachusetts-Amherst.
Amariglio, Jack, and Antonio Callari. 1989. "Marxian Value Theory and the Problem of the Subject: The Role of Commodity Fetishism." *Rethinking Marxism* 2, 3 (Fall): 31–60.
Amariglio, Jack, Stephen A. Resnick, and Richard Wolff. 1988. "Class, Power, and Culture." In *Marxism and the Interpretation of Culture*, ed. by C. Nelson and L. Grossberg. Urbana and Chicago: University of Illinois Press, 487–501.
Amariglio, Jack, and David Ruccio. 1995. "Postmodern Marxism, and the Critique of Modern Economic Thought." In *Marxism in the Postmodern Age: Confronting the New World Order,* ed. by A. Callari, S. Cullenberg, and C. Biewener. New York: Guilford Press, 13–23.
Anderson, Michael. 1995. *Approaches to the History of the Western Family, 1500–1914*. Cambridge: Cambridge University Press.
Anderson, Perry. 1974. *Passages from Antiquity to Feudalism*. London: New Left Books.
———. 1975. *Lineages of the Absolute State*. London: New Left Books.
Arato, Andrew, and Eine Gebhardt. 1978. *The Essential Frankfurt School Reader*. New York: Urizen Books.
Avineri, Shlomo. 1969. *The Social and Political Thought of Karl Marx*. Cambridge: Cambridge University Press.
Bailes, Kendall E. 1978. *Technology and Society Under Lenin and Stalin*. Princeton: Princeton University Press.
Balibar, Etienne. 1977. *On the Dictatorship of the Proletariat*, trans. by Grahame Lock. London: New Left Books.
Ball, Alan M. 1990. *Russia's Last Capitalists: The Nepmen, 1921–1929*. Berkeley: University of California Press.
———. 1996. *And Now My Soul is Hardened: Abandoned Children in Soviet Russia, 1918–1930*. Berkeley: University of California Press.
Barber, John, and R. W. Davies. 1994. "Employment and Industrial Labour." In *The Economic Transformation of the Soviet Union*, ed. by R. W. Davies, Mark Harrison, and S. G. Wheatcroft. Cambridge: Cambridge University Press, 81–105.
Barber, John, and Mark Harrison. 1991. *The Soviet Home Front, 1941–1945*. London and New York: Longman.
Barrett, Michele. 1980. *Women's Oppression Today*. London: Verso.
Baykov, Alexander. 1947. *The Development of the Soviet Economic System*. New York: Macmillan.

Bellis, Paul. 1979. *Marxism and the USSR: The Theory of Proletarian Dictatorship and Marxist Analysis of Soviet Society.* London: Macmillan.
Belov, Fedor. 1955. *The History of a Soviet Collective Farm.* New York: Frederick A. Praeger.
Benjamin, Walter. 1986. *Reflections,* trans. by Edmund Jephcott. New York: Schocken Books.
Bergson, Abram. 1961. *The Real National Income of Soviet Russia Since 1928.* Cambridge: Harvard University Press.
Berliner, Joseph. 1957. *Factory and Manager in Soviet Industry.* Cambridge: Harvard University Press.
———. 1976. *The Innovation Decision in Soviet Industry.* Cambridge: MIT Press.
Berman, Marshall. 1983. *All That is Solid Melts Into Air: The Experience of Modernity.* London: Verso.
Bernstein, Eduard. 1961. *Evolutionary Socialism.* New York: Schocken Books.
Bettelheim, Charles. 1975. *Economic Calculation and Forms of Property: An Essay on the Transition between Capitalism and Socialism.* New York: Monthly Review Press.
———. 1976a. *Economic Calculation and Forms of Property,* intro. by Barry Hindess. London: Pluto Press.
———. 1976b. *Class Struggles in the USSR: First Period, 1917–1923,* trans. by B. Pearce. New York: Monthly Review Press.
———. 1978. *Class Struggles in the USSR: Second Period, 1923–1930,* trans. by B. Pearce. New York: Monthly Review Press.
———. 1985. "The Specificity of Soviet Capitalism." *Monthly Review* 37 (September): 43–56.
Bim, Alexander S., Derek C. Jones, and Thomas E. Weisskopf. 1993. "Hybrid Forms of Enterprise Organisation in the Former USSR and the Russian Federation." *Comparative Economic Studies* XXXV, 1 (Spring): 1–38.
Blackwell, William L. 1968. *The Beginnings of Russian Industrialization, 1800–1860.* Princeton: Princeton University Press.
Blum, Jerome. 1961. *Lord and Peasant in Russia.* Princeton: Princeton University Press.
Bohac, Rodney D. 1991. "Widows and the Russian Serf Community." In *Russia's Women: Accommodation, Resistance, Transformation,* ed. by Barbara Evans Clements, Barbara Alpern Engel, and Christine D. Worobec. Berkeley: University of California Press, 95–112.
Bonnell, Victoria E., ed. 1983. *The Russian Worker: Life and Labor Under the Tsarist Regime.* Berkeley: University of California Press.
———. 1997. *Iconography of Power: Soviet Political Posters Under Lenin and Stalin.* Berkeley: University of California Press.
Boss, Helen. 1990. *Theories of Surplus and Transfer: Parasites and Producers in Economic Thought.* Boston: Unwin Hyman.
Bottomore, Tom. 1990. *The Socialist Economy.* New York: Guilford Press.
Bottomore, Tom, and Patrick Goode. 1978. *Austro-Marxism.* Oxford: Clarendon Press.
Brezhnev, Leonid. 1974. "Speech to the 17th Komsomol Congress, April 23." *Moscow News* 17 (1216).
Brinton, Maurice. 1970. *The Bolsheviks and Workers' Control, 1917–1921: The State and Counter Revolution.* London: Solidarity.
Buick, Adam, and John Crump. 1986. *State Capitalism: The Wages System Under New Management.* Houndmills and London: Macmillan.
Bukharin, Nikolai. 1925. *Historical Materialism: A System of Sociology.* New York: International Publishers.
Bukharin, Nikolai, and Evgeny Preobrazhensky. 1969. *The ABC of Communism,* trans. by E. and C. Paul. Baltimore: Penguin.
Burbank, Jane. 1986. *Intelligentsia and Revolution: Russian Views of Bolshevism, 1917–1922.* New York: Oxford University Press.
Callinicos, Alex. 1991. *The Revenge of History: Marxism and the East European Revolutions.* University Park: Pennsylvania State University Press.
Carr, Edward Hallett. 1954. *The Interregnum 1923–1924.* New York: Macmillan.

———. 1958. *Socialism in One Country 1924-1926*, vol. 1. New York: Macmillan.
———. 1985. *The Bolshevik Revolution 1917-1923*, vol.2. New York: W. W. Norton.
Carr, Edward Hallett, and R. W. Davies. 1969. *Foundations of a Planned Economy 1926-1929*, vol. 1, part 2. London: Macmillan.
Carrere d'Encausse, Helene. 1982. *Lenin: Revolution and Power*. London and New York: Longman.
———. 1981. *Stalin: Order Through Terror*. London and New York: Longman.
Castoriadis, Cornelius. 1988. *Political and Social Writings*, vol. 1, trans. by David Ames Curtis. Minneapolis: University of Minnesota Press.
———. 1993. *Political and Social Writings*, vol. 3, trans. by David Ames Curtis. Minneapolis: University of Minnesota Press.
Chambre, Henri. 1974. *L'evolution du marxisme sovietique: theorie economique et droit*. Paris: Seuil.
Chandler, Alfred D., Jr. 1962. *Strategy and Structure: Chapters in the History of the American Industrial Enterprise*. Cambridge: MIT Press.
Chapman, Janet G. 1963. *Real Wages in Soviet Russia Since 1928*. Cambridge: Harvard University Press.
Chase, William J. 1990. *Workers, Society and the Soviet State: Labor and Life in Moscow, 1918-1929*. Urbana-Champagne: University of Illinois Press.
Chattopadhyay, Paresh. 1994. *The Marxian Concept of Capital and the Soviet Experience*. Westport and London: Praeger.
Chavance, Bernard. 1980. *Le capital socialiste: histoire critique de l'economie politique du socialisme*. Paris: Le Sycomore.
Chayanov, A. V. 1966. *The Theory of Peasant Economy*. Homewood: Richard D. Irwin.
———. 1986. *The Theory of Peasant Economy*. Madison: University of Wisconsin Press.
Childe, V. Gordon. 1950. "The Urban Revolution." *Town Planning Review* 21: 1, 3-17.
———. 1952. "The Birth of Civilization." *Past and Present* 2: 1-10.
Clark, Katerina. 1986. "Political History and Literary Chronotope: Some Soviet Case Studies." In *Literature and History: Theoretical Problems and Russian Case Studies*, ed. by Gary Saul Morson. Stanford: Stanford University Press, 230-246.
Clark, M. Gargner. 1956. *The Economics of Soviet Steel*. Cambridge: Harvard University Press.
Clements, Barbara Evans. 1991. "Later Developments: Trends in Soviet Women's History, 1930 to the Present." In *Russia's Women: Accommodation, Resistance, Transformation*, ed. by Barbara Evans Clements, Barbara Alpern Engel, and Christine D. Worobec. Berkeley: University of California Press, 267-278.
Cliff, Tony. 1974. *State Capitalism in Russia*. London: Pluto Press.
Cohen, Stephen F. 1977. "Bolshevism and Stalinism." In *Stalinism*, ed. by Robert C. Tucker. New York: W. W. Norton, 3-29.
———. 1980. *Bukharin and the Bolshevik Revolution: A Political Biography, 1888-1938*. Oxford: Oxford University Press.
———. 1985. *Rethinking the Soviet Experience: Politics and History Since 1917*. New York: Oxford University Press.
———. 1992. "What's Really Happening in Russia?" *The Nation* 254, 8 (March 2): 259-268.
Conyngham, William. 1973. *Industrial management in the Soviet Union*. Stanford: Hoover Institution Press.
Corrigan, Philip, Harvie Ramsay, and Derek Sayer. 1978. *Socialist Construction and Marxist Theory: Bolshevism and its Critique*. New York: Monthly Review Press.
Crisp, Olga. 1976. *Studies in the Russian Economy Before 1914*. London: Macmillan.
Cullenberg, Stephen. 1992. "Socialism's Burden: Toward a 'Thin' Definition of Socialism." *Rethinking Marxism* 5 (Summer): 64-83.
Danes, Sharon M., Olga N. Doudchenko, and Ludmilla V. Yasnaya. 1994. "Work and Family Life." In *Families Before and After Perestroika: Russian and U. S. Perspective*, ed. by James W. Maddock, M.

Janice Hogan, Anatolyi I. Antonov, and Mikhail W. Mastovsky. New York: Guilford Press, 156–185.

Davies, R. W. 1980. *The Soviet Collective Farm, 1929–1930*. Cambridge: Harvard University Press.

———, ed. 1991. *From Tsarism to the New Economic Policy*. Ithaca: Cornell University Press.

———. 1993. "The Management of Soviet Industry, 1928–41." In *Social Dimensions of Soviet Industrialization*, ed. by William G. Rosenberg and Lewis H. Siegelbaum. Bloomington and Indianapolis: Indiana University Press, 105–123.

———. 1994. "Industry." In *The Economic Transformation of the Soviet Union, 1913–1945*, ed. by R. W. Davies, M. Harrison, and S. G. Wheatcroft. Cambridge: Cambridge University Press, 131–157.

Davies, R. W., Mark Harrison, and S. G. Wheatcroft eds. 1994. *The Economic Transformation of the Soviet Union, 1913–1945*. Cambridge: Cambridge University Press.

Davis, Christopher M. 1990. "Economics of Soviet Public Health, 1921–1930." In *Health and Society in Revolutionary Russia*, ed. by Susan Gross Solomon and John F. Hutchinson. Bloomington: Indiana University Press, 146–174.

Day, Richard B. 1973. *Leon Trotsky and the Politics of Economic Isolation*. Cambridge: Cambridge University Press.

———. 1995. *Cold War Capitalism: The View From Moscow, 1945–1975*. Armonk and New York: M. E. Sharpe.

Delphy, Christine. 1984. *Close to Home: A Materialist Analysis of Women's Oppression*, trans. by Diane Leonard. Amherst: University of Massachusetts Press.

DeMartino, George. 1992. "Modern Macroeconomic Theories of Cycles and Crisis: A Methodological Critique." Ph.D. diss., Dept. of Economics, University of Massachusetts-Amherst.

Denitch, Bogdan. 1990. *The End of the Cold War*. Minneapolis: University of Minnesota Press.

Deutscher, Isaac. 1968. *Stalin: A Political Biography*. New York: Oxford University Press.

Diskin, Jonathan. 1990. "Classical Marxian Economic Theory and the Concept of Socialism." Ph.D. diss., Dept. of Economics, University of Massachusetts-Amherst.

Djilas, Milovan. 1983. *The New Class*. San Diego, New York, London: Harvest (Harcourt Brace and Company).

Dobb, Maurice. 1938. *Political Economy and Capitalism*. New York: International Publishers.

———. 1963. *Studies in the Development of Capitalism*. New York: International Publishers.

———. 1966. *Soviet Economic Development Since 1917*. Rev., enl. ed. New York: International Publishers.

———. 1973. *Theories of Value and Distribution Since Adam Smith*. Cambridge: Cambridge University Press.

Dudintsev, Vladimir. 1957. *Not By Bread Alone*, trans. by Edith Bone. New York: E. P. Dutton.

Dunayevskaya, Raya. 1971. *Marxism and Freedom*. London: Pluto Press.

———. 1992. *The Marxist-Humanist Theory of State-Capitalism: Selected Writings by Raya Dunayevskaya*. Chicago: News and Letters.

Dunham, Vera S. 1976. *In Stalin's Time: Middleclass Values in Soviet Fiction*. Cambridge: Cambridge University Press.

Dunn, Ethel. 1977. "Russian Rural Women." In *Women in Russia*, ed. by Dorothy Atkinson, Alexander Dallin, and Gail Warshovsky Lapidus. Stanford: Stanford University Press.

du Plessix Gray, Francine. 1990. *Soviet Women: Walking the Tightrope*. New York: Doubleday.

Ellman, Michael. 1984. *Collectivisation, Convergence and Capitalism*. London: Academic Press.

Ellman, Michael, and Vladimir Kontorovich, eds. 1998. *The Destruction of the Soviet Economic System: An Insider's View*. Armonk and London: M. E. Sharpe.

Engels, Frederick. 1962. *Anti-Duhring: Herr Eugen Duhring's Revolution in Science*. Moscow: Foreign Languages Publishing House.

———. 1969a. *Socialism: Utopian and Scientific*. New York: International Publishers.

———. 1969b. *The Origin of the Family, Private Property, and the State.* New York: International Publishers.
Erlich, Alexander. 1960. *The Soviet Industrialization Debate, 1924–1928.* Cambridge: Harvard University Press.
Fainsod, Merle. 1989. *Smolensk Under Soviet Rule.* Boston: Unwin Hyman.
Farnsworth, Beatrice Brodsky. 1977. "Bolshevik Alternatives and the Soviet Family: The 1926 Marriage Law Debate." In *Women in Russia,* ed. by Dorothy Atkinson, Alexander Dallin, and Gail Warshovsky Lapidus. Stanford: Stanford University Press, 139–165.
Figes, Orlando. 1989. *Peasant Russia, Civil War: The Volga Countryside in Revolution, 1917–1921.* Oxford: Clarendon Press.
Fine, Ben, and Laurence Harris. 1979. *Rereading Capital.* New York: Columbia University Press.
Fitzpatrick, Sheila. 1984. "Cultural Revolution as Class War." In *Cultural Revolution in Russia, 1928–1931,* ed. by Sheila Fitzpatrick. Bloomington: Indiana University Press, 8–40.
———. 1994a. *The Russian Revolution.* 2d ed. Oxford and New York: Oxford University Press.
———. 1994b. *Stalin's Peasants: Resistance and Survival in the Russian Village After Collectivization.* Oxford: Oxford University Press.
Foner, Philip S., ed. 1984. *Clara Zetkin: Selected Writings.* New York: International Publishers.
Fraad, Harriet, Stephen A. Resnick, and Richard D. Wolff. 1994. *Bringing It All Back Home.* London and Boulder: Pluto Press and Westview Press.
Gabriel, Satya. 1989. "Ancients: A Marxian Theory of Self-Exploitation." Ph.D. diss., Dept. of Economics, University of Massachusetts-Amherst.
———. 1990. "Ancients: A Marxian Theory of Self-Exploitation." *Rethinking Marxism* 3, 1 (Spring): 85–106.
Gabriel, Satya, and Michael Martin. 1992. "China: the Ancient Road to Communism?" *Rethinking Marxism* 5, 1 (Spring): 56–77.
Gaddy, Clifford G. 1996. *The Price of the Past: Russia's Struggle with the Legacy of a Militarized Economy.* Washington: Brookings Institution Press.
Galai, Shmuel. 1973. *The Liberation Movement in Russia, 1900–1905.* Cambridge: Cambridge University Press.
Garnett, Rob. 1994. "Value, Man, and Markets in Modern Economic Discourse." Ph.D. diss., Dept. of Economics, University of Massachusetts-Amherst.
Geoghegan, Vincent. 1987. *Utopianism and Marxism.* London and New York: Methuen.
Godelier, Maurice. 1972. *Rationality and Irrationality in Economics,* trans. by B. Pierce. London: New Left Books.
———. 1977. *Perspectives in Marxist Anthropology,* trans. by R. Brain. Cambridge: Cambridge University Press.
Goldman, Wendy Z. 1993. *Women, the State, and Revolution: Soviet Family Policy and Social Life, 1917–1936.* Cambridge: Cambridge University Press.
Gorlin, Alice. 1985. "The Power of Soviet Industrial Ministers." *Soviet Studies* 37, 3: 353–370.
Goscilo, Helena. 1993. "*Domostroika* or *Perestroika*? The Construction of Womanhood in Soviet Culture Under Glasnost." In *Late Soviet Culture: From Perestroika to Novostroika,* ed. by Thomas Lahusen and Gene Kuperman. Durham and London: Duke University Press, 233–288.
Granick, David. 1954. *Management of the Industrial Firm in the USSR.* New York: Columbia University Press.
———. 1960. *The Red Executive.* Garden City, NY: Doubleday and Company.
Gregory, Paul. 1970. *Socialist and Nonsocialist Industrialization Patterns.* New York: Praeger Publishers.
———. 1990. *Restructuring the Soviet Economic Bureaucracy.* Cambridge: Cambridge University Press.
Gregory, Paul, and Robert C. Stuart. 1990. *Soviet Economic Structure and Performance.* New York: Harper and Row.

———. 1998. *Russian and Soviet Economic Performance and Structure.* 6th ed. Reading: Addison-Wesley.

Grossman, Gregory. 1973. "The Industrialization of Russia and the Soviet Union." In *The Fontana Economic History of Europe,* vol. 4-2, ed. by Carlo M. Cipolla. London: Collins/Fontana, 486-531.

———. 1977. "The Second Economy of the USSR." *Problems of Communism* 26 (September-October): 25-40.

———. 1989. "The Second Economy: Boon or Bane for the Reform of the First Economy." In *Economic Reforms in the Socialist World,* ed. by Stanislaw Gomulka, Yong-Chool Ha, and Cae-One Kim. Armonk: M. E. Sharpe, 79-96.

Guerman, Mikhail. 1979. *Art of the October Revolution.* New York: Harry M. Abrams Publishers.

Hall, S. 1985. "Signification, Representation, Ideology: Althusser and the Post-Structuralist Debates." *Critical Studies in Mass Communication* 2, 2 (June): 91-114.

Hardach, Gerd, Dieter Karras, and Ben Fine. 1979. *A Short History of Socialist Economic Thought,* trans. by James Wickham. New York: St. Martins Press.

Harrington, M. 1990. *Socialism: Past and Future.* New York: Penguin Books.

Harrison, Mark. 1991. "The Peasantry and Industrialization." In *From Tsarism to the New Economic Policy,* ed. by R. W. Davies. Ithaca: Cornell University Press, 104-124.

———. 1994. "National Income." In *The Economic Transformation of the Soviet Union, 1913-1945,* ed. by R. W. Davies, Mark Harrison, and S. G. Wheatcroft. Cambridge: Cambridge University Press, 38-56.

Hegel, G. W. F. 1949. *The Phenomenology of Mind,* trans. by J. B. Baillie. 2d ed., revised. London: George Allen and Unwin.

Hilferding, R. 1950. "State Capitalism or Totalitarian State Economy." In *Verdict of Three Decades,* ed. by J. Sternberg. New York: Duell, Sloane and Pierce, 446-453.

Hill, Christopher. 1971. *Lenin and the Russian Revolution.* London: Penguin.

Hill, Ian H. 1975. "The End of the Russian Peasantry? The Social Structure and Culture of the Contemporary Soviet Agricultural Population." *Soviet Studies* 27, 1 (January): 109-127.

Hilton, Rodney. 1976. *The Transition from Feudalism to Capitalism.* London: New Left Books.

Hindess, Barry and Paul Hirst. 1975. *Pre-Capitalist Modes of Production.* London and Boston: Routledge and Kegan Paul.

Hindus, Maurice. 1988. *Red Bread.* Bloomington and Indianapolis: Indiana University Press.

Hobsbawm, E. J. 1964. "Introduction." In *Karl Marx, Pre-capitalist Economic Formations.* New York: International Publishers.

Hochschild, Arlie. 1989. *The Second Shift: Inside the Two-Job Marriage.* New York: Viking.

Holloway, Mark. 1966. *Heavens on Earth.* New York: Dover Publications.

Horkheimer, M. 1978. "The Authoritarian State." In *The Essential Frankfurt School Reader,* ed. by A. Arato and E. Gebhardt. New York: Urizen Books, 95-117.

Hoschschild, Adam. 1994. *The Unquiet Ghost: Russians Remember Stalin.* New York: Viking.

Hough, Jerry, and Merle Fainsod. 1979. *How the Soviet Union Is Governed.* Cambridge: Harvard University Press.

Hubbard, Leonard E. 1939. *The Economics of Soviet Agriculture.* London: Macmillan.

James, C. L. R. 1986. *State Capitalism and World Revolution.* Chicago: Charles H. Kerr.

Jasny, Naum. 1967. *The Socialized Agriculture of the USSR.* Stanford: Stanford University Press.

Jay, Martin. 1973. *The Dialectical Imagination.* Boston: Little Brown.

Jensen, R. 1982. "The Transition from Primitive Communism: The Wolof Social Formation of South Africa." *Journal of Economic History* 42 (March): 69-76.

Jerome, W., and Adam Buick. 1967. "Soviet State Capitalism? The History of an Idea." *Survey: A Journal of Soviet and East European Studies* 26 (January): 58-71.

Jessop, Bob. 1982. *The Capitalist State.* New York: New York University Press.

Kaminski, Bartolomiej. 1991. *The Collapse of State Socialism: The Case of Poland*. Princeton: Princeton University Press.
Karcz, Jerzy. 1971. "From Stalin to Brezhnev: Soviet Agricultural Policy in Historical Perspective." In *The Soviet Rural Community*, ed. by James Miller. Chicago: University of Chicago Press, 36–70.
Kautsky, Karl. 1910. *The Class Struggle (Erfurt Program)*, trans. by William E. Bohn. Chicago: Charles H. Kerr.
———. 1971. *The Class Struggle*. New York: W. W. Norton & Co.
Keep, John L. H. 1995. *Last of the Empires: A History of the Soviet Union, 1945–1991*. Oxford: Oxford University Press.
Kerblay, Basile. 1983. *Modern Soviet Society*, trans. by Rupert Swyer. New York: Pantheon.
Kingsbury, Susan M., and Mildred Fairchild. 1935. *Factory, Family, and Women in the Soviet Union*. New York: G. P. Putnam.
Kitching, Gavin. 1998. "The revenge of the Peasant? The Collapse of Large-Scale Russian Agriculture and the Role of the Peasant." *The Journal of Peasant Studies* 26, 1 (October): 43–81.
Kollontai, Alexandra. 1977. *Selected Writings*, trans. by Alix Holt. New York: W. W. Norton.
Kon, Igor. 1993. "Sexuality and Culture." In *Sex and Russian Society*, ed. by Igor Kon and James Riordan. Bloomington: Indiana University Press, 15–44.
Kon, Igor, and James Riorden. 1993. *Sex and Russian Society*. Bloomington: Indiana University Press.
Kornai, Janos. 1992. *The Socialist System: The Political Economy of Communism*. Princeton: Princeton University Press.
Kotz, David M. 1997. *Revolution from Above: The Demise of the Soviet System*. New York and London: Routledge.
Kumar, Krishan. 1991. *Utopianism*. Minneapolis: University of Minnesota Press.
Kuromiya, Hiroaki. 1990. *Stalin's Industrial Revolution: Politics and Workers, 1928–1932*. Cambridge: Cambridge University Press.
Kuron, J., and K. Modzelewski. 1972. *Open Letter to Party Members*, trans. by G. Paul. New York: Pathfinder Press.
Lane, David. 1978. *Politics and Society in the USSR*. 2d ed. New York: New York University Press.
———. 1985a. *Soviet Economy and Society*. Oxford: Blackwell.
———. 1985b. *State and Politics in the USSR*. New York: New York University Press.
Lange, O., and F. M. Taylor. 1964. *On the Economic Theory of Socialism*. New York: McGraw-Hill.
Lapidus, Gail Warshovsky. 1977. "The Brezhnev Regime and Directed Social Change: Depoliticization as Political Strategy." In *The Twenty-Fifth Congress of the CPSU*, ed. by Alexander Dallin. Stanford: Hoover Institution Press, 26–38.
———. 1978. *Women in Soviet Society*. Berkeley: University of California Press.
Lefort, Claude. 1986. *The Political Forms of Modern Society*. Cambridge: Polity Press.
Lenin, V. I. 1932. *The Threatening Catastrophe and How to Fight It*. New York: International Publishers.
———. 1956. *The Development of Capitalism in Russia*. Moscow: Foreign Languages Publishing House.
———. 1959. *Alliance of the Working Class and the Peasantry* (Articles and Speeches). Moscow: Foreign Languages Publishing House.
———. 1961. *Selected Works*, vol. 3. Moscow: Foreign Languages Publishing House.
———. 1964. *Questions of the Socialist Economic Organisation of the Economy*. Moscow: Progress Publishers.
———. 1965. *Collected Works*, vol. 27. Moscow: Progress Publishers.
———. 1967. *On Socialist Economic Organisation*. 2d ed., rev. Moscow: Progress Publishers.
———. 1969. *State and Revolution*. New York: International Publishers.
Leonhard, Wolfgang. 1984. *The Kremlin and the West: A Realistic Approach*, trans. by H. E. Chehabi. New York: W. W. Norton.

Lerner, Abba. 1959. *The Economics of Control*. New York: Macmillan.
Levitas, Ruth. 1990. *The Concept of Utopia*. Syracuse: Syracuse University Press.
Lewin, Moshe. 1975. *Russian Peasants and Soviet Power*. New York: W. W. Norton.
———. 1977. "The Social Background of Stalinism." In *Stalinism: Essays in Historical Interpretation*, ed. by Robert C. Tucker. New York: W. W. Norton, 111–136.
———. 1984. "Society, State, and Ideology during the First Five-Year Plan." In *Cultural Revolution in Russia, 1928–1931*, ed. by Sheila Fitzpatrick. Bloomington: Indiana University Press, 41–77.
———. 1985. *The Making of the Soviet System*. New York: Pantheon.
Lichtheim, George. 1969. *The Origins of Socialism*. New York and Washington: Frederick A. Praeger.
Lukes, Steven. 1984. "Marxism and Utopianism." In *Utopias*, ed. by Peter Alenander and Roger Gill. La Salle, Ill.: Open Court Publishing, 153–167.
———, ed. 1986. *Power*. New York: New York University Press.
Lyaschenko, Peter I. 1949. *History of the National Economy of Russia to the 1917 Revolution*. New York: Macmillan.
Mace, David, and Vera Mace. 1963. *The Soviet Family*. New York: Doubleday.
Male, D. J. 1971. *Russian Peasant Organization Before Collectivization*. Cambridge: Cambridge University Press.
Mandel, David. 1994. *Rabotyagi: Perestroika and After Viewed from Below*. New York: Monthly Review Press.
Mandel, Ernest. 1968. *Marxist Economic Theory*, vol. 2, trans. by Brian Pearce. New York: Monthly Review Press.
———. 1985. "Marx and Engels on Commodity Production and Bureaucracy." In *Rethinking Marxism*, ed. by Stephen A. Resnick and Richard D. Wolff. New York: Autonomedia, 223–258.
Manuel, Frank, and Fritzie Manuel. 1979. *Utopian Thought in the Western World*. Cambridge: The Belknap Press of Harvard University Press.
Marx, Karl. 1933. *The Civil War in France*. New York: International Publishers.
———. 1968. *The Economic and Philosophic Manuscripts of 1844*. New York: International Publishers.
———. 1969. *Theories of Surplus Value*, part 1. Moscow: Progress Publishers.
———. 1971. *Theories of Surplus Value*, part 3. Moscow: Progress Publishers.
———. 1973. *Grundrisse*, trans. by M. Nicolaus. New York: Vintage Books.
———. 1986. *Critique of the Gotha Programme*. New York: International Publishers.
———. 1990. *Capital*, vol. 1. London: Penguin Books.
———. 1991. *Capital*, vol. 3. London: Penguin Books.
———. 1992. *Capital*, vol. 2. London: Penguin Books.
Marx, Karl, and Frederick Engels. 1975. *Selected Correspondence*. Moscow: Progress Publishers.
———. 1978. "Manifesto of the Communist Party." In *The Marx-Engels Reader*, ed. by R. Tucker. New York: W. W. Norton, 469–500.
Massell, Gregory. 1974. *The Surrogate Proletariat: Moslem Women and Revolutionary Strategies in Soviet Central Asia, 1919–1929*. Princeton: Princeton University Press.
Matossian, Mary. 1968. "The Peasant Way of Life." In *The Peasant in Nineteenth Century Russia*, ed. by Wayne S. Vucinich. Stanford: Stanford University Press.
Mattick, Paul. 1969. *Marx and Keynes: The Limits of the Mixed Economy*. Boston: Porter Sargent.
Mawdsley, Evan, and Stephen White. 2000. *The Soviet Elite from Lenin to Gorbachev*. Oxford: Oxford University Press.
McCrank, Lawrence J. 1997. "Religious Orders and Monastic Communalism in America." In *America's Communal Utopias*, ed. by Donald Pritzer. Chapel Hill and London: University of North Carolina Press, 204–252.
McIntyre, Robert J. 1992. "The Phantom of the Transition: Privatization of Agriculture in the Former

Soviet Union and Eastern Europe." *Comparative Economic Studies* XXXIV, 3–4 (Fall-Winter): 81–95.

Medvedev, Roy. 1973. *Let History Judge*. New York: Vintage Books.

———. 1975. *On Socialist Democracy*, trans. by Ellen de Kadt. London: Macmillan.

Meillassoux, C. 1972. "From Reproduction to Production." *Economy and Society* 1, 1: 93–105.

Merl, Stephen. 1991. "Socio-economic Differentiation of the Peasantry." In *From Tsarism to the New Economic Policy*, ed. by R. W. Davies. Ithaca: Cornell University Press, 47–65.

———. 1993. "Social Mobility in the Countryside." In *Social Dimensions of Soviet Industrialization*, ed. by William G. Rosenberg and Lewis H. Siegelbaum. Bloomington: Indiana University Press, 41–62.

Meyer, Alfred G. 1991. "The Impact of World War I on Russian Women's Lives." In *Russia's Women: Accommodation, Resistance, Transformation*, ed. by Barbara Evans Clements, Barbara Alpern Engel, and Christine J. Worobec. Berkeley: University of California Press, 208–224.

Millar, James. 1981. *The ABCs of Soviet Socialism*. Urbana: University of Illinois Press.

———. 1990. *The Soviet Economic Experiment*. Urbana: University of Illinois Press.

Moody, S. S. 1991. "Fallen Star." *The New Republic* (September 9): 21–25.

Moorstein, Richard, and Raymond Powell. 1966. *The Soviet Capital Stock, 1928–1962*. Homewood: Richard D. Irwin.

More, Thomas. 1964. *Utopia*. New Haven and London: Yale University Press.

Muqiao, X. 1981. *China's Socialist Economy*. Beijing: Foreign Languages Press.

Nordhoff, Charles. 1970. *The Communist Societies of the United States*. New York: Schocken Books.

Nove, Alec. 1983. *The Economics of Feasible Socialism*. London: Allen and Unwin.

———. 1989. *An Economic History of the USSR*. London: Penguin.

Ollman, Bertell. 1979. *Social and Sexual Revolution*. Boston: South End Press.

Pavlovsky, George. 1968 (1930). *Agricultural Russia on the Eve of the Revolution*. New York: Howard Fertig.

Pinsker, Boris, and Larisa Piyasheva. 1992. "Property and Freedom." In *Perils of Perestroika: Viewpoints from the Soviet Press, 1989–1991*, ed. by Isaac J. Tarasulo. Wilmington: SR Books, 163–175.

Pitzer, Donald E. 1984. "Collectivism, Community and Commitment: America's Religious Communal Utopias from the Shakers to Jonestown." In *Utopias*, ed. by Peter Alexander and Roger Gill. Lasalle, Ill.: Open Court Publishing, 119–135.

———, ed. 1997. *America's Communal Utopias*. Chapel Hill and London: University of North Carolina Press.

Pollock, Friedrich. 1978. "State Capitalism: Its Possibilities and Limitations." In *The Essential Frankfurt School Reader*, ed. by Andrew Arato and Eike Gebhardt. New York: Urizen Books.

Prawer, S. S. 1976. *Karl Marx and World Literature*. Oxford: Oxford University Press.

Preobrazhensky, Evgeny. 1966. *The New Economics*, trans. by B. Pearce. Oxford: Clarendon Press.

Ramer, Samuel C. 1990. "Feldshers and Rural Health Care in the Early Soviet Period." In *Health and Society in Revolutionary Russia*, ed. by Susan Gross Solomon and John F. Hutchinson. Bloomington: Indiana University Press, 121–145.

Resnick, Stephen A., and Richard D. Wolff. 1986. "What Are Class Analyses?" In *Research in Political Economy* 9, ed. by P. Zarembka. Greenwich: JAI Press, 1–32.

———. 1987. *Knowledge and Class*. Chicago: University of Chicago Press.

———. 1988. "Communism: Between Class and Classless." *Rethinking Marxism* 1 (Spring): 14–48.

———. 1993. "State Capitalism in the USSR? A High-Stakes Debate." *Rethinking Marxism* 6, 2 (Summer): 46–68.

———. 1994. "The Reagan-Bush Strategy: Shifting Crises from Enterprises to Households." In *Bringing It All Back Home*, ed. by Harriet Fraad, Stephen A. Resnick, and Richard D. Wolff. London and Boulder: Pluto Press and Westview Press, 88–111.

Rey, Pierre-Philippe. 1975. "The Lineage Mode of Production." *Critique of Anthropology* 3 (Spring): 27-79.

Riasanovsky, Nicholas V. 1984. *A History of Russia*. 4th ed. New York: Oxford University Press.

Richman, Barry. 1965. *Soviet Management*. Englewood Cliffs: Prentice-Hall.

Rizzi, B. 1985. *The Bureaucratization of the World*, trans. and intro. by A. Westoby. New York: The Free Press.

Roberts, Bruce. 1981. "Value Categories and Marxian Method: A Different View of Value-Price Transformation." Ph.D. diss., Dept. of Economics, University of Massachusetts-Amherst.

———. 1987. "Marx after Steedman: Separating Marxism from 'Surplus Theory'" *Capital and Class* 32 (Fall): 84-103.

Roll, E. 1946. *A History of Economic Thought*. Rev. ed. New York: Prentice-Hall.

Rorty, Richard. 1992. "The Intellectuals and the End of Socialism." *Yale Review* 80, 1 and 2 (April): 1-16.

Rose, Margaret A. 1984. *Marx's Lost Aesthetic: Karl Marx and the Visual Arts*. Cambridge: Cambridge University Press.

Rowbotham, Sheila. 1974. *Women, Resistance, and Revolution*. New York: Vintage.

———. 1992. *Women in Movement: Feminism and Social Action*. New York and London: Routledge, Chapman, and Hall.

Ruccio, David. 1984. "Optimal Planning Theory and Theories of Socialist Planning." Ph.D. diss., Dept. of Economics, University of Massachusetts-Amherst.

———. 1986a. "Essentialism and Socialist Planning: A Methodological Critique of Optimal Planning Theory." In *Research in the History of Economic Thought and Methodology*, ed. by W. Samuels. Greenwich: JAI Press, 85-108.

———. 1986b. "Planning and Class in Transitional Societies." In *Research in Political Economy* 9, ed. by P. Zarembka. Greenwich: JAI Press, 235-252.

Rumyantsev, Alexei. 1969. *Categories and Laws of the Political Economy of Communism*, trans. by D. Danemanis. Moscow: Progress Publishers.

Sahlins, M. 1972. *Stone Age Economics*. Chicago: Aldine, Atherton, Inc.

Saitta, D., and Keene, A. 1985. "Concepts of Surplus and the Primitive Economy: A Critique and Reformulation." Paper presented at Annual Meeting of Society for American Anthropologists, May.

Scott, Hilda. 1974. *Does Socialism Liberate Women?* Boston: Beacon Press.

Service, Elman R. 1975. *Origins of the State and Civilization*. New York: W. W. Norton.

Shanin, Teodor. 1986. *The Roots of Otherness: Russia's Turn of the Century*. New Haven and London: Yale University Press.

Shcheglov, Lev. 1993. "Medical Sexology." In *Sex and Russian Society*, ed. by Igor Kon and James Riordan. Bloomington: Indiana University Press, 152-164.

Shearer, David R. 1996. *Industry, State, and Society in Stalin's Russia*. Ithaca and London: Cornell University Press.

Sherman, Howard. 1969. *The Soviet Economy*. Boston: Little, Brown.

———. 1995. *Reinventing Marxism*. Baltimore and London: Johns Hopkins University Press.

Shlapentokh, Vladimir. 1989. *Public and Private Life of the Soviet People: Changing Values in Post-Stalin Russia*. New York: Oxford University Press.

Siegelbaum, Lewis, and Ronald G. Suny. 1994. *Making Workers Soviet*. Ithaca: Cornell University Press.

Silver, Geoffrey. 1987. "Marxisms, Socialisms and Communisms: An Analysis and Reformulation of Economic Development and Comparative Systems Theories." Ph.D. diss., Dept. of Economics, University of Massachusetts-Amherst.

Sirianni, Carmen J. 1982. *Workers Control and Socialist Democracy: The Soviet Experience*. London: Verso.

Solomon, Susan Gross. 1990. "Social Hygiene and Soviet Public Health, 1921–1930." In *Health and Society in Revolutionary Russia,* ed. by Susan Gross Solomon and John F. Hutchinson. Bloomington: Indiana University Press, 175–199.

Sproul, Claire. 1994. "Mastering the Other: An Ecofeminist Analysis of Neoclassical Economics." Ph.D. diss., Dept. of Economics, University of Massachusetts-Amherst.

Spulber, Nicolas. 1964. *Soviet Stragety for Economic Growth.* Bloomington: Indiana University Press.

———. 1969. *The Soviet Economy.* New York: W. W. Norton.

Stalin, Joseph. 1939. *From Socialism to Communism in the Soviet Union: Report to Eighteenth Congress of the CPSU(B).* New York: International Publishers.

———. 1954. *Problems of Leninism.* Moscow: Foreign Languages Publishing House.

Steinmetz, George. 1997. "Social Class and the Re-emergence of the Radical Right in Contemporary Germany." In *Reworking Class,* ed. by John R. Hall. Ithaca: Cornell University Press, 335–368.

Stites, Richard. 1978. *The Women's Liberation Movement in Russia.* Princeton: Princeton University Press.

———. 1989. *Revolutionary Dreams: Utopian Vision and Experimental Life in the Russian Revolution.* New York: Oxford University Press.

Sutela, Pekka. 1991. *Economic Thought and Economic Reform in the Soviet Union.* Cambridge: Cambridge University Press.

Sweezy, Paul, and Charles Bettelheim. 1971. *On the Transition to Socialism.* New York: Monthly Review Press.

———. 1985a. "After Capitalism—What?" *Monthly Review* 37 (July-August): 98–111.

———. 1985b. "Specificity of Soviet Capitalism, Rejoinder." *Monthly Review* 37 (September): 56–61.

Szymanski, Albert. 1979. *Is the Red Flag Flying?* London: Zed Press.

Taylor, John G. 1979. *From Modernization to Modes of Production.* London: Macmillan.

Terray, Emmanuel. 1972. *Marxism and Primitive Societies.* New York: Monthly Review Press.

Thompson, Edward. P. 1963. *The Making of the English Working Class.* New York: Vintage Books.

Thurston, Robert W. 1996. *Life and Terror in Stalin's Russia 1934–1941.* New Haven and London: Yale University Press.

Tian-Shanskaya, Olga Semyonova. 1993. *Village Life in Late Tsarist Russia,* trans. and ed. by David L. Ransel and Michael Levine. Bloomington: Indiana University Press.

Trotsky, Leon. 1924. *Problems of Life,* trans. by Z. Vengerova. London: Methuen.

———. 1961. *Terrorism and Communism.* Ann Arbor: University of Michigan Press.

———. 1970. *Women and the Family.* New York: Pathfinder.

———. 1972. *The Revolution Betrayed: What is the Soviet Union and Where Is It Going?* New York: Pathfinder.

Tugan-Baranowsky, Mikhail I. 1966. *Modern Socialism in its Historical Development.* New York: Russell and Russell.

———. 1970. *The Russian Factory in the 19th Century,* trans. from the 3d Russian ed. by Arthur and Clara S. Levin. Homewood: Richard D. Irwin.

Turner, Bryan. 1978. *Marx and the End of Orientalism.* London: George Allen and Unwin.

Vanek, Jaroslav, ed. 1975. *Self-Management: Economic Liberation of Man.* Harmondsworth: Penguin.

Varga, Eugene. 1939. *Two Systems: Socialist Economy and Capitalist Economy,* trans. by R. Page Arnot. New York: International Publishers.

Vickers, Douglas. 1994. *Economics and the Antagonism of Time.* Ann Arbor: University of Michigan Press.

Viola, Lynn. 1987. *The Best Sons of the Fatherland: Workers in the Vanguard of Soviet Collectivization.* New York: Oxford University Press.

Volin, Lazar. 1970. *A Century of Russian Agriculture.* Cambridge: Harvard University Press.

von Laue, Theodore H. 1963. *Sergei Witte and the Industrialization of Russia.* New York: Columbia University Press.

Vucinich, Wayne S., ed. 1968. *The Peasant in Nineteenth Century Russia.* Stanford: Stanford University Press.
Wallerstein, Immanuel. 1979. *The Capitalist World Economy.* Cambridge: Cambridge University Press.
Watters, Francis M. 1968. "The Peasant and the Village Commune." In *The Peasant in Nineteenth Century Russia,* ed. by Wayne S. Vucinich. Stanford: Stanford University Press, 133–157.
Weissman, Neil B. 1990. "Origins of the Soviet Health Administration: Narkomnzdrav, 1918–1928." In *Health and Society in Revolutionary Russia,* ed. by Susan Gross Solomon and John F. Hutchinson. Bloomington: Indiana University Press, 97–120.
Wesson, Robert. 1963. *Soviet Communes.* New Brunswick: Rutgers University Press.
Wheatcroft, S. G. 1991. "Agriculture." In *From Tsarism to the New Economic Policy,* ed. by R. W. Davies. Ithaca: Cornell University Press, 79–103.
Wheatcroft, S. G., and R. W. Davies. 1994. "Agriculture." In *The Economic Transformation of the Soviet Union,* ed. by R. W. Davies, Mark Harrison, and S. G. Wheatcroft. Cambridge: Cambridge University Press, 106–130.
Williams, Raymond. 1977. *Marxism and Literature.* Oxford: Oxford University Press.
Wittfogel, Karl. 1963. *Oriental Despotism.* New Haven: Yale University Press.
Wolff, Richard D. 1995. "Markets Do Not a Class Structure Make." In *Marxism in the Postmodern Age,* ed. by Antonio Callari, Stephen Cullenberg, and C. Biewener. New York: Guilford Press, 394–401.
Wolff, Richard D., and Stephen A. Resnick. 1987. *Economics: Marxian versus Neoclassical.* Baltimore and London: Johns Hopkins University Press.
Wolff, Richard D., Bruce Roberts, and Antonio Callari. 1982. "Marx's (not Ricardo's) Transformation Problem: A Radical Reconceptualization." *History of Political Economy* 16 (Fall): 431–436.
———. 1984. "A Marxian Alternative to the Traditional 'Transformation Problem.'" *Review of Radical Political Economics* 16 (Summer-Fall): 115–135.
*The Woman Question: Selections from the Writings of Karl Marx, Frederick Engels, V. I. Lenin, and Joseph Stalin.* 1951. New York: International Publishers.
Zimbalist, Andrew, and Howard Sherman. 1984. *Comparing Economic Systems.* Orlando and London: Academic Press.

# Index

administration
 of resources, 32–36
 of values, 92–94, 213–20, 283–84
agriculture
 ancient structures in, 137–39, 147, 151, 152, 175–79, 213–26, 244, 249–50, 262, 288–90
 under Bolsheviks, 156–57
 communist structures in, 19, 69–70, 243–57, 261
 under Czar, 137–42
 decline in, 314–15
 feudal structures in, 134–36
 interaction with industry, 157–79, 209–12
 state ownership in, 69, 257, 315
Afghanistan invasion, 282, 321
alienation, 61–62
Althusser, Louis, 292
anti-Marxian critics, 118
appropriators of surplus labor
 communal, 23
 and communist class structures, 13–16
 contradictions and, 40–42, 222–26
 decentralized, 16–20
 and producers, 16
 and state capitalism, 105–106
*arenda* movement, 296–97
artel farms, 248
"Authoritarian State, The" (Horkheimer), 113–14

Balkan wars of 1990s, 120
Belov, Fedor, 246
Bernstein, Eduard, 6, 7
Bettelheim, Charles, 112, 123
blindness to class, 70–74, 124–25, 185–92, 322–23

Bolsheviks
 potential of, 4
 and state capitalism, x, 108–11
Brezhnev, Leonid, 288, 302, 305, 314
Buick, Adam, 115–16
Bukharin, N. I., 106, 112, 193, 221

*Capital* (Marx), 13–14, 86, 229, 292–93
capital accumulation, 168
capitalism
 corporate, 14–15
 and exploitation, 13–14
 forms of, ix–x, 13, 86–88, 96
 vs. markets, 92–94
 oscillation between private and state, 99–101, 114–15, 282–83, 318–25
centralization, 16–20
Cahttopadhyay, Paresh, 112
Chavance, Bernard, 116, 123
children, treatment of, 23, 190, 192, 194, 197–99
Christianity, communal, 18, 143
class
 alternative concepts of, 8–10
 blindness to, 70–74
 and markets, 59–65
 power as definition of, 6–9
 power relation to, 65–71
 property as definition of, 5–7
 property relation to, 52–59
 surplus labor definition of, *see* surplus labor definition of class
class structures
 coexisting, 135–53, 268–69
 conflicts among, 31, 161, 201–202
 interaction of, 143–46, 162–64
 multiple, 140–43, 145, 148–49, 268

## 348 — Index

class structures, ancient
  in agriculture, 137-39 147, 151, 152, 175-79, 213-26, 244, 249-50, 262, 288-90
  conditions of existence of, 22-23, 136-38, 195
  and democracy, 67
  and exploitation, 13-14
  in households, 137-39, 185-202, 294-95
  in industry, 138, 141, 143
class structures, communist
  in agriculture, 19, 243-57, 261, 322
  cultural conditions of, 17, 20-24
  economic conditions of, 16-20, 23-24, 31-37
  forms of, 8-16, 51-79
  in households, 17-23, 185-92
  in industry, 32-36
  and markets, 59-65
  political conditions of, 17, 24-30, 37-42
  and property, 53-59
  state subsumed to, 40
class structures, feudal
  in agriculture, 134-36
  conditions of existence, 26, 89-90, 146-47, 195
  and exploitation, 13-14
  under Czar, 133-39
  in households, 134-37, 186-202, 264-65, 294-95
class structures, private capitalist
  in agriculture, 140-41, 177-79, 216-17, 317-19
  and alienation, 61-62
  conditions of existence of, 5-6, 21-22, 85-86
  emergence of, 140-42, 149-50
  and exploitation, 13-14
  forms of, 86-88, 317-18
  in industry, 141-53, 217-19, 317-18
  and state, 30-31
  vs. state capitalism, 99-101
class structures, state capitalist
  in agriculture, 213-26
  conditions of existence of, 86-88, 229-30, 316
  forms of, 88
  in industry, 90, 109, 215-22, 227-30, 257-67
  vs. socialism x, 98-99, 104-26
  subsumed class distributions in, 95-102
  in U.S.S.R. , 85-91

*Class Struggle* (Kautsky), 5
class struggles
  and distribution of surplus, 14-15
  vs. non-class, 37
  among structures, 31, 144-45, 175-79
  within structures, 31
"classless" society, 7, 11, 71-74
Cold War, 281, 299-302
collective farms
  and ancient structures, 244, 249-50, 262
  and capitalist structures, 237-43, 282-84
  and communist structures, 19, 69-70, 163, 243-57, 261, 322
  and NEP, 226-27
  and private plots, 240-41, 254-55, 262
  and terms of trade, 249-53, 273-75
  types of, 244
commodities
  and capitalism, 87
  "communist," 59-60
communes
  communist structures in, 186
  farms as, 163, 248
  in households, 185-92, 194
  village, 134, 138, 140, 142-43, 148
communism
  "classless," 7, 11, 71-74
  and communist structures, 14-15, 54-65
  conceptions of, 3-8
  concrete, 13-42
  definitions of, 74-76
  forms of, 51-79
  markets under, 32-33, 59-65
  non-Marxian accounts of, 3-4, 7-8
  power under, 6-9, 40
  "primitive," 19
  property under, 5-6, 11-13, 25-26
  religious, 18, 143
  vs. socialism, x, 3, 74-79
  state under, 37-42
  vs. state capitalism, 4
  utopia and, 3, 10-13
"communist" as adjective, 59-60
Communist Party
  centralization of, 305
  collapse of, 281
  corruption of, 306-308
  distributions to, 167
  and households, 187
  as subsumed class, 41, 240-41

conditions of existence
   of ancient structures, 136–38, 195
   of communist structures, 13–42, 56
   of feudal structures, 89–90, 195
   of private capitalist structures, 85–86
   of state capitalist structures, 86–88, 229–30, 316
Constitution of 1977, 288
consumption
   by industrial workers, 224–25, 266–68, 303
   private/individual, 266, 314
   types of, 258–59
contradictions
   class and nonclass, 5, 12–13, 316–17
   producer/appropriator, 40–42
   appropriator/receiver, 222–26
   among structures, 20, 42, 55, 201–202, 249–51
   within structures, 42
Council of Ministers
   as board of directors, 166
   as receivers and distributors, 163–64, 166–69, 237, 243, 272–73
   and Stalinism, 272–73
   as state capitalists, 157, 237, 319
crises
   class and nonclass, 12–13, 316–17
   of households, 192–94, 201–202, 320–21
   "scissors," 175–78, 215, 222–26
   among structures, 162–64
   within structures, 319
Crump, John, 115–16
cultural processes
   class concept in, 290–94
   and communism, 17, 20–24
   and despotism, 70
   postwar, 286–98
   and unemployment, 63–64
Czarist state, 133–53, 159–61

decentralization, 7, 16–20, 136–37, 301, 303–306
definition, problems of of, 74–79
democracy
   types of, 66–68
   and socialism, 6–7, 75, 118
   utopian, 12
despot communism, 68–70
detente, 286–88, 302–303
determinism, 8–9, 39
dialectics, 72

dictatorship of the proletariat, 77–79, 112
distribution of surplus labor, 13–16, 32–36, 54–57, 95–102, 163–64
divorce, 194–95, 197–99
Dudintsev, Vladimir, 291
Dunayevskaya, Raya, 111

economic conditions of communist structures, 16–24, 30–37
economic thought, Soviet, 295–96
Engels, Frederick, 5, 27, 105, 107, 189
enterprises
   allocation among, 32–33
   capitalist, 54–55
   and communism, 20–24, 28–29, 55–57, 61–64
   competition among, 94–95
   feudal, 135
   private, 87, 94
   profitability of, 35
   waste in, 314–15
   worker-owned, 55–59
*Evolutionary Socialism* (Bernstein), 6
exchange, unequal, 219–22, 265–66, 311–12
exploitation
   and capitalisms, 86–88
   and communism, 21–22, 25, 63–64
   definition of, 13–14
   household, 264, 320–21
   Stalinist, 264–66
   and the state, 38–39
   state-enterprise, 95–96
   of women, 201, 320

Family Code of 1918, 193–94
fascism, 113–14, 325
feldshers, 200
feminism, 187–88, 201, 320
five-year plans, 119, 198, 200, 266–67
Frankfurt School, 113–15
freedoms and unfreedom, 26–27, 89–90
fundamental class processes
   and communism, 14–16, 23, 31–33
   in Czarist state, 143–53
   kinds of, 20
   in Soviet state, 167–69
   and struggles, 31

Glavki subagencies, 207–208
"goods famine," 225

Gorbachev, Mikhail, 282, 282, 292, 314, 317, 322–24
Gosplan, 167–68
grain market, 219–26

Hilferding, Rudolph, 118–19
Hindess, Barry, 123
Hirst, Paul, 123
Horkheimer, Max, 113–14
households
　ancient structures in, 137–39
　communist structures in, 17–23, 36, 69, 185–92
　conflict within, 22, 185, 194–202, 264, 320–21
　crises of, 192–94, 201–202, 320–21
　feudal structures in, 134–37, 142, 148–50, 186–202, 264–65, 320
　multiple class positions in, 145, 148–49
　value and, 36
housework, socialized, xiii, 190

*Imperialism, the Highest Stage of Capitalism* (Lenin), 105
industry
　interaction with agriculture, 157–79, 209–12, 225–27
　under Bolsheviks, 156–57
　feudal, 132
　ministries of, 90
　rural, 225–26
　under Stalin, 257–67
　state capitalist, 109, 168–69, 227–30
　and surplus, xii, 227–29
　women in, 194, 198–99
integral statism, 113–14
international trade, 220, 296, 310–12, 324–25
"invisible hand" theory, 57

James, C. L. R., 113
job security, 308–309

Kautsky, Karl, 5, 7, 105
Kerblay, Basile, 312–13
Kirchheimer, Otto, 113
Kollontai, Alexandra, 190
Kornai, Janos, 301, 305
Krushchev, N., 288, 300, 303

*kulak* farmers, xiii, 176, 213, 224
Kuron, J., 115, 123–24

labor power
　consumed by managers, 95
　value of, 92, 60–61, 92, 262–63
　and wages, 170–71
Larin, 244
laws
　and collective ownership, 25–30, 247
　and communist state, 39–40, 61
　on households, 193–94, 199
Left, the, 74
"Left Communists," 111
Lenin, V. I.
　and class structures, x
　determinism of, 39
　and dictatorship of proletariat, 77–79
　on peasantry, 147, 150
　and NEP, 176
　on the state, 37–40
　and state capitalism, 105–11, 165
　on women, 189, 192
*Leninism* (Zinoviev), 111
Lewin, Moshe, 244

machine tractor stations (MTS), 239, 251, 272
managers
　and administration of resources, 32–36
　and noncommunist class structures, 18–19
　secret deals by, 243
markets
　administered prices in, 33–34, 213–26
　and class, 59–65
　and communist structures, 32–33, 59–65
　and decentralizing of power, 7
　private prices in, 213–26, 288–89
　and values, 92–94
Martov, 106–107
Marx, Karl
　on capitalist structures, 86, 229–30
　on "classless" society, 7, 11, 71–74
　on communist structures, ix–x
　on freedoms and unfreedom, 26–27
　on market capital, 62–63
　on state capital, 105
　on surplus labor and class, ix, 8–9, 99, 124–26
　value theory of, 33–36, 60, 92–94

Marxian tradition
  authors' approach to, x–xi
  and boundaries of society, 43–44
  definitions in, 74–79
  and household, 187–89
  limitations of, 71–74
  vs. Marxism, xii–xiii, 5–8, 99
  state capitalism debates in, 105–19
  value theory in, 33–36, 60, 93–94
  U.S.S.R. in, 107–108
Mattick, Paul, 116–17
Mayakovsky, Vladimir, 186
medical care, 199–200
Mensheviks, 106–107
merchants
  private, xiii, 196, 213–26
  state, 61, 219–26, 243, 250–52
*mir* (village communes), 134, 138, 140, 142–43, 148, 248
Modzelewski, K., 115, 123–24
More, Thomas, 11

necessary labor, 71–74
Nepmen (private merchants), xiii, 212, 214–19, 222–26, 229
New Economic Policy (NEP), 108, 157, 167, 172, 175–79, 191–93, 206, 209–16, 226–30, 313
non-class positions, multiple, 146–47
non-class processes
  and communist structures, 10, 21–42
  contradictions in, 5, 12–13, 36–37, 269, 316–17
  and Council of Ministers, 167
  revenues as, 143–46, 216, 283–84, 311, 316–17
  in Stalinism, 268–73
  struggles in, 36–37
*Not By Bread Alone* (Dudintsev), 291

Old Believers, 143
oligarchy, 66, 68–70
*Origin of Family, Private Property, and the State* (Engels), 189
Ossipova, Elvira, 201
overdetermination, 4, 9, 12, 16, 70

planning
  circumvention of, 305–307
  "fetishism" of, 111

  inefficiencies of, 243, 305
  and property distribution, 52
  and values, 91–92
Poland, state power in, 119–20
Pollock, Friedrich, 113–14
power
  as definition of class, 6–9, 119–26
  definitions of, 120–21
  essentialization of, 122–26
  non-class processes of, 44
  vs. property definition, 6–7, 110–13
  vs. surplus labor definition, 8–9, 70–71, 110–26
  social distribution of, 65–71, 119–25, 153
Prebisch, Raul, 220
Preobrazhensky, Evgeny, 229–30
prices
  administered, 33–34, 92–94, 213–26, 249–51, 258–75, 283–84
  market, 33–34, 213–26, 245–46, 288–89
  in Soviet state, 119–20
  vs. values, 92, 170–71
private plots
  and collective farms, 178–79, 251–52, 254, 262
  and wages, 141
  under Stalin, 238–42
productive vs. unproductive labor, 72, 294, 307–309
productivity, 36, 248–49, 243, 307, 313–14
profit rates, 34–35, 93–94
property
  and class, 52–59
  as definition of class, 5–7, 74–75, 110
  collective, 5–6, 11–13, 52–53
  vs. power definition, 6–7, 110–13
  private, 5, 52–53, 105–107
  state, 13–16
Putin, 292, 297, 317, 322–24

Renner, Karl, 105
revolution
  in class structures, 97–98
  and social harmony, 6
Revolution of 1905, 148, 150
Revolution of 1917
  lack of class change after, 97–98, 151–53
  and social organization of surplus, xii
rotation of individuals through class positions, 67–69

## Index

scissors crises, 175–78, 215, 222–26
second economy
    class structures in, 312, 289–90
    relation to official, 312–13, 316–17, 319
Sectarians, 143
self-employment, 22–23
self-management by workers, 96–97, 121–22, 296–97, 301
serfdom, 133–39
sexuality, 189–90, 197–98
slave society, 13–14, 26, 89–90
Smith, Adam, 6, 57
social democracy, 66–68, 118
social formation
    and interactive class structures, 146, 162
    problem of naming, 42–44, 76–79
socialism
    classical views of, 5–8
    vs. communism, x, 3, 74–79
    definitions of, 74–76
    and democracy, 6–7, 67–68
    and dictatorship of proletariat, 77–79
    non-Marxian accounts of, 7–8
    vs. state capitalism, ix–x, 98–99, 104–26
*Socialism Scientific and Utopian* (Engels), 5
socialization, 105–106
Soviet state
    capitalist class structure of, ix–x, 4, 85–91, 104–19
    collapse of, x, 318–25
    critics of, xii–xiii, 118
    decentralization in, 301–308
    as failed, 74–75
    power in, 119–20
    social formation in, 42–44, 76–79
    lack of surplus-related study of, 9, 52, 70–71
Stalin, Joseph
    and agriculture, 19, 119, 238–39, 244
    and Council of Ministers, 166
    and planning, 111
    purges of, 287
    and state capitalism, x, 107–108
Stalinism
    contradictions under, 238–43
    class and non-class processes of, 268–73
    critiques of, 292
    as term, 68, 268

state
    as appropriator, 18–20
    and capitalism, 30–31
    and communism, 13–16, 37–42
    distribution by, 32–36
    downsizing of, 317
    and feudalism, 133–39
    and markets, 63–65
    and prices, 92–94, 213–26
    and revolution, 6
state equation
    crises depicted by, 162–64, 316–17
    Czarist, 158–62
    Soviet, 162–74, 210–12, 216–20
subsumed class processes
    and bureaucracy, 29–30, 34–37, 41, 95–102, 243
    and capital accumulation, 243
    under Czar, 143–47, 159–61
    defined, 14–16
    and collective farms, 251
    and household, 36
    and private merchants, 196, 213–26
    and property, 53–59
    and state merchants, 61, 219–26, 243, 250–52
surplus labor
    in ancient structures, 13–14, 24
    and boundaries of society, 43
    in capitalist structures, 94
    in communist structures, 13–16, 34–35
    defined, 8–10
    as definition of class, *See*, surplus labor definition of class
    in feudal structures, 42–43, 134–36
    vs. necessary labor, 71–74
    and power, 110–26
    and property 52–59
    social organization and, xii, 8–10, 14–16
surplus labor definition of class
    authors' focus on, ix–x, 4–5
    Marx on, 124–26
    vs. power definition, 8–9, 70–71, 110–26
    and property, 52–59
    vs. property definition, 110–13
    and value theory, 32–36

tax
    Czarist, 160

reduction of, 309
turnover, 283
terms of trade, 215–29, 249–53, 273–75, 283, 326
*toz* farms, 244
Trotsky, Leon, 108–11

unemployment, 63–64
United States
    capitalist theory in, 21–22
    competition with, 299–304, 321
use values, 15, 32, 72
U.S.S.R. history
and Marxism, xii–xiii, 4
and power processes, 98
surplus labor analysis of, 125–26
utopia, 3, 10–13
*Utopia* (More), 11

value theory
    and agriculture/industry relation, 210–12, 220–29, 249–50, 259–62, 283–84
    and class analysis, 32, 60–61
    and military expenditures, 325–26
    and state administered prices and values, 92–94, 213–29, 283–84
    and state capitalism, 92–94, 316–17, 325–26
values
    administered exchange, 92–94, 283–84
    ancient, 252, 262
    capitalist market, 33–35
    communist administered, 33–35
    of labor power, 15 60–61, 92, 262–63
    market exchange, 32, 273–75
    vs. prices, 33–34, 92, 213–16
    state administered, 33–34, 213–20

Veronina, Olga, 201
Veshenka, the, 157, 166, 169–75, 207–209, 222, 227–28
Vol'fson, S. 194

wages
    and administered surplus value, 35
    agricultural, 141
    and alienation, 61–62
    falling, 262–66
    and food prices, 213–14
    and labor power, 170–71
    and planning, 91–92
    and private plots, 141
    theory on, 293–95
    women's, 194, 198
war communism, 100, 164–65, 169–74, 206–209
Wedemeyer, Joseph, 71
Witte, Serge, 148, 150
World War One, 151, 184–85
World War Two, 282, 285
*Women and Society* (Lenin), 189
women's roles, 22–23, 184–202, 253–54, 264–65, 320
workers
    alienation of, 61–62
    as heroes, 263, 272
    and property, 54–59
    self-management of, 96–97, 121–22, 296–97, 301
    under state capitalism, 105–11

Yeltsin, Boris, 282, 292, 296, 317, 322, 324

Zetkin, Clara, 189–90
Zinoviev, G., 111